AF834567

VOLUME EIGHT

ADVANCES IN TRANSPORT POLICY AND PLANNING

Social Issues in Transport Planning

VOLUME EIGHT

ADVANCES IN TRANSPORT POLICY AND PLANNING

Social Issues in Transport Planning

Edited by

RAFAEL H. M. PEREIRA

Institute for Applied Economic Research (Ipea), Brazil

GENEVIÈVE BOISJOLY

Polytechnique Montréal, Canada

ELSEVIER

ACADEMIC PRESS

An imprint of Elsevier

Academic Press is an imprint of Elsevier
50 Hampshire Street, 5th Floor, Cambridge, MA 02139, United States
525 B Street, Suite 1650, San Diego, CA 92101, United States
The Boulevard, Langford Lane, Kidlington, Oxford OX5 1GB, United Kingdom
125 London Wall, London, EC2Y 5AS, United Kingdom

First edition 2021

Copyright © 2021 Elsevier Inc. All rights reserved.

No part of this publication may be reproduced or transmitted in any form or by any means, electronic or mechanical, including photocopying, recording, or any information storage and retrieval system, without permission in writing from the publisher. Details on how to seek permission, further information about the Publisher's permissions policies and our arrangements with organizations such as the Copyright Clearance Center and the Copyright Licensing Agency, can be found at our website: www.elsevier.com/permissions.

This book and the individual contributions contained in it are protected under copyright by the Publisher (other than as may be noted herein).

Notices
Knowledge and best practice in this field are constantly changing. As new research and experience broaden our understanding, changes in research methods, professional practices, or medical treatment may become necessary.

Practitioners and researchers must always rely on their own experience and knowledge in evaluating and using any information, methods, compounds, or experiments described herein. In using such information or methods they should be mindful of their own safety and the safety of others, including parties for whom they have a professional responsibility.

To the fullest extent of the law, neither the Publisher nor the authors, contributors, or editors, assume any liability for any injury and/or damage to persons or property as a matter of products liability, negligence or otherwise, or from any use or operation of any methods, products, instructions, or ideas contained in the material herein.

ISBN: 978-0-12-822982-8
ISSN: 2543-0009

For information on all Academic Press publications
visit our website at https://www.elsevier.com/books-and-journals

Publisher: Zoe Kruze
Acquisitions Editor: Sam Mahfoudh
Developmental Editor: Naiza Ermin Mendoza
Production Project Manager: James Selvam
Cover Designer: Matthew Limbert

Typeset by STRAIVE, India

ELSEVIER Book Aid International
Working together to grow libraries in developing countries
www.elsevier.com • www.bookaid.org

Contents

Contributors

Jesus M. Barajas
University of California, Davis, CA, United States

Elizabeth C. Delmelle
Department of Geography and Earth Sciences, University of North Carolina at Charlotte, Charlotte, NC, United States

Claire Dungey
Durham University, Durham, United Kingdom

Emily Grisé
School of Urban and Regional Planning, University of Alberta, Edmonton, AB, Canada

Astrid Kemperman
Eindhoven University of Technology, Eindhoven, The Netherlands

Jacqueline M. Klopp
Center for Sustainable Urban Development, Earth Institute, Columbia University, New York, NY, United States

Giulio Mattioli
Transport Research Group, Department of Spatial Planning, TU Dortmund University, Dortmund, Germany

Niek Mouter
Delft University of Technology, Faculty of Technology, Policy and Management, Transport and Logistics Group, Delft, The Netherlands

Daniel Oviedo
Development Planning Unit, University College London, London, United Kingdom

Gina Porter
Durham University, Durham, United Kingdom

Tanu Priya Uteng
Department of Mobility and Organisation, Institute of Transport Economics (TOI), Oslo, Norway

Cherise Roberts
School of Urban and Regional Planning, University of Alberta, Edmonton, AB, Canada

Ruth Shortall
Delft University of Technology, Faculty of Technology, Policy and Management, Transport and Logistics Group, Delft, The Netherlands

Pauline van den Berg
Eindhoven University of Technology, Eindhoven, The Netherlands

Dea van Lierop
Department of Human Geography & Spatial Planning, Utrecht University, Utrecht, The Netherlands

E.O.D. Waygood
Polytechnique Montréal, Montréal, QC, Canada

Preface: Social issues in transport planning

Rafael H. M. Pereira[a] **and Geneviève Boisjoly**[b]
[a]Institute for Applied Economic Research—Ipea, Brasília, Brazil
[b]Polytechnique Montréal, Montréal, QC, Canada

The field of transport planning has been historically dominated by a technical perspective. In its origins, the planning of modern cities and regions was largely developed by engineers with a technocratic understanding of how transportation systems should work, primarily geared toward efficiency (Banister, 2002; Hanson and Giuliano, 2004). Over the last few decades, the field gradually became more interdisciplinary with growing contributions from scholars and professionals from various backgrounds such as geography, urban planning, economics, and sociology (Hickman et al., 2015; Uteng and Cresswell, 2008; Vickerman, 2021). Transport planning became more diverse. This gave visibility to a variety of social issues that pervade human mobility systems as well as to the political processes that exist alongside the technical aspects of planning.

Concerns about social issues are not new in transport studies. In the late 1960s, a growing number of researchers started to investigate transport inequalities related to access to job opportunities and car dependence (Kain, 1968; Rosenbloom and Altshuler, 1977; Wachs and Kumagai, 1973) and the distribution of transport subsidies (Abe, 1975; Hanson, 1992; Hefner, 1972). Earlier studies have also examined issues of fairness in transport decision-making processes (Booth and Richardson, 2001; Grant, 1975) and social and racial inequalities in exposure to environmental externalities (Appleyard and Lintell, 1972; Forkenbrock and Schweitzer, 1999). Several studies and reports were published as postwar urban structure changes driven by car-oriented planning exacerbated issues of race, poverty, and unemployment (Kain and Meyer, 1970; O'Regan and Quigley, 1998; Pignatar and Falcocch, 1969; Sanchez, 2008). The early literature on social issues in transportation were very much concerned with transport poverty, giving particular attention to the growing importance of public transport systems in catering to the needs of transit-dependent populations, usually low-income and minority households. Since the late 1960s, we have seen a growing number of more diverse and intricate social issues emerge from how our cities and transport systems are organized.

The *aim* of this book is to present an up-to-date and critical review of some of the most pressing and sometimes overlooked social issues identified by scholars and practitioners working on transport planning. The book gathers a collection of chapters that cover a diverse range of topics such as transport poverty and car dependence, transit-induced gentrification, accessibility, gender, race, children's mobility, the governance of paratransit, equity in project appraisal as well as customer satisfaction with public transport, and the potential of research methodologies in promoting more inclusive and participatory transport planning. The book also presents a rich interdisciplinary perspective on these issues based on the expertise of authors from diverse backgrounds and speaking from different contexts, including Latin America, Africa, South Asia, Europe, and North America.

Which social issues are considered worthy of public attention in the transport planning process depends on local and historical context. In particular, it depends on the conceptions of a just city and mobility system embedded in the social norms and institutions of each society. This is because every social issue only becomes recognized as a social problem that requires policy attention inasmuch as its manifestation goes against our aspirations of justice and against our understanding of how ethics should be applied to transport planning (van Wee, 2011). While the idea of justice is constantly evolving, there is growing consensus that a full understanding of justice in modern societies involves moral concerns with equity, democracy, and diversity (Davoudi and Brooks, 2014; Fainstein, 2010; Kymlicka, 2002). Ultimately, every social issue faced by transport planners and scholars is related to how these three pillars of justice can be understood in the field of transport planning (Pereira and Karner, 2021).

The concern with *equity* is centered around distributive justice (Pereira et al., 2017). It relates to how social and economic inequalities are shaped by the institutions and rules that govern society. Questions of equity draw attention to the distributional outcomes of policies. Equity concerns provoke us to question what social groups benefit or lose from transportation policies, for example, in terms of accessibility gains or in terms of health damage due to exposure to pollution. Government policies have a crucial role to play in social democracies through the provision of public goods and services. This is particularly true in the provision of mass transportation infrastructure and services, which often involves the mobilization of substantial resources and construction of large infrastructure projects, which cannot be easily provided in a decentralized manner through local communities. In this sense, public transport services and investments will remain one of the key drivers that can shape spatial inequalities of development and opportunities in cities (Tonkiss, 2013), making the study of equity in transport policies particularly important.

Meanwhile, the concern with *democracy* focuses on the fairness of governance, political participation, and decision-making processes. It is based on the core principle that everyone's voice should be equally heard, with particular attention to the need to engage with communities to develop the public policies that shape the built environment and transport systems around them (Bickerstaff et al., 2002; Davoudi and Brooks, 2014). In this sense, the democracy pillar of justice challenges us to move beyond periodic voting and to overcome technocratic top-down planning practices by engaging communities in the coproduction of urban space and governmental policies.

Finally, the concern with *diversity* involves the recognition of group-based differences, rights, needs, values, and identities as well as promoting diversity in decision-making processes (Verlinghieri and Schwanen, 2020; Young, 1990). It requires us to acknowledge that participatory democracy is constantly marked by structural imbalances of wealth and power that marginalize certain groups and favor others in their ability to influence policy decisions that produce urban space (Enright, 2019). The pillar of diversity reminds us that justice is also fundamentally about the uplifting of minorities and marginalized communities, and that justice involves a constant political dispute over which rights, needs, and entitlements should be recognized and for whom.

This book speaks directly about this broad understanding of transport justice and how it applies to a variety of social issues present in transport planning. The reader of this book will notice that each chapter addresses a pressing social issue in transport and touches on one or more of the three pillars of transport justice mentioned above. The first three chapters shed light on the *diversity of needs and experiences* around individuals' mobility and discuss how specific groups are considered in—often marginalized from—current transport planning practices and frameworks.

In Chapter 1 "The roots of racialized travel behavior" Jesus M. Barajas presents an in-depth review of the transport inequities that place Black, Indigenous, and people of color at disadvantage in terms of mobility and access to opportunities, with a focus on the United States. The author clearly shows that these patterns partly result from historical and contemporary racism at play at the systemic and individual levels. To start with, racial inequities are strongly rooted in transport planning and urban development policies, which have brought about major distributional inequities in the benefits and burdens of transportation systems (Bullard, 2004; Rothstein, 2017; Sanchez and Wolf, 2007). But the transport inequities go well beyond the configuration of the land use and transport systems. Barajas puts forward several examples to illustrate other (often less tangible) ways in which racism limits individuals in their everyday mobility. These include disproportionate policing arising from racial bias, issues of safety and security in communities of color as well as suspicion arising from individuals perceived as being "out of place" in a neighborhood. This chapter highlights why race-neutral planning processes often exacerbate racial disparities, but it also draws attention to the shortcomings of planning practices and theories that solely focus on distributional effects. It then concludes on the need and challenges to appropriately account for race, namely, by considering the broader context and domains that affect travel behavior and policies, and calling for a recognition of history and experiences.

An issue that has been historically overlooked by urban and transport planners is how to make planning sensitive to the needs of women, despite women constituting roughly 50% of urban populations (Akyelken, 2020; Hanson, 2010; Uteng and Cresswell, 2008). Chapter 2 "Gender gaps in urban mobility and transport planning" by Tanu Priya Uteng presents an extensive review on the topic of gender and transport and highlights the existing gaps in this important social issue. Drawing from empirical materials of research and practice from both the Global North and the Global South, Uteng critically reviews the findings around gendered mobilities and reflects on some of the challenges to mainstream gender in transport and urban planning. The chapter starts by summarizing a range of evidence on the gendered differences in travel behavior. Compared to men, women tend to have more complex travel patterns across space and time of the day. Women also tend to do shorter trips, more trip chaining, and are more likely to use active and public transport modes and to be accompanied by small children. As noted by Uteng, these differences emerge due to the interlinks between several factors. These include how women generally have lower access to private transport resources such as cars, the ways in which trip patterns are shaped by women's more complex and intricate scheduling of activities related to non-work activities such as care work, and how women's perceptions of safety have a stronger influence on their travel choices or lack thereof. The chapter draws attention to the profound equity implications of how women's mobility and access to opportunities are often limited due to economic, geographic, time-based, and fear-based exclusion. Finally, the work of Uteng highlights how the predominant male bias in transport planning and even in travel data collection methods and analysis is deeply rooted in a lack of diversity, with little participation of women in the transport sector as employees, as decision-makers in key policy positions, and as educators.

Another social group that receives relatively little attention from transport researchers and planners are children (Mitra, 2013; Waygood et al., 2019). This is the topic covered in Chapter 3 "The social dimensions of children's travel," written by E.O.D. Waygood, Pauline van den Berg, and Astrid Kemperman. The authors review an extensive literature on children's travel behavior and how it relates to social interactions and connections within a neighborhood, well-being, and life satisfaction. Since transport planning largely concentrates on the needs of adults (namely, car travel), a declining proportion of children are able to travel independently in several cities of the world. Yet, the authors gather a variety of evidence that independent travel by children is associated with multiple positive physical and mental health outcomes. By supporting social interactions and greater social capital, independent travel contributes to greater trip satisfaction and overall social well-being. This chapter therefore recommends the design of child-friendly neighborhoods (that facilitate independent travel by children), by promoting active transport and including children in the planning process. Further, the authors highlight the broader social impacts that transport can have on one's life and make a call for researchers and planners to recognize the particular needs of children in urban and transport planning to promote more inclusive cities for all.

The second series of chapters in this book discusses the complex and multidimensional interrelationships that contribute to transport inequities. These chapters review how land use and transport development processes, together with institutional and governance structures, foster transport inequities, placing socially disadvantaged groups at risk of transport poverty and social exclusion.

A central concern from transport researchers and planners is the multiple and overlapping dimensions of transport poverty, particularly in the context of car-dependent neighborhoods and cities (Lucas et al., 2016; Mattioli et al., 2020). This is the topic covered in Chapter 4 "Transport poverty and car dependence: A European perspective," where Giulio Mattioli makes important links between these issues and questions of transportation equity and justice. Mattioli reviews the conceptual debates around transport equity by discussing the notion of transport poverty from a broad and holistic perspective. As such, the chapter highlights that transport poverty is a multidimensional concept that encompasses inequities and distributional issues, in terms of both burdens and benefits. By covering the multiple overlapping dimensions of transport poverty (mobility poverty, transport affordability, accessibility poverty, and exposure to externalities), the chapter demonstrates the wide reach of transport poverty across population groups, particularly in Europe and North America. Further, Mattioli emphasizes that transport poverty cannot be understood separately from the societal processes that led to the context of car dependence. As such, in the Global North, and increasingly in the Global South, car access and car use has become a prerequisite for many households to access services and opportunities and to fully participate in the society. This results in several challenges for transport disadvantaged communities not only in terms of mobility, transport affordability, and accessibility, but also in terms of transport externalities associated with car-dominant transport systems.

Transport inequities in rapidly growing cities of the Global South are a pressing concern for transport researchers and planners. In Chapter 5 "Making the links between accessibility, social and spatial inequality, and social exclusion: A framework for cities in Latin America," Daniel Oviedo reviews empirical research on transport provision and poverty and spatial inequalities in access in Latin America, revealing how transport and urban planning contributed to the social exclusion of the poor in the urban peripheries. Drawing on the splintering urbanism and social exclusion frameworks, Oviedo provides a conceptual frame to understand the drivers behind—and impacts of—the lack of accessibility experienced by socially disadvantaged groups. Splintering urbanism, which refers to the differentiated provision of infrastructure based on power, wealth, and influence, is helpful in understanding how power and wealth have influenced, and still influence, the development of infrastructure in Latin America. The frameworks used by Oviedo in the chapter helps us understand the paths through which Latin American urbanization has led to well-connected spaces for the elite while leaving areas and communities without political power at the margins of the development processes. Such fragmented development results in a reinforcing cycle of transport disadvantage and inequities, where socially disadvantaged groups are progressively excluded from networks and connected spaces. The proposed framework also illustrates how informal transport, housing, and employment strategies work against the structural processes of exclusion. By reviewing transport, development, and urban studies, this chapter demonstrates the necessity to consider the multiple dimensions of social exclusion.

As discussed in the previous chapters, the provision of public transport is key to supporting social equity and inclusion by improving accessibility to opportunities. However, the implementation of new transport infrastructure can also lead to gentrification and have negative impacts by pushing out low-income residents and local businesses, harming the populations that would benefit the most from these new infrastructure (Delmelle and Nilsson, 2020; Nilsson and Delmelle, 2020; Padeiro et al., 2019). This topic is thoroughly reviewed by Elizabeth C. Delmelle in Chapter 6 "Transit-induced gentrification and displacement: The state of the debate." The chapter reviews the theoretical foundations and empirical evidence associated with neighborhood changes brought about by investments in rail transit. Delmelle questions the idea that transit alone is responsible for this phenomenon. As such, she exposes mixed findings that have been put forward in previous studies, emphasizing that gentrification-like changes are often marginal and very difficult to quantify. More importantly, Delmelle highlights the importance of the local context in determining how new transport investments will influence the changes in a neighborhood, as well as the need for more disaggregated research to effectively capture the causal effects of transport investments. Again, the complex interrelationships between transport infrastructure, neighborhood change, travel behavior, and well-being are highlighted as key questions to address the equity concerns over who are the winners and losers from transport investments.

The complex interplays between transport systems, urban development, and political institutions are further discussed by Jacqueline M. Klopp in Chapter 7 "From 'Para-Transit' to Transit? A Review of the Politics of Popular Transport." The chapter sheds a critical light on the current debates around what is commonly referred to as paratransit of informal transport (e.g., privately or cooperatively owned minibus and taxi systems). The author illustrates that while these forms of transport are typically marginalized and depicted as "chaotic" and "unplanned" by researchers and planners, more and more efforts are placed into integrating these forms of transport in transport planning (Behrens et al., 2016; Cervero and Golub, 2007; Klopp and Cavoli, 2019). Klopp thereby refers to them as popular transport rather than paratransit or informal transport, which tends to hold a negative connotation. While the literature reviewed in this chapter increasingly recognizes the potential role of popular transit as first-last mile options, the question remains of how to effectively work with these modes and engage with their users and stakeholders. If, on the one hand, popular transport has a key role to play in promoting more inclusive cities and transport systems by catering to the needs of low- and middle-income classes, it also poses numerous governance challenges. Some of these challenges discussed in the chapter include the lack of data, labor exploitation, and a profound misunderstanding of operations and issues at stake, and also more broadly the politics around them as well as common attitudes among policy makers. Having demonstrated the complexity of the challenges around the politics and power relations underlying popular transport the author calls for a holistic approach to the governance and planning of these modes in order to promote more equitable and just mobility systems.

The previous chapters emphasized the limitations of current practices in addressing inequities in transport planning. The last three chapters provide insights on emerging methods that can contribute to foster more inclusive land use and transport systems.

Customer satisfaction surveys are commonly conducted by transport agencies as a means to identify the diverse needs and experiences of specific population groups (Eboli and Mazzulla, 2010; van Lierop et al., 2018). Yet, there is little systematic understanding of how this type of data is collected and analyzed to help improve overall passenger satisfaction and long-term loyalty. This is the literature gap covered by Cherise Roberts, Emily Grisé, and Dea van Lierop in Chapter 8 "What are we doing with all that satisfaction data? Evaluating public transport customer satisfaction data collection and analysis techniques." The chapter focuses on public transport satisfaction data and market segmentation, and how it can contribute to or limit the ability of policy makers to address the needs of all segments of the population, particularly the hard-to-reach minorities. The authors draw attention to some of the advantages and drawbacks of various techniques used by public transport agencies to collect satisfaction data, including intercept and phone surveys, online questionnaires, focus groups, and interviews. While quantitative approaches allow reaching a greater number of individuals, achieving representativeness remains a challenge. As for qualitative methods, they allow identifying concerns that are not exposed with quantitative methods and are specifically relevant to highlight experiences of specific, often marginalized, groups. Overall, the authors recommend that a mix of techniques be used to ensure that the perceptions of marginalized groups are captured. Further, the authors insist that careful attention must be placed on the data that is collected and how it is analyzed to effectively capture the differences across segments. This chapter complements the other chapters in the book by providing a practical perspective on how agencies' practices can foster or hinder the recognition of marginalized groups in planning.

One of the most common tasks in transport planning involves assessing the potential positive and negative impacts of transport policy options. While cost–benefit analysis (CBA) has been the first go-to method used by academics and practitioners for this task, CBA is quite limited in that it does not account for social and distributional impacts of transport projects (Hickman and Dean, 2018; Mouter, 2020, 2021; van Wee, 2012). This is the starting point of Chapter 9 "Social and distributional impacts in transport project appraisals" by Ruth Shortall and Niek Mouter. In this chapter, Shortall and Mouter discuss some fundamental limitations of CBA to account for social impacts and ethical concerns of transport policies, and review the recent developments that seek to overcome the shortcomings of CBA. As discussed by the authors, CBA has been criticized for ignoring that the formation of preferences is inherently a social process that goes beyond a purely economic rationality of individual agents. The chapter also discusses the equity implications of CBA for being fundamentally guided by utilitarian and consequentialist moral reasoning, and by the individual willingness to pay paradigm that often deviates from public preferences. Recent innovations in welfare economics to overcome some of these CBA limitations are also covered in the chapter. These include participatory value evaluation and deliberative monetary valuation, which bring together citizens' participation and social interactions to help inform the allocation of scarce public resources. Shortall and Mouter move on to summarize the core elements of multicriteria assessment and deliberative appraisal methods, and review several cases in which they have been used in transport policy appraisal. Both methods can improve the valuation of transport impacts and public goods by taking into account multiple viewpoints and dimensions of well-being that are difficult to translate into monetary terms, and deliberative appraisal methods in particular also can foster democratic participation and pluralistic perspectives through reasoned discussions between participants. This chapter helps us understand the potentials and pitfalls of various appraisal methods and warns us that the capacity of each of these methods to genuinely promote a more equitable and democratic transport planning that fosters diversity depends on how participation processes are organized and facilitated.

Finally, in Chapter 10 "Innovative field research methodologies for more inclusive transport planning: Review and prospect," Gina Porter and Claire Dungey focus on how innovative field research methodologies can support more inclusive transport planning. The authors contrast the technocratic approaches (typically centered on large-scale quantitative data and methodologies) with the need to understand and address the perceptions and experiences of marginalized populations. To do so, effectively engaging with potential users, especially the ones that are marginalized within current practices, is crucial. At the same time, the authors caution that participatory research needs to be carried out with careful consideration of the landscapes of power, politics, and vested interests. The chapter covers a wide range of field research methodologies, including in-person interviews and focus groups, go-along methods, coinvestigation practices (excluding researchers' direct presence on the field), joint research and interventions as well as digital methodologies. The authors provide a wealth of examples where such methodologies have allowed uncovering challenges experienced by specific groups and providing a nuanced understanding, as well as challenges that go beyond the infrastructure and services as such (e.g., what surrounds the trips in terms of sociality, the urban fabric, etc.). The material presented in the chapter illustrates the importance of these innovative field research methodologies to empower communities as peer researchers. It also shows the potential role of such methodologies to have a real impact in policy design to further the recognition of the diversity and needs of local communities in local policy making. The authors acknowledge that these approaches are not straightforward and present their own set of challenges, but clearly demonstrate the potential of these methodologies and the relevance of overcoming these challenges. It is our hope that it will bring more researchers to engage with such methodologies, thereby contributing to the development of more inclusive research and planning practices.

The full set of chapters in this book cover some of the most challenging social issues in transport planning, which speak directly to the three pillars of transport justice summarized in this introduction: equity, democracy, and diversity. The chapters highlight the complexity of the social aspects of transport, given their multidimensional, multiscalar, and often less tangible nature. Social issues are interconnected with broader concerns of governance and political institutions, inequalities, social exclusion, and urban development, while at the same time being intimately related to very personal experiences. A common element that spontaneously emerged across the chapters in this book is the acknowledgment that researchers and practitioners need to take more holistic approaches, together with a diverse set of methodologies, to properly address those pressing social issues in local urban and transport planning. Such multidisciplinary approaches and frameworks are essential to tackle the complex interplay between institutions, culture, individuals, planning agencies, transport networks, land use development, etc., in order to make transport planning more inclusive and just.

This book is a call for action for researchers, planners, and decision-makers to not be afraid to dig into these complex issues and to take upon the associated challenges. Addressing these issues demands that we go beyond mainstream traditional methods and practices. Doing so requires a lot of effort, resources, and time to make changes toward more progressive and inclusive planning practices. But it is our hope that this book will inspire researchers and practitioners in engaging with pressing social issues, and that it will motivate the research and planning communities to develop, adapt, and apply innovative approaches.

References

Abe, M.A., 1975. Distributional equity and optimal pricing of urban transport. J. Transp. Econ. Policy 9 (2), 178–185.

Akyelken, N., 2020. Transport for women: who decides what women need? Transp. Rev. 40 (6), 687–688. https://doi.org/10.1080/01441647.2020.1799162.

Appleyard, D., Lintell, M., 1972. The environmental quality of city streets: the residents' viewpoint. J. Am. Inst. Plann. 38 (2), 84–101. https://doi.org/10.1080/01944367208977410.

Banister, D., 2002. Transport Planning, second ed. Routledge.

Behrens, R., McCormick, D., Mfinanga, D., 2016. Paratransit in African Cities: Operations, Regulation and Reform. Routledge.

Bickerstaff, K., Tolley, R., Walker, G., 2002. Transport planning and participation: the rhetoric and realities of public involvement. J. Transp. Geogr. 10 (1), 61–73.

Booth, C., Richardson, T., 2001. Placing the public in integrated transport planning. Transp. Policy 8 (2), 141–149. https://doi.org/10.1016/S0967-070X(01)00004-X.

Bullard, R.D., 2004. The anatomy of transportation racism. In: Bullard, R.D., Johnson, G.S., Torres, A.O. (Eds.), Highway Robbery. South End Press, pp. 15–32.

Cervero, R., Golub, A., 2007. Informal transport: a global perspective. Transp. Policy 14, 445–457. https://doi.org/10.1016/j.tranpol.2007.04.011.

Davoudi, S., Brooks, E., 2014. When does unequal become unfair? Judging claims of environmental injustice. Environ. Plan. A 46 (11), 2686–2702. https://doi.org/10.1068/a130346p.

Delmelle, E., Nilsson, I., 2020. New rail transit stations and the out-migration of low-income residents. Urban Stud. 57 (1), 134–151.

Eboli, L., Mazzulla, G., 2010. How to capture the passengers' point of view on a transit service through rating and choice options. Transp. Rev. 30 (4), 435–450.

Enright, T., 2019. Transit justice as spatial justice: learning from activists. Mobilities 14 (5), 665–680.

Fainstein, S.S., 2010. The Just City. Cornell University Press, Ithaca.

Forkenbrock, D.J., Schweitzer, L.A., 1999. Environmental justice in transportation planning. J. Am. Plann. Assoc. 65 (1), 96–112. https://doi.org/10.1080/01944369908976036.
Grant, J.A., 1975. Urban transportation and decision making—a comparison of three case studies in Britain. Transportation 4 (2), 123–142.
Hanson, M.E., 1992. Automobile subsidies and land use: estimates and policy responses. J. Am. Plann. Assoc. 58 (1), 60–71. https://doi.org/10.1080/01944369208975535.
Hanson, S., 2010. Gender and mobility: new approaches for informing sustainability. Gend. Place Cult. 17 (1), 5–23.
Hanson, S., Giuliano, G., 2004. The Geography of Urban Transportation. Guilford Press.
Hefner, J., 1972. Efficiency, equity and pricing in mass transit system. Rev. Black Polit. Econ. 2 (3), 38–44. Scopus. https://doi.org/10.1007/BF03040606.
Hickman, R., Dean, M., 2018. Incomplete cost–incomplete benefit analysis in transport appraisal. Transp. Rev. 38 (6), 689–709.
Hickman, R., Bonilla, D., Givoni, M., Banister, D., 2015. Handbook on Transport and Development. Edward Elgar.
Kain, J.F., 1968. Housing segregation, negro employment, and metropolitan decentralization. Q. J. Econ. 82 (2), 175–197.
Kain, J., Meyer, J., 1970. Transportation and poverty. Public Interest 18, 75–87.
Klopp, J.M., Cavoli, C., 2019. Mapping minibuses in Maputo and Nairobi: engaging paratransit in transportation planning in African cities. Transp. Rev. 39, 657–676. https://doi.org/10.1080/01441647.2019.1598513.
Kymlicka, W., 2002. Contemporary Political Philosophy: An Introduction, second ed. Oxford University Press, Oxford.
Lucas, K., Mattioli, G., Verlinghieri, E., Guzman, A., 2016. Transport poverty and its adverse social consequences. Proc. Inst. Civ. Eng. Transp. 169 (6), 353–365.
Mattioli, G., Roberts, C., Steinberger, J.K., Brown, A., 2020. The political economy of car dependence: a systems of provision approach. Energy Res. Soc. Sci. 66, 101486.
Mitra, R., 2013. Independent mobility and mode choice for school transportation: a review and framework for future research. Transp. Rev. 33 (1), 21–43.
Mouter, N., 2020. Standard transport appraisal methods. In: Advances in Transport Policy and Planning, vol. 6. Elsevier.
Mouter, N., 2021. New methods, reflections and application domains in transport appraisal. In: Advances in Transport Policy and Planning, vol. 7. Elsevier.
Nilsson, I., Delmelle, E.C., 2020. Impact of new rail transit stations on neighborhood destination choices and income segregation. Cities 102, 102737.
O'Regan, K., Quigley, J., 1998. Accessibility and economic opportunity. Retrieved from SSRN http://escholarship.org/uc/item/37h6t700#page-1.
Padeiro, M., Louro, A., da Costa, N.M., 2019. Transit-oriented development and gentrification: a systematic review. Transp. Rev. 39 (6), 733–754.
Pereira, R.H.M., Karner, A., 2021. Transportation equity. In: Vickerman, R. (Ed.), International Encyclopedia of Transportation, vol. 1. Elsevier Ltd, United Kingdom, pp. 271–277.
Pereira, R.H.M., Schwanen, T., Banister, D., 2017. Distributive justice and equity in transportation. Transp. Rev. 37 (2), 170–191. https://doi.org/10.1080/01441647.2016.1257660.
Pignatar, L., Falcocch, J., 1969. Transportation needs of low-income families. Traffic Q. 23 (4), 505–525.
Rosenbloom, S.A., Altshuler, A., 1977. Equity issues in urban transportation. Policy Stud. J. 6 (1), 29–39.
Rothstein, R., 2017. The Color of Law: A Forgotten History of How Our Government Segregated America. Liveright Publishing Corporation, New York; London.

Sanchez, T.W., 2008. Poverty, policy, and public transportation. Transp. Res. A Policy Pract. 42 (5), 833–841.
Sanchez, T.W., Wolf, J.F., 2007. Environmental justice and transportation equity: a review of MPOs. In: Bullard, R.D. (Ed.), Growing Smarter: Achieving Livable Communities, Environmental Justice, and Regional Equity. MIT Press, Cambridge, MA and London, UK, pp. 249–271.
Tonkiss, F., 2013. Cities by Design: The Social Life of Urban Form. Polity Press.
Uteng, T.P., Cresswell, T., 2008. Gendered Mobilities. Ashgate, Aldershot.
van Lierop, D., Badami, M., El-Geneidy, A., 2018. What influences satisfaction and loyalty in public transport? A review of the literature. Transp. Rev. 38 (1), 52–72. https://doi.org/10.1080/01441647.2017.1298683.
van Wee, B., 2011. Transport and Ethics: Ethics and the Evaluation of Transport Policies and Projects. Edward Elgar Pub, Cheltenham.
van Wee, B., 2012. How suitable is CBA for the ex-ante evaluation of transport projects and policies? A discussion from the perspective of ethics. Transp. Policy 19 (1), 1–7.
Verlinghieri, E., Schwanen, T., 2020. Transport and mobility justice: evolving discussions. J. Transp. Geogr. 87, 102798.
Vickerman, R. (Org.). (2021). International Encyclopedia of Transportation (first ed.). Elsevier.
Wachs, M., Kumagai, K., 1973. Physical accessibility as a social indicator. Socioecon. Plann. Sci. 7 (5), 437–456. https://doi.org/10.1016/0038-0121(73)90041-4.
Waygood, E.O.D., Friman, M., Olsson, L., Mitra, R., 2019. Transport and Children's Wellbeing. Elsevier, pp. 237–252.
Young, I.M., 1990. Justice and the Politics of Difference. Princeton University Press, Princeton.

CHAPTER ONE

The roots of racialized travel behavior

Jesus M. Barajas*
University of California, Davis, CA, United States
*Corresponding author: e-mail address: jmbarajas@ucdavis.edu

Contents

Abstract

Transportation inequities, particularly in the United States, result in part from historical and contemporary racism in planning, policy, urban development, decision making, and societal institutions. They have limited the mobility and access to opportunity for Black, Indigenous, and people of color, and shaped the ways that they travel. This chapter reviews the literature on racial and ethnic identity in travel behavior, examining the history and claims of transportation injustice. The chapter explores the barriers that historically marginalized communities experience as a result of disproportionate policing, safety and security issues, and neighborhood othering and belonging—that is, inviting suspicion because a person appears to be "out of place" in a neighborhood. It concludes by making the case for why transportation planners must consider race and racism explanatory factors in travel and why race-neutral planning processes exacerbate disparities.

Keywords: Travel behavior, Race, Policing, Safety, Transportation planning, Mobility justice

Advances in Transport Policy and Planning, Volume 8
ISSN 2543-0009
https://doi.org/10.1016/bs.atpp.2021.06.007
Copyright © 2021 Elsevier Inc.
All rights reserved.

1. Introduction

Between 1936 and 1966, Victor Hugo Green published an annual travel guide called *The Negro Motorist Green Book*. The book listed hotel accommodations, restaurants, and other travel services that would cater to Black Americans during a time of legal segregation as they road-tripped across the United States. Post-World War II prosperity lead to the rapid rise of automobile ownership across the United States and with it, a sense of freedom to travel recreationally and set sights to distant destinations. But the existence of the *Green Book* serves as a reminder that as the automobile took hold of the landscape, policy, and cultural image of the country, Black Americans were routinely denied access to the full benefits of the car (Sorin, 2021). "African Americans' desire and fitness for citizenship were tethered to and divined in their participation in automobility," Cotton Seiler (2006, p. 1092) wrote, and Jim Crow laws in the South—laws that enforced racial segregation—and racial prejudice everywhere made it impossible for them to achieve that full citizenship. Private businesses of all types restricted mobility through "whites only" services, preventing Black people from being in spaces not designated for them, while the government did the same through racially motivated policing and violence. Similar dynamics were in play for other marginalized groups as well; for example, Carpio (2019) has argued that mobility of all forms, from the automobile to the larger forces of migration and new urban developments, shaped racial hierarchies during the 20th century among Japanese, Mexican, and other immigrant groups in southern California—a region nearly defined by its obsession with the automobile and perpetual motion. Racial identities,[a] because they have often been the basis by which mobility was restricted, have influenced travel experiences.

The *Green Book* and similar guidebooks responded to the needs caused by individualized, but widespread, racial animus. But systematic racism in government decision making also limited the mobility of Black people and other people of color on a scale much broader than vacation travel. A long list of deliberate actions transpired to make this the case from the dawn of the highway era to today: residential segregation that prevented people of color from

[a] I use the terms "race" and "racial identities" synonymously with "ethnicity" in this chapter. While Hispanic or Latino identity is an ethnicity rather than a race, for example, Latinos in the United States have been racialized as Brown regardless of culture or country of origin (García, 2020).

moving to suburbs characterized by nearly unlimited automobility; the purposeful construction of highways through Black neighborhoods as a means of urban renewal; and transit funding formulas that have favored rail construction, disfavored bus operating expenses, and offered higher subsidies for commuter rail that overwhelming serve white passengers, just to name a few examples (Bullard, 2004; Garrett and Taylor, 1999; Rothstein, 2017). These planning and engineering processes have led to distributive injustices—people of color have received fewer benefits and shouldered higher burdens from transportation investment—as well as procedural injustices, because people of color have had little voice and representation when these decisions have been made. Since the 1960s, civil rights and environmental justice legislation have forced transportation agencies to acknowledge and identify racial disparities in an attempt to prevent such injustices from continuing to happen, but scholars have argued that the mere identification of inequities and mitigation of disproportionate impact do little to remedy the consequences of historical decisions that caused the disparities in the first place (Karner et al., 2020; Martens, 2017; Sheller, 2018).

This historical context helps explain how race and identity shape travel behavior today. In this chapter, I detail the roots of racialized travel behavior in the United States and make the case for why transportation planners must consider race and racism as explanatory factors in travel and why race-neutral planning processes exacerbate disparities. I then share additional historical background of how race and racism have been embedded in historical transportation decision making processes. I next describe three issues in which racial identity is especially salient: policing and the law, safety and security, and the ideas of belonging and othering. Finally, I conclude with implications for changes in transportation practice and policy. Together, these issues comprise what planner and researcher Brown (2021) has termed "arrested mobility" and call on the transportation community to both understand and remedy injustice.

2. The limitations of race-neutral travel behavior analysis

Travel behavior can be thought as a set of realized practices in response to the availability of transportation resources and a supportive context for enabling travel. The determinants of travel behavior are complex; the assumption most widely used in travel demand forecasting is that travelers make choices consistent with economic rationality, perhaps subject to some heterogeneity in preferences across the population (Ben-Akiva and Lerman, 1985; Meyer and Miller, 2001). People will choose transportation modes, travel routes, and destinations according to the options that will cost them the least amount or time or money. Those decisions are bound by the resources they have; a person cannot drive, for example, if they do not have access to a vehicle. But economic rationality is not the only or the best way to characterize travel behavior. Scholars from traditions in psychology and public health have shown that other attributes and domains affect decisions: attitudes, subjective norms, perceptions of the ability to carry out a behavior, sociocultural relationships, individual characteristics, and the built and natural environments feature in various theoretical models of travel behavior (Ajzen, 1991; Handy and Xing, 2011; Sallis et al., 2006; Schneider, 2013). Racial identity figures into these domains because many past decisions were discriminatory on the basis of race, but race is rarely acknowledged as a causal factor in travel behavior.

Traditional planning methods are not equipped to analyze transportation through a racialized framework because race is undertheorized in explanatory analyses or deliberately omitted from quantitative transportation models. Racial categories are used as descriptive variables when identifying impacts, such as by measuring whether a new transit line will provide access to a majority Latino neighborhood or whether a certain share of Black drivers will experience travel time savings from a freeway expansion. But these analyses do not measure why, for example, access to transit may not induce Latino residents in the neighborhood to use the system or why Black drivers may not want the freeway expansion in the first place. Travel demand models used to develop long range transportation plans exclude race as an explanatory—or even control—factor because analysts have argued that while we observe differences in travel patterns by race, race does not *cause* those differences and so its inclusion as a variable in explaining behavior is inappropriate (Karner and Niemeier, 2013). These omissions, deliberate or not, are often reflections of the disciplinary and personal backgrounds and priorities of transportation professionals (Lowe, 2021; Vigar, 2017).

Nevertheless, racial identity does matter when explaining travel behavior because of the way race operates as a social construct, particularly, but not exclusively, in the United States. It is true that one does not find themselves unable to afford a car because of phenotype; income is the direct determinant. But a Black shopper might be denied credit or quoted a higher price because an auto dealer discriminates, making race an indirect causal factor

(Ayres and Siegelman, 1995; Rice and Schwartz, 2018). Likewise, inability to walk or bike places may be impossible because of a lack of connectivity due to physical barriers such as highway infrastructure. Again, that does not happen because one has dark skin, but because decision-makers disproportionately placed freeway infrastructure in communities of color (Adkins et al., 2017). And the criminalization of Black and brown bodies places even further barriers on mobility from outside the transportation domain (Seo, 2019). An updated model of travel behavior would explicitly center racial identity and racism as explanatory factors because of the ways they intersect with other individual characteristics, the social environment, the built environment, and the regulatory frameworks in which those domains are embedded (Fig. 1). This conceptual model proposes that individual factors, such socioeconomic characteristics and travel constraints, attitudes and perceptions toward transportation and land use characteristics, social networks, and urban form together with the physical environment are interrelated and influence one another (Barajas, 2016; Handy and Xing, 2011). Those factors influence the ways people move around. But the web of relationships is affected by wide-ranging policies and regulations, which in turn have been shaped by the ways that racism have pervaded public decision making. For these reasons, race-neutral transportation planning risks reinforcing, rather than resolving, systemic injustices.

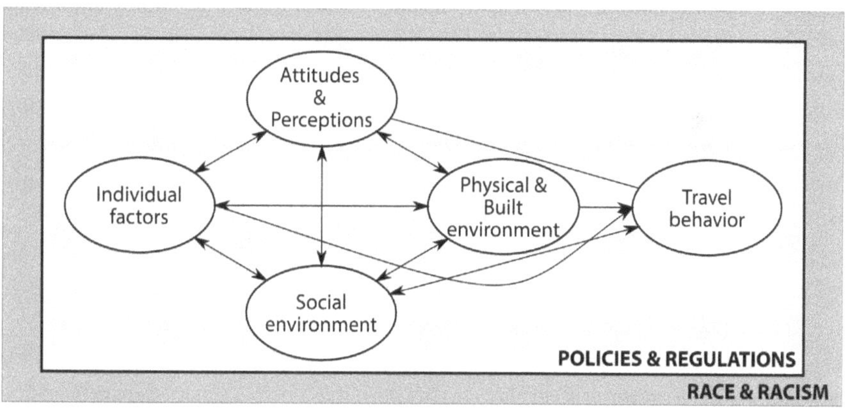

Fig. 1 A proposed conceptual framework of travel behavior, centering race and racism as explanatory factors for travel behavior. *Adapted from Handy, S., Xing, Y., 2011. "Factors correlated with bicycle commuting: a study in six small U.S. Cities." Int. J. Sustain. Transp. 5 (2), 91–110. https://doi.org/10.1080/15568310903514789 and Barajas, J.M., 2016. "Making Invisible Riders Visible: Motivations for Bicycling and Public Transit Use Among Latino Immigrants." University of California, Berkeley, CA. Dissertation.*

3. Mobility and its limits from yesterday to today

Transportation is just one manifestation of mobility, which can be characterized not only by day-to-day travel but also by migration and the flows of ideas. Freedom and mobility have been twin ideals in the United States from its colonial roots. Settling on the shores of a "new" world by moving from the old brought freedoms eventually codified in the constitution of the new country. After independence, settlers marched continually westward across the continent, establishing trading towns, forming organized territories, and eventually joining the union as an integral part of the US. But this perpetual mobility has always come at the expense of people who are Indigenous, Black, or people of color. Colonial encroachment on Native lands led to death and displacement as white settlers warred with and forcibly removed entire peoples from their ancestral homes (Dunbar-Ortiz, 2014). The links between freedom and mobility were especially clear in the antebellum South; enslaved Africans could go only where slaveholders said they could go. Should they have chosen to go beyond those limits, enslaved people were returned and punished for deigning to be mobile. The Fugitive Slave Act of 1850 saw to it that agents of the federal government were to act as the police of "fugitives from service or labor" no matter where in the jurisdiction of the United States they escaped to (Campbell, 1970).

The conclusion of the US Civil War brought the end of slavery but not the end of restrictions on Black mobility. While Black men were accorded the same rights and privileges as white men under the law, entrenched white power in the South prohibited them from exercising those rights in fact. Real property promised by the federal government to African Americans after emancipation was never delivered, and a system of sharecropping in which renters paid for their homes by returning a portion of their crop to the landowner chained most Black farmers to the land and curtailed economic mobility (Royce, 1993). For those with means to survive outside of this form of economic slavery, Black mobility was restricted at different scales, especially after the end of the Reconstruction era in the late 1870s. Under Jim Crow laws, public and private spaces became segregated, wherein the movement of Black people was policed at a micro-scale. Some of the first segregated spaces were rail cars. It was in defiance of this segregation that *Plessy v. Ferguson* was brought before the Supreme Court in 1896, after Homer Plessy, an African American man, refused to move from a whites-only train car in Louisiana and was arrested. In that case, the Court held that separate facilities were constitutional so long as they were equal, entrenching the restrictions on Black movement with the force of law (Woodward, 1964).

Between the late 1800s and the 1960s, transportation continued to be at the heart of the struggles for freedom and mobility under the specter of institutional racism and state policing power. Indeed, one of the initial sparks of the Civil Rights Movement was the Montgomery Bus Boycott, a protest against the treatment of Black people as second-class citizens on public transportation (Bullard, 2004). Even after laws enforcing racial segregation on transportation were struck down by the Supreme Court, southern states refused to acknowledge them and continued to enforce the invalidated discriminatory statutes. This prompted the Freedom Rides in 1961, where racially integrated teams rode interstate buses in the South to bring attention to continued segregation (Arsenault, 2006). Eventually, the Freedom Riders prevailed and the Interstate Commerce Commission, which regulated buses and trains that cross state lines, began to enforce its anti-segregation policies.

4. The reconfiguring of communities of color and justice responses

4.1 The racism of transportation infrastructure development

Although the Freedom Rides and other Civil Rights actions helped end segregation on public and private carriers, discrimination and racial policing in transportation persists today. The automobile is now the vehicle by which many people experience today's issues of transportation inequity, from policing to safety. The car has become the quintessential symbol of freedom across the globe; car ownership grew by an average of 4.6% year-over-year in the second half of the 20th century, and by an even greater 7.5% in developing countries (Dargay et al., 2007). Empirical evidence in transportation psychology has shown strong and reinforcing links between positive affect, such as pride, status, and independence, and car use (Moody and Zhao, 2020; Steg et al., 2001). Some scholars have argued that we are now living in a "system of automobility," in which "automobility has reshaped citizenship and the public sphere via the mobilization of civil societies" (Sheller and Urry, 2000, p. 739). As I will argue later, biased policing of this automobility constrains drivers of color to being less than full participants in society.

It is hard to understate the injustices for people of color caused by the automobile and auto-centric development in the United States. (See Fig. 2 for a

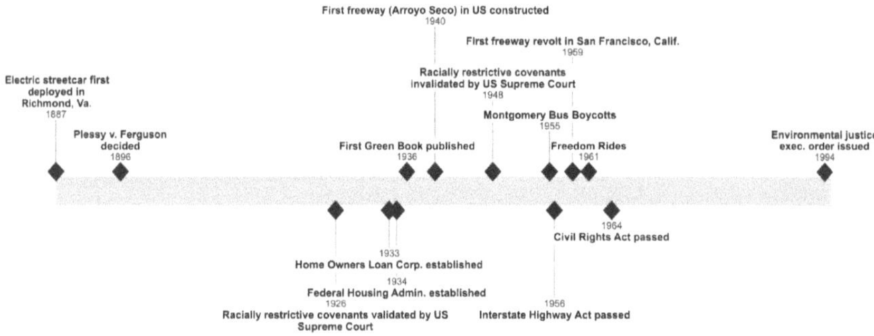

Fig. 2 Selected events relevant to racialized experiences in transportation.

timeline.) The stage was set through housing and land use policies that fostered racial segregation in the early part of the 20th century, followed by the use of transportation infrastructure as a means for urban renewal (Rothstein, 2017). The suburbs could not have been built—and the white flight to them could not have occurred—without the benefit of transportation infrastructure. New suburban homes were generally built along electric streetcar or trolley lines, run by private corporations and sometimes subsidized by housing developers themselves to ensure access to their developments (Jackson, 1985). In many places, however, homes would not be sold to African Americans either because zoning codes explicitly forbade it at the municipal level or because racially restrictive covenants on housing deeds prevented it at the individual level (Rothstein, 2017). Both means of discrimination in the housing market were invalided by the US Supreme Court in separate cases, though local governments, developers, and real estate agents continued to find indirect ways to segregate.

The federal government was also complicit in the project of racial segregation. As more homes were being built but as economic conditions worsened in the Great Depression, the United States established two new housing programs to spur home ownership: the Home Owners Loan Corporation (HOLC), which issued its own loans, and the Federal Housing Administration (FHA), which insured bank-issued mortgages. Because the federal government was on the hook in case of default, they needed a way to ensure that the properties backed by the loans were of sufficient quality to maintain their values (Rothstein, 2017). The appraisals were based primarily on the characteristics of the neighborhoods, color-coded on maps from the "best" neighborhoods (green) to "hazardous" neighborhoods (red), and guarantees would not be applied for loans to borrowers in the red neighborhoods ("redlining"). The assessment of neighborhood quality was almost invariably judged by the preponderance of the racial groups that lived there, using terms such as "infiltration" and "undesirable" to describe African Americans, Asians, and other people of color and immigrant groups as akin to forms of environmental pollution (Nelson et al., 2021). In this way, official programs severely limited the opportunities of Black residents and other people of color to own and improve homes, depressing their values through redlining.

The low economic value of land only compounded racially motivated decisions to site new freeway infrastructure in predominately Black neighborhoods and neighborhoods of color. While highway construction began not long after the public began purchasing autos en masse, road-building got a boost after the passage of the Federal-Aid Highway Act of 1956. The law ushered in the Interstate Highway era in which the federal government pledged to pay 90 cents on the dollar for every project built. In many cases, that infrastructure was deliberately designed to traverse Black neighborhoods, both before and after the Act's implementation, in the name of slum clearance and urban renewal (Bullard, 2004; Rothstein, 2017). The new auto-oriented infrastructure displaced Black residents and other people of color groups for the benefit of commuters who came into the city by day and left for the suburbs at night. Freeways built in St. Paul, Minn., Miami, New Orleans, Los Angeles, and elsewhere destroyed the fabric of tight-knit Black and Latino communities or otherwise redefined the landscape of the residents who remained (Avila, 2014). The legacy of New York City commissioner Robert Moses, who above all shaped the city as we know it today, has been well documented for its racist effects there. He bulldozed through low-income neighborhoods and deliberately built parkway overpasses low enough that public transit vehicles could not take city residents to beaches and outlying parks as just two examples (Caro, 1975; Lewis, 2013). The commissioner was able to get legislation passed to prohibit buses and commercial vehicles from using state parkways—originally designed to be linear parks with to recreational destinations on Long Island, but quickly turned into commuter routes. He coupled law with the permanence of construction to ensure that buses that served mostly Black city residents would never be able to use those parkways; none of the 204 bridges spanning the parkways exceeded 13 ft in height, the standard size of a city bus (Caro, 1975). Some have argued that the bridge heights were consistent with earlier parkway designs, but the average height of the first bridges built under Moses were significantly lower than previous examples (Campanella, 2017).

While limited-access highways were the main culprit in the displacement of Black residents and other people of color via transportation, rail infrastructure developed for the benefit of suburb-to-city commuters harmed communities in some instances as well. The San Francisco Bay Area Rapid Transit (BART) system was oriented around getting office workers from the farther reaches of the region into San Francisco. And while the rail system ran above ground down the heart of West Oakland's Black business district, it was undergrounded in wealthier parts of the urban core like San Francisco and North Berkeley (Golub et al., 2013). Few modern-day projects are as explicitly destructive to residential and commercial infrastructure, but the fabric of communities of color has been disrupted by the gentrification and displacement processes associated with transit and bicycle investment (Flanagan et al., 2016; Lubitow and Miller, 2013; Padeiro et al., 2019; Zuk et al., 2018).

4.2 Justice frameworks in transportation

The deliberate destruction of Black, Indigenous, and People of Color communities via transportation infrastructure no longer happens on the scale that it once did. Multiracial coalitions formed to lead freeway revolts beginning in the late 1950s and, in a series of hard-fought wins, led to the cancellation or rerouting of infrastructure and some recognition of the harms that construction caused (Avila, 2014; Mohl, 2004). These and other struggles for transportation justice can be thought of as precursors to the environmental justice movement. The movement was born when residents of majority Black Warren County, North Carolina, one of the poorest counties in the state, protested construction of a landfill meant to contain toxic waste that had been illegally dumped along rural highway shoulders (McGurty, 2000). Much like in the fight for civil rights two decades earlier, transportation was central to contested claims about the unfair distribution of goods and harms toward people of color and the recognition of people to make those claims (Schlosberg, 2009).

Together with traditional community organizing, frameworks of environmental justice, environmental racism, and transportation racism have been used by advocates in their struggles for fair transportation systems. In part, this is helped by federal law and policies: Title VI of the Civil Rights Act and the Environmental Justice executive order together prohibit discrimination of the receipt of federal funds on the basis of race and direct federal agencies to ensure no group protected by the laws receives disproportionate benefits or experiences disproportionate burdens. Transportation advocates have used evidence of racial disparities and organized campaigns to achieve goals such as lower transit fares and more parity in funding for bus and rail modes (Grengs, 2005; Mann, 2004), elimination of diesel buses from Black neighborhoods (Bullard et al., 2004), defeating the long-blocked expansion of transit service into a majority Black, high-poverty county (Karner and Duckworth, 2019), and greater investment in cycling programs and infrastructure in Latino communities (Lubitow et al., 2016; Moore-Monroy et al., 2016). Although these wins are worthy of celebration, they reflect only incremental and site-specific improvements in equitable transportation. They do not begin to achieve deep structural change and belie the near futility that justice advocates have faced when seeking government remedy because of the state's entrenched interests in maintaining the status quo (Karner et al., 2020; Pulido, 2017).

The imprint of the historical processes reviewed earlier remain to limit mobility and opportunity for people of color, despite the small wins to achieve a fairer distribution of resources and the policies that purport to protect that fair distribution. These practices and systems have yielded a long list of distributional inequities in the benefits and burdens of transportation as well as in the processes of transportation planning: people of color have lower access to vehicles and transportation service, jobs and opportunities, active transportation infrastructure and new mobility services, and suffer from poorer health outcomes related to emissions and inactive travel (Bastiaanssen et al., 2020; Braun et al., 2019; Grengs, 2012; Ihlanfeldt and Sjoquist, 1998; Karner et al., 2016; Lee et al., 2017; Mueller et al., 2015; Rowangould, 2013). Environmental justice policy and civil rights legislation that seek to ensure racial equity in transportation access look to the future but do not assure "restorative justice" or reparations for past harms, which several scholars have argued is a logical goal emanating from civil rights legislation (Marcantonio et al., 2017; Martens and Golub, 2018). Multiple barriers exist to this sort of affirmative action: geographic equity considerations often mean that urban areas—the locations of most historical damage from transportation planning—receive less than a fair share of transportation funding; the composition of regional transportation boards often does not reflect the diversity among their constituents; and racial equity criteria are sparingly used when prioritizing transportation projects (Krapp et al., 2021; Manaugh et al., 2015; Martens and Golub, 2018; Sanchez and Wolf, 2007; Sciara and Wachs, 2007). Some scholars have proposed that a way forward for transportation justice in planning practice is to shift the object of equity from the distribution of mobility or resources to the distribution of accessibility (Levine et al., 2019; Martens, 2017; Pereira et al., 2017). By seeking to raise average access across groups while also minimizing access disparities, those who have been left behind by previous planning practices will see their fortunes rise to a greater degree (Martens et al., 2012; Pereira et al., 2017).

Other scholars have argued that achieving justice requires a shift in focus from measuring and comparing transportation outcomes to addressing a variety of other injustices that people of color face when it comes to free movement. Sheller (2018) has proposed *mobility justice* as a critical theoretical framework that builds upon environmental justice, spatial justice, and transportation justice and which considers movement as the fundamental object of justice. Because we are creatures who spend our lives on the move, Sheller argues, understanding disparities in access to transportation is not enough to achieve justice: "Beyond access to transport, we need to understand the ways in which uneven mobilities produce differentially enabled (or disabled) subjects and differentially enabling (or disabling) spaces" (Sheller 2018, p. 28). While distributive justice has been the main means by which transportation theorists and practitioners have conceived of fairness in the transportation system (e.g., Martens, 2017; Pereira and Karner, 2021; Pereira et al., 2017), a mobility justice perspective points out distribution is just one of many inequities that people of color face. Recognition of groups and expertise, access to power and decision making, and the valuation of knowledge are all facets of planning in which people of color have been denied full participation (Sheller, 2018). A transportation system based on mobility justice thus calls on practitioners and advocates to center race and identity in their processes, acknowledge and seek to repair harm, look beyond modes of transportation to people and their needs, and value community experiences as essential data for decision making (Untokening Collective, 2017). Mobility justice perspectives also highlight hidden connections to transportation, such as educational equity (Bierbaum et al., 2021) and gendered and intersectional violence in transportation systems (Ding et al., 2020; Loukaitou-Sideris et al., 2020; Lubitow et al., 2020).

5. Understanding the intersections of race, racism, and travel behavior

The history of racist practices, both individual and systemic, has affected the way that people of color lived and moved about. Land use and transportation systems segregated people and inflicted significant damage to neighborhoods, and methods and theories that planners have used have shown to be inadequate in providing remedy for these actions. While the questions of which groups benefit from and are burdened by transportation fall under the purview of transportation professionals, many issues that influence how people travel are not explicitly transportation-related. And yet these issues speak to how race is central to travel. This section will address three of these issues: policing and the law, safety and security, and neighborhood belonging.

5.1 Mobility, policing, and race

Traffic enforcement stops are the most common form of interaction between the police and the public in the United States. In 2015, over 53 million residents had some form of police contact. Roughly 62% of those contacts occurred while people were driving a vehicle, riding as a passenger in a vehicle, or as a result of traffic crash (Davis et al., 2018). Put another way, about one in every eight drivers are stopped by the police every year (Epp et al., 2014). But those stops are not equally distributed across the population; about twice as many, or one in four, Black drivers are stopped annually (Epp et al., 2014).

Historians and legal scholars have argued that the proliferation of contact between police and everyday residents was singularly driven by interests related to the automobile. In the first instance, automobiles reordered who had rights to the road. Until the 1920s, there were few if any strict laws regulating street use. Pedestrians, horse-drawn carriages, bicycles, trams, and the few cars that existed all intermingled on city streets.[b] As the automobile became more ubiquitous, however, and as the number of traffic crashes increased as a result, laws that had previously favored pedestrians shifted to ensure the smooth flow of automobiles, spearheaded by auto-interest groups. In short, these changes led to the invention and criminalization of jaywalking[c] and shaped the hierarchy on the streets (Norton, 2011).

[b] One of the best illustrations of street use in that day is the short film "A Trip Down Market Street," shot in 1906. The film captures a scene from the perspective of a streetcar traveling down Market Street in San Francisco toward the ferry building, with horse-drawn carriages, pedestrians, bicycles, and cars all navigating the street together in the same space. Several restored and edited versions of the film are available online; one of them is at https://www.youtube.com/watch?v=8YRbMMqj0qw.

[c] Even the term jaywalking has classist undertones, being derived from the word "jay," a slang term for an ignorant or provincial person.

While the proliferation of the automobile prompted changes in the way that street space was regulated, another profound change in policing came about with the way that courts viewed traffic stops with respect to constitutional rights. American jurisprudence came to see automobiles as conveying little privacy to individuals, cementing the right to privacy within one's home as legally different from a right to privacy on public roadways (Seo, 2019). This lessened right to privacy extends to most police stops in the public right of way and has led to extensive use of stop-and-frisk—that is, a brief stop where police pat down a suspect if they have a reasonable suspicion of a crime having occurred—as a policing tool. Opponents of stop-and-frisk, such as the NAACP (the National Association for the Advancement of Colored People, the most prominent civil rights organization in the US), warned of its consequences for Black people, borne out by the evidence of disproportionate application in cities like New York and Chicago (ACLU of Illinois, 2015; Fagan et al., 2010; Howell, 2016). Courts have also reasoned that officers should be given the benefit of the doubt as to what constitutes a legitimate traffic stop. Because nearly every vehicle action could be read as a violation of the law in some regard, the decision to pull over a vehicle is almost always within reason. While race cannot be used as the reason to initiate the stop, evidence of disparate racial impacts would not necessarily be enough to prevent stops. In other words, if the police wanted to profile individuals by race, they could—so long as the professed reason for the traffic stop was any violation of the vehicle code (Baumgartner et al., 2018; Seo, 2019).

Abundant evidence bears out the fact that people of color are stopped more often by the police (Epp et al., 2014; Harris, 1999; Pierson et al., 2020; Warren et al., 2006). Young Black men are taught how to deal with this reality when they drive, walk, or otherwise move about so as to not endanger their lives during an encounter (Gandbhir and Foster, 2015). Evidence of difference is not necessarily evidence of bias, however; scholars have used a number of techniques to investigate the degree to which Black and Brown drivers are disproportionately subject to police scrutiny relative to their counterparts. One body of work has examined the initiation of the stops themselves. When they occur is important. In one study, Pierson et al. (2020) compiled a database of nearly 100 million traffic stops from over 50 state and municipal police departments. Black drivers were stopped more often than white drivers, while Latino drivers were stopped less often. To assess whether the differences in stop rates were evidence of bias, the researchers used an adjustment technique known as the "veil of darkness" by estimating the likelihood an individual was stopped, controlling for the time of day, under the assumption that officers who stop individuals at night cannot observe skin color as well they can during daylight hours. There was a substantial drop in the proportion of Black drivers stopped after dark, giving evidence for racial discrimination based on this test (Pierson et al., 2020).

For what reason the stops occur is also important. Police may stop drivers for either safety reasons, such as speeding or driving under the influence, or for discretionary reasons, such as a broken tail light or a lapsed registration, that do not have immediate safety consequences (Epp et al., 2014). Safety stops exhibit a lower incidence of discriminatory patterns compared to discretionary stops (Baumgartner et al., 2018). When a police department in North Carolina shifted its traffic enforcement emphasis to safety stops in an effort to reduce serious motor vehicle crashes, both the total number of traffic stops and the ratio of stops involving Black drivers to white drivers decreased, as did the number of vehicle crashes (Fliss et al., 2020). Traffic stops have long been used as a crime deterrent as advocated by the "broken windows" theory of policing (Wilson and Kelling, 1982), a theory that posits that a preponderance of minor crimes like vandalism contribute to major ones, but the authors found that the number of crimes did not increase relative to control cities. The same logic applies to pedestrian and bicycle stops. Citations are disproportionately issued in Black and Latino neighborhoods and the vast majority are given minor infractions such as riding a bike on the sidewalk or walking along a roadway (Barajas, 2019; Wisniewski, 2018).

A second body of work has examined the outcomes of the stops; specifically, the likelihood with which drivers would be searched during the stop. The evidence for racial bias is convincing. Across 55 million traffic stops and in every state for which they had data, the racial disparities in who was searched were large and consistent. On average, Black drivers were searched twice as often as white or Latino drivers (Baumgartner et al., 2017). A study that focused on the 5 million traffic stops that occurred in Illinois and North Carolina found that Black and Latino drivers were searched more often than white drivers, and men in all racial and ethnic categories were searched than women, controlling for racial and socioeconomic neighborhood characteristics (Shoub et al., 2020). In another study of 20 million observations from Illinois examining both racial and gender characteristics of drivers, one researcher found that the higher the degree to which someone fit the profile of a young, Black, poor male, the more likely they were to have been searched after a traffic stop and the less likely they were to have received a warning instead of a citation (Christiani, 2020). Finally, a study of 40 million police stops across four states found that Black men were more likely to be stopped and searched but less likely to be found with contraband, particularly when the stop was initiated for discretionary rather than safety reasons (Roach et al., 2020).

Latinos also face scrutiny on the streets, further complicated by immigration policy. Immigration restrictions have tightened in the wake of the increasing priority placed on counterterrorism efforts since September 11, 2001, although anti-immigrant narratives have persisted throughout US history. In several states, including Arizona, Mississippi, and Alabama, legislatures passed what colloquially have been called "show me your papers" laws, in which local police were empowered to ask people they stopped whether they were lawfully present in the United States. US Immigration and Customs Enforcement can establish memoranda of agreement with local and state law enforcement agencies to allow them to act as federal immigration officers when they detain individuals under the 287(g) program. No matter the statues under which the police operate, the additional powers granted to police act to limit the mobility of all immigrants, documented or not, because of the racial profiling associated with such programs. Many undocumented immigrants fear leaving the home or alter their travel to avoid detection, resulting in lost opportunities, including work and access to health care (Maldonado et al., 2016; Stuesse and Coleman, 2014; Toomey et al., 2014). Some of these policies may account for travel behavior differences, such as the lower likelihood of commuting by car among undocumented immigrants (Allen and Wang, 2020).

5.2 Safety and security

Transportation safety research and practice is concerned with preventing collisions between vehicles and other vehicles, pedestrians, and cyclists. Historically, the solution to this problem has been to try to eliminate fatal consequences of inevitable human error via engineering countermeasures, for example, by creating "clear zones" devoid of fixed objects that drivers can crash into regardless of whether the road is a high-speed freeway or in an dense urban area (Dumbaugh and Gattis, 2005). This sort of design, along with improvements in car safety standards, has reduced injury outcomes for drivers but has done little to nothing to reduce the danger for vulnerable road users (Noland, 2003). In response, researchers and advocates have proposed an alternative approach known as "safe systems" that takes driver error into account by slowing speeds, encouraging safe behavior, and designing safe roads (Dumbaugh et al., 2020). In practice, the safe systems approach is implemented as Vision Zero, first established in Sweden and subsequently adopted around the world, and shifts some of the onus for safety onto road system designers (Cushing et al., 2016).

The Vision Zero approach is also a data-driven approach to safety planning, wherein cities use information about the most dangerous traffic locations to prioritize interventions. Many Vision Zero cities find that a disproportionate number of high-crash intersections and corridors are in communities of color (City and County of San Francisco, 2015; City of Chicago, 2017; City of Los Angeles, 2015), likely because of infrastructure disparities documented earlier. National-level statistics also bear out the disproportionate safety burden that people of color face (Fig. 3). Black road users especially are overrepresented in pedestrian and bicycle fatalities relative to their share in the population, trips taken, and miles traveled using statistics from the two most recent national travel surveys, in 2009 and

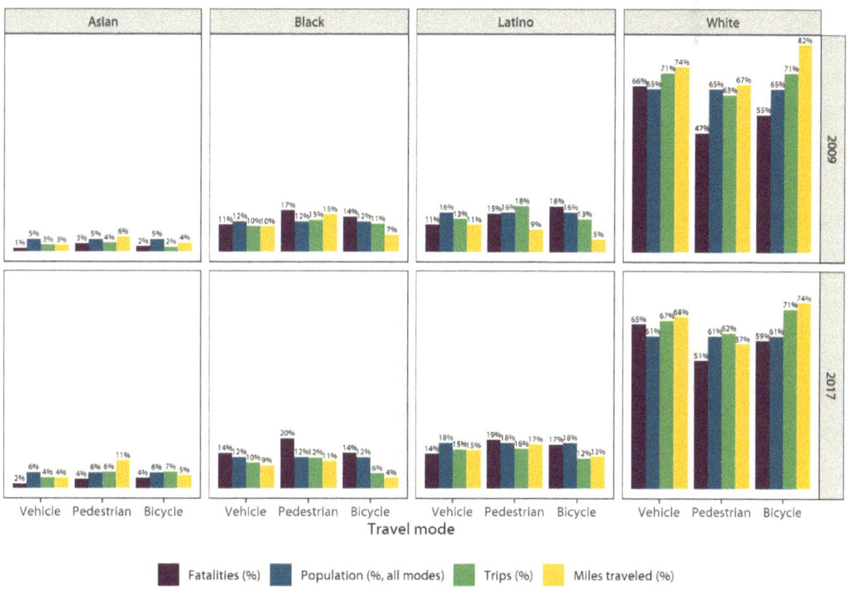

Fig. 3 Share of road fatalities compared to population, trips made, and miles traveled by race/ethnicity and year. Denominator excludes unidentified race/ethnicity. *Data sources: National Highway Traffic Safety Administration, 2019. "Fatality Analysis Reporting System (FARS)." https:/www.nhtsa.gov/research-data/fatality-analysis-reporting-system-fars; U. S. Census Bureau, 2020. "American Community Survey 5-Year Estimates: 2014–2018." https://www.census.gov/programs-surveys/acs; Federal Highway Administration, 2017. "National Household Travel Survey." https:/nhts.ornl.gov.*

2017. Likewise, the most dangerous corridors for pedestrians are in majority Black and Latino neighborhoods (Schneider et al., 2021). The reasons for these disparities include biases in infrastructure funding and implementation in communities of color and increased vulnerability associated with personal travel, such as night-shift workers who travel during darkness and new immigrants who are not yet accustomed to US traffic norms (Braun et al., 2019; Chen et al., 2012; Cradock et al., 2009; Lee et al., 2016; Smith et al., 2017; Yu, 2014).

But safety carries a double meaning. People in communities of color are often equally or more concerned with personal security, or safety from violence. Pedestrians and cyclists, who travel in "exposed" modes, may be at greatest risk (Appleyard and Ferrell, 2017). A study of New Jersey residents in Black and Latino communities found that cyclists and non-cyclists alike rated fear of robbery or assault as the second-highest rated barrier to cycling after fear of traffic collisions (Brown, 2016). In a study measuring the efficacy of a bicycle education and training program on overweight Black and Latino adults, researchers found that about two-thirds of participants rated fear of crime as a barrier to cycling. The intervention helped reduce that barrier relative to a control group in the short term, but after a longer term follow-up, the difference was no longer significant (Schneider et al., 2018). To counter potential danger from interpersonal violence, cyclists in low-income communities and communities of color may adopt different cycling behaviors than cyclists in other communities, preferring to cycle on busier streets where they are most visible rather than on quieter streets that may be safer from traffic (Lusk et al., 2019).

Residents of communities of color and low-income communities also rate high crime as significant barriers to walking and accessing transit (Barajas, 2020; Coren et al., 2021), and these barriers may be even higher for women and gender non-conforming individuals (Loukaitou-Sideris et al., 2020; Lubitow et al., 2020). An educational intervention in which participants learned about systemic strategies for improving pedestrian safety found no change in perceptions of crime as barriers to walking in the short-term; roughly 60% of participants described danger from crime as a barrier to walking both before and after the workshop (Barajas et al., 2019). Interpersonal violence compounds the danger from the ever-present street violence, creating even greater vulnerabilities for those who have few other options to walking or cycling (Lachapelle and Noland, 2015). The possibilities of danger are particularly salient for youth of color. While planning research and practice tends to emphasize changes in the built environment to promote walkability and safe routes to school, young students describe shootings, gang members, and "broken windows"–type disorder as significant barriers to walking to school in inner-city neighborhoods (Banerjee et al., 2014; Jamme et al., 2018).

5.3 Neighborhood context: Othering and belonging

While feelings of insecurity arise from crime rates and the danger of the unknown, barriers to travel also exist for people who draw suspicion because they are judged not to belong in a particular place. One explanation for the pervasive nature of racial profiling in police stops is the racial threat hypothesis. The hypothesis suggests that elites seek to impose greater control on the Black population as it grows because of the political, economic, and criminal threats they pose (e.g., Eitle et al., 2002). In some places, there is evidence that this theory may hold for traffic stops, where more stops occur in areas with more Black or Latino residents (Ingram, 2007; Roh and Robinson, 2009). But others have found compelling evidence for a different "race-out-of-place" theory, in which drivers who are assumed to be interlopers to the neighborhood are treated as more suspect. Scholars have found that Black drivers are more likely to be stopped in predominately white neighborhoods and vice versa for white drivers (Novak and Chamlin, 2012; Rojek et al., 2012). An version of this theory grounded in economics is the postindustrial policing thesis, which suggests that gentrifying neighborhoods or cities with growing creative class economies will increase social order policing for relatively minor infractions of the law (Laniyonu, 2018; Newberry, 2021; Sharp, 2014).

The implications of not belonging in a neighborhood are increased surveillance of people of color by both police and private citizens on the one hand, and their suspicion of planning efforts on the other, heightened by the twin concerns of gentrification and displacement. Particularly with respect to cycling and recreational facilities, communities of color have viewed new infrastructure with skepticism because they perceive the investment to have come only after economic redevelopment of their neighborhoods had begun (Hoffmann and Lugo, 2014; Lubitow and Miller, 2013). Mainstream bicycle advocacy, too, has promoted cycling from the perspective of the young, middle-class, white professional returning to the city, while ignoring the circumstances of people of color and laborers who have relied on cycling in the absence of safe infrastructure (Hoffmann, 2016; Lugo, 2018; Sheller, 2015). These histories have manifested in differences in the use of such facilities. Marginalized cyclists, for example, have substituted "human infrastructure," or their accumulated knowledge of and experiences with the city, to navigate when hard infrastructure was non-existent, relying on paths they know to be safe even if designated routes were built (Lugo, 2013). In the case of new recreational facilities, people of color who cycle or walk along paths self-segregate away from gentrifying neighborhoods to avoid inviting suspicion and run-ins with the police (Harris et al., 2020a,b).

The perception of non-auto users as "others" is also evident in public transit in the United States. There are both income and race divides both between public transit riders and users of other modes and within public transit modes themselves. Data from the 2017 National Household Travel Survey show that transit riders are on the whole poorer than users of other modes, while bus riders have a median household income below poverty wages compared to six-figure household incomes for rail riders. The majority of transit riders are people of color, compared to less than half of all other modes. Again, there are stark differences between bus riders and rail riders: people of color make up almost three-quarters of bus riders, compared to almost one-half of subway and light-rail riders and one-third of commuter rail riders (Federal Highway Administration, 2017). These demographic patterns are hard to disentangle from a general stigma against public transportation (Schweitzer, 2014); some neighborhood residents oppose new transit service because they fear the "other" who rides it (Weitz, 2008), while transit riders of color themselves perceive discrimination on the part of other riders or transit officials as barriers to use (Barajas et al., 2018; Liu and Schachter, 2007; Lubitow et al., 2017).

6. Conclusions and policy implications

A long history of racist practices, including individual discrimination and systemic exclusion from the right to safe and free movement via government policy, has led to profound disparities in the benefits and burdens of transportation for people of color in the United States. One can trace how questions of mobility, transportation, and race have been intertwined across eras—from colonial settlement through slavery and Jim Crow to the civil rights movement and beyond to modern-day urban and transportation planning—and observe how that has placed limits on access and opportunity for marginalized people. This history also gives perspective on how policing, insecurity, and othering work to limit the mobility of people of color.

The effects of distributional inequities together with policing are lost economic opportunities, poor health outcomes, and even death in "arrested mobility" (Brown, 2021) for Black people and other people of color. Taken together, the links between history, planning, and policing also give context for why race and racism is a fundamental determinant of travel behavior. Focusing on race and racism in transportation research and practice helps guide how to approach achieving a more just transportation system.

First, it is important to account for race not just as a control variable in transportation models, but to center it in analysis to appropriately account for its effects on travel behavior. This includes incorporating information about racial identity in any models that are used to support planning and policy efforts. It also includes identifying *how* information about race is specified. The way we measure and interpret race can change how we fundamentally understand the relationships between measurement and outcome. For example, when analyzing effects of race, default comparisons to a white reference population reproduces the notion that white groups are the norm (Johfre and Freese, 2021). Point estimates of impacts without attention to the distribution of those impacts can lead to misleading results and can misstate the effects of inventions across populations of concern (Bills and Walker, 2017). In some cases, such as traffic collisions, race information is not always collected or released, making it impossible to make claims about or develop remedies to unjust conditions. As new data sources proliferate, it is important to understand how the data points are collected or contributed and to acknowledge and address the inherent biases prior to allowing them to guide decisions (Williams, 2020). And while proper quantitative data about race can aid in better decision making, it is important to remember that not all data can be captured by numbers—lived experiences are valid qualitative data points—and that analysts' own positionalities contribute biases and errors in the research and modeling process (Lowe, 2021).

Second, adopting a broader perspective about equity and justice is fundamental to achieving fairer transportation systems. The history described earlier helps convey why transportation inequity is more than a problem of benefits and burdens, and why some theories of transportation justice that focus on individuals and on access alone fall short. Mobility justice requires more than just ensuring equal distribution of infrastructure, resources, and service; it "calls for recognition, participation, deliberation, and procedural fairness to be up for discussion, adjustment, and repair" (Sheller, 2018, p. 28). Advocates of mobility justice in transportation practice encourage planners and decision-makers to reckon with history, to value community experience and knowledge, and to recognize that identity is linked to vulnerability (Untokening Collective, 2017). Transportation planning built on such principles requires fundamental shifts in the relationship between governments and communities, moving beyond perfunctory community engagement and working on solutions that prioritize equitable outcomes over mere mitigation of existing inequalities and findings of no disparate impact.

Finally, a focus on race in transportation highlights the need to work outside of professional silos to recognize how other domains affect travel and how policies to improve or enhance transportation may have unintended consequences. For example, many plans that seek to improve transportation safety rely on traffic enforcement as a fundamental component of the overall strategy (e.g., City of Chicago, 2017). But any policy that calls for additional policing places people of color—and Black people especially—at disproportionate risk despite the benefits from crash reductions. Some efforts are beginning to walk back the role of police in safety after a greater attention to racial injustice in the United States was sparked in the summer 2020 protests; national policy advocates have called for replacing additional traffic enforcement with more safely designed streets (Shahum, 2020; Transportation Alternatives, 2020), the state of Virginia has taken steps to decriminalize jaywalking (Wilson, 2021), and several US cities are reforming the way the police are involved in traffic stops. More recently, connections between transportation and public health professionals have been strengthened; stronger links between transportation and community development may also produce stronger conditions for transportation justice.

Acknowledgments

Many thanks to Miriam Solis, Geneviève Boisjoly, and Rafael H. M. Pereira for their invaluable critiques and comments.

References

ACLU of Illinois, 2015. Stop and Frisk in Chicago. https://www.aclu-il.org/sites/default/files/wp-content/uploads/2015/03/ACLU_StopandFrisk_6.pdf.

Adkins, A., Makarewicz, C., Scanze, M., Ingram, M., Luhr, G., 2017. Contextualizing walkability: do relationships between built environments and walking vary by socioeconomic context? J. Am. Plan. Assoc. 83 (3), 296–314. https://doi.org/10.1080/01944363.2017.1322527.

Ajzen, I., 1991. The theory of planned behavior. Organ. Behav. Hum. Decis. Process. 50 (2), 179–211. Theories of Cognitive Self-Regulation https://doi.org/10.1016/0749-5978(91)90020-T.

Allen, R., Wang, J., 2020. Immigrant legal status and commute mode choice for Hispanics in the United States. J. Am. Plan. Assoc. 86 (3), 284–296. https://doi.org/10.1080/01944363.2020.1724818.

Appleyard, B.S., Ferrell, C.E., 2017. The influence of crime on active & sustainable travel: new geo-statistical methods and theories for understanding crime and mode choice. J. Transp. Health 6 (September), 516–529. https://doi.org/10.1016/j.jth.2017.04.002.

Arsenault, R., 2006. Freedom riders: 1961 and the struggle for racial justice. In: Pivotal Moments in American History. Oxford University Press, Oxford, New York.

Avila, E., 2014. The folklore of the freeway: race and revolt in the Modernist City. In: A Quadrant Book. University of Minnesota Press, Minneapolis.

Ayres, I., Siegelman, P., 1995. Race and gender discrimination in bargaining for a new car. Am. Econ. Rev. 85 (3), 304–321. https://www.jstor.org/stable/2118176.

Banerjee, T., Uhm, J.A., Bahl, D., 2014. Walking to school: the experience of children in inner City Los Angeles and implications for policy. J. Plan. Educ. Res. 34 (2), 123–140. https://doi.org/10.1177/0739456X14522494.

Barajas, J.M., 2016. Making Invisible Riders Visible: Motivations for Bicycling and Public Transit Use Among Latino Immigrants. Dissertation, University of California, Berkeley, Berkeley, CA.

Barajas, J.M., 2019. Traffic citations in Chicago: implications for pedestrian and bicycle equity. In: Presented at the 49th Urban Affairs Association Conference, Los Angeles, April 25.

Barajas, J.M., 2020. Supplemental infrastructure: how community networks and immigrant identity influence cycling. Transportation 47 (June), 1251–1274. https://doi.org/10.1007/s11116-018-9955-7.

Barajas, J.M., Agrawal, A.W., Chatman, D.G., 2018. Immigration, income, and public transit perceptions: findings from an intercept survey. J. Public Transp. 21 (2), 1–18. https://doi.org/10.5038/2375-0901.21.2.1.

Barajas, J.M., Beck, K.M., Cooper, J.F., Lopez, A., Reynosa, A., 2019. How effective are community pedestrian safety training workshops? short-term findings from a program in California. J. Transp. Health 12 (March), 183–194. https://doi.org/10.1016/j.jth.2019.01.002.

Bastiaanssen, J., Johnson, D., Lucas, K., 2020. Does transport help people to gain employment? A systematic review and meta-analysis of the empirical evidence. Transp. Rev. 40 (5), 607–628. https://doi.org/10.1080/01441647.2020.1747569.

Baumgartner, F.R., Christiani, L., Epp, D.A., Roach, K., Shoub, K., 2017. Racial disparities in traffic stop outcomes. Duke F. L. & Soc. Change 9, 21–54. https://heinonline.org/HOL/P?h=hein.journals/dukef9&i=22.

Baumgartner, F.R., Epp, D.A., Shoub, K., 2018. Suspect Citizens: What 20 Million Traffic Stops Tell Us About Policing and Race. https://public.ebookcentral.proquest.com/choice/publicfullrecord.aspx?p=5473139.

Ben-Akiva, M., Lerman, S.R., 1985. Discrete Choice Analysis: Theory and Application to Travel Demand. MIT Press, Cambridge, MA.

Bierbaum, A.H., Karner, A., Barajas, J.M., 2021. Toward mobility justice: linking transportation and education equity in the context of school choice. J. Am. Plan. Assoc. 87 (2), 197–210. https://doi.org/10.1080/01944363.2020.1803104.

Bills, T.S., Walker, J.L., 2017. Looking beyond the mean for equity analysis: examining distributional impacts of transportation improvements. Transp. Policy 54 (February), 61–69. https://doi.org/10.1016/j.tranpol.2016.08.003.

Braun, L.M., Rodriguez, D.A., Gordon-Larsen, P., 2019. Social (in)equity in access to cycling infrastructure: cross-sectional associations between bike lanes and area-level sociodemographic characteristics in 22 large U.S. Cities. J. Transp. Geogr. 80 (October), 102544. https://doi.org/10.1016/j.jtrangeo.2019.102544.

Brown, C.T., 2016. Fear: a silent barrier to bicycling in black and brown communities. ITE J. (September), 22–24. https://nacto.org/wp-content/uploads/2017/03/2016_Brown_Fear-A-Silent-Barrier-to-Bicycling-in-Black-and-Hispanic-Communities.pdf.

Brown, C.T., 2021. Arrested mobility. In: Presented at the 100th Annual Meeting of the Transportation Research Board, January 25.

Bullard, R.D., 2004. The anatomy of transportation racism. In: Bullard, R.D., Johnson, G.S., Torres, A.O. (Eds.), Highway Robbery. South End Press, pp. 15–32.

Bullard, R.D., Johnson, G.S., Torres, A.O., 2004. Dismantling transit racism in Metro Atlanta. In: Bullard, R.D., Johnson, G.S., Torres, A.O. (Eds.), Highway Robbery. South End Press, pp. 49–73.

Campanella, T.J., 2017. The True Measure of Robert Moses (and His Racist Bridges). Bloomberg CityLab. July 9, 2017 https://www.bloomberg.com/news/articles/2017-07-09/robert-moses-and-his-racist-parkway-explained.

Campbell, S.W., 1970. The Slave Catchers: Enforcement of the Fugitive Slave Law, 1850–1860. University of North Carolina Press, Chapel Hill.

Caro, R.A., 1975. The Power Broker: Robert Moses and the Fall of New York. Vintage Books, New York.

Carpio, G., 2019. Collisions at the Crossroads: How Place and Mobility Make Race. University of California Press, Oakland, California.

Chen, C., Lin, H., Loo, B.P.Y., 2012. Exploring the impacts of safety culture on immigrants' vulnerability in non-motorized crashes: a cross-sectional study. J. Urban Health 89 (1), 138–152. https://doi.org/10.1007/s11524-011-9629-7.

Christiani, L., 2020. Intersectional stereotyping in policing: an analysis of traffic stop outcomes. Politics Groups and Identities, 1–23. https://doi.org/10.1080/21565503.2020.1748064.

City and County of San Francisco, 2015. Vision Zero San Francisco Two-Year Action Strategy. San Francisco.

City of Chicago, 2017. Vision Zero Chicago Action Plan 2017–2019. http://visionzerochicago.org/wp-content/uploads/2016/05/17_0612-VZ-Action-Plan_FOR-WEB.pdf.

City of Los Angeles, 2015. Vision Zero Los Angeles: 2015–2025. Los Angeles.

Coren, C., Lowe, K., Barajas, J.M., 2021. Commuting in context: a qualitative study of transportation challenges for disadvantaged job seekers in Chicago, IL. In: 100th Annual Meeting of the Transportation Research Board, Washington, D.C.

Cradock, A.L., Troped, P.J., Fields, B., Melly, S.J., Simms, S.V., Gimmler, F., Fowler, M., 2009. Factors associated with federal transportation funding for local pedestrian and bicycle programming and facilities. J. Public Health Policy 30 (S1), S38–S72. https://doi.org/10.1057/jphp.2008.60.

Cushing, M., Hooshmand, J., Pomares, B., Hotz, G., 2016. Vision Zero in the United States versus Sweden: infrastructure improvement for cycling safety. Am. J. Public Health 106 (12), e1–e3. https://doi.org/10.2105/AJPH.2016.303466.

Dargay, J., Gately, D., Sommer, M., 2007. Vehicle ownership and income growth, worldwide: 1960–2030. Energy J. 28 (4), 143–170. https://doi.org/10.5547/ISSN0195-6574-EJ-Vol28-No4-7.

Davis, E., Whyde, A., Langton, L., 2018. Contacts Between Police and the Public, 2015. NCJ 251145, US Department of Justice, Washington, D.C.

Ding, H., Loukaitou-Sideris, A., Agrawal, A.W., 2020. Sexual harassment and assault in transit environments: a review of the English-language literature. J. Plan. Lit. 35 (3), 267–280. https://doi.org/10.1177/0885412220911129.

Dumbaugh, E., Gattis, J.L., 2005. Safe streets, livable streets. J. Am. Plan. Assoc. 71 (3), 283–300. https://doi.org/10.1080/01944360508976699.

Dumbaugh, E., Saha, D., Merlin, L., 2020. Toward safe systems: traffic safety, cognition, and the built environment. J. Plan. Educ. Res. 0739456X20931915 https://doi.org/10.1177/0739456X20931915.

Dunbar-Ortiz, R., 2014. An Indigenous Peoples' History of the United States. Beacon Press, Boston.

Eitle, D., D'Alessio, S.J., Stolzenberg, L., 2002. Racial threat and social control: a test of the political, economic, and threat of black crime hypotheses. Soc. Forces 81 (2), 557–576. https://doi.org/10.1353/sof.2003.0007.

Epp, C.R., Maynard-Moody, S., Haider-Markel, D.P., 2014. Pulled Over: How Police Stops Define Race and Citizenship. The Chicago Series in Law and Society, The University of Chicago Press, Chicago, London.

Fagan, J., Geller, A., Davies, G., West, V., 2010. Street stops and broken windows revisited: the demography and logic of proactive policing in a safe and changing city. In: Rice, S.K., White, M.D. (Eds.), Race, Ethnicity, and Policing: New and Essential Readings. NYU Press, pp. 309–348.

Federal Highway Administration, 2017. National Household Travel Survey. https://nhts.ornl.gov.

Flanagan, E., Lachapelle, U., El-Geneidy, A., 2016. Riding tandem: does cycling infrastructure investment mirror gentrification and privilege in Portland, OR and Chicago, IL? Res. Transp. Econ. 60 (December), 14–24. https://doi.org/10.1016/j.retrec.2016.07.027.

Fliss, M.D., Baumgartner, F.R., Delamater, P., Marshall, S., Poole, C., Robinson, W., 2020. Re-prioritizing traffic stops to reduce motor vehicle crash outcomes and racial disparities. Inj. Epidemiol. 7 (1), 3. https://doi.org/10.1186/s40621-019-0227-6.

Gandbhir, G., Foster, B., 2015. A Conversation With My Black Son. The New York Times. https://www.nytimes.com/video/opinion/100000003575589/a-conversation-with-my-black-son.html.

García, I., 2020. Cultural insights for planners: understanding the terms Hispanic, Latino, and Latinx. J. Am. Plan. Assoc. 86 (4), 393–402. https://doi.org/10.1080/01944363.2020.1758191.

Garrett, M., Taylor, B., 1999. Reconsidering social equity in public transit. Berkeley Plan. J. 13 (1), 6–27. https://escholarship.org/uc/item/1mc9t108.

Golub, A., Marcantonio, R.A., Sanchez, T.W., 2013. Race, space, and struggles for mobility: transportation impacts on African Americans in Oakland and the East Bay. Urban Geogr. 34 (5), 699–728. https://doi.org/10.1080/02723638.2013.778598.

Grengs, J., 2005. The abandoned social goals of public transit in the Neoliberal City of the USA. City 9 (1), 51–66. https://doi.org/10.1080/13604810500050161.

Grengs, J., 2012. Equity and the social distribution of job accessibility in detroit. Environ. Plann. B Plann. Des. 39 (5), 785–800. https://doi.org/10.1068/b36097.

Handy, S., Xing, Y., 2011. Factors correlated with bicycle commuting: a study in six small U.S. Cities. Int. J. Sustain. Transp. 5 (2), 91–110. https://doi.org/10.1080/15568310903514789.

Harris, D.A., 1999. The stories, the statistics, and the law: why driving while black matters. Minn. L. Rev. 84, 265–326.

Harris, B., Rigolon, A., Fernandez, M., 2020a. To them, we're just kids from the hood': citizen-based policing of youth of color, 'white space,' and environmental gentrification. Cities 107 (December), 102885. https://doi.org/10.1016/j.cities.2020.102885.

Harris, B., Schmalz, D., Larson, L., Fernandez, M., Griffin, S., 2020b. Contested spaces: intimate segregation and environmental gentrification on Chicago's 606 trail. City Community 19 (4), 933–962. https://doi.org/10.1111/cico.12422.

Hoffmann, M.L., 2016. Bike Lanes Are White Lanes: Bicycle Advocacy and Urban Planning. University of Nebraska Press, Lincoln.

Hoffmann, M.L., Lugo, A.E., 2014. Who is 'world class'? transportation justice and bicycle policy. Urbanities 4 (1), 45–61. http://www.anthrojournal-urbanities.com/docs/tableofcontents_6/5-%20Hoffmann-Lugo.pdf.

Howell, K.B., 2016. The costs of broken windows policing: twenty years and counting. Cardozo Law Rev. 37 (3), 1059–1073.

Ihlanfeldt, K.R., Sjoquist, D.L., 1998. The spatial mismatch hypothesis: a review of recent studies and their implications for welfare reform. Hous. Policy Debate 9 (4), 849–892. https://doi.org/10.1080/10511482.1998.9521321.

Ingram, J.R., 2007. The effect of neighborhood characteristics on traffic citation practices of the police. Police Q. 10 (4), 371–393. https://doi.org/10.1177/1098611107306995.

Jackson, K., 1985. Crabgrass Frontier: The Suburbanization of the United States. Oxford University Press, New York.

Jamme, H.-T.W., Bahl, D., Banerjee, T., 2018. Between 'broken windows' and the 'eyes on the street:' walking to school in inner city San Diego. J. Environ. Psychol. 55 (February), 121–138. https://doi.org/10.1016/j.jenvp.2018.01.004.

Johfre, S.S., Freese, J., 2021. Reconsidering the reference category. Sociol. Methodol. 0081175020982632 https://doi.org/10.1177/0081175020982632.

Karner, A., Duckworth, R., 2019. 'Pray for transit': seeking transportation justice in Metropolitan Atlanta. Urban Stud. 56 (9), 1882–1900. https://doi.org/10.1177/0042098018779756.

Karner, A., Niemeier, D., 2013. Civil rights guidance and equity analysis methods for regional transportation plans: a critical review of literature and practice. J. Transp. Geogr. 33 (December), 126–134. https://doi.org/10.1016/j.jtrangeo.2013.09.017.

Karner, A., Rowangould, D., London, J., 2016. We Can Get There From Here: New Perspectives on Transportation Equity. National Center for Sustainable Transportation, Davis, CA. https://ncst.ucdavis.edu/wp-content/uploads/2016/12/NCST_EquityWhitePaper-FINAL.pdf.

Karner, A., London, J., Rowangould, D., Manaugh, K., 2020. From transportation equity to transportation justice: within, through, and beyond the state. J. Plan. Lit. 35 (4), 440–459. https://doi.org/10.1177/0885412220927691.

Krapp, A., Barajas, J.M., Wennink, A., 2021. Equity-oriented criteria for project prioritization in regional transportation planning. Transp. Res. Rec. J. Transp. Res. Board.

Lachapelle, U., Noland, R.B., 2015. Inconsistencies in associations between crime and walking: a reflection of poverty and density. Int. J. Sustain. Transp. 9 (2), 103–115. https://doi.org/10.1080/15568318.2012.742947.

Laniyonu, A., 2018. Coffee shops and street stops: policing practices in gentrifying neighborhoods. Urban Aff. Rev. 54 (4), 898–930. https://doi.org/10.1177/1078087416689728.

Lee, M.L., Howard, M.E., Horrey, W.J., Liang, Y., Anderson, C., Shreeve, M.S., O'Brien, C.S., Czeisler, C.A., 2016. High risk of near-crash driving events following night-shift work. Proc. Natl. Acad. Sci. 113 (1), 176–181. https://doi.org/10.1073/pnas.1510383112.

Lee, R.J., Sener, I.N., Jones, S.N., 2017. Understanding the role of equity in active transportation planning in the United States. Transp. Rev. 37 (2), 211–226. https://doi.org/10.1080/01441647.2016.1239660.

Levine, J., Grengs, J., Merlin, L.A., 2019. From Mobility to Accessibility: Transforming Urban Transportation and Land-Use Planning. Cornell University Press, Ithaca, New York.

Lewis, T., 2013. Divided Highways: Building the Interstate Highways, Transforming American Life. Cornell University Press, Ithaca, NY.

Liu, R.(.R.)., Schachter, H.L., 2007. Mobility information needs of immigrants with limited English proficiency (LEP) in New Jersey. J. Immigr. Refug. Stud. 5 (2), 89–108. https://doi.org/10.1300/J500v05n02_05.

Loukaitou-Sideris, A., Brozen, M., Pinski, M., Ding, H., 2020. Documenting #MeToo in public transportation: sexual harassment experiences of University students in Los Angeles. J. Plan. Educ. Res. 0739456X20960778 https://doi.org/10.1177/0739456X20960778.

Lubitow, A., Miller, T.R., 2013. Contesting sustainability: bikes, race, and politics in Portlandia. Environ. Justice 6 (4), 121–126. https://doi.org/10.1089/env.2013.0018.

Lubitow, A., Zinschlag, B., Rochester, N., 2016. Plans for pavement or for people? The politics of bike lanes on the 'Paseo Boricua' in Chicago, Illinois. Urban Stud. 53 (12), 2637–2653. https://doi.org/10.1177/0042098015592823.

Lubitow, A., Rainer, J., Bassett, S., 2017. Exclusion and vulnerability on public transit: experiences of transit dependent riders in Portland, Oregon. Mobilities 12 (6), 924–937. https://doi.org/10.1080/17450101.2016.1253816.

Lowe, K., 2021. Undone science, funding, and positionality in transportation research. Transp. Rev. 41 (2), 192–209. https://doi.org/10.1080/01441647.2020.1829742.

Lubitow, A., Abelson, M.J., Carpenter, E., 2020. Transforming mobility justice: gendered harassment and violence on transit. J. Transp. Geogr. 82 (January), 102601. https://doi.org/10.1016/j.jtrangeo.2019.102601.

Lugo, A.E., 2013. CicLAvia and human infrastructure in Los Angeles: ethnographic experiments in equitable bike planning. J. Transp. Geogr. 30, 202–207. https://doi.org/10.1016/j.jtrangeo.2013.04.010.

Lugo, A.E., 2018. Bicycle/Race: Transportation, Culture & Resistance. https://search.ebscohost.com/login.aspx?direct=true&scope=site&db=nlebk&db=nlabk&AN=2182760.

Lusk, A.C., Willett, W.C., Morris, V., Byner, C., Li, Y., 2019. Bicycle facilities safest from crime and crashes: perceptions of residents familiar with higher crime/lower income neighborhoods in Boston. Int. J. Environ. Res. Public Health 16 (3), 484. https://doi.org/10.3390/ijerph16030484.

Maldonado, M.M., Licona, A.C., Hendricks, S., 2016. Latin@ immobilities and altermobilities within the U.S. Deportability Regime. Ann. Am. Assoc. Geogr. 106 (2), 321–329. https://doi.org/10.1080/00045608.2015.1106304.

Manaugh, K., Badami, M.G., El-Geneidy, A.M., 2015. Integrating social equity into urban transportation planning: a critical evaluation of equity objectives and measures in transportation plans in North America. Transp. Policy 37 (January), 167–176. https://doi.org/10.1016/j.tranpol.2014.09.013.

Mann, E., 2004. Los Angeles bus riders derail the MTA. In: Bullard, R.D., Johnson, G.S., Torres, A.O. (Eds.), Highway Robbery. South End Press, pp. 33–48.

Marcantonio, R.A., Golub, A., Karner, A., Nelson, L., 2017. Confronting inequality in metropolitan regions: realizing the promise of civil rights and environmental justice in metropolitan transportation planning. Fordham Urban Law J. 44 (4), 1017. https://ir.lawnet.fordham.edu/ulj/vol44/iss4/4.

Martens, K., 2017. Transport Justice: Designing Fair Transportation Systems. Routledge, Taylor & Francis Group, New York, NY.

Martens, K., Golub, A., 2018. A fair distribution of accessibility: interpreting civil rights regulations for regional transportation plans. J. Plan. Educ. Res. 0739456X18791014 https://doi.org/10.1177/0739456X18791014.

Martens, K., Golub, A., Robinson, G., 2012. A justice-theoretic approach to the distribution of transportation benefits: implications for transportation planning practice in the United States. Transp. Res. A Policy Pract. 46 (4), 684–695. https://doi.org/10.1016/j.tra.2012.01.004.

McGurty, E.M., 2000. Warren County, NC, and the emergence of the environmental justice movement: unlikely coalitions and shared meanings in local collective action. Soc. Nat. Resour. 13 (4), 373–387. https://doi.org/10.1080/089419200279027.

Meyer, M.D., Miller, E.J., 2001. Urban Transportation Planning, second ed. McGraw-Hill.

Mohl, R.A., 2004. Stop the road: freeway revolts in American Cities. J. Urban Hist. 30 (5), 674–706. https://doi.org/10.1177/0096144204265180.

Moody, J., Zhao, J., 2020. Travel behavior as a driver of attitude: car use and car pride in U.S. Cities. Transp. Res. F: Traffic Psychol. Behav. 74 (October), 225–236. https://doi.org/10.1016/j.trf.2020.08.021.

Moore-Monroy, M., Wilkinson-Lee, A., Lewandowski, D., Armenta, A., 2016. No Hay Peor Lucha Que La Que No Se Hace: re-negotiating cycling in a Latino Community. In: Golub, A., Hoffman, M.L., Lugo, A.E., Sandoval, G.F. (Eds.), Bicycle Justice and Urban Transformation: Biking for All? Routledge Equity, Justice and the Sustainable City, Routledge, New York, NY, pp. 217–230.

Mueller, N., Rojas-Rueda, D., Cole-Hunter, T., de Nazelle, A., Dons, E., Gerike, R., Götschi, T., Panis, L.I., Kahlmeier, S., Nieuwenhuijsen, M., 2015. Health Impact assessment of active transportation: a systematic review. Prev. Med. 76 (July), 103–114. https://doi.org/10.1016/j.ypmed.2015.04.010.

Nelson, R.K., Winling, L.D., Marciano, R., Connolly, N., 2021. Mapping Inequality: Redlining in New Deal America. Accessed January 7, 2021 https://dsl.richmond.edu/panorama/redlining/.

Newberry, J.L., 2021. Policing strategies and potential targets: the influence of gentrification and crime on the stoppage of blacks and Hispanics in New York City. Papers Appl. Geogr. 7 (1), 34–49. https://doi.org/10.1080/23754931.2020.1814848.

Noland, R.B., 2003. Traffic fatalities and injuries: the effect of changes in infrastructure and other trends. Accid. Anal. Prev. 35 (4), 599–611. https://doi.org/10.1016/S0001-4575(02)00040-4.

Norton, P.D., 2011. Fighting traffic: the dawn of the motor age in the American city. In: Inside Technology. MIT Press, Cambridge, Mass. London.

Novak, K.J., Chamlin, M.B., 2012. Racial threat, suspicion, and police behavior: the impact of race and place in traffic enforcement. Crime Delinq. 58 (2), 275–300. https://doi.org/10.1177/0011128708322943.

Padeiro, M., Louro, A., da Costa, N.M., 2019. Transit-oriented development and gentrification: a systematic review. Transp. Rev. 39 (6), 733–754. https://doi.org/10.1080/01441647.2019.1649316.

Pereira, R.H.M., Karner, A., 2021. Transportation equity. In: Vickerman, R. (Ed.), International Encyclopedia of Transportation, first ed. Elsevier Science, pp. 271–277.

Pereira, R.H.M., Schwanen, T., Banister, D., 2017. Distributive justice and equity in transportation. Transp. Rev. 37 (2), 170–191. https://doi.org/10.1080/01441647.2016.1257660.

Pierson, E., Simoiu, C., Overgoor, J., Corbett-Davies, S., Jenson, D., Shoemaker, A., Ramachandran, V., et al., 2020. A large-scale analysis of racial disparities in police stops across the United States. Nat. Hum. Behav. 4 (7), 736–745. https://doi.org/10.1038/s41562-020-0858-1.

Pulido, L., 2017. Geographies of race and ethnicity II: environmental racism, racial capitalism and state-sanctioned violence. Prog. Hum. Geogr. 41 (4), 524–533. https://doi.org/10.1177/0309132516646495.

Rice, L., Schwartz Jr., E., 2018. Discrimination When Buying a Car: How the Color of Your Skin Can Affect Your Car-Shopping Experience. National Fair Housing Alliance, Washington, DC. https://nationalfairhousing.org/wp-content/uploads/2018/01/Discrimination-When-Buying-a-Car-FINAL-1-11-2018.pdf.

Roach, K., Baumgartner, F.R., Christiani, L., Epp, D.A., Shoub, K., 2020. At the intersection: race, gender, and discretion in police traffic stop outcomes. J. Race Ethnicity and Politics, 1–23. https://doi.org/10.1017/rep.2020.35.

Roh, S., Robinson, M., 2009. A geographic approach to racial profiling: the microanalysis and macroanalysis of racial disparity in traffic stops. Police Q. 12 (2), 137–169. https://doi.org/10.1177/1098611109332422.

Rojek, J., Rosenfeld, R., Decker, S., 2012. Policing race: the racial stratification of searches in police traffic stops. Criminology 50 (4), 993–1024. https://doi.org/10.1111/j.1745-9125.2012.00285.x.

Rothstein, R., 2017. The Color of Law: A Forgotten History of How Our Government Segregated America. Liveright Publishing Corporation, New York, London.

Rowangould, G.M., 2013. A census of the US near-roadway population: public health and environmental justice considerations. Transp. Res. Part D: Transp. Environ. 25 (December), 59–67. https://doi.org/10.1016/j.trd.2013.08.003.

Royce, E.C., 1993. The origins of southern sharecropping. In: Labor and Social Change. Temple University Press, Philadelphia.

Sallis, J.F., Cervero, R.B., Ascher, W., Henderson, K.A., Kraft, M.K., Kerr, J., 2006. An ecological approach to creating active living communities. Annu. Rev. Public Health 27, 297–322. https://doi.org/10.1146/annurev.publhealth.27.021405.102100.

Sanchez, T.W., Wolf, J.F., 2007. Environmental justice and transportation equity: a review of MPOs. In: Bullard, R.D. (Ed.), Growing Smarter: Achieving Livable Communities, Environmental Justice, and Regional Equity. MIT Press, Cambridge, MA and London, UK, pp. 249–271.

Schlosberg, D., 2009. Defining Environmental Justice: Theories, Movements, and Nature. 1. publ. in paperback, Oxford University Press, Oxford.

Schneider, R.J., 2013. Theory of routine mode choice decisions: an operational framework to increase sustainable transportation. Transp. Policy 25, 128–137. https://doi.org/10.1016/j.tranpol.2012.10.007.

Schneider, R.J., Kusch, J., Dressel, A., Bernstein, R., 2018. Can a twelve-week intervention reduce barriers to bicycling among overweight adults in low-income latino and black communities? Transport. Res. F: Traffic Psychol. Behav. 56 (July), 99–112. https://doi.org/10.1016/j.trf.2018.03.023.

Schneider, R.J., Sanders, R., Proulx, F., Moayyed, H., 2021. United States fatal pedestrian crash hot spot locations and characteristics. J. Transp. Land Use 14 (1), 1–23. https://doi.org/10.5198/jtlu.2021.1825.

Schweitzer, L., 2014. Planning and social media: a case study of public transit and stigma on twitter. J. Am. Plan. Assoc. 80 (3), 218–238. https://doi.org/10.1080/01944363.2014.980439.

Sciara, G.-C., Wachs, M., 2007. Metropolitan transportation funding: prospects, progress, and practical considerations. Public Works Manag. Policy 12 (1), 378–394. https://doi.org/10.1177/1087724X07303987.

Seiler, C., 2006. So that we as a race might have something authentic to travel by': African American automobility and cold-war liberalism. Am. Q. 58 (4), 1091–1117. https://doi.org/10.1353/aq.2007.0015.

Seo, S.A., 2019. Policing the Open Road: How Cars Transformed American Freedom. Harvard University Press, Cambridge, Massachusetts.

Shahum, L., 2020. Acting for Racial Justice & Just Mobility. Vision Zero Network. June 8, 2020 https://visionzeronetwork.org/acting-for-racial-justice-just-mobility/.

Sharp, E.B., 2014. Politics, economics, and urban policing: the postindustrial city thesis and rival explanations of heightened order maintenance policing. Urban Aff. Rev. 50 (3), 340–365. https://doi.org/10.1177/1078087413490397.

Sheller, M., 2015. Racialized mobility transitions in Philadelphia: connecting urban sustainability and transport justice. City Soc. 27 (1), 70–91. https://doi.org/10.1111/ciso.12049.

Sheller, M., 2018. Mobility Justice: The Politics of Movement in the Age of Extremes. Verso, London, Brooklyn, NY.

Sheller, M., Urry, J., 2000. The city and the car. Int. J. Urban Reg. Res. 24 (4), 737–757. https://doi.org/10.1111/1468-2427.00276.

Shoub, K., Epp, D.A., Baumgartner, F.R., Christiani, L., Roach, K., 2020. Race, place, and context: the persistence of race effects in traffic stop outcomes in the face of situational, demographic, and political controls. J. Race Ethnicity and Politics 5 (3), 481–508. https://doi.org/10.1017/rep.2020.8.

Smith, M., Hosking, J., Woodward, A., Witten, K., MacMillan, A., Field, A., Baas, P., Mackie, H., 2017. Systematic literature review of built environment effects on physical activity and active transport—an update and new findings on health equity. Int. J. Behav. Nutr. Phys. Act. 14 (1), 158. https://doi.org/10.1186/s12966-017-0613-9.

Sorin, G., 2021. Driving While Black: African American Travel and the Road to Civil Rights. Liverlight, New York.

Steg, L., Vlek, C., Slotegraaf, G., 2001. Instrumental-reasoned and symbolic-affective motives for using a motor car. Transport. Res. F: Traffic Psychol. Behav. 4 (3), 151–169. https://doi.org/10.1016/S1369-8478(01)00020-1.

Stuesse, A., Coleman, M., 2014. Automobility, immobility, altermobility: surviving and resisting the intensification of immigrant policing. City Soc. 26 (1), 51–72. https://doi.org/10.1111/ciso.12034.

Toomey, R.B., Umaña-Taylor, A.J., Williams, D.R., Harvey-Mendoza, E., Jahromi, L.B., Updegraff, K.A., 2014. Impact of Arizona's SB 1070 immigration law on utilization of health care and public assistance among Mexican-origin adolescent mothers and their mother figures. Am. J. Public Health 104 (S1), S28–S34. https://doi.org/10.2105/AJPH.2013.301655.

Transportation Alternatives, 2020. The Case for Self-Enforcing Streets. New York https://static1.squarespace.com/static/5cab9d9b65a707a9b36f4b6c/t/5eec1235fe73d720da412589/1592529462229/CaseForSelfEnforcingStreets.pdf.

Untokening Collective, 2017. Untokening 1.0—Principles of Mobility Justice. http://www.untokening.org/updates/2017/11/11/untokening-10-principles-of-mobility-justice.

Vigar, G., 2017. The four knowledges of transport planning: enacting a more communicative, trans-disciplinary policy and decision-making. Transp. Policy 58 (August), 39–45. https://doi.org/10.1016/j.tranpol.2017.04.013.

Warren, P., Tomaskovic-Devey, D., Smith, W., Zingraff, M., Mason, M., 2006. Driving while black: bias processes and racial disparity in police stops. Criminology 44 (3), 709–738. https://doi.org/10.1111/j.1745-9125.2006.00061.x.

Weitz, R., 2008. Who's afraid of the big bad bus? NIMBYism and popular images of public transit. J. Urban. 1 (2), 157–172. https://doi.org/10.1080/17549170802221500.

Williams, S., 2020. Data Action: Using Data for Public Good. The MIT Press. https://doi.org/10.7551/mitpress/12261.001.0001.

Wilson, K., 2021. Virginia Policy Could End Jaywalking Stops. Streetsblog USA (blog). January 4, 2021 https://usa.streetsblog.org/2021/01/04/virginia-policy-could-end-jaywalking-stops/.

Wilson, J.Q., Kelling, G.L., 1982. Broken Windows: The Police and Neighborhood Safety. The Atlantic. March 1982 https://www.theatlantic.com/magazine/archive/1982/03/broken-windows/304465/.

Wisniewski, M., 2018. Black Neighborhoods Still See Most Bike Tickets, Police Data Show. Chicago Tribune. February 12, 2018, sec. Column http://www.chicagotribune.com/news/columnists/wisniewski/ct-met-bike-tickets-getting-around-20180211-story.html.

Woodward, C.V., 1964. Plessy v. Ferguson: The Birth of Jim Crow. American Heritage. April 1964 https://www.americanheritage.com/plessy-v-ferguson.
Yu, C.-Y., 2014. Environmental supports for walking/biking and traffic safety: income and ethnicity disparities. Prev. Med. 67 (October), 12–16. https://doi.org/10.1016/j.ypmed.2014.06.028.
Zuk, M., Bierbaum, A.H., Chapple, K., Gorska, K., Loukaitou-Sideris, A., 2018. Gentrification, displacement, and the role of public investment. J. Plan. Lit. 33 (1), 31–44. https://doi.org/10.1177/0885412217716439.

CHAPTER TWO

Gender gaps in urban mobility and transport planning

Tanu Priya Uteng*
Department of Mobility and Organisation, Institute of Transport Economics (TOI), Oslo, Norway
*Corresponding author: e-mail address: tanu.priyauteng@toi.no

Contents

Abstract

Though we have ample amount of research evidence to prove that women's needs, usage and preferences for urban transport systems differ from men, we lack a clear understanding on the different variables involved in this equation and further, how these variables affect each other and are evolving with time. Simplistic assertions can be carved out in debates surrounding private car vs public transport use, but the ways in which current transport systems enable or disable women are complex, multi-faceted and context specific. It is also debatable if the current format of the ICT-enabled "smart" mobilities can address gendered needs. This paper presents main findings emerging from a literature review on the topic and highlights important gaps existing in the current framings of urban and transport planning, both from the perspectives of research and practice. Examples are drawn from both Global North and Global South.

Keywords: Gender gaps, Transport, Urban mobility, Smart city, Smart mobilities, Mode choice, Safety and security, Data, Engineering education, Space consumption

Advances in Transport Policy and Planning, Volume 8
ISSN 2543-0009
https://doi.org/10.1016/bs.atpp.2021.07.004
Copyright © 2021 Elsevier Inc.
All rights reserved.

1. Introduction

Gender, urban mobility and transport planning share a deeply intertwined relationship and yet this relationship is poorly understood, discussed and has little to no impact on policymaking. Most transport planning decisions are based on "revealed" urban mobility while the "hidden," "irregular" and "potential" mobility almost never enters mainstream discussions in the field of urban and transport planning. It is remarkable that planning field has continued to ignore women, constituting roughly 50% of any urban population, and is replete with similar planning fallacies across the globe. Initiatives like building a gender equal city in Vienna (Austria) or a gendered urban planning and mobility interface being developed in Malmo (Sweden) (Svanfelt, 2018) are few and far between. Constrained accessibility for women has led to diminishing results on a number of development goals—education, health, employment, welfare and general well-being (e.g., Borker, 2017; Hamlin, 2004; Kantor, 2002; Sweet and Kanaroglou, 2016). Further, the sectors of energy and transport which practically underpin all development agendas have traditionally operated in strict engineering domains and the societal and gendered ramification of the under-delivery of these services have not been understood and remain unaddressed.

It is additionally important to highlight that the global development agenda being targeted through the 17 sustainable development goals or the SDGs,[a] a collection of independent but interconnected goals designed to give the planet a better future, will also be ineffective if development does not specifically target the topic of gendered mobilities. The following SDGs will simply not be achieved if we do not build a consistent focus on gender and development in the domains of urban and transport planning: Gender equality (SDG 5), Good health and well-being (SDG 3), Reduced inequalities (SDG 10), Sustainable cities and communities (SDG 11), Climate action (SDG 13), and Partnerships for the goals (SDG 17). A specific target associated with goals include SDG Target 5.2 goal on "the elimination of all forms of violence against all women and girls in public and private spheres." Further, urban transportation is seen as a key component of inclusive cities. SDG 11.2 states that by 2030, there must be the provision of access to safe, affordable, accessible and sustainable transport systems for all,

[a] THE 17 GOALS | Sustainable Development (un.org)

improving road safety, notably by expanding public transport, with special attention to the needs of those in vulnerable situations, women, children, persons with disabilities and older persons.

In order to achieve these goals, we first need to understand the current status of the topic of gender and daily mobilities, and the ways in which it should be taken forward to be able to meet the targets set in SDGs. Studies conducted across the world present some consistent findings and it is astonishing that though the shape and size of these findings vary, the core elements are repetitive:

i. Walking, public transport (both formal and informal) and, in some contexts, intermediate means of transport (IMTs)[b] are the most frequent and important transportation modes for women in developing countries (e.g., Priya Uteng, 2011; Priya Uteng and Turner, 2019).

ii. Though both license holding and access to cars for women has increased in the past decades, there is still a preference for walking and public transport among women (e.g., Clark et al., 2016; Hjorthol, 2008; Scheiner and Holz-Rau, 2017).

iii. Women's travels are, in general, complex (higher trip-chaining), multipurpose and resource-constrained (e.g., Paleti et al., 2011; Scheiner and Holz-Rau, 2017).

iv. Fear of sexual harassment and personal security remain great concerns in negotiating daily mobilities (e.g., Ceccato and Loukaitou-Sideris, 2020).

v. Women on low-income suffer a disproportionately high loss of employment opportunities in face of slum eviction and relocation primarily due to constricted mobilities (e.g., Salon and Gulyani, 2010).

vi. Public transport and IMTs inevitably gets lower focus than road/highways/bridge building projects, thus putting women's needs to further disadvantage (Priya Uteng and Lucas, 2017).

vii. Cultural restrictions placed on mobility of girls and women in accessing public spaces influences the time, space, and duration of women's movements. Extreme cultural restrictions necessitate a context-specific and inclusive approach to women's mobility and transport (e.g., Delatte, 2018).

[b] Local transport solutions like wheelbarrows, hand carts, bicycles, tricycles, animal-powered transport, motorcycles and power tiller trailers have been categorized as intermediate means of transport (IMTs). These increase transport capacity and reduce drudgery at relatively low cost, solving local transport problems (Starkey, 2001).

viii. Smart mobilities and smart cities agendas are developing in a techno-cratic, gender-blind fashion (e.g., Kawgan-Kagan, 2015; Lenz, 2017).

In order to be truly relevant as both academic and policy disciplines, there is a need to build focus on context specificities to "mainstream" gender in transport, and urban planning domains. We need to understand the existing gaps to be able to answer *what needs to be done differently* in terms of infrastructure and service delivery design, provision, and promotion to prioritize equity in urban/transport planning. For example:

i. How can gendered needs and travel patterns be made part of drafting transport and spatial development policies?

ii. How to address the topic of safety and security of women in public spaces in a streamlined and structured manner? What kind of practical tools are needed for both decision makers and citizens to address different gender concerns in accessing and using safe and secure transport systems?

iii. What are the current mobility needs of women in light of the context—gendered roles, jobs, emerging trends etc.?

iv. What kind of policies and investment will ensure that accessibility based on sustainable modes like walking, bicycling and public transport, is increased?

v. What are the reasons behind gender-blind transport policies?

vi. How is land use and associated accessibility affecting gendered mobility in urban and peri-urban areas?

vii. How are trips being recorded—1-day, 1-week or other forms of trip diaries? Are there any records of which trips are being supplemented/complemented or substituted by mobile phones?

viii. Are smart mobilities and smart cities able to deliver gender-equitable services?

Since "gender" needs to be inserted in an already complex planning field comprising multiple, and often overlapping issues related to collecting data, analyses, drafting and implementing policies and programs, there are no readily available theories to plug in for creating a gender equitable city. Therefore, it is necessary to acknowledge the existing complexities and build on a host of theories and analyses. A combination of socio-psychological and feminist theories, socio-technical transition theory, mobility biographies and social practice theory framework can be used to kick-off the framing of women's transport needs, usage and implications for future planning.

This chapter presents a literature review on the topic of "Gender and Transport" and reflects on the existing gaps to bring this important social issue in the field of transport planning to the fore. Though the chapter does not delve into theories, I urge the readers to explore different theories based on the gaps highlighted in this chapter. Interlocking of gender and transport can be studied from multiple angles, for example, looking at the existing data gaps, gaps in governance and decision-making, technological gaps etc. Section 2 presents a list of selected themes to build a generic discussion on current gender gaps in urban mobility and transport planning. Section 3 concludes the study and puts forth some thoughts for future research and policymaking.

2. Gender gaps in urban mobility and transport planning

2.1 Gendered travel behavior

Women exhibit complex and intricate scheduling activities in both time and space (Hanson, 2010; Kwan, 1999; Susilo and Dijst, 2009). A combination of structural conditions, like cities designed to cater for motorized mobility, and socio-economic conditions like constrained access to resources among women reduce their possibilities for solving this complex scheduling problem. This has led to a markedly different travel behavior of women as expressed in the following variations:

2.1.1 Trip purposes

Despite the rise in female participation in higher education and paid employment in the last decades, gendered roles have not witnessed any dramatic shifts. It is thus not surprising that low mobility levels and time–space constraints, such as childcare obligations, are two important factors explaining why women tend to work closer to home and use more public transport, compared to their male counterparts (e.g., Priya Uteng, 2006; Susilo and Maat, 2007). Since a high share of women are either unemployed, working part time or working in close vicinity of their homes along with balancing their household responsibilities, it is noted that women make fewer job and business trips, but more shopping and escort (children, and elderly) trips (e.g., Best and Lanzendorf, 2005; Ghate and Tiwari, 2019). This has led to more varied/complex activity patterns of women (e.g., Scheiner and Holz-Rau, 2017). Law (1999) had pointed out that differences in access to resources of time, money, skills and technology had led to markedly different travel patterns for women, which in turn created differentiated labor market and space-time opportunities. But despite this warning, not much has changed in the last two decades in the practice of transport planning.

2.1.2 Trip chains

Both the incidence and complexity of trip-chaining is higher among women (e.g., Heinen and Chatterjee, 2015; Paleti et al., 2011; Scheiner and Holz-Rau, 2017). Given this complex trip-chaining and a lack of access to private transport resources like cars etc., women remain comparitively more dependent on the availability of public transport network. Even in the 1980s, when this topic was barely making its presence felt, King (1980) argued that while travel choices for men primarily depend on travel time, the variables of "availability" and "affordability" are the crucial issues for women. Further, women are likely to use public transport twice as often as men. However, it has been noted that in advanced economies, the gender gap in public transport use has been reducing over time as more women joined the fleet of car drivers (Hjorthol, 2008; Susilo and Maat, 2007). But even with these converging trends, the preference and collective use of public transport by women remains much higher as compared to men.

2.1.3 Daytime distribution and concentration of trips

Personal security concerns are one of the most important challenges for women. Both due to security concerns and as a matter of preference, women go out by night and late evenings less often (e.g., Scheiner, 2013). Given that women are involved in various different combinations of employment like flexible, part-time jobs, home-based enterprises etc., or in many incidences, not employed in paid positions, women travel less often in rush hour. In light of these facts, women's trips get distributed over the day and the often-used variable of peak hour traffic to justify road expansion schemes seems to be misjudged considering gendered travel patterns.

2.1.4 Licensing and car availability

Traditionally, license and car availability has been higher for men (e.g., Hjorthol, 2008) but in recent works undertaken in the Global North, it is noticed that both licensing and car availability are converging for men and women (e.g., Scheiner, 2018). But despite this trend, a longitudinal study from Germany shows that women have considerably lower access to the car than their male partners in low-car households (i.e., when couples share a car), and their power to increase access either by bringing home money, or by doing out-of-home household work, is more limited than male power (Scheiner, 2019). This is further illustrated through the case of Sweden where although the gender gap in terms of driving has reduced and a convergence is taking place, the gap remains (Susilo et al., 2018).

A decline in gender difference over the generations appears most substantially in the group of partnered/married families without children (a drop from 48% in the 1930s to 18% in the 1970s). The women of the 1980s and 1990s generations still have on average 10% less car driving share than men, although that number is 30% for the 1940s generation. These trends indicate that although more women have started driving, the gender gap in terms of driving still remains. Meanwhile, in most countries in the Global South, both licensing and car availability are primarily restricted to men and these trends do not seem to be converging over time between the genders (Priya Uteng and Lucas, 2017; Priya Uteng and Turner, 2019).

2.1.5 Trip distances and trip duration

Research studies across the globe highlight that both trip distance and trip duration have been shorter for women. This is especially the case for work trips but holds true for other purposes as well (e.g., Hjorthol, 2008; Scheiner et al., 2011). Further, women participate less in long distance work- or business-related travel. On average, women have shorter travel time and more non-work activities than their male counterparts (e.g., Transport for London, 2012). But recent studies point toward a convergence taking place in this arena as well and the term "gender turnaround" in distances traveled by young people is also being used in the Global North (Tilley and Houston, 2016).

2.1.6 Traditional transport modes and upcoming modes like shared-bikes, shared-cars and other app-based rental/sharing services

Studies suggest that women generally use public transport, walk or cycle more than men to perform their daily activities (Priya Uteng, 2011; Priya Uteng and Cresswell, 2008). Priya Uteng (2011) notes that a consistent finding all over the world is that women depend primarily on public transport to meet their travel needs. For example, 88.7% of women in Palembang, Indonesia depend primarily on public transport. In addition to big buses, women in Global South are also more likely to use other modes of paratransit, such as becak (tricycle), Ojek/boda-boda (taxi-motorcycle) and minibuses (oplet, mikrolet etc.). Women are also more dependent than men on cycle-rickshaws in India, minibuses in Latin America, and combitaxes and minibuses in African cities like Car Rapides (Ndiaga Ndiayes) in Senegal. Further, the use of informal Public Transport is dominant in the Global South owing to a nexus between restricted or no supply of formal transport[c] on the desired routes, timing and affordability issues (Salazar Ferro et al., 2013; Schalekamp and Behrens, 2010; Vahidi and Yan, 2016). There also exists a strong coupling between high share of female employment in the informal sector and their dependence on informal transport. For example, it is noted that more than 70% of the households in Dar-es-Salaam who depend on informal livelihoods use the informal modes of transport such as minibuses, motorcycles and tricycles as their primary transport mode (Joseph et al., 2020).

On a different note, there has been a renewed focus on cycling during the unfolding of Covid-19 pandemic in 2020–21. It is likely that this trend will lead to further bolstering of cycling strategies and plans in urban areas across the globe. Emergence of shared bikes, *E*-scooters and other upcoming shared modes will also subsequently be brought in the purview of Mobility-as-a-service (MaaS) paradigm. It is here that we need to understand how gender intersects with the uptake of both current and new forms of sustainable modes. It has been reported that both recorded and perceived danger on the road prevents women from commuting by bicycle (METPEX, 2013; Susilo and Cats, 2014). Further, Lam (2019) highlights that women have a stronger preference for safer forms of cycling infrastructure, and they prefer protected cycle lanes away from motorized traffic as it increases their perception of safety (Aldred et al., 2016; Garrard et al., 2008; Lam and Cosgrave, 2019; Pucher et al., 2010).

Krizek et al. (2005) showed that women were more likely than men to cycle for shopping, making errands and visiting friends, while they were less likely to cycle on their commute. Studies have also found that the built environment such as land use characteristics, physical layout and design of transport networks and facilities influence the travel behavior of men and women differently (e.g., Law, 1999; Waygood and Susilo, 2011). Additionally, wherever cycling is a part of the travel culture, and in places with cycling levels greater than 7%, female bicyclists are both better represented and bicycle longer distances (e.g., Goel et al., 2021; Götschi et al., 2015; Pucher and Buehler, 2006; Pucher et al., 2011a). Goel et al. (2021) send a cautionary warning that a focus beyond the commute to work is needed to address equity concerns around age and gender (Collins and Tisdell, 2002; Shaw et al., 2020). Findings based on a comparative analysis of 17 countries across

[c] The retreat of the state from provision of (formal) public transportation has been noted in multiple African countries, and due to this failure, privately owned informal transport systems of varying sizes and modes (buses, vans, jeepneys, motorcycles etc.) have come to dominate the urban transport landscape of the continent (Agyapong and Ojo, 2018).

6 continents (Goel et al., 2021) imply that in low-cycling cities, developing cycling infrastructure based on the demands, or revealed cycling behavior, of middle-aged men commuting to work may perpetuate gender and age inequalities.

Lack of knowledge about bicycle maintenance and the need to combine multiple trips also deters women from cycling. Bicycling for women emerges as a direct outcome of spatial planning issues related to safety and cycling infrastructure. A 2018 study from Stockholm, based on time-series data from 1985 to 2015, highlighted that while the gender gap in car use and bicycling "closed completely" in the inner city of Stockholm, the gap continues to exist the outer and suburban areas (Bastian and Börjesson, 2018). Similar findings have emerged from other parts of the world as well (Abasahl et al., 2018; European Parliament, 2012; Sovacool et al., 2018). It has been found that countries with high levels of cycling and good gender representation like Germany, Japan, and the Netherlands have provided infrastructure for cyclists such as protected cycle paths and secure parking facilities, and these provisions are typically complemented with motor traffic reduction and calming in residential neighborhoods, mixed land-use, and transport policies that discourage use and ownership of cars, such as higher taxes on car purchase and fuel, and limited parking spaces (Berent and Nagahiro, 2017; Goel et al., 2021; Pucher and Buehler, 2008; Pucher et al., 2010). Low-cycling countries like USA and Australia are also marked by low provision of cycling supportive infrastructure along with a lack of policies to deter car use (Buehler, 2011; Goel et al., 2021; Pucher et al., 2011a,b). While cultural constraints and other factors determine that there is a glaring gender divide in cycling in many low-and-middle income countries, a car-centric planning approach along with an alarmingly high traffic accident rate deters the emergence of cycling as an option in future for either gender. Goel et al. (2021) note that Bogota city in Colombia, with the highest cycling level among low-cycling countries, is an encouraging example, where cycling infrastructure supported by political will and advocacy groups have resulted in improved levels of cycling in the recent times (Rosas-Satizábal and Rodriguez-Valencia, 2019).

Women are also more likely than men to walk. Though the proportion is higher is the Global South, this fact is well-established in the Global North as well. For example, 22% of women, compared to 12% of men, walk their children to school, and a comparatively higher share of women (53%) walk to work/school/college in London (Transport for London, 2012). Despite these numbers, the theme of walkability is yet to mature and establish itself in the field of transport planning. A singular focus on providing for cars has had adverse effects on not only women but the world economy at large. In Morocco, for example, 80% of women surveyed in 2010 affirmed that lack of transport provision limited their autonomy (CoMun, 2014). In Jordan, 40% of women reported turning down employment opportunities exclusively due to lack of access to affordable and acceptable modes of transport (Delatte, 2018). A McKinsey report from 2015 concluded that women's employment is the driver for global economic growth and closing the gender gap could deliver $12–28 trillion of additional GDP in 2025 (Woetzel et al., 2015).

Given this backdrop, the "smart" agenda needs to be drawn up with caution and careful planning. Available statistics on the use of carsharing (Kawgan-Kagan, 2015), and uber services (Lenz, 2017) have already established that the uptake of the new mobility trends which are based on personal car usage is higher among men but ride-based services which mimic demand-responsive transport and facilitate complex trip-chaining have a larger uptake among women (refer Table 1 and Fig. 1). For example,

Table 1 Gender split among private customers of various car-sharing providers in Europe in 2010.

Car-sharing provider and/or location	Share of male customers	Share of female customers	Source
Cambio, Brussels (Belgium)	58%	42%	Taxistop, cambio, 2009
Several providers	58%	42%	Italian Ministry of Environment, 2009
Three providers in London (UK)	69%	31%	Synovate, 2006
Mobility, Switzerland	53%	47%	Bundesamt für Energie (Swiss Federal Office of Energy), 2006
Two providers in Frankfurt (Germany)	63%	37%	traffiQ, 2007
Ten providers in Germany	58%	42%	Wuppertal Institute 2007

From Loose, W., 2010. Aktueller Stand des Car-Sharing in Europa. In: Endbericht D 2.4 Arbeitspaket 2. Bundesverband CarSharing e.V., http://www.carsharing.info/images/stories/pdf_dateien/wp2_endbericht_deutsch_final_4.pdf (accessed 15.04.19): 54, quoted in Lenz, B., 2017. Smart mobility—for all? Gender issues in the context of new mobility concepts, paper presented in Workshop 1. In: Gendering Smart Mobilities, Nos-Sh Workshop Series, 24–25 August. Institute of Transport Economics TØI, Oslo, Norway.

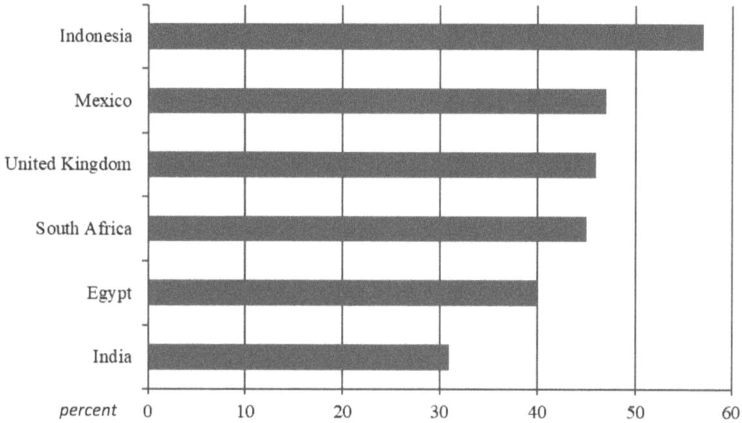

Fig. 1 Share of female Uber service riders 2017. *From IFC (International Finance Corporation) and Accenture, 2018. Driving Toward Equality: Women, Ride-Hailing, and the Sharing Economy. IFC, Washington D.C.: 33, quoted in Lenz, B., 2017. Smart mobility—for all? Gender issues in the context of new mobility concepts, paper presented in Workshop 1. In: Gendering Smart Mobilities, Nos-Sh Workshop Series, 24–25 August. Institute of Transport Economics TØI, Oslo, Norway.*

84% of the car-sharers in Berlin are men (Kawgan-Kagan, 2015) while data from Brazil shows that women represent over 60% of ride-hailing users (Warwar and Pereira, 2021).

Gender differences can also be found in the uptake of bike sharing schemes (Fig. 2). A recent study from Oslo (Priya Uteng et al., 2019) highlights that men and women demonstrate clear differences in the usage and preference for the shared bike system in Oslo. Analyses revealed that women were relatively more concentrated on the outer fringes of the city in terms of spatial distribution of both their residential and employment locations, but the provision of docking stations for shared bikes was concentrated in the city center. This spatial mismatch between employment/residential location and provision of centralized docking stations greatly affected the initial uptake of bike sharing scheme. It seems that in the initial phases, low provision of shared bikes in the peripheral areas might have led to an underutilization of the bike sharing scheme by women in Oslo. This locational deficit of docking stations was subsequently corrected and the usage of shared bikes among women went up following this correction. However, gendered differences persisted, and it was noticed that while men primarily used shared bikes for the purpose of access and egress, women used shared bikes for multi-purpose trips. The system, however, was not designed to allow longer

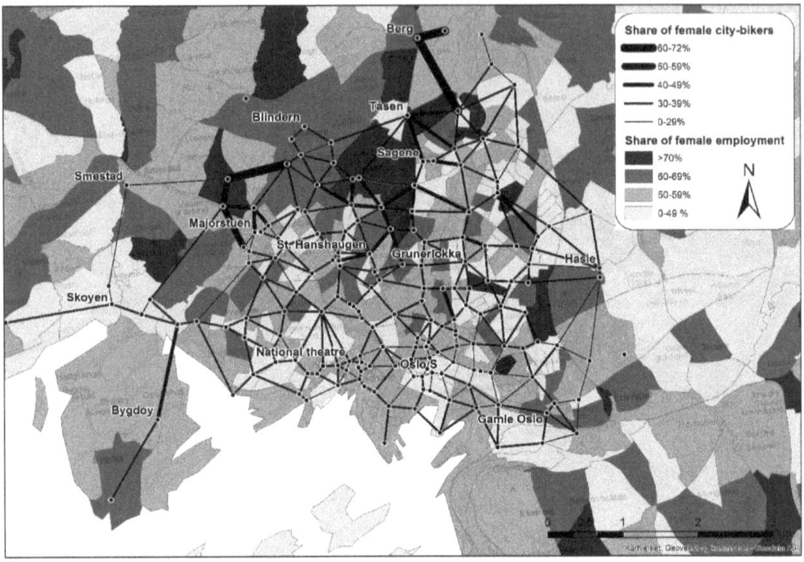

Fig. 2 Route mapping of shared bikes vis-à-vis share of female employment. *From Priya Uteng, T., Espegren, H.M., Throndsen T.S., Bocker, L., 2019. The gendered dimension of multi-modality: exploring the bike sharing scheme of Oslo. In: Priya Uteng, T., Levin, L., Rømer Christensen, H. (Eds.), Gendering Smart Mobilities. Routledge, Abingdon and New York.*

usage of these shared bikes (cap of 45 min rental time period) and thus inevitably affected women more than men.

Lam (2019) discusses the case of London and it is seen that despite increased investment in cycling infrastructure and overall growth in cycling over the past two decades, gender gap in cycling persists. The case of cycle superhighways vs. the quietways points toward the existence of the layers of systemic and structural inequalities that produce uneven urban cycling experiences (Fig. 3). The author (ibid) states "… implicit male bias is present in London's treatment of cycling infrastructure, representations of 'cycling' and 'cyclists' and 'smart' cycling innovations. Consequently, London's cycling interventions raise the profile of already-visible, privileged cyclists (predominantly white, middle-class, able-bodied men) for whom cycling is a lifestyle choice, while erasing those for whom cycling is an economic or spatial necessity." But these gaps are evident in other parts of the world as well, where there is clear chasm between how cycling infrastructure is being designed and funded and the "sustainable" logics borrowed to fund these projects. Questions regarding the potential users and beneficiaries of these state-driven projects are rarely analyzed in the pre-feasibility stages of such

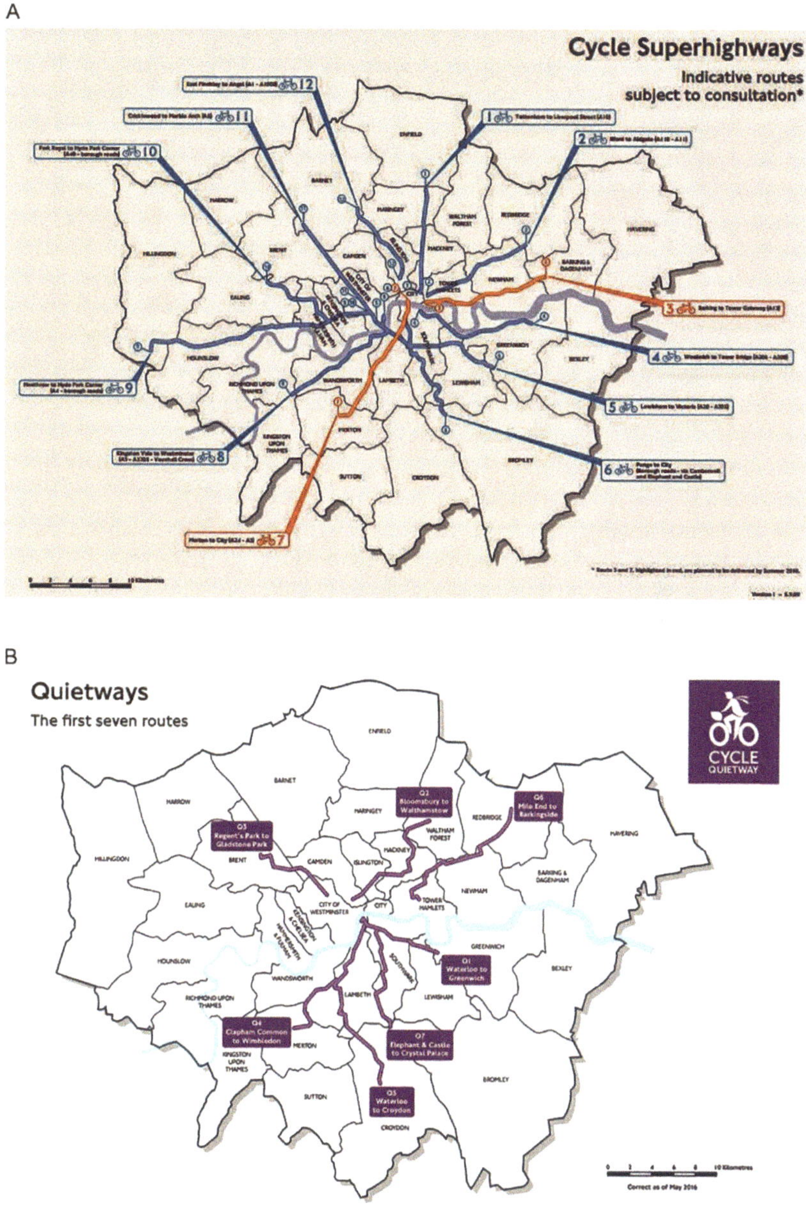

Fig. 3 Cycle superhighways and quietways of London. *From Transport for London, https://tfl.gov.uk/modes/cycling/routes-and-maps*

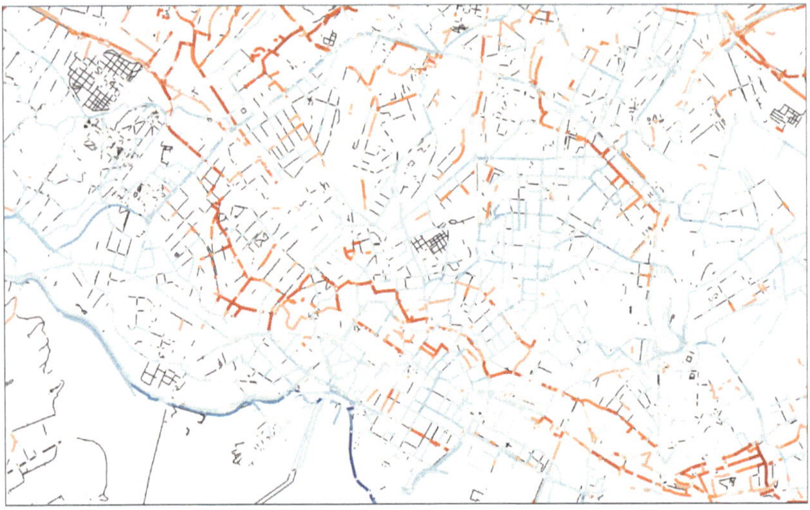

Fig. 4 Difference in bicycling route preference between men and women in Oslo. The colors illustrate the gendered distribution of preferences for particular routes and roads for bicycling. The color blue represents a relatively higher share of men bicyclists while strong red color highlights female bicycling shares and preferences. *From de Jong, T., Fyhri, A., Priya Uteng, T., 2018. Gender Gap—Perception of Safety and Cycling Use, Workshop 2: Smart Mobilities—Walking and Biking, Nos-Sh Workshop Series, 21 April. University of Copenhagen, Copenhagen, Denmark.*

projects. The case of Oslo, presented in Fig. 4, shows a neat overlay of bicycle highways and its usage by men (coded in blue) while women continue to prefer streets with low traffic in calmer parts of the city.

This brief sketch on gendered travel behavior points toward prioritizing sustainable modes like walking, cycling and public transport over providing for cars and making access to safe traveling conditions a top priority. For the Global South, provision of public transport primarily takes through informal transport and only minimally through state-driven formal transport systems. It is thus imperative that informal public transport options like shuttle bus, jitneys, boda-boda etc., is included in the different hierarchies of transport planning—from national, regional to local transport plans. Further, there is a need to directly address the issue of affordability. Affordability (and thereby accessing public transport) is a major impediment for low-income women. This is further compounded if the employment space of women living in slum and squatter settlements are hit by resettlement programs. Programs to address daily mobility issues needs to be cross-fertilized with other welfare programs like training, provision of micro-credit, location of special economic zones and factories, see for example, the case of female workers in the Bangladeshi garment manufacturing industry (Absar, 2000; Kabeer, 2004). Women-only services, free bicycle distribution (e.g., Muralidharan and Prakash, 2013) and other innovative solutions can have positive impacts on low-income women's access to education, employment and health opportunities, but these programs need to be carefully sieved through to understand who are the final beneficiaries and ensure that the benefits percolate down to the female population.

2.2 Current travel data collection methods and analysis

Routinized data collection, access to data, and suitable analyses have continuously imposed some major challenges in highlighting the gendered nature of travel behavior. Even though travel behavior data is periodically collected in most countries in the Global North, disaggregated gendered analyses do not form a part of pre-feasibility studies guiding major transport infrastructure projects and are seldom reckoned as a foundational strategy in transport decision making processes. There is, however, a categorical lack of routinized data collection in low- and middle-income countries, and often data collection is driven by international infrastructure firms interested in road building projects (Priya Uteng and Turner, 2019). Additionally, the 1-day trip diary format of data collection on travel behavior does not catch the entire range and complexity of women's daily mobility performances, as it inevitably omits women whose travel patterns might vary across a week. Furthermore, most transport systems in low- and middle-income countries consist primarily of privately owned and operated minibus and motorbike taxis with few formal mass transit systems. Data is typically collected with respect to major infrastructure investments or projects, and fails to cover the entire network. Focus is typically on routes that will be displaced or where the authorities will need to address the paratransit or informal service operators (Klopp and Cavoli, 2019). Additionally, data is often not shared and limited to departmental silos. The range and variety of data that needs to be collected is also largely amiss in planning and policymaking discussions. For example, 92% of the world's low- and middle-income cities either do not have or highly incomplete transit maps (Krambeck, 2015). Klopp and Cavoli (2019) argue that using technology to collect data on existing routes (for both formal and informal public transport) and providing access to the collated information on mapped routes and services would greatly enhance gendered equity and access.

Apart from lack of routinized data collection and disaggregated analyses, a lack of clarity over which methods to employ to analyze the collected data poses an additional challenge. Typically, data collected by government authorities fail to blend quantitative and qualitative methods to both collect and analyze data, whereas in reality, both are needed to understand the gendered nuances of travel behavior. Research domain is slowly and steadily progressing toward blending the qualitative and quantitative methods but even in this case, a 2019 TRB workshop noted that research itself may also be suffering from gender bias. Conclusions from this workshop highlighted that a certain level of gender bias exists in data collection based on researchers' pre-defined prejudices, stereotyped and furthered traditional assumptions about women's traveling behaviors. This includes judgments that women travel in off peak periods (for shopping, escorting young children etc.) while they are themselves going to school, university or work. Consequently, they are traveling as much in peak hours as off-peak hours in the urban areas. Similar thoughts are presented by Akyelken (2020) in her editorial note in Transport Reviews.

Accessibility to employment, health and education opportunities have tangible economic benefits and though these numbers can be converted into economic indicators, such indicators aren't readily available. Given this backdrop, gender-based accessibility indicators do not inform current cost-benefit analyses (CBA) exercises, even though CBA are the cornerstones of transport decision-making. In the current technocratic outlook of the transport field which hinges on assessments like CBA, I posit that if gender and accessibility-based indicators are taken into the cost benefit assessments, then chances of prioritizing transport infrastructure facilitating public transport, walking and cycling will be substantially increased. Such exercises will also serve the ambition of creating liveable cities and assist in fulfilling the SDGs at large. Both in order to keep a tab on evolving travel behavior and to develop indicators as discussed above, travel data needs to be routinely collected and analyzed.

Data collection is a complex and resource-consuming exercise and thus a number of context-specific variables need to be discussed before data on travel behavior is collected. Additionally, disaggregated data analyses need to be made a priority in the transport field. For example, given the predominance of walking among women in the Global South, it will be no surprise that a greater number of (pedestrian) women might be dying in traffic accidents and yet a sex disaggregated analysis of traffic deaths remains unavailable. Disaggregated data analyses are also needed to ascertain the spatiality and temporality dimensions of both traffic and travel behaviors.

The knowledge generated through periodic assessments and estimations of the macroeconomic and welfare effects of creating accessible (education, health and employment) opportunities, could potentially benefit two important groups of existing heavyweights among policy makers and government stakeholders—(i) officials responsible for evaluating road construction programs as economic investments and (ii) welfare sector officials focused on promoting gender equality, social development and poverty reduction. For the first set of officials, core area of interest revolves around the relationship between the provision of road infrastructure and national income growth as measured by GDP metrics while the second group is interested in social development outcomes. These two analytical perspectives are seldom brought together to complement each other. Through creating the simple, standardized and context-informed methodology for the measurement of economic and social impact of road building and other transport intervention programs, both sets of policy concerns can be monitored.

2.3 Governance challenges

In a recent shift in both research and policy-making fields, the interlocking of different urban and transport issues is being recognized and arguments for integrative governance are gaining grounds (Tønnesen et al., 2020). But there is a gap in understanding how different transport policies relate to (i) each other at different scales, (ii) different sectors and (iii) needs of different population groups, and how these gaps produce specific gendered outcomes. The first point refers to the intra-sectoral levels of governance, which links the hierarchies of national, regional and local planning. It is often seen that there is lack of clarity over ways to translate national policies to local level programs and solutions. Global ambitions on climate targets need special mention here. Ways in which climate related goals exclude gendered analyses is detrimental to both policy arenas. For example, national agendas on lowering transport emissions in urban areas is popularly being used to facilitate uptake of electric cars. This move fails to recognize that a mere focus on shifting to electric cars will not be socially sustainable since car-based design solutions will fail to facilitate for women as their daily mobility is primarily not car-based. In a case study based on the electric car capital of the world, Oslo, Priya Uteng et al. (2021) found that despite a commitment to achieve climate goals at the national, regional and local levels, it is unlikely that Oslo will achieve its climate goals in the transport sector as the variables of gender and aging have been overlooked in setting both the future mobility and climate agendas.

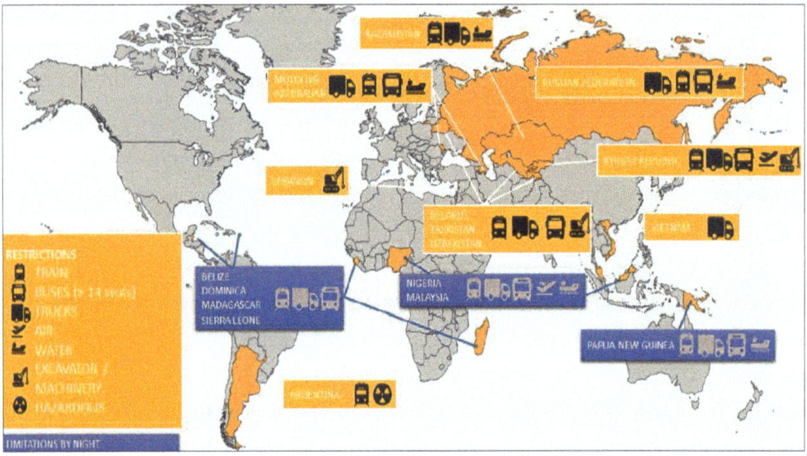

Photo 1 Legal restrictions on women's employment in the transport sector. *Ukraine removed restrictions after the data collection period ended. *From Iqbal, S., 2018. Women, Business and the Law. The World Bank, Washington D.C.*

Secondly, the link between policies related to other social development sectors like employment, education and health and the transport sector needs to be highlighted and bolstered. The case of female employment within the transport sector itself presents an important example. Women face high levels of discrimination to both enter and work in the transport sector (Photo 1), which is often supported by restrictive laws in some developing countries. Typically, women are either absent or marginally present in the transport sector. Women are less likely to find employment in the transport sector at large, but this is especially pronounced for the developing economies. This inadvertently results in rendering women's needs invisible, even in the provision of informal transport which is largely market responsive and highly adaptable.

The case of Dantewada, India[d] presents an important interface between the deep-rooted inadequacies of the transport system and cultural/sectoral constraints on female drivers (Photo 2). The tribal women of this remote rural area organized themselves through self-help groups to combat the lack of any form of public transport connectivity. They funneled government-sponsored

[d] http://www.newindianexpress.com/thesundaystandard/2018/feb/03/chhattisgarh-e-rickshaws-drive-a-change-in-the-lives-of-dantewadas-tribal-women-1767909.html
https://www.firstpost.com/india/women-in-dantewada-take-up-on-themselves-to-solve-transport-woes-drive-e-rickshaws-to-tackle-bad-infrastructure-4425347.html

Photo 2 E-rickshaws and tribal women of Dantewada, India. *From The New India Express, http://www.newindianexpress.com/thesundaystandard/2018/feb/03/chhattisgarh-e-rickshaws-drive-a-change-in-the-lives-of-dantewadas-tribal-women-1767909.html.*

Photo 3 Female (informal) transport workers in Kenya. *From Kamau, A., 2018. Women transport workers: social protection and labour issues. In: Proceedings of the Eastern Africa Women in Transportation Conference, Nairobi, Kenya.*

subsidy schemes to purchase and run *E*-rickshaws connecting the female population to rural markets, schools etc.

Another case, drawn from Kenya, highlights how increasing female participation in the (informal) transport sector as owners, drivers, touts, stage clerks and fleet managers is challenging the largely male dominated transport sector of the country (Kamau, 2018) (Photo 3). But lack of formal social protection schemes does not render it as an attractive long-term option.

However, there is a large symbolic value that female employees in the transport sector carry which needs to be protected to open this sector for future female employment. The case of female bus conductors in the city of Bengaluru in India serves the same logic (Campbell, 2019). Since these female conductors are working on state-run buses and consequently beneficiaries of social protection schemes, they have not only received encouragement from their families to join a previously socially-banned sector for women but have managed to shift the popular perception of society at large regarding female employees in the transport sector (ibid).

Women are poorly represented at all levels of employment and decision making, across all modes and subsectors (SuM4ALL, 2019). This is especially true for operations with most senior positions still being held by men. Attracting, keeping, and advancing women in the transportation workforce is of key interest in both the developed and developing parts of the world (ITF, 2002; Turnbull, 2013). A key barrier is the high levels of violence, discrimination and sexual harassment within the transport working environment. The International Transport Workers Federation states that its member unions across all modes globally, show that sexual harassment is widespread in the sector (ITF, 2002). Additionally, due to a lack of diversity in the sector, women staff risk increased levels of sexual harassment both by the passengers and their co-workers. A survey by European Transport Federation (ETF, 2019) reveals that violence against women at work is a widespread and growing problem in transport, affecting women's occupational safety, health and wellbeing at work.

These cases highlight that firstly, given the predominance of informal transport systems in the developing countries, this sector can be a potential source of employment for women. Secondly, in order to combat existing social taboos and facilitate a safe employment space for women in the transport sector, Kamau's (2018) questions need to be integrated in inter-sectoral governance mechanism: *Can we design and integrate social and physical protection for women transport workers? How can this be guaranteed? Are their services being valued? What is the evidence?*.

2.4 Gender lens in engineering education

Engineering education is deeply embedded in a framework which looks at design and production of projects from cost-savings and technical efficiency perspective, and the field remains heavily male-dominated. For example, in UK, 91% of engineering professionals are male (IET, 2015, p. 22) and this figure is more or less an accurate estimate of the global skewness in this profession. Such skewed distribution has inevitably rendered a scenario where both the problems and the solutions are drawn from a male perspective. Even a perfunctory gaze over the history of transport planning will establish the dominance of a system which designed its tools (for example, transport models) to promote car use and actively promoted the expansion of cities based primarily on automobility. The field remains deeply embedded in the engineering domain, and it is no surprise that the transport systems are bereft of problem structuring and decision-making which takes a social perspective of transport issues.

In a critical review of current engineering education, Lam and Cosgrave (2017, 2019) argue that the present binary thinking inscribes an implicit androcentric bias which ignores women's experiences and fails to plan for not only women, but people with disabilities, the elderly, and children. Both engineering and planning education need to address this systemic bias to incorporate a wide array of experiences in designing processes, products and solutions.

The authors (ibid) prescribe that a social science gearing of the transport field at large should adopt a gender lens both in theory and practice. The theoretical framing of engineering education should be made intersectional, acknowledging the multiplicity of identities and how engineering designs may produce uneven urban experiences. Simultaneously, a gender lens in practice must focus on both the lifecycle of an engineer as well as the lifecycle of an engineering project.

Given this backdrop, the emergence of smart cities and smart mobilities need to broaden its scope to be able to incorporate a needs-based understanding in designing of smart solutions. For example, transport systems need to be integrated with urban design solutions to understand how variations in street lighting and layouts affect people's perceptions of personal security. Additionally, the most established macro tools like the 4-step transport models, widely used in advising road capacity augmentation programs etc., need to be linked with the micro-level accessibility tools to find how macro and micro decisions can be aligned to promote sustainable modes like walking, cycling and public transport. Current engineering and planning education remain disjointed and is unable to impart such a layered thinking process.

2.5 Safety and security issues and perception of risk leading to economic, geographic, time-based, and fear-based exclusion

Studies have consistently shown that incidences of gender-based violence, assault and harassment (GBVAH) are closely interlinked with accessing and using public transport. This phenomenon is widespread in both the developed and developing parts of the world (Ceccato and Paz, 2017; Gekoski et al., 2015; Goulds et al., 2018; Stringer, 2007; Twyford, 2017).[e] A large-scale survey of street harassment in 42 cities around the world in 2015 revealed that approximately 84% (from a sample of 16,600 female respondents spread across the world) had experienced street harassment for the first time before they were 17 years old (Hollaback! and The ILR School, 2015). In India, 91% of women felt that public transport was very unsafe, unsafe or somewhat unsafe (Shah and Raman, 2019). In Loukaitou-Sideris and Ceccato's recent book (Loukaitou-Sideris and Ceccato, 2020), the Lagos (Nigeria) case study found that female college students were 2.2 times more likely to experience non-verbal sexual violence than males.

Loukaitou-Sideris (2009) examined the relationship between the built environment and women's fear of public transportation systems and compiled a comprehensive literature review, based on examples drawn primarily from the US, on fear of transit/public transport. Their review highlights that safety concerns have strong contextual determinants—public lighting, characteristics of sidewalks, isolation and neighborhood characteristics. Another study, by Quinones (2020), underscores the ways in which women in

[e] To quote a few examples, 55% of women reported that they were concerned about traveling to educational institutions after dark in Kigali, Rwanda (UN Women, 2013). In Kenya, 54% of women interviewed in 2015 said they had experienced some form of gender-based violence while using public transportation. And a staggering 99% of the women surveyed in the UN Women study in 2013 in Egypt had experienced sexual harassment, most commonly touching or groping, which involved harassment in public spaces inclusive of public transport and streets. The study showed that public transport and the general street environment were both vulnerable areas. Almost 70% of women in a survey conducted by the EBRD in 2016 (EBRD, 2016) were dissuaded from using the train to commute to work because of safety concerns in Egypt. These concerns were mostly a response to a high incidence of sexual harassment in public transport. For Mexico City, it has been reported that institutional programs had a limited effect on stopping abusive behavior and sexual harassment of women in the public transit system, and 65% of female riders who had been targeted and victimized continued to be reluctant to report incidents (Thomas Reuters Foundation, 2014). In Buenos Aries, 89% of the women interviewed had experienced sexual harassment on public transport; almost half of the women interviewed had been harassed in the year prior to the survey (Allen et al., 2019).

Bogotá, Colombia, experience sexual harassment in public space with special reference to public transport (inside vehicles, on stations/stops and walking routes to and from their origins or destination). According to Verma et al. (2017), women's perceptions of safety while traveling on buses influences their modal preference for buses. Fear and safety concerns cause women to shift from public transportation to less sustainable, private modes of travel. Often, women make decisions on where they go or which jobs they accept based on feelings of safety. Thus, the lack of safety has repercussions that extend beyond acts of violence and affect the socio-economic growth of a considerable demographic in society. Ensuring sufficient street lighting and toilets is the bare minimum that urban planners and engineers can do to facilitate women's safety and mobility, and yet, this need remains largely unmet. Street lighting, for example, is very much a gendered issue—more street lighting makes women feel safer. In a cost-cutting measure after the 2008 economic recession, many US cities reduced the amount of lighting on city streets, which had an insignificant fiscal impact but a disproportionately detrimental impact on women's mobility and safety (Hazelton, 2017). If engineers and planners view street lighting as a technical, engineering project without any consideration of how safety is gendered, they ignore the realities of street harassment and violence against women.

Quinones (2020) emphasizes that there are three main sections of any journey where women are at risk—(i) the "first" and "last" mile, (ii) public transport waiting areas and (iii) in vehicle (road or rail based). In one of the most extensive international surveys on the topic, it was found that over 82% of the respondents reported taking a different route home/to their destination to avoid GBVAH (Hollaback! and The ILR School, 2015). This is confirmed in other studies as well (Allen et al., 2019; Borker, 2017; Roy and Bailey, 2021).

Acts of harassment against women in urban transport vary in their degree, spatiality and temporality, ranging from sexual harassment, assault or violence on city streets, at public transport stations to inside the vehicles. Harassment itself exists on a continuum (visual, verbal and physical) that may be almost invisible to men, including acts like leering, sexual comments, photography, intimidation, groping, threats, and other nuisances or crimes with sexual undertones (Allen, 2015). These perceived and actual threats of violence have constrained female mobility to a great extent which not only has social ramifications but serious economic repercussions as well (Woetzel et al., 2015).

A gap in collection of data on GBVAH, combined with under-reporting incidences of sexual harassment on transport systems, and a lack of clarity on, or a total absence of, reporting mechanisms and responsibility allocation, has ensured that GBVAH continues to exist across the world. The situation is compounded in Global South due to the dominance of informal modes of transport. The under-representation of women working in the transport sector, both at the decision-making and operational levels, has also contributed to the "invisibility" of this problem. It has also been noted that the operators, drivers and conductors of these informal modes of transport are often active participants in perpetuating GBVAH.

Lack of sectoral coordination in addressing the issue of GBVAH is another major impediment found across the globe. Under the UN-Habitat's Safer Cities Program, the local UN-Habitat Office in Warsaw, Poland conducted a Women's Safety Audit pilot project in 2007 (Buckingham, 2007). Eight female participants comprising women from the Warsaw municipality, police headquarters, UN-Habitat office, Chamber of Town Planners, a local NGO, and the media were involved in the audit of the Srodmiescie district in Warsaw's city center. Participants identified concerns related to lighting, signage, receiving emergency assistance, infrastructural maintenance, and urban amenities. They also suggested improvements to enhance the safety and design of the neighborhood and recommended to create mixed-use spaces in the neighborhood to attract more human presence. A Making Places Safer study in three London neighborhoods noted that the following factors make women feel safer: Good street lighting; clear sight lines to public spaces by cutting back shrubs; giving pedestrians priority; legible public signage; and most importantly, public places occupied by a diverse range of people (Loomans, 2017).

Spatial and transport projects need to prioritize creating safe spaces at both macro and micro levels. At the macro level, emerging mapping techniques through interactive portals like Safetipin apps[f] and safety auditing routines can be employed to map unsafe areas. It is important to flag that these mapping exercises without a protocol to redress these unsafe areas will be a wasted endeavor, and therefore protocols need to be established on how to transform these unsafe areas, routes etc. into safe, accessible areas. To illustrate a case at the micro level, spaces within the public transport can be discussed. Sexual harassment within these spaces is a routine in many parts of the world and yet there are no established protocols on where and how to

[f] https://safetipin.com/our-apps/; Safetipin (2017).

report such abuses. A simple way forward could be to train the bus drivers and bus conductors to deal with situations of sexual harassment and report it further. However, when the driver or conductor themselves are found to be culprits, punitive measures need to be in place for dealing with such actions.

In terms of sexual violence, assault or harassment—almost the entire range of these incidents are widely underreported, and there is a general perception among the victims that reporting is emotionally degrading and leads to nothing (Allen et al., 2019). This is supported by accounts of women who have tried to report an incident and have faced several difficulties not only in finding where to report the incident, but also that the reporting process was often insensitive and time consuming. A study from Bogotá, Colombia showed that sexual harassment in public transport—and public spaces—is widespread in the city, and sexual harassment incidents are primarily underreported (Quinones, 2020). At a global level, security agencies do not have female or trained staff to take the report. A lack of trust in the authorities and police is found to be widespread, and one of the primary reasons why most of these incidents (90% or more) remain underreported across Latin America (Allen et al., 2019; Quinones, 2020).

Though most urban areas lack a clear monitoring framework and routinized feedback mechanisms, there are certain examples to draw on. In Sierra Leone, the government created two key indicators to monitor the implementation of an inclusive project (Arroyo and Diallo, 2020). The first one measures users' satisfaction—disaggregated by gender and including questions about reliability, safety, accessibility, comfort, customer service, and sexual harassment. The other indicator measures how many women change from informal to formal public transport services. This change is used as a proxy to measure progress on the reduction of sexual harassment risk, given that women are harassed five times less frequently on formal public transport (World Bank, 2019). Additionally, UN Habitat's (2019) practical tool is a rare example of tool for policymakers and practitioner within the African region, that explicitly focuses on addressing sexual harassment within public transport. The toolkit sets out a series of actions that transport operators and policy makers can take in order to deliver a more gender equitable transport system as well as specifically addressing sexual harassment on public transport within the context of urban Kenya. These actions range from establishing high levels of customer service standards, introducing zero-tolerance policies toward sexual harassment of passengers and staff, introducing passenger vehicles that are accessible for people with disabilities and a range of other uses and implementing employment policies that are secure and are compatible with family responsibilities. The UN Women Safe Cities program (UN Women, 2019) worked with city authorities and NGOs in Torreon, Mexico, to institutionalize grievance mechanisms, bolster the capacity of the municipal government and transport agencies to respond to sexual harassment, and improve legal sanctions.

The need to mix soft and hard measures in addressing this topic cannot be emphasized enough. For example, campaigns targeting sexual harassment and assault on public transport have been found to be instrumental in raising awareness, encouraging women to report incidents and "speak up," inform public about initiatives to reduce such behavior, appeal for witnesses to come forward and publicize pictures of suspects. Examples range from campaigns like Massachusetts Bay Transportation Authority's (MBTA) 2008 public awareness campaign using large scale posters which was revived in 2013[g]; "*Take Back the Metro*" in Paris (launched in 2014) leading to nationwide campaign "Stop, enough is enough" ("Stop ça suffit") in 2015; "Know the Difference" campaign in the UK which included different headlines like "*Back to Mine. Back Off,*" "*Get it On. Get off Me,*" "*Flirt. Harass,*" "*Harmless Fun. Sexual Assault*"—followed by the same central message: "*Real Men Know the Difference. And so does the Law*"; Belgium's "*Touche Pas à Ma Pote!*" ("*Don't Touch my Girl Friend*") campaign including posters with images of big yellow hands with the message written on them in pink etc., are few examples in how campaigns have been used in the Global North. The case of Mexico City provides us valuable material to state that soft measures can be successfully launched in developing economies as well. As part of Mexico City's initiatives, INMUJERES—the federal institute for gender equality and equal opportunities for women—started advertising campaigns which used a combination of posters, billboards and bumper stickers reading "*It is our right to travel without fear.*" To add a grounding to this claim, a free 24-h hotline number to report harassment was displayed below the slogan. Gekoski et al. (2015)

[g] A public awareness campaign, using large scale posters across the transport network, was launched in 2008 by the Massachusetts Bay Transportation Authority (MBTA). It encouraged victims to report incidents to the police, emphasizing that certain behavior was not acceptable and would be treated seriously by the authorities. In 2013, the campaign was revived after numerous reports of indecent exposure and public masturbation on trains were reported. The new posters, which were displayed on trains and buses, featured photographs of both men and women holding up their hands, pointing at offenders, and crossing their arms. Slogans on the posters included messages such as: "Respect my space," "Keep your hands off me," and "No means no." One poster, with the slogan "Keep your privates private," carried the following warning against public exposure: "Want the whole world to see you? No problem. I can snap your photo with my See Something, Say Something app, and send it to Transit Police."

build on success stories of these campaigns, including MBTA's anti-harassment advertising campaign. Evaluation conducted 4 years post MBTA's campaign launch indicated that the number of sex offenses *reported* on the MBTA increased by 32% and the number of *arrests* for sex offenses increased by 96% after the launch of the campaign.

Gekoski et al. (2015) quite aptly warn against the approach where campaigns blame or shame women for sexual harassment and assault. Such campaigns and their subsequent failures have been recorded in Iran, Singapore, and Canada outlining the importance of a methodological approach based on extensive consultations before launching campaigns on such a sensitive topic.

2.6 Space organization and consumption

Given the huge variations in how urban areas have evolved and are currently being organized in different parts of the world, the topic of built environment and its interlocking with gendered travel behavior and perceptions on security needs to be studied in a context-specific manner. A recent study from UN-Women found that informal settlements are increasingly becoming feminized with a relatively higher concentration of female living in slums in the Global South (Azcona et al., 2020). Further, relocation decisions impact livelihoods of women to a much greater extent than men and it is found that access to opportunities which suits the livelihood profile of slum women is hardly ever recognized in relocation decisions (Bryceson et al., 2003; Desai et al., 2017; Gupta and Sharma, 2000; Priya Uteng, 2011). The existing mismatch between current and proposed accessibility levels afforded to women needs to be both recognized and addressed in urban planning decisions guiding development of new areas. Ideally, mixed land use is best suited from a gendered perspective. But gender itself is not a uniform variable and needs to be analyzed from the lens of intersectionality. It is here that decisions on slum relocation etc., must be carefully sieved through the potential impacts on low-income women.

Another parameter related to space organization and consumption is linked to the topic of circular economy. Though there are an astounding number of urban and transport studies on the topics of circular economy, sustainable resource consumption and sharing, the gendered variations of these topics remain poorly understood. The synergies between shared mobility and multifunctional space solutions considering gendered uptake needs further unpacking. We lack knowledge on how "shared" qualities and characteristics of the built environment affect consumption and sustainable behaviors of men vs women. Consequently, planners simply do not have the tools to develop and implement effective area development strategies, measures and policies that can lead to more sharing and circularity of resources (Kębłowski et al., 2020; Obersteg et al., 2019; Petit-Boix and Leipold, 2018). Gender analyses can be an integral element in informing planning and decision-making processes to promote plans with respect to creating shared spaces and shared mobility solutions to serve as an accelerator in promoting sustainable consumption in urban areas. Additionally, Covid-19 pandemic has highlighted the unpreparedness at all levels of governance to deal with such crisis situations. I posit that vigilant sharing and suitable framework conditions might play an important role for revised consumption patterns, which will inevitably benefit women across all strata of the society.

Both urban and transport fields need to actively engage with creating framework conditions that enable transitions, address the institutional and regulatory bottlenecks and create policies and strategies that are simultaneously relevant for environment and economic domains (like integrated circular economy in urban areas) and social arenas (equity in access). Intersectoral exchanges on resource consumption needs to be established to foster the ethos that circular economy is as much about reduction of resource use as it is about shared and circular use of resources, i.e., within an urban context, a shift to shared mobility and multifunctional space uses will support both these goals as well as lead to significant improvements in public health and quality of life when governed in the right way. The current travel behavior of women highlights that they are already champions in this arena and provision of right structures will assist in maintaining these consumption patterns.

3. Discussion and conclusion

Transport planning is undertaken primarily under the framework of Comprehensive Mobility Plan (CMP) across the globe. Preparation of CMP is a technical exercise following the "predict and provide" optimization principles for travel demand and further validated through cost-benefit analyses (ADB, 2008). Multiple studies have reiterated the shortcomings of this approach, as the embedded technocratic focus fails to incorporate user needs and behavior in transport infrastructure planning and provision (Diaz Olvera et al., 2013; Porter et al., 2019). Further, gender is seldom considered in transportation planning, and transportation is seldom included in the gender policy agendas, leading to a systemic and systematic gap in procedures guiding transportation (and urban) design, planning and provision of services.

Evidently, while the field of urban planning and transport is grappling with how to balance the economic and environmental agendas, it is at a loss to recognize the social ramifications of transport planning decisions. This chapter attempted to bridge this gap by expanding on the gendered nature of mobility consumption and existing gaps in ensuring that sustainable mobility patterns are maintained rather than obliterated in the long run. The differentiated nature of impacts or ways in which the different demographic groups are affected by transport decisions need to be both understood and taken into cognizance while framing urban and transport planning decisions. Studies undertaken on gendered mobilities across the world reveal that women are already champions of sustainable travel behavior and yet continue to be ignored. Issues pertaining to GBVAH are seldom recognized in mainstream transport planning. Through becoming gender-responsive, the sector can effectively cater to the three pillars of sustainable development—economic, environment, and social, but a consistent focus is required to address the 4As—affordability, accessibility, availability, acceptability—for addressing the sustainability goals. Integrating the 4As in future policies and programs should be based on careful sieving of the current transport system's interlocking with women's employment, education, access to health, training facilities and the overall nexus between "production" and "reproduction" (i.e., paid employment and unpaid domestic care work). Essentially, we lack knowledge on the politics of how, when, and why gender either gets or does not get embodied in urban transport. The term "politics" here does not ascribe exclusively to the semantics of the word itself, but refers to the definitions, structures, processes, protocols and outlook of the transport field. For example, given the traditional focus on hard infrastructure, how will ICT-enabled "smart" technologies be put to use in future transport designs and solutions?

At a global level, we witness a continued absence or meager presence of women employees in the transport sector. Though reasons range from security concerns, cultural inappropriateness to the technical dominance of the field, the gains of employing women in the transport field are manifold. Apart from becoming a source of employment for women, their presence will influence the current norms and the field might evolve to be more mindful of women's needs and preferences. Traditionally, the norms governing transport sector remains heavily male dominated in terms of both employment and its technical orientation. There is a clear need to integrate female presence at the level of decision-making to actualize the principles of inclusive and liveable cities.

From a static domain of primarily road-building exercises, the field of urban transportation is being pushed into adopting a more dynamic and fast-changing outlook. However, the insertion of evolving technologies leaves little room for a static approach and thus transitions both from a policy and practice perspective are required to keep pace with emerging solutions like Mobility-as-a-system (MaaS) which builds on linking both traditional and upcoming modes of transport. But there is again a technocratic approach in the overall framing of policies which is evident in an active promotion of electric cars to exemplify a shift from non-renewables to renewable source of energy. The primary unit of "car" is being kept as a constant variable which is certainly problematic. Given the prevalent norms in the transport field, focus on hard infrastructure persists and modes like walking, bicycling, safe and secure public transport and their social-psychological ramifications benefitting women's daily mobilities are routinely ignored. Practice theory, for example, could be employed here to highlight and explain user adoption of innovations and provide for a richer understanding of the micro-phenomena that takes place on different life stages (both affecting men and women) by which these stages can be targeted in the right manner. Considering the practices adopted by women at large, the process of recruitment and retention of new technologies needs to be better understood. In the parlance of practice theory, how a practice such as walking, bicycling and public transport usage can undergo formation and reformation in a manner that it can sustain itself needs to be both studied and allowed to shape future transportation policies and programs.

One of the greatest impediments concerns routinized data collection and analyses protocols. A majority of the countries in Global South do not have such protocols and data is often collected on an adhoc basis, often to justify road and bridge-building exercises. Even though data on travel behavior is routinely collected in the Global North, gender-based analyses are not routinely undertaken and consequently do not have any major influence on decision making. The resultant "invisibility" on how lack of suitable transport options link with other sectors and how these missing links specifically affect women has led to a continued state of under development in many parts of the world. For example, links between transport and housing policies should be inserted in land use, housing and relocation decisions. Even in the research world, few studies have looked at the interactions between urban housing policies and accessibility with respect to subsidized housing, establishment of resettlement colonies and loss of livelihoods of women.

To conclude, a behavior change model which can address the incidences of current travel behavior, GBVAH, spatial and temporal dimensions, data collection, inter-sectoral coordination etc., should be created to respond to the interlocking of structural, behavioral and physical elements affecting the daily mobilities of women. A behavior change model should be more encompassing than being framed simply in terms of designing interventions to target men's behavior. The overall framework of behavior change would need to target both general population as well as policymakers given the inertia found in both popular and institutional culture governing the topic of gender and transport.

References

Abasahl, F., Kelarestaghi, K.B., Ermagun, A., 2018. Gender gap generators for bicycle mode choice in Baltimore college campuses. Travel Behav. Soc. 11, 78–85. https://doi.org/10.1016/j.tbs.2018.01.002.

Absar, S.S., 2000. Conditions, concerns and needs of garment workers in Bangladesh. Dev. Bull. 51, 82–84.

ADB Asian Development Bank, 2008. Comprehensive Mobility Plans (CMPs): Preparation Toolkit [Internet]. Available at: https://sti-india-uttoolkit.adb.org/mod1/index.html.

Agyapong, F., Ojo, T.K., 2018. Managing traffic congestion in the Accra Central Market, Ghana. J. Urban Manag. 7, 85–96. Available at https://doi.org/10.1016/j.jum.2018.04.002.

Akyelken, N., 2020. Transport for women: who decides what women need?. Transp. Rev. 40 (6), 687–688. https://doi.org/10.1080/01441647.2020.1799162.

Aldred, R., Woodcock, J., Goodman, A., 2016. Does more cycling mean more diversity in cycling? Transp. Rev. 36 (1), 28–44.

Allen, H., 2015. Safe and Sound—An International Review of Gender, Personal Security and Public Transport [Internet]. FIA Foundation. Available at: https://www.researchgate.net/publication/326588267_SAFE_AND_SOUND_INTERNATIONAL_RESEARCH_ON_WOMEN%27S_PERSONAL_SAFETY_ON_PUBLIC_TRANSPORT.

Allen, H., Cárdenas, G., Pereyra, L., Sagaris, L., 2019. Ella Se Mueve Segura (ESMS)—A Study and Toolkit on women's Personal Security in Three Latin American Cities. CAF and FIA Foundation, Caracas. Available at: http://scioteca.caf.com/handle/123456789/1405.

Arroyo, F.A., Diallo, B., 2020. Invisible Travelers: 3 Lessons From Freetown to Transform Urban Transport—And Your City [Internet]. Available at: https://blogs.worldbank.org/ppps/invisible-travelers-3-lessons-freetown-transform-urban-transport-and-your-city?cid=tai_tt_transport_en_ext%3Fcid%3DSHR_BlogSiteShare_EN_EXT.

Azcona, G., Bhatt, A., Duerto Valero, S., Priya Uteng, T., 2020. Harsh Realities: Marginalized Women in Cities of the Developing World. UN Women, New York. Available at: https://www.unwomen.org/en/digital-library/publications/2020/02/harsh-realities-marginalized-women-in-cities-of-the-developing-world.

Bastian, A., Börjesson, M., 2018. The city as a driver of new mobility patterns, cycling and gender equality: travel behaviour trends in Stockholm 1985–2015. Travel Behav. Soc. 13, 71–87. https://doi.org/10.1016/j.tbs.2018.06.003.
Berent, P., Nagahiro, Y., 2017. Understanding the nature of walking and cycling for transport in Japan. Mem. Fac. Eng. 58, 25–43.
Best, H., Lanzendorf, M., 2005. Division of labour and gender differences in metropolitan car use: an empirical study in Cologne, Germany. J. Transp. Geogr. 13 (2), 109–121. https://doi.org/10.1016/j.jtrangeo.2004.04.007.
Borker, G., 2017. Safety First: Perceived Risk of Street Harassment and Educational Choices of Women. Available at: https://girijaborker.files.wordpress.com/2017/11/borker_jmp.pdf.
Bryceson, D.F., Maunder, D.A.C., Mbara, T.C., Kibombo, R., Davis, A.S.C., Howe, J.D.G.F., 2003. Sustainable Livelihoods, Mobility and Access Needs. Report No. TRL544. TRL, Croethorne. Available at: http://citeseerx.ist.psu.edu/viewdoc/download?doi=10.1.1.590.5152&rep=rep1&type=pdf.
Buckingham, S., 2007. Addressing Women's Urban Safety Through the Right to the City: UN-Habitat's Women Safety Audit Pilot Project in Warsaw, Poland. Available at: http://base.d-p-h.info/es/fiches/dph/fiche-dph-8058.html.
Buehler, R., 2011. Determinants of transport mode choice: a comparison of Germany and the USA. J. Transp. Geogr. 19 (4), 644–657. https://doi.org/10.1016/j.jtrangeo.2010.07.005.
Campbell, M., 2019. Smart as agency and human interaction: exploring the work of women bus conductors in Bengaluru, India. In: Priya Uteng, T., Levin, L., Rømer Christensen, H. (Eds.), Gendering Smart Mobilities. Routledge, Abingdon and New York.
Ceccato, V., Loukaitou-Sideris, A. (Eds.), 2020. Transit Crime and Sexual Violence in Cities: International Evidence and Prevention. Routledge, Abingdon.
Ceccato, V., Paz, Y., 2017. Crime in São Paulo's metro system: sexual crimes against women. Crime Prev. Community Saf. 19 (3–4), 211–226. https://doi.org/10.1057/s41300-017-0027-2.
Clark, B., Lyons, G., Chatterjee, K., 2016. Understanding the process that gives rise to household car ownership level changes. J. Transp. Geogr. 55, 110–120.
Collins, D., Tisdell, C., 2002. Gender and differences in travel life cycles. J. Travel Res. 41 (2), 133–143. https://doi.org/10.1177/004728702237413.
CoMun, 2014. Reseau Marocain de Transport Public—Etat des lieux synthetique du transport public dans les villes membres du REMA-TP. Available at http://www.comun.net/maroc/les-reseaux-thematiques/rema-tp-transportpublic/etat-des-lieux-et-benchmarking.
Delatte, A., 2018. Women in transport international outlook, workshop 3. In: Smart Mobilities, Planning and Policy Processes—Gender and Diversity Mainstreaming, Nos-Sh Workshop Series, 17–18 September. VTI, Stockholm, Sweden.
Desai, R., Parmar, V., Mahadevia, D., 2017. Resettlement, mobility and women's safety in cities. IIC Q. 43 (3–4), 65–76.
Diaz Olvera, L., Plat, D., Pochet, P., 2013. The puzzle of mobility and access to the city in sub- Saharan Africa. J. Transp. Geogr. 32, 56–64.
ETF, 2019. Online Survey on How to Make Transport Fit for Women to Work in [Internet]. Available at: https://www.etf-europe.org/launch-of-the-etf-survey-on-what-the-transport-sector-needs-to-be-more-attractive-for-women/.
European Parliament, P. D. C, 2012. The Role of Women in the green Economy—The Issue of Mobility. Available at: (europa.eu).
Garrard, J., Rose, G., Lo, S.K., 2008. Promoting transportation cycling for women: the role of bicycle infrastructure. Prev. Med. 46 (1), 55–59.

Gekoski, A., Gray, J., Horvath, M., Edwards, M.A.H., Emirali, S., Adler, J.R., 2015. What Works' in Reducing Sexual Harassment and Sexual Offences on Public Transport Nationally and Internationally: A Rapid Evidence Assessment. British Transport Police and Department for Transport, London. Available at: https://eprints.mdx.ac.uk/15219/.

Ghate, A.T., Tiwari, G., 2019. A Gendered Perspective of the Phenomenon of 'No Travel to Work' in Indian Cities: A Case Study of Jaipur City, Paper Presented at WCTR Conference, 26–31 May. IIT Mumbai, India.

Goel, R., Goodman, A., Aldred, R., Nakamura, R., Tatah, L., Garcia, L.M.T., Zapata-Diomedi, B., Herick de Sa, T., Tiwari, G., de Nazelle, A., Tainio, M., Buehler, R., Götschi, T., Woodcock, J., 2021. Cycling behaviour in 17 countries across 6 continents: levels of cycling, who cycles, for what purpose, and how far? Transp. Rev. https://doi.org/10.1080/01441647.2021.1915898.

Götschi, T., Tainio, M., Maizlish, N., Schwanen, T., Goodman, A., Woodcock, J., 2015. Contrasts in active transport behaviour across four countries: how do they translate into public health benefits? Prev. Med. 74, 42–48.

Goulds, S., Tanner, S., Kalms, N., Matthewson, G., 2018. Portfolio: 'Unsafe in the City: The Everyday Experiences of Girls and Young Women'. Plan International, Surrey, UK.

Gupta, S., Sharma, A.K., 2000. A causal analysis of public sector working women's mobility in Navi Mumbai: lessons for policy formulation. In: *CODATU IX Conference Proceedings*, Mexico, 11-14th April 2000.

Hamlin, C., 2004. Preventing Fistula: Transport's Role in Empowering Communities for Health in Ethiopia. Available at Preventing fistula: transport's role in empowering communities for health in Ethiopia | Eldis.

Hanson, S., 2010. Gender and mobility: new approaches for informing sustainability. Gend. Place Cult. 17 (1), 5–23.

Hazelton, J., 2017. The shocking connection between street harassment and street lighting. In: The Establishment. July 24, 2017. Available at: https://theestablishment.co/the-shocking-connection-between-street-harassment-and-street-lighting-5db8497ef653.

Heinen, E., Chatterjee, K., 2015. The same mode again? An exploration of mode choice variability in Great Britain using the National Travel Survey. Transp. Res. A Policy Pract. 78, 266–282.

Hjorthol, R.J., 2008. Daily mobility of men and women—a barometer of gender equality? In: Uteng, T.P., Cresswell, T. (Eds.), Gendered Mobilities. Ashgate.

Hollaback! and The ILR School, 2015. Street Harassment: The Largest International Cross-Cultural Study [Internet]. Available at https://www.ilr.cornell.edu/worker-institute/news/ilr-and-hollaback-release-largest-analysis-street-harassment-date.

IET. The Institution of Engineering and Technology, 2015. 2015 IET Skills Survey. Available at: IET Skills Survey 2015 (theiet.org).

ITF, 2002. Women Transporting the World. An ITF Resource Book for Trade Union Negotiators in the Transport Sector. Available at: https://www.itfglobal.org/sites/default/files/resources-files/Womenworld.pdf.

Joseph, L., Neven, A., Martens, K., Kweka, O., Wets, G., Janssens, D., 2020. Activity participation and perceptions on informal public transport and bus rapid transit in Dar Es Salaam. Transp. Res. Rec. 2674 (11), 573–583.

Kabeer, N., 2004. Globalization, labor standards, and women's rights: dilemmas of collective (in) action in an interdependent world. Fem. Econ. 10 (1), 3–35.

Kamau, A., 2018. Women transport workers: social protection and labour issues. In: *Proceedings of the Eastern Africa Women in Transportation Conference*, Nairobi, Kenya.

Kantor, P., 2002. A sectoral approach to the study of gender constraints on economic opportunities in the informal sector in India. Gend. Soc. 16 (3), 285–302.

Kawgan-Kagan, I., 2015. Early adopters of carsharing with and without BEVs with respect to gender preferences. Eur. Transp. Res. Rev. 7 (4), 1–11. https://doi.org/10.1007/s12544-015-0183-3.
Kębłowski, W., Lambert, D., Bassens, S., 2020. Circular economy and the city: an urban political economy agenda. Cult. Organ. 26 (2), 142–158.
King, R., 1980. Residential location, travel mode and income: the likely effects of changes in housing cost and transport cost in Melbourne. In: Australian Road Research Board Internal Report 311-1. Retrieved from http://trid.trb.org/view.aspx?id=1207067.
Klopp, J., Cavoli, C., 2019. Mapping minibuses in Maputo and Nairobi: engaging paratransit in transportation planning in African cities. Transp. Rev. 39 (5), 657–676.
Krambeck, H., 2015. Mapping Manila Transit: A New Approach to Solving Old Challenges. Connections: Transport & ICT. World Bank.
Krizek, K.J., Johnson, P.J., Tilahun, N., 2005. Gender differences in bicycling behavior and facility preferences. In: Rosenbloom, S. (Ed.), Research on Women's Issues in Transportation. Transportation Research Board, Washington, DC, pp. 31–40.
Kwan, M., 1999. Gender and individual access to urban opportunities: a study using space-time measures. Prof. Geogr. 51 (2), 210–227.
Lam, T., 2019. Cycling London: an intersectional feminist perspective. In: Priya Uteng, T., Levin, L., Rømer Christensen, H. (Eds.), Gendering Smart Mobilities. Routledge, Abingdon and New York.
Lam, T., Cosgrave, E., 2017. Toward a Gender Lens in (Civil) Engineering for Cities, Working Paper. Available at Towards+a+Gender+Lens+in+Engineering.pdf (squarespace.com.
Lam, T., Cosgrave, E., 2019. Gender inclusive climate action in cities. In: A Report for C40 Cities Women4Climate Initiative. Available at W4C_REPORT_Gender Inclusive Climate Action in Cities_BD.pdf.
Law, R., 1999. Beyond 'women and transport': towards new geographies of gender and daily mobility. Prog. Hum. Geogr. 23 (4), 567–588.
Lenz, B., 2017. Smart mobility—for all? Gender issues in the context of new mobility concepts, paper presented in Workshop 1. In: Gendering Smart Mobilities, Nos-Sh Workshop Series, 24–25 August. Institute of Transport Economics TØI, Oslo, Norway.
Loomans, T., 2017. Designing Safe Cities for Women. Available at: http://www.smartcitiesdive.com/ex/sustainablecitiescollective/designing-safe-cities-women/1052876/.
Loukaitou-Sideris, A., 2009. How to Ease Women's Fear of Transportation Environments: Case Studies and Best Practices. Mineta Transportation Institute, College of Business, San Jose, CA.
Loukaitou-Sideris, A., Ceccato, V., 2020. Sexual violence in transit environments: aims, scope, and context. In: Ceccato, V., Loukaitou-Sideris, A. (Eds.), Transit Crime and Sexual Violence in Cities: International Evidence and Prevention. Routledge, Abingdon.
METPEX, 2013. Identification of User Requirements Concerning the Definition of Variables to be Measured by the METPEX Tool (Deliverable 2.3 of the METPEX Project). EU Commissions.
Muralidharan, K., Prakash, N., 2013. Cycling to School: Increasing Secondary School Enrollment for Girls in India, Working Paper 19305. National Bureau of Economic Research, Cambridge. Available at: https://www.nber.org/papers/w19305.
Obersteg, A., et al., 2019. Urban regions shifting to circular economy: understanding challenges for new ways of governance. Urban Plan. 4 (3), 19–31. https://doi.org/10.17645/up.v4i3.2158.
Paleti, R., Pendyala, R.M., Bhat, C.R., Konduri, K.C., 2011. A Joint Tour-Based Model of Tour Complexity, Passenger Accompaniment, Vehicle Type Choice, and Tour Length. Technical Paper. Arizona State University, Tempe, AZ.

Petit-Boix, A., Leipold, S., 2018. Circular economy in cities: reviewing how environmental research aligns with local practices. J. Clean. Prod. 195, 1270–1281.
Porter, G., Abane, A., Lucas, K., 2019. User needs and practices: a position paper. In: VREF Program Mobility and Access in African Cities. Future Urban Transport.
Priya Uteng, T., 2006. Mobility: discourses from the non-western immigrant groups in Norway. Mobilities 1 (3), 435–462.
Priya Uteng, T., 2011. Gender-Related Issues Affecting Daily Mobility in the Developing Countries. The World Bank, Washington DC.
Priya Uteng, T., Cresswell, T. (Eds.), 2008. Gendered Mobilities. Ashgate, Aldershot, Routledge.
Priya Uteng, T., Knapskog, M., Uteng, A., Maridal, S., 2021. Addressing climate policy-making and gender in transport plans and strategies. The case of Oslo. In: Magnusdottir, G.L., Kronsell, A. (Eds.), Gender, Intersectionality and Climate Institutions in Industrialised States. Routledge, Abingdon and New York. https://doi.org/10.4324/9781003052821.
Priya Uteng, T., Lucas, K., 2017. The trajectories of urban mobilities in the global south: an introduction. In: Priya Uteng, T., Lucas, K. (Eds.), Urban Mobilities in the Global South. Taylor & Francis, Routledge, Abingdon and New York.
Priya Uteng, T., Turner, J., 2019. Addressing the linkages between gender and transport in low- and middle-income countries. Sustainability 11 (17), 4555.
Priya Uteng, T., Espegren, H.M., Throndsen, T.S., Bocker, L., 2019. The gendered dimension of multi-modality: exploring the bike sharing scheme of Oslo. In: Priya Uteng, T., Levin, L., Rømer Christensen, H. (Eds.), Gendering Smart Mobilities. Routledge, Abingdon and New York.
Pucher, J., Buehler, R., 2006. Why Canadians cycle more than Americans: a comparative analysis of bicycling trends and policies. Transp. Policy 13 (3), 265–279.
Pucher, J., Buehler, R., 2008. Making cycling irresistible: lessons from the Netherlands, Denmark and Germany. Transp. Rev. 28 (4), 495–528. https://doi.org/10.1080/01441640701806612.
Pucher, J., Dill, J., Handy, S., 2010. Infrastructure, programs, and policies to increase bicycling: an international review. Prev. Med. 50, 106–125. https://doi.org/10.1016/j.ypmed.2009.07.028.
Pucher, J., Garrard, J., Greaves, S., 2011a. Cycling down under: a comparative analysis of bicycling trends and policies in Sydney and Melbourne. J. Transp. Geogr. 19 (2), 332–345. https://doi.org/10.1016/j.jtrangeo.2010.02.007.
Pucher, J., Buehler, R., Merom, D., Bauman, A., 2011b. Walking and cycling in the United States, 2001-2009: evidence from the national household travel surveys. Am. J. Public Health 101 (SUPPL. 1), 310–317. https://doi.org/10.2105/AJPH.2010.300067.
Quinones, L.M., 2020. Sexual harassment in public transport in Bogotá. Transp. Res. A Policy Pract. 139, 54–69.
Rosas-Satizábal, D., Rodriguez-Valencia, A., 2019. Factors and policies explaining the emergence of the bicycle commuter in Bogotá. Case Stud. Transp. Policy 7 (1), 138–149.
Roy, S., Bailey, A., 2021. Safe in the City? Negotiating safety, public space and the male gaze in Kolkata, India. Cities 117. https://doi.org/10.1016/j.cities.2021.103321.
Safetipin, 2017. Using Data to Build Safer Cities: Delhi, Bogota, Nairobi. Available at: http://safetipin.com/resources/files/Report%20Cities%20Alliance.pdf.
Salazar Ferro, P., Behrens, R., Wilkinson, P., 2013. Hybrid urban transport systems in developing countries: portents and prospects. Res. Transp. Econ. 39, 121–132.
Salon, D., Gulyani, S., 2010. Mobility, poverty, and gender: travel 'choices' of slum residents in Nairobi, Kenya. Transp. Rev. 30 (5), 641–657.

Schalekamp, H., Behrens, R., 2010. Engaging paratransit on public transport reform initiatives in South Africa: a critique of policy and an investigation of appropriate engagement approaches. Res. Transp. Econ. 29, 371–378.

Scheiner, J., 2013. Gender roles between traditionalism and change: time use for out-of-home activities and trips in Germany, 1994-2008. In: Gerike, R., Hülsmann, F., Roller, K. (Eds.), Strategies for Sustainable Mobilities: Opportunities and Challenges. Ashgate, Farnham, pp. 79–102.

Scheiner, J., 2018. Gender, travel and the life course. Thoughts about recent research, Workshop 3: Smart Mobilities. In: Planning and Policy Processes—Gender and Diversity Mainstreaming, Nos-Sh Workshop Series, 17–18 September. VTI, Stockholm, Sweden.

Scheiner, J., 2019. Couples, the car, and the gendering of the life course: what ordinary trip diary data from the past may tell us about smart mobilities in the future. In: Priya Uteng, T., Levin, L., Rømer Christensen, H. (Eds.), Gendering Smart Mobilities. Routledge, (Abingdon and New York.

Scheiner, J., Holz-Rau, C., 2017. Women's complex daily lives: a gendered look at trip chaining and activity pattern entropy in Germany. Transportation 44 (1), 117–138.

Scheiner, J., Sicks, K., Holz-Rau, C., 2011. Gendered activity spaces: trends over three decades in Germany. Erdkunde 65 (4), 371–387.

Shah, S., Raman, A., 2019. What Do Women and Girls Want from Urban Mobility Systems? Ola Mobility Institute.

Shaw, C., Russell, M., Keall, M., MacBride-Stewart, S., Wild, K., Reeves, D., Bentley, R., Woodward, A., 2020. Beyond the bicycle: seeing the context of the gender gap in cycling. J. Transp. Health 18, 100871. https://doi.org/10.1016/j.jth.2020.100871.

Sovacool, B.K., Kester, J., Noel, L., de Rubens, G.Z., 2018. The demographics of decarbonizing transport: the influence of gender, education, occupation, age, and household size on electric mobility preferences in the Nordic region. Glob. Environ. Chang. 52, 86–100. https://doi.org/10.1016/j.gloenvcha.2018.06.008.

Starkey, P., 2001. Local transport solutions—people, paradoxes and progress: lessons arising from the spread of intermediate means of transport. In: Sub-Saharan Africa Transport Policy Program Working Paper Series (SSATP) No. 56. World Bank, Washington, DC. © World Bank https://openknowledge.worldbank.org/handle/10986/17694. License: CC BY 3.0 IGO.

Stringer, S.M., 2007. Hidden in Plain Sight: Sexual Harassment and Assault in the new York City Transport System. Manhattan Borough President Office, New York.

Susilo, Y.O., Cats, O., 2014. Exploring key determinants of travel satisfaction for multi-modal trips by different travellers' groups. Transp. Res. A 67, 366–380.

Susilo, Y.O., Dijst, M., 2009. How far is too far? Travel time ratios for activity participations in the Netherlands. J. Transp. Res. Rec. 2134, 89–98.

Susilo, Y.O., Maat, K., 2007. The influence of built environment to the trends in commuting journeys in the Netherlands. Transportation 34, 589–609.

Susilo, Y.O., Liu, C., Börjesson, M., 2018. Examination across gender, life-cycle, and generations: the changes of activity-travel participation in Sweden over 30 years, Workshop 3. In: Smart Mobilities, Planning and Policy Processes—Gender and Diversity Mainstreaming, Nos-Sh Workshop Series, 17–18 September. VTI, Stockholm, Sweden.

SuM4ALL Sustainable Mobility for All, 2019. Global Roadmap of Action toward Sustainable Mobility. Washington DC. Available at: http://pubdocs.worldbank.org/en/350451 571411004650/Global-Roadmap-of-Action-Toward-Sustainable-Mobility.pdf.

Svanfelt, D., 2018. Some gender equality and equity planning cases in urban planning in Malmö, or how I became a transport feminist, Workshop 3. In: Smart Mobilities, Planning and Policy Processes—Gender and Diversity Mainstreaming, Nos-Sh Workshop Series, 17–18 September. VTI, Stockholm, Sweden.

Sweet, M., Kanaroglou, P., 2016. Gender differences: the role of travel and time use in subjective well-being. Transp. Res. F 40, 23–34.

Tilley, S., Houston, D., 2016. The gender turnaround: young women now travelling more than young men. J. Transp. Geogr. 54, 349–358.

Tønnesen, A., Knapskog, M., Priya Uteng, Øksenholt, K.V., 2020. The integration of active travel and public transport in Norwegian policy packages: a study on 'access, egress and transfer' and their positioning in two urban contractual agreements. Res. Transp. Bus. Manag, 100546. https://doi.org/10.1016/j.rtbm.2020.100546.

Transport for London, 2012. Annual report and statement of accounts, 2012. Retrieved from https://www.tfl.gov.uk/cdn/static/cms/documents/annual-report-and-statement-of-accounts-2013.pdf.

Turnbull, P., 2013. Promoting the Employment Women in the Transport Sector—Obstacles and Policy Options, ILO Working Paper No. 298. Available at https://www.ilo.org/wcmsp5/groups/public/- - -ed_dialogue/- - -sector/documents/publication/wcms_234880.pdf.

Twyford, R., 2017. Report: Project Guardian—Public Awareness Campaign Rationale. Project Guardian, London.

UN Habitat, 2019. Gender Sensitive Mini-Bus Services & Transport Infrastructure for African Cities: A Practical Toolkit. Available at: https://unhabitat.org/sites/default/files/download-manager-files/Gender%20Toolkit.pdf.

UN Women, 2013. Kigali Safe City for Women and Girls: Baseline Survey Report.

UN Women, 2019. Safe cities and safe public spaces for women and girls. In: Global Flagship Initiative International Compendium of Practices. Ending Violence Against Women Section.

Vahidi, H., Yan, W., 2016. How is an informal transport infrastructure system formed? Towards a spatially explicit conceptual model. In: Open Geospatial Data, Software and Standards 1; 2016. Available at https://doi.org/10.1186/s40965-016-0009-9.

Verma, M., Manoj, M., Rodeja, N., Verma, A., 2017. Service gap analysis of public buses in Bangalore with respect to women safety. Transp. Res. Procedia 25, 4322–4329.

Warwar, L., Pereira, R.H.M., 2021. Mobilidade por aplicativo no Brasil: Características e padrões de consumo. In: Callil, V., Costanzo, D. (Eds.), Mobilidade por aplicativo: Estudos em cidades brasileiras, first ed. Centro Brasileiro de Análise e Planejamento Cebrap, pp. 12–42.

Waygood, E.O.D., Susilo, Y., 2011. Distinguishing universal truth from country-specific influences on children's sustainable travel: a comparison of children in the UK and the Osaka regional area. J. East. Asia Soc. Transp. Stud. 9, 271–286.

Woetzel, J., Madgavkar, A., Ellingrud, K., Labaye, E., Devillard, S., Kutcher, E., Manyika, J., Dobbs, R., Krishnan, M., 2015. The Power of Parity: How Advancing Women's Equality Can Add $12 Trillion to Global Growth [Internet]. Available at: https://www.mckinsey.com/featured-insights/employment-and-growth/how-advancing-womens-equality-can-add-12-trillion-to-global-growth.

World Bank, 2019. Sierra Leone Integrated Resilient Urban Mobility Project. World Bank, Washington DC, p. 2019. Available at: https://ppiaf.org/documents/5803/download?otp=b3RwIzE1ODI0MTAxMjM=.

CHAPTER THREE

The social dimensions of children's travel

E.O.D. Waygood[a,]*, Pauline van den Berg[b], and Astrid Kemperman[b]
[a]Polytechnique Montréal, Montréal, QC, Canada
[b]Eindhoven University of Technology, Eindhoven, The Netherlands
*Corresponding author: e-mail address: owen.waygood@polymtl.ca

Contents

Abstract

The social dimension of children's lives is an essential part of growing up. A generation ago, researchers examined how transport influenced children's social lives in their communities. Those findings suggested that increased traffic diminished children's opportunities for social interactions. Since that time though, little research has considered this dimension of their lives. Most recent research on children and transport has focused on explaining modal choice for trips to school, or their independent mobility and relationships to physical activity. The research that has been conducted on the social dimension of children's travel has found that it helps children foster relationships with friends and adults, contributing to their social capital. Social capital in turn, along with good social environments in general, is linked to increased likelihoods of traveling by active modes and independent travel. Interaction with friends during a trip also improves satisfaction with trips and is linked to improved moods. This chapter will summarize relevant work

Advances in Transport Policy and Planning, Volume 8
ISSN 2543-0009
https://doi.org/10.1016/bs.atpp.2021.06.002
Copyright © 2021 Elsevier Inc.
All rights reserved.

on the social dimension of children's travel, discuss the potential to expand knowledge on the subject, and present results from a recent quantitative study examining the complex interaction of children's travel and their social interactions.

Keywords: Children's travel, Social dimensions, Social interactions, Social environment, CIM

1. Introduction

Transport planning and research often focuses on time and safety. Both of these are important parts of our lives, but as one author (Abu-Ghazzeh, 1998) wrote, "planners need... to elevate the street in the residential neighborhood from a mere traffic channel to a social institution for children." The street is where children can play (if traffic is controlled), where they meet their neighbors and friends, and generally where they can observe and participate in the social life of their community. However, this crucial part of transport is rarely addressed (Mitra and Abbasi, 2019).

If you ask a child about important aspects of their life, chances are friends will be mentioned. Children seek out friends for social interactions and play, whether imaginative or physical. Such activities contribute to the child's health and wellbeing—being physically active with other children to improve physical health and developing social bonds to improve social and mental health (Biddle et al., 2019; Wu et al., 2017). Yet, the majority of research on children's travel focuses on modal choice for trips to school (Larouche et al., 2018; Rothman et al., 2018; Villa-González et al., 2018). The social components of travel for children are seldom studied such as traveling to meet friends and interact, or traveling with friends. The first of those two examples relates to transport's role in facilitating *access* to desirable destinations (e.g., a friend's house or place to play together). The latter relates to the *intrinsic* component of travel; what goes on while one is traveling.

In order to meet with friends, some travel is required by at least one person. Sometimes that travel is facilitated by an adult, while at other times it is independent of them. When considering whether such trips are conducted with or without an adult, factors such as distance and traffic safety are extremely important, along with social safety. Social safety often relates to how well one is connected to their neighbors, and this has been found to be influenced by how one gets around, street design, and traffic levels (e.g., Biddulph, 2012; Grannis, 2011; Waygood and Friman, 2015). In such studies, walking promotes connections as children are more likely to see other members of their community as they travel around (Waygood and Friman, 2015) and interact with them (Waygood et al., 2017a). Streets that limit traffic support such social interactions (Waygood and Friman, 2015) likely by better supporting such movement, but it may also play a role in creating a small geographical boundary to their neighborhood (Grannis, 2011). Further, streets that limit traffic are also found to promote play by allowing children to use such public spaces (Biddulph, 2012). Finally, lower levels of traffic are associated with more connections with others who share the same street (Appleyard, 1980), but also with connecting to others while children travel (Waygood and Friman, 2015). The impact of traffic levels on social interactions can be considered an *external* component of transport.

Feeling connected to one's community (e.g., the sense that you belong and have social bonds with your community) is also an important contribution to wellbeing in of itself (e.g., Elgar et al., 2011). As authors Lennard and Lennard (2000) write, "to walk down the street and be recognized and greeted... conversations and encounters and special events that give meaning to the urban environment." As such, we can see that desirable social activities—meeting with friends, connecting with neighbors—is dependent on either parental free time or the freedom to travel if children are to walk, see others, and develop social bonds. However, the latter movement (independent travel) can be dependent on good social conditions such as being connected to other parents (Prezza et al., 2001). Those good social conditions themselves are apparently developed through connections made by children or through walking with them (Grannis, 2011).

This chapter will discuss previous research on children's travel that relate to these different facets of the social domain such as connecting to others, play, and social well-being in the section "Children's social wellbeing and transport." It will then present results from a recent study on children's social interactions and transport. The final section reflects on gaps and further avenues to investigate in this important part of children's lives.

2. Children's social wellbeing and transport

The social domain of children's wellbeing relates to sociological perspectives (Pollard and Lee, 2003). It includes social relationships with friends, family, their community, and society. It also relates to the support that these groups offer whether that be emotional or practical in nature including the sense of safety given by knowing that others are around that can help. Social relationships are a key component of children's lives, and thus developing and maintaining them are critical considerations for transport (Waygood, 2019) as it relates to their quality of life. Having social interactions and a sense of belonging greatly contribute to the wellbeing of adolescents and young children (Park, 2004; Pretty et al., 1996). This chapter focuses on children, but the positive influences of a good social environment can also be seen in adults' travel (van den Berg et al., 2017; Weijs-Perrée et al., 2015).

Transport affects children's social wellbeing through three means-of-influence: access, intrinsic, and external (Waygood et al., 2017b). As mentioned above, transport allows for children to *access* destinations where they may meet with community members and friends, it allows them time to interact with friends and family while moving from one place to another (*intrinsic*), but it can also negatively impact socializing and play primarily through traffic (*external*). Through incidental social interactions that occur while traveling (typically by foot), people cross paths with their neighbors, starting, developing, or maintaining social connections (Grannis, 2011). Those social connections are demonstrated to positively support physical and subjective wellbeing (Helliwell and Putnam, 2004). With respect to children's travel, those social connections are linked to greater independent and active travel by children (McDonald et al., 2010; Prezza et al., 2001), and in complement to that, children's independent travel is linked to more incidental interactions with the community (Prezza et al., 2001; Waygood et al., 2017a) and building social capital (Prezza and Pacilli, 2007; Weller and Bruegel, 2009). Thus, an important point is to know that children are not just receivers of social capital, but also build their own and expand their parents' (Waygood, 2019).

The social dimension of transport can also be seen from other perspectives. Baslington (2008) wrote of travel socialization where children learn about how to act and travel through experiences and observations of others. In frameworks of children's independent mobility such as that proposed by Mitra and Manaugh (2019), children's travel is influenced by the social environment which includes community, neighbors, and friends. Measures of a neighborhood that relate to the social domain would include social cohesion and trust which are found to influence active travel in studies (e.g., Ikeda et al., 2019; Johansson, 2006), and directly on parental perceptions of safety (van den Berg et al., 2020). Carver et al. (2013) argue that policies to improve social trust are essential improve active transport. Related to that is the concept of "stranger danger," which has been examined in children's travel research for some time now, though often when distance and traffic danger are included those factors are not significant (e.g., Timperio et al., 2006).

At the household level, the social environment can relate to perceived norms of how children get around. One influence that is not explicitly mentioned in Mitra and Manaugh's (2019) framework is the role of social norms. If most children are traveling by a certain mode, people may naturally assume that this is the "correct" behavior. Such an influence has been examined by authors such as Sidharthan et al. (2011) who suggested that clustering influences that they observed were likely a result of parents interacting among themselves and creating local social norms related to children's travel. Knowing other children who walk or cycle can lead to greater active travel (Veitch et al., 2017), and having peer support can increase active travel (Panter et al., 2010). An intervention with children aged 5–6 years old demonstrated that changing social norms and practicing walking with children and their caregivers can increase walking and modify perceptions of social norms (Humberto et al., 2021). Although not specifically a social norm, having other children to walk with was shown to influence active travel (Salmon et al., 2007). In a review, Carver et al. (2008), mention the likely influence of social norms, but also the concept of social traps that was introduced by Tranter (2006). That concept relates to the problem where parents may follow the norms of other parents, and if that is to drive, they contribute to the problem of creating danger and also of consuming their own time. Wanting to reduce their travel time, parents may chauffeur their children by motor vehicle, however, that results in the parent using their own time every day to drive the child, which is not the case for active modes as children, once adept, can then perform such trips independently, thus requiring no time by the parents. The contrast in time spent by parents in travel with or for children is highlighted in a few studies that show in cases of independent travel, parental time on average is quite low and mostly for "family" trips as opposed to trips that are solely to chauffeur the child (Mattsson, 2002; Waygood, 2009).

A generation ago, researchers examined how transport influenced children's social lives in their communities. Those findings suggested that increased traffic diminished children's opportunities for social interactions. The means that transport influences the social domain of children's transport also relate to what Lynch (Lynch, 1981) wrote about how children relate to and gain a sense of control over their environment. He wrote that it can be through four means: presence, use and action, appropriation, and disposition. *Presence* relates to being in a location, requiring access and that traffic can limit this. *Use and action* relates to not only being in a place, but doing some activity (using the space), and again traffic can limit this. *Appropriation* requires that the children feel that the space belongs to them, and this can occur through frequent use, but also modifying the space (whether that be through drawing on the infrastructure, moving/adding street furniture, or some other such action). Finally, *disposition* relates to connections with the community at is pertains to allowing other children to join in and participate in activities. Much of this can be seen in the use of streets as play spaces (Abu-Ghazzeh, 1998; Biddulph, 2012; Mitra and Abbasi, 2019).

Early research on children's travel included examining how traffic was impacting children (e.g., Berg and Medrich, 1980; Gaster, 1991; Lynch and Banerjee, 1976) and why children were losing independence (i.e, Hillman et al., 1990; van Vliet, 1983). In the studies by Lynch, Berg and Medich, and that by Gaster, the relationship between traffic (and how traffic changes the built environment) and children's lives were examined. Lynch examined children's lives in different cities (globally dispersed), Berg and Medich examined children's lives in four different neighborhoods whereas Gaster examined children's lives over three generations. In all cases, whether temporarily (Gaster) or spatially (Lynch; Berg and Medich), the finding was that as traffic increased, children's play and travel were restricted. From Gaster's work, it could be implied that facilitating car travel essentially necessitated designated play areas (parks), a reduction in free play, and a move toward children's lives being focused on organized activities with constant adult supervision.

Less focus was given to the social domain (e.g., connecting to friends and their community, traveling with friends, etc.) of children's travel in studies on children's independent travel. However, some authors acknowledged that a lack of independent travel likely limited how frequently children met to play with others (Hillman et al., 1990; van Vliet, 1983). Hillman et al., included questions related to whether children could reach parks and conduct social visits independently, and in 1971 found that the vast majority could in both the UK and West Germany. Their follow-up study in 1990 found that only a minority of children in primary school in the UK could travel to destinations other than school alone, though this was higher in West Germany. In a follow-up study of children in the UK and Germany, Shaw et al. (2013) found that in most cases, this percentage had further decreased. Thus the trend appears to be a decrease in children having freedom of access to friends over time.

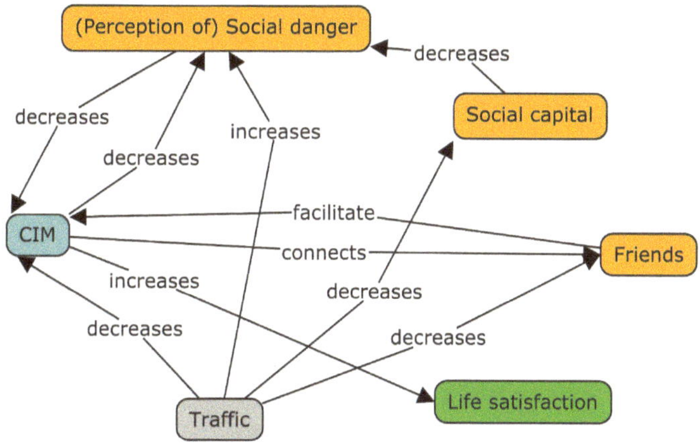

Fig. 1 Conceptual framework of transport and the social domain (CIM = Children's Independent mobility; links between the social domains are not shown so as to limit the complexity of the image).

The social dimension is an important part of children's travel, not only with respect to stimulating trips (e.g., to meet friends, to do activities), but also how it relates to community life and life satisfaction. In Fig. 1, a conceptual framework of relationships between different aspects of the social domain (social danger, social capital, friends) and transport (children's independent mobility (CIM), traffic) is shown. Previous research demonstrates that children who perceive social danger to be higher do not typically walk or travel independently (Alparone and Pacilli, 2012; Pacilli et al., 2013; Prezza and Pacilli, 2007). Thus, the perception of danger can restrict such movement (Mitra, 2013). In the other direction though, is research (Pacilli et al., 2013) that suggests that children who travel independently meet and get to know their neighbors better and thus have a more positive view. That social capital supports parents when they are deciding whether or not to let children travel independently (McDonald et al., 2010; Pacilli et al., 2013; Prezza et al., 2010). Knowing that other children and parents are there to help if needed is often given as a reason to allow CIM (e.g., Bonner, 1997). Weller and Bruegel (2009) also argue that children actively develop their own social capital, and Grannis (Grannis, 2011) finds that children facilitate greater community connections by making connections with other neighborhood children through play within their range of independent travel, and those connections can lead to parents knowing each other. However, social capital may be poorly defined when it comes to children (Morrow, 1999; Waygood, 2019). Measures related to simple social interactions during travel are also positively associated to active and independent travel (Bringolf-Isler et al., 2008; Carver et al., 2005). Again, children who travel independently and by active modes are more likely to see people in their community (Waygood and Friman, 2015; Waygood et al., 2017a), thus likely building their social capital. Reaching friends is often found to be done on foot (Veitch et al., 2017) and knowing where to find friends is linked to CIM (Lim and Barton, 2010).

Examining how those different factors relate to each other is complex. Recently, a study on children's travel to school in the Netherlands demonstrated links between social connections made while traveling and perceptions of the social environment (Waygood et al., 2021). Using a Bayesian Belief Network, the relationships between these various influences and measures can be seen. This methodology begins with a proposed model, and determines whether measures have influences, and suggests the direction of the influence. That study found that the shorter the children's commuting distance, the higher the reported social connection frequency with other children was. Greater social connection frequency was positively linked to greater perceptions of social cohesion, and that was in turn positively linked to perceptions of social safety. Active travel was strongly linked to distance and travel without parents, or CIM.

On the other side of the coin is traffic. Trips conducted by motorized vehicles are generally found to have negative social consequences. Travel in cars is sometimes talked about by parents as a time to socialize with their children, and children are found to also mention this, but most children appreciate active modes for the chance to socialize and play with friends (Egli et al., 2020) and traveling by car can be seen as isolating them from friends (Barker et al., 2009). In the case of a chance to socialize with their children, this can obviously also be done while walking, which would allow for greater connection between the parent and child (e.g., looking at each other) and increasing connections to the community as mentioned above. In some locations, the built environment may restrict what is possible for active and independent travel which could lead to the car being seen as a means to connect. Traffic also consumes the space that children may use to play and socialize (Abu-Ghazzeh, 1998; Berg and Medrich, 1980; Biddulph, 2012; Gaster, 1991; Hüttenmoser, 1995) through both danger and noise. Travel by car was also strongly negatively associated to simply seeing people and seeing people that children knew while traveling (Waygood and Friman, 2015). Thus, the advantage that these modes have in terms of speed, have negative consequences on children's community and social connections.

3. Social interactions and travel survey

In the fall of 2018 (October), students from grade five (ages 9 through 12) in six schools spread across Quebec City participated in a study on children's social interactions and travel. The schools were chosen to represent three distinct types of built environment previously identified in Quebec City, namely: central city, old suburbs, and new suburbs. In total 183 students (and their parents) gave permission to use their survey responses which were completed at their schools. The study collected data on social interactions during trips, how children traveled and the frequency to play with friends, the size of local and non-local social networks, frequency of interactions with social network, the use of virtual interactions and social media, as well as satisfaction with life, friends, and their community. In this chapter, descriptive results are presented with respect to travel and those measures of the social dimension. The different components discussed are: life satisfaction and social domains (friends, community), connections with neighbors, and connections with friends.

3.1 Measuring children's independent mobility (CIM)

A measure of children's independent mobility was created using questions based on mode (walk, bicycle, bus), level of independence (cannot go alone, with friends, alone), and by daylight or at night. As these "licenses" are not all equal, a weighting was developed based on how common the license was (Fig. 2). A less common activity is considered to be more difficult or require

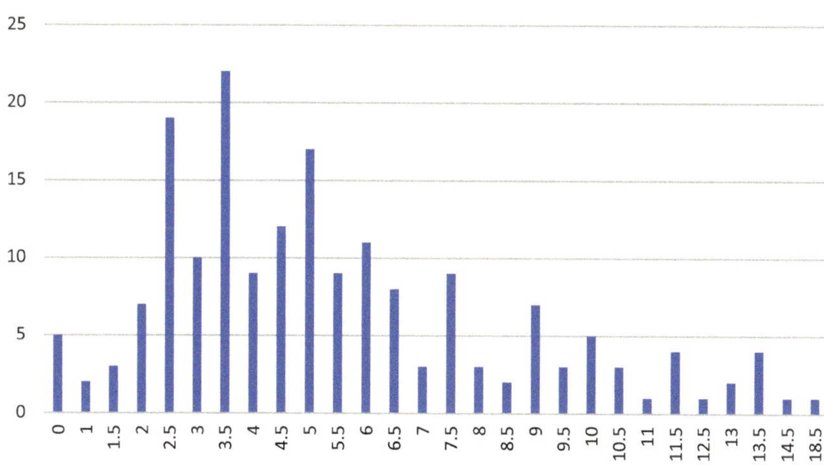

Fig. 2 Distribution of CIM index results.

additional training and skills. For example, for the case of walking during the day (alone or with friends), the majority of children reported having this license. As most children do this, and thus it can be considered an "easy" activity and its value was 0.5. In the case of cycling during the day, less than half of children had this license. As a minority of children have this license, the behavior is considered to be more advanced and difficult, so the value was 1.0. In the case of cycling at night, less than 1/3 of children had this license, so it's value was 1.5. Taking the bus alone was one of the least common, so it's value was given 2. Finally, the distance that a child was allowed to travel alone was added (0 = not allowed; 1 = neighborhood area (<15-min walk); 2 = surrounding neighborhoods (15 to <30-min walk); 3 = further). A simple summation of the CIM measures and only the distance variable were tested against the measures discussed below (e.g., life satisfaction, satisfaction with different social domains, connecting with friends), but the index value (based on the point system discussed here) was the most useful measure for distinguishing differences.

3.2 Measuring social networks

The size of the children's social network was estimated through a number of questions to get at both the size and the strength of the networks. As outlined in Grannis (2011), social connections with others can start with simply seeing others and recognizing them, and then move through to acknowledging the person (e.g., nodding one's head, saying hello), to talking with the person, to visiting each other's homes, and to doing activities together (in a neutral/public location). These last two might vary by culture, but in the case of children the thought was that they call on other children to play frequently by going to the other child's home in a less formal manner than an arranged activity together. The size of the network was categorical: 0 people, 1–2 people, 3–5 people, 6–10 people, more than 10 people. This was further divided into children and adults. For the social network of children, further questions were asked about where they play with other children. For the social network of adults, further questions were asked about the number of adults that they could ask for help if needed.

A distinction was made between local and non-local social networks. Again, based on Grannis (2011), the geographic location of the children's connections was distinguished between local and non-local based on his finding that after an intersection, community networks drop off.

Fig. 3 Image used to highlight the concept of the same street between two intersections.

As a result, local was defined for the children as being on the same block or the block facing their home, but remaining within two intersections. The term "near my home" was used in the survey and Fig. 3 was included.

Finally, the frequency of social interactions was determined through questions on the types mentioned above: see, acknowledge, wave, talk with them, visit, and do activities together. The levels of frequency were: never, a few times a year, a few times a month, a few times a week, every day. Here, the questions related to "neighborhood" to simplify the task for the children, but the question was distinct for neighborhood children and neighborhood adults.

3.3 Parents and the influence of local transport social norms

Along with the survey for the children, parents were asked to voluntarily complete an additional questionnaire. Of the 183 children, 93 parents completed that survey as it was completely voluntary. That questionnaire had a question that aimed to get at the influence of social norms on travel behavior. The question described two different travel contexts and asked how their children would likely travel in such situations. More details on those scenarios are given below in the relevant section.

4. Analysis and results

The analysis follows the conceptual framework proposed above where interactions between travel and various measures of the social domain are proposed.

4.1 Life satisfaction and social domains

Questions on satisfaction were asked using a nine-point Likert scale. The questions related to the domains of friends, community, school, trips, family, and life in general. The correlations between three different domains with life satisfaction are shown in Table 1 (these three are used as theoretically, a link between their satisfaction and travel can be made). As can be seen, positive and moderate strength relationships exist between all measures.

The CIM index value was weakly correlated with the satisfaction with trips (0.159, $p < 0.05$). The CIM index value is not directly correlated with life satisfaction or any other measure of satisfaction in this study. That result reflects findings from previous studies on children's trip and life satisfaction where CIM was directly related to trip satisfaction, but only indirectly to life satisfaction (Waygood et al., 2019). Friman et al. (2019) examined travel satisfaction to school with life satisfaction and also found similar results where travel satisfaction to school was directly correlated with life satisfaction.

4.2 Connections with neighbors

As mentioned in Section 3, several questions were asked with respect to the types and frequencies of connections with neighbors both on the same block and those who live off their block following research in the USA by Grannis (Grannis, 2011) which demonstrated that community connections are higher on the block and fall off after intersections. The results of those questions on social network size (walk: Table 2; car: Table 3) and frequency of interaction (walk: Table 4; car: Table 5) were compared with the reported frequency of travel by walking and travel by car in the previous week. All relationships were tested using chi-squared tests of independence and the

Table 1 Correlations between satisfaction of three domains of children's lives with their life satisfaction.

	Satisfaction with trips	Satisfaction with friends	Satisfaction with community	Satisfaction with life
Trips	1			
Friends	0.24	1		
Community	0.216	0.355	1	
Life	0.295	0.363	0.408	1

Obs. All relationships were significant at $p < 0.01$.

Table 2 The odds ratio of Social network size by frequency of walking as compared to children not in the category.

Location	Level of connection	Number of people	Walk 6 or more days/wk (odds ratio)	Walk 3 or more days/wk (odds ratio)
Children—Off block	Know names	3+ names	2.49	2.42
		6+ names	2.34	2.52
	Talk with them	3+ names	2.22	2.24
		6+ names	2.93	2.62
	Do activities together	3+ names	2.96	4.91
		6+ names	3.17	4.97

Table 3 Social network size by frequency of car use.

Location	Level of connection	Number of people	Car: 6 or more days/wk. (odds ratio)	Car: 3 or more days/wk. (odds ratio)
Children on block	Wave	0 people	1.08	NS
		<3–5 people	NS	1.44
	Know names	0 people	0.91	NS
		<3–5 people	1.05	1.38
	Do activities together	0 people	1.11	1.50
		<3–5 people	0.81	1.49
Children off block	Wave	0 people	1.81	2.25
		<3–5 people	1.30	1.59
	Know names	0 people	1.59	2.83
		<3–5 people	1.67	2.19
	Talk with them	0 people	1.23	2.39
		<3–5 people	1.10	1.83

Continued

Table 3 Social network size by frequency of car use.—cont'd

Location	Level of connection	Number of people	Car: 6 or more days/wk. (odds ratio)	Car: 3 or more days/wk. (odds ratio)
Adults on block	Say hi	0 people	0.63	0.71
		<3–5 people	0.58	1.48
	Know their names	0 people	1.05	1.05
		<3–5 people	0.70	1.45
	Talk with them	0 people	0.87	1.28
		<3–5 people	0.64	1.08
	Visit them	0 people	1.36	1.59
		<3–5 people	0.72	1.21
Adults off block	Wave	0 people	0.78	1.50
		<3–5 people	0.89	0.92

NS = Not significant difference.

Table 4 Frequency of different types of interactions with children in the neighborhood by frequency of walking.

Type of interaction	Frequency	Walk 6+ days/wk	Walk 3+ days/wk
Say hi to other children	>multiple times/month	1.04	1.50
	Everyday	1.77	2.24
Talk with other children	>multiple times/month	1.74	2.45
	Everyday	2.31	3.64
See adults	>multiple times/month	1.07	0.75
	Everyday	1.94	1.02
Play in alley		1.88	2.33

Table 5 Frequency of different types of interactions with children in the neighborhood by frequency of car use.

Type of interaction	Frequency of interaction	Car 6+ days/wk	Car 3+ days/wk
See children	Never	3.77	2.77
	<multiple times/month	4.29	2.89
	<multiple times/week	2.45	1.84
Wave to children	Never	3.04	1.65
	<multiple times/month	3.06	1.54
	<multiple times/week	2.16	1.18
Say hi to children	Never	1.94	1.06
	<multiple times/month	1.92	N.S.
	<multiple times/week	1.83	N.S.
Talk with other children	Never	3.30	1.64
	<multiple times/month	4.25	1.93
	<multiple times/week	4.18	2.06
Visit other children	Never	1.96	N.S.
	<multiple times/month	1.95	N.S.
	<multiple times/week	1.35	0.92
Do activities together with other children	Never	3.05	1.57
	<multiple times/month	2.89	1.42
	<multiple times/week	1.62	N.S.
Play	Never	2.02	1.09
Play	At park	0.74	0.94

statistically significant results are reported in the tables using odds ratios to represent the size of the effect.

4.2.1 The social network size

Children were asked with how many people (children and adults separately) they had some social connection at the local and non-local level.

As a reminder, the levels of social connections were: wave, vocally acknowledge, know their name, talk with them, visit them, and do activities with them. The number of people were: 0 people, 1–2 people, 3–5 people, 6–10 people, and more than then. Local was anyone on the same street or block as discussed in Section 3. The analysis examined whether the frequency of mode use might relate to those measures. Only walking and car use were examined as sufficient numbers of children used those modes.

Correlations between the frequency of walking and social network size was examined at two levels: for children who walked nearly every day, and for children who walked 3 or more days a week. In both cases they are compared to those who do not fall into that category.[a] For the network size, the findings did not show any significant differences for connections at the block (local) level for either children or adult connections, and only differences for children were found at the off-block (non-local) level. The findings suggest that children who walk more frequently reported stronger connections with children who do not live on their same block (knowing their names, talking with them, and doing activities together). What this may suggest is that children of this age who walk frequently are likely doing it further abroad than just their immediate block and that this results in stronger connections to those who are perhaps at the larger neighborhood level. Such results likely link to those of previous studies where children who travel by foot and independently are more likely to see people that they know (Waygood et al., 2017a) and meet with friends more often (Prezza et al., 2001).

For the frequency of car use, the same two measures were used, but for the social network, it is a limited size that is examined (0 people and under 3 people) as the relationships are positively correlated for smaller social networks (Table 3). If results for having larger networks are examined, a negative relationship is found (i.e., less likely to have a larger network size). As compared with walking, more statistically valid results are found at both the local and non-local levels and for children and adult networks. For the child social network, children who frequently travel by car are generally more likely to have no connections or connections to only a few children as measured by knowing the names of other children. They are less likely to have local children with whom they do activities, and less likely to talk with

[a] Dummy variables were created for those two categories, and chi-squared analyses were conducted separately for each variable. i.e., a test was conducted for children who walk 6 or more days a week versus others, and a test was conducted for children who walk 3 or more days a week versus others.

children that are off their block. For the adult social network, most results relate to the local level. Here, children who frequently travel by car are more likely to have no or very small networks at the local level. The only statistically valid result for off-block was that they were less likely to wave to other adults. These results reflect previous findings where travel by car was negatively associated to incidental social interactions such as seeing and having some interaction with people we know (Waygood and Friman, 2015; Waygood et al., 2017a).

4.2.2 Frequency of social connections

For the frequency of social interactions, the possible responses were: never, a few times a year, a few times a month, a few times a week, and every day. The levels of interactions were: see, a salutation, wave, talk with them, visit them, and do activities with them. The questions were asked with respect to child and adult social networks. Here, the geographic level was the "neighborhood." No definition was given to the children of what a neighborhood encompassed.

For walking (Table 4), children who walk more say hello and talk with other children more frequently. They are also more likely to frequently see adults that they know, again likely reflecting the results of previous studies on incidental social interactions (Waygood and Friman, 2015; Waygood et al., 2017a) and social environmental influences on children's travel (Carver et al., 2005; Waygood et al., 2021).

The role of back alleys as a place to play with friends was associated with children who walk more. Such areas in the province of Quebec are often found in older mixed-use and dense neighborhoods. They typically contain traffic restraining components such as speed bumps and sometimes bollards (Figs. 4–6). As such, they offer public spaces that are near to the home, where children are (generally) free from traffic danger, and where activities such as cycling, basketball, drawing, and general running around can be observed (ref. Images). Such areas reflect findings from other low-car-access areas in previous studies (e.g., Abu-Ghazzeh, 1998; Biddulph, 2012; Hüttenmoser, 1995).

For car use (Table 5), the frequency of social interactions is again measured with respect to less frequent so that a "more likely" result can be discussed. No statistically significant results were found with respect to adult interactions. However, with respect to the frequency of interactions with other children in the neighborhood, numerous relationships are found. Children who frequently travel by car are more likely to have no interactions or very seldom (less than a few times per week) ones for seeing, waving,

Fig. 4 Children of various ages setting up rules of a game.

Fig. 5 Back alleys can act as a low traffic area where children are safe to wander and practice cycling.

Fig. 6 Back alleys allow children to gather, socially interact, and be physically active without worrying about traffic.

saying hi (though only for those who nearly always travel by car), talking with other children, visiting other children, and doing activities with other children. As well, they are more likely to play at the park with other neighborhood children. However, they are less likely to report never playing with other neighborhood children. Overall though, the results are likely in contrast to what many parents may believe about how the car facilitates children's play with friends. True, children who often travel by car were less likely to never play with other neighborhood children, but in terms of frequency of interactions at nearly all levels, they are less likely to do so.

4.3 Children's independent mobility and social connections

As children's frequency of travel by walking and driving were found to be correlated to numerous social connection measures, the influence of the right to travel alone is examined here. A child who is allowed to travel alone presumably has greater freedom to explore their neighborhood and meet up with other children.

In Table 6, the statistically significant results (odds ratios) for the measure of children's independent mobility (CIM) are presented with respect to a

Table 6 Odds ratios for CIM and connections with community children.

Question block	Detail	Possible responses	Odds ratio
Interactions with children			
Immediate block			
	Wave	No one, 1–2 people, 3–5 people, 6–10 people, more than 10	1.12
	Say hi	No one, 1–2 people, 3–5 people, 6–10 people, more than 10	1.08
	Know the names	No one, 1–2 people, 3–5 people, 6–10 people, more than 10	1.1
	Speak with them	No one, 1–2 people, 3–5 people, 6–10 people, more than 10	1.09
	Visit	No one, 1–2 people, 3–5 people, 6–10 people, more than 10	1.11
Nearby blocks			
	Say hi	No one, 1–2 people, 3–5 people, 6–10 people, more than 10	1.1
	Know their name	No one, 1–2 people, 3–5 people, 6–10 people, more than 10	1.12
	Speak with them	No one, 1–2 people, 3–5 people, 6–10 people, more than 10	1.09
	Visit them	No one, 1–2 people, 3–5 people, 6–10 people, more than 10	1.09
	Do activities together	No one, 1–2 people, 3–5 people, 6–10 people, more than 10	1.11
Play location			
	Street	Yes/no	1.15
	Back alley	Yes/no	1.12
	Park	Yes/no	1.15
	Vacant area	Yes/no	1.11
Interactions with adults			
	Say hi	No one, 1–2 people, 3–5 people, 6–10 people, more than 10	1.11
	Know their names	No one, 1–2 people, 3–5 people, 6–10 people, more than 10	1.11

Table 6 Odds ratios for CIM and connections with community children.—cont'd

Question block	Detail	Possible responses	Odds ratio
Help from adults			
	Immediate block	No one, 1 or 2, 3 to 5, 6 or more	1.12
	Surrounding blocks	No one, 1 or 2, 3 to 5, 6 or more	1.17

Note: All results have a significance of $p < 0.05$; ordered logistic models were used for measures with multiple responses and binary logistic regression was used for binary responses.

number of community connection measures. As can be seen, in most cases there is a positive association between CIM and the number of people that the child has such interactions with. For example, for most of the measures on the immediate block, a child with greater CIM has 10% higher likelihood of interacting (visiting, knowing the names of others, etc.) with their community. These results build on previous research that showed that trips where children are walking or are independent (of an adult) are much more likely to have incidental interactions (Waygood et al., 2017a). Here, it can be seen that this extends beyond those incidental interactions of waving, a salutation, or stopping to chat, but shows that CIM is also linked to having a larger local network with whom visits and activities are conducted. Having higher CIM is also linked to higher likelihoods of playing in local public spaces (it was not significant for playing at home or in a yard). Having CIM is not linked to many different interactions with adults either on the immediate block or surrounding blocks, but was associated to children saying hi and knowing the names of more local adults (i.e., those on the immediate block or facing street). Finally, having higher CIM is linked to knowing more adults who live on the same block or in the surrounding blocks who could help if their own parents were not available. That result would relate to findings where social capital helps children's CIM.

These results of the CIM are in line with findings by Waygood et al. (2020) of children's travel and social interactions (physically present and virtual) in Canada, Japan, and Sweden. In that study, children with higher CIM reported a greater likelihood of meeting a friend at various destinations which reflects the finding of this study on visiting and doing activities together. As well, children with higher CIM were found to have a greater variety of places where they would meet friends. These children were more likely to report higher frequency of meeting with friends outside of school.

Table 7 The frequency and main mode of travel to meet with friends on weekdays.

	Weekdays			Weekend	
	1 day	**2–3 days**	**4–5 days**	**1 day**	**2 days**
Walk	58%	75%	79%	59%	66%
Bike	10%	5%	4%	6%	3%
Car	27%	18%	13%	34%	31%
Other	4%	1%	2%	2%	0%

4.4 Meeting up with friends

Children were asked about the frequency of meeting with friends outside of school, and how they reached them. In all cases, children were most likely to report going by foot to meet with friends. As the frequency of meeting with friends increased, so did the share of such trips by foot increase (Table 7). Further, the majority of trips to meet friends were either done independently (37%) or with friends (27%). As the trips are mostly done on foot and independently, having friends in close proximity is likely important. The same trends were found for weekends.

The index for CIM was not found to be related to meeting with friends. However, children who are allowed to have some CIM (i.e., travel independently within their neighborhood or more) were five times more likely to meet with friends more times per week. The interpretation of this may be that it is not necessary to have licenses to travel by bicycle or bus to meet up with friends (captured and given value in the CIM index), but simply being allowed to travel by foot in at least their neighborhood. This is supported by the result shown above where most children meet their friends by foot.

4.5 Communication

In the final section of the survey, the children were asked about how they communicated with friends outside of school (Table 8), how they *actually* communicate with friends when there is something important to discuss, and how they *prefer* to communicate when there is something important to discuss (Table 9). As can be seen, the majority of children communicate more than weekly with friends by being physically together, the next two most common are telephone and text messaging (34%). When children have something important to discuss, nearly three-quarters will discuss in person, then a quarter use a telephone, and texting drops to 18% (children could

Table 8 Frequency of communication outside of school with friends by different communication mediums.

	Physically present	Web site	Text messages	Telephone	Cell-phone "app"	*E*-mail	Video
Never	22.4	68.31	47.54	29.51	60.66	73.77	61.2
Monthly	6.56	3.83	9.84	14.21	5.46	12.57	10.93
Weekly	9.84	5.46	8.74	22.4	7.1	4.37	10.38
Often	25.68	10.93	13.66	22.4	13.11	5.46	8.74
Daily	35.52	11.48	20.22	11.48	13.66	3.83	8.74

Table 9 Actual versus preferred medium of communication when the child has something important to discuss (for actual, they could choose multiple responses, for preferred they could only choose one response).

	Physically present	Web site	Text messages	Telephone	Cell-phone "app"	E-mail	Video
Actual (% of all responses)	130 (36%)	15 (4%)	66 (18%)	89 (24%)	40 (11%)	15 (4%)	9 (2%)
Preferred (% of all responses)	118 (56%)	5 (2%)	27 (13%)	42 (20%)	8 (4%)	6 (3%)	6 (3%)

choose more than one medium). When it comes to the preferred means of communicating, the same trend can be seen with most preferring to be physically present (56%), followed by telephone (20%) and texting (13%). This would suggest that facilitating children's independent travel should also allow them to discuss important topics with their peers, which is important for their development and mental health. This is likely reflected in studies of children and their use of social media. In a study on adolescents by (Kamargianni and Polydoropoulou, 2014), technologies were found to facilitate meeting up, rather than as a replacement. For children aged 10–11, a study conducted in Canada, Sweden, and Japan found similar results where children who used social media more frequently, were also associated with greater CIM and meeting face-to-face with other children (Waygood et al., 2020). Having access to a cellphone may also increase children's independent travel as it allows the child (or the parent) to make contact with a parent (or vice versa) when they want or need. It should also be noted that in that study, Canadian children used social media less frequently than Swedish children, but more so than the Japanese children. As such, the results of the study reported here may be different for countries where communication technology use is different.

4.6 Parents and social norms

The parents were asked a variety of questions and those pertinent to this chapter are reported here. One key question for this chapter is the influence of social norms. To address this, the parents were asked to respond how their child would travel in two situations: one where most children walk or cycle places; one where children nearly never walk or cycle places. The question was phrased: Imagine you move to a new location where you notice that most children seem to walk and cycle; Imagine you move to a new location where it seems that most children never walk or cycle places. The parents could choose as many different modes as they wanted. As can be seen in Table 10, the likelihood that the child would be allowed to go by active modes decreases and the likelihood that the child could travel alone decreases as well between the contexts where the norm changes away from active travel. This result is by no means definitive, as it cannot control for various other influences. Parents would likely assume that in the context where children actively travel independently, that one can assume that it is safe to do so. In the other context, the opposite may be assumed.

Table 10 Parents responses to two social norm situations.

	Norm is active travel	**Norm is to not use active modes**
MODE for child's travel		
Walk	94%	57%
Bike	96%	52%
Scooter	32%	17%
Bus	9%	29%
Car	13%	65%
COMPANION		
Alone	67%	37%
Friend	81%	48%
Sibling	54%	42%
Adult	34%	72%

However, this is part of the influence of social norms—people assume that there is a reason why others do that behavior, that others have put the time and effort into making the best choice.

4.7 Overview of results

Taken as a whole, the results of this study continue to support findings that allowing children freedom to travel and limiting car-based travel can help improve their social networks and increase the frequency of activities with other children. When thinking of activities for children, some people may focus on organized activities such as soccer practice, but free play among children is also important. Studies of children find that those who are independent and do free play with local children are better at conflict resolution, for example, (Hüttenmoser, 1995). Children who actively and independently travel gain greater overall physical activity (Schoeppe et al., 2013) which is likely both through the active travel, but also facilitating higher frequencies of play. Increasing evidence suggests that active and independently travel also links to better social connections (this study; Pacilli et al., 2013; Prezza et al., 2010; Weller and Bruegel, 2009) and these are important to children in numerous ways (Holland et al., 2007) including supporting better wellbeing (Helliwell and Putnam, 2004). As such, further efforts should be made to examine how transport affects these measures of wellbeing that are much less studied than physical impacts (Waygood, 2019; Waygood et al., 2017b).

5. Conclusion

This chapter summarized the growing field of the social domain of children's travel and presented results from a recent study examining how transport relates to social interactions and connections with one's community and friends outside of school. Previous work and the research reported here generally demonstrate that independent travel positively relates to trip satisfaction and that trip satisfaction positively relates to life satisfaction. It likely does so by facilitating trips to meet with friends. Active and independent travel positively relate to social interactions, be they either incidental during trips or meeting with friends. Further, such travel supports or is supported by greater social capital. Even though modern technology exists to easily contact and even see friends "live," children still prefer to be with their peers, and that facilitating CIM would likely support them when they want to talk about serious topics. As such, the overall findings would suggest that improving children's ability to travel independently and actively will increase their overall social wellbeing.

As this research is only regaining interest, many research avenues exist to explore. A more in-depth study of the interaction between CIM and home-based activities such as video games or other screen-related activities is of interest as such sedentary activities are associated with negative mental health outcomes (e.g., Stiglic and Viner, 2019). Different cultures approach interactions between children and adults in the street differently. In some cultures, the idea is that children shouldn't speak to adults that they don't know, whereas in others, greeting others, even those that you don't know in your neighborhood is encouraged (Waygood and Taniguchi, 2020). How that relates to children's independent mobility and safety is not well known, nor implications for psychological outcomes, though some research suggests that promoting fear in children about strangers leads to negative mental health outcomes (Prezza and Pacilli, 2007).

Designing neighborhoods that are child-friendly, that facilitate CIM, is an avenue for continued research. Authors such as Freeman and Tranter (2011) discuss how various aspects of the built environment relate to children. In the above research differences by built environment were not examined and this is an avenue to explore. Involving children in the process of planning is an important part of improving conditions for them. Studer (2018) wrote a book on how to include children in design charrettes, and Witten and Field (2019) discuss the inclusion of children in planning in New Zealand.

Questions of equity should also be examined where children in more disadvantaged neighborhoods may suffer greater threats from traffic (Waygood et al., 2017b), and distances to schools and parks may be longer. A specific focus on how to improve conditions for children in these more marginalized conditions is needed. One approach is to reduce the danger of motor vehicle traffic which includes restricting traffic where children are likely to be, such as around schools (Waygood and Taniguchi, 2020).

Another crucial part of research is to examine how parents view different types of neighborhoods. Parents may think that large yards and space are good for children, but the research suggests that such areas do not support CIM and social interactions as distances increase, motor vehicle traffic (and speeds) increase, and thus reliance on parent's free time to escort children decreases their freedom to roam and meet with friends.

References

Abu-Ghazzeh, T.M., 1998. Children's use of the street as a playground in Abu-Nuseir, Jordan. Environ. Behav. 30 (6), 799–831.

Alparone, F.R., Pacilli, M.G., 2012. On children's independent mobility: the interplay of demographic, environmental, and psychosocial factors. Child. Geogr. 10 (1), 109–122.

Appleyard, D., 1980. Livable streets: protected neighborhoods? Ann. Am. Acad. Pol. Soc. Sci. 451 (1), 106–117.

Barker, J., Kraftl, P., Horton, J., Tucker, F., 2009. The road less travelled—new directions in children's and young people's mobility. Mobilities 4 (1), 1–10.

Baslington, H., 2008. Travel socialisation: a social theory of travel mode behaviour. Int. J. Sustain. Transp. 2 (2), 91–114.

Berg, M., Medrich, E.A., 1980. Children in four neighborhoods: the physical environment and its effect on play and play patterns. Environ. Behav. 12 (3), 320–348.

Biddle, S.J., Ciaccioni, S., Thomas, G., Vergeer, I., 2019. Physical activity and mental health in children and adolescents: an updated review of reviews and an analysis of causality. Psychol. Sport Exerc. 42, 146–155.

Biddulph, M., 2012. Street design and street use: comparing traffic calmed and home zone streets. J. Urban Des. 17 (2), 213–232.

Bonner, K., 1997. A Great Place to Raise Kids: Interpretation, Science, and the Urban-Rural Debate. McGill-Queen's University Press, Quebec.

Bringolf-Isler, B., Grize, L., Mäder, U., Ruch, N., Sennhauser, F.H., Braun-Fahrländer, C., 2008. Personal and environmental factors associated with active commuting to school in Switzerland. Prev. Med. 46 (1), 67–73.

Carver, A., Salmon, J., Campbell, K., Baur, L., Garnett, S., Crawford, D., 2005. How do perceptions of local neighborhood relate to Adolescents' walking and cycling? Am. J. Health Promot. 20 (2), 139–147.

Carver, A., Timperio, A., Crawford, D., 2008. Playing it safe: the influence of neighbourhood safety on children's physical activity—a review. Health Place 14 (2), 217–227.

Carver, A., Watson, B., Shaw, B., Hillman, M., 2013. A comparison study of children's independent mobility in England and Australia. Child. Geogr. 11 (4), 461–475.

Egli, V., Mackay, L., Jelleyman, C., Ikeda, E., Hopkins, S., Smith, M., 2020. Social relationships, nature, and traffic: findings from a child-centred approach to measuring active school travel route perceptions. Child. Geogr. 18 (6), 667–683. https://doi.org/10.1080/14733285.2019.1685074.

Elgar, F.J., Davis, C.G., Wohl, M.J., Trites, S.J., Zelenski, J.M., Martin, M.S., 2011. Social capital, health and life satisfaction in 50 countries. Health Place 17 (5), 1044–1053.

Freeman, C., Tranter, P.J., 2011. Children and their Urban Environment: Changing Worlds. Routledge.

Friman, M., Westman, J., Olsson, L.E., 2019. Children's life satisfaction and satisfaction with school travel. Child Indic. Res. 12 (4), 1319–1332.

Gaster, S., 1991. Urban children's access to their neighborhood: changes over three generations. Environ. Behav. 23 (1), 70–85.

Grannis, R., 2011. From the Ground Up: Translating Geography into Community through Neighbor Networks. Princeton University Press.

Helliwell, J.F., Putnam, R.D., 2004. The social context of well-being. Philos. Trans. R. Soc. Lond. B Biol. Sci. 359, 1435–1446.

Hillman, M., Adams, J., Whitelegg, J., 1990. One False Move… A Study of Children's Independent Mobility. Policy Studies Institute, London.

Holland, J., Reynolds, T., Weller, S., 2007. Transitions, networks and communities: the significance of social capital in the lives of children and young people. J. Youth Stud. 10 (1), 97–116.

Humberto, M., Moura, F., Giannotti, M., 2021. Can outdoor activities and inquiry sessions change the travel behavior of children and their caregivers? Empirical research in public preschools in São Paulo (Brazil). J. Transp. Geogr. 90, 102922.

Hüttenmoser, M., 1995. Children and their living surroundings: empirical investigations into the significance of living surroundings for the everyday life and development of children. Child. Environ. 12 (4), 403–413.

Ikeda, E., Hinckson, E., Witten, K., Smith, M., 2019. Assessment of direct and indirect associations between children active school travel and environmental, household and child factors using structural equation modelling. Int. J. Behav. Nutr. Phys. Act. 16 (1), 32.

Johansson, M., 2006. Environment and parental factors as determinants of mode for children's leisure travel. J. Environ. Psychol. 26 (2), 156–169.

Kamargianni, M., Polydoropoulou, A., 2014. Gender differences in on-line social networking and travel behavior of adolescents. In: 5th International Conference on Women's Issues in Transportation.

Larouche, R., Mammen, G., Rowe, D.A., Faulkner, G., 2018. Effectiveness of active school transport interventions: a systematic review and update. BMC Public Health 18 (1), 206.

Lennard, H.L., Lennard, S.H.C., 2000. The Forgotten Child: Cities for the Well-Being of Children. Gondolier Press.

Lim, M., Barton, A.C., 2010. Exploring insideness in urban children's sense of place. J. Environ. Psychol. 30 (3), 328–337.

Lynch, K., 1981. A Theory of Good City Form. MIT Press, Cambridge, MA.

Lynch, K., Banerjee, T., 1976. Growing up in cities. New Soc. 37 (722), 281–284.

Mattsson, K.T., 2002. Children's (in)dependent mobility and parents' chauffeuring in the town and the countryside. Tijdschr. Econ. Soc. Geogr. 93 (4), 443–453.

McDonald, N.C., Deakin, E., Aalborg, A.E., 2010. Influence of the social environment on children's school travel. Prev. Med. 50 (Suppl. 0), S65–S68.

Mitra, R., 2013. Independent mobility and mode choice for school transportation: a review and framework for future research. Transplant. Rev. 33 (1), 21–43.

Mitra, R., Abbasi, Z., 2019. Bringing back play to urban streets. In: Waygood, E.O.D., Friman, M., Olsson, L., Mitra, R. (Eds.), Transport and Children's Wellbeing. Elsevier, pp. 237–252.

Mitra, R., Manaugh, K., 2019. A social-ecological conceptualization of children's mobility. In: Waygood, E.O.D., Friman, M., Olsson, L.E., Mitra, R. (Eds.), Transportation and Children's Well-Being. Elsevier, Amsterdam, pp. 81–100.

Morrow, V., 1999. Conceptualising social capital in relation to the well-being of children and young people: a critical review. Sociol. Rev. 47 (4), 744–765.

Pacilli, M.G., Giovannelli, I., Prezza, M., Augimeri, M.L., 2013. Children and the public realm: antecedents and consequences of independent mobility in a group of 11-13-year-old Italian children. Child. Geogr. 11 (4), 377–393.

Panter, J.R., Jones, A.P., van Sluijs, E.M.F., Griffin, S.J., 2010. Attitudes, social support and environmental perceptions as predictors of active commuting behaviour in school children. J. Epidemiol. Community Health 64 (01), 41–48.

Park, N., 2004. The role of subjective well-being in positive youth development. Ann. Am. Acad. Pol. Soc. Sci. 591, 14.

Pollard, E., Lee, P., 2003. Child well-being: a systematic review of the literature. Soc. Indic. Res. 61 (1), 59–78.

Pretty, G.M., Conroy, C., Dugay, J., Fowler, K., Williams, D., 1996. Sense of community and its relevance to adolescents of all ages. J. Community Psychol. 24 (4), 365–379.

Prezza, M., Pacilli, M.G., 2007. Current fear of crime, sense of community, and loneliness in italian adolescents: the role of autonomous mobility and play during childhood. J. Community Psychol. 35 (2), 151–170.

Prezza, M., Pilloni, S., Morabito, C., Sersante, C., Alparone, F.R., Giuliani, M.V., 2001. The influence of psychosocial and environmental factors on children's independent mobility and relationship to peer frequentation. J. Community Appl. Soc. Psychol. 11 (6), 435–450.

Prezza, M., Alparone, F.R., Renzi, D., Pietrobono, A., 2010. Social participation and independent mobility in children: the effects of two implementations of "we go to school alone". J. Prev. Interv. Community 38 (1), 8–25.

Rothman, L., Macpherson, A.K., Ross, T., Buliung, R.N., 2018. The decline in active school transportation (AST): a systematic review of the factors related to AST and changes in school transport over time in North America. Prev. Med. 111, 314–322.

Salmon, J., Salmon, L., Crawford, D.A., Hume, C., Timperio, A., 2007. Associations among individual, social, and environmental barriers and children's walking or cycling to school. Am. J. Health Promot. 22 (2), 107–113.

Schoeppe, S., Duncan, M.J., Badland, H., Oliver, M., Curtis, C., 2013. Associations of children's independent mobility and active travel with physical activity, sedentary behaviour and weight status: a systematic review. J. Sci. Med. Sport 16 (4), 312–319.

Shaw, B., Watson, B., Frauendienst, B., Redecker, A., Jones, T., Hillman, M., 2013. Children's Independent Mobility: A Comparative Study in England and Germany (1971–2010). Policy Studies Institute, London, UK.

Sidharthan, R., Bhat, C.R., Pendyala, R.M., Goulias, K.G., 2011. Model for children's school travel mode choice accounting for effects of spatial and social interaction. Transp. Res. Rec. 2213, 78–86.

Stiglic, N., Viner, R.M., 2019. Effects of screentime on the health and well-being of children and adolescents: a systematic review of reviews. BMJ Open 9 (1), e023191. https://doi.org/10.1136/bmjopen-2018-023191.

Studer, D., 2018. Put Play to Work: Engaging Children in the Design Process through Play-Based Charrettes. Self-published, Victoria, Canada.

Timperio, A., Ball, K., Salmon, J., Roberts, R., Giles-Corti, B., Simmons, D., Baur, L.A., Crawford, D., 2006. Personal, family, social, and environmental correlates of active commuting to school. Am. J. Prev. Med. 30 (1), 45–51.

Tranter, P., 2006. Overcoming social traps. In: Gleeson, B., Sipe, N. (Eds.), Creating Child Friendly Cities: new Perspectives and Prospects. Routledge, pp. 121–135.

van den Berg, P., Sharmeen, F., Weijs-Perrée, M., 2017. On the subjective quality of social interactions: influence of neighborhood walkability, social cohesion and mobility choices. Transp. Res. A Policy Pract. 106, 309–319.

van den Berg, P., Waygood, E.O.D., van de Craats, I., Kemperman, A., 2020. Factors affecting parental safety perception, satisfaction with school travel and mood in primary school children in the Netherlands. In: Transportation Research Board (TRB) 99th Annual Meeting, Washington, D.C.

van Vliet, W., 1983. Children's travel behavior. Ekistics 298 (50), 61–65.

Veitch, J., Carver, A., Salmon, J., Abbott, G., Ball, K., Crawford, D., Cleland, V., Timperio, A., 2017. What predicts children's active transport and independent mobility in disadvantaged neighborhoods? Health Place 44, 103–109.

Villa-González, E., Barranco-Ruiz, Y., Evenson, K.R., Chillón, P., 2018. Systematic review of interventions for promoting active school transport. Prev. Med. 111, 115–134.

Waygood, E.O.D., 2009. What is the role of mothers in transit-oriented development? The case of Osaka–Kyoto–Kobe, Japan. In: Women's Issues in Transportation 4th International Conference. Transportation Research Board, Irvine California, pp. 163–178.

Waygood, E.O.D., 2019. Transport and social wellbeing. In: Waygood, E.O.D., Friman, M., Olsson, L.E., Mitra, R. (Eds.), Transport and Children's Wellbeing. Elsevier, Amsterdam, pp. 61–80.

Waygood, E.O.D., Friman, M., 2015. Children's travel and incidental community connections. Travel Behav. Soc. 2 (3), 174–181.

Waygood, E.O.D., Taniguchi, A., 2020. Japan: maintaining high levels of walking. In: Transport and Children's well-being. Elsevier, pp. 297–316.

Waygood, E.O.D., Friman, M., Olsson, L.E., Taniguchi, A., 2017a. Children's incidental social interaction during travel: international case studies from Canada, Japan, and Sweden. J. Transp. Geogr. 63, 22–29.

Waygood, E.O.D., Friman, M., Olsson, L.E., Taniguchi, A., 2017b. Transport and child well-being: an integrative review. Travel Behav. Soc. 9 (Suppl. C), 32–49.

Waygood, E.O.D., Friman, M., Taniguchi, A., Olsson, L.E., 2019. Children's life satisfaction and travel satisfaction: evidence from Canada, Japan, and Sweden. Travel Behav. Soc. 16, 214–223.

Waygood, E.O.D., Olsson, L.E., Taniguchi, A., Friman, M., 2020. The role of children's independent mobility and social media use for face-to-face social interaction with friends. Transportation 47 (4), 1987–2009.

Waygood, E.O.D., Kemperman, A., van de Craats, I., van den Berg, P., 2021. Social aspects of children's travel in the Netherlands. In: Transportation Research Board 2021 Annual Meeting, Washington, D.C. (online).

Weijs-Perrée, M., van den Berg, P., Arentze, T., Kemperman, A., 2015. Factors influencing social satisfaction and loneliness: a path analysis. J. Transp. Geogr. 45, 24–31.

Weller, S., Bruegel, I., 2009. Children's place in the development of neighbourhood social capital. Urban Stud. 46 (3), 629–643.

Witten, K., Field, A., 2019. Engaging children in neighborhood planning for active travel infrastructure. In: Waygood, E.O.D., Friman, M., Olsson, L.E., Mitra, R. (Eds.), Transportation and Children's Well-Being. Elsevier, Amsterdam, pp. 199–216.

Wu, X.Y., Han, L.H., Zhang, J.H., Luo, S., Hu, J.W., Sun, K., 2017. The influence of physical activity, sedentary behavior on health-related quality of life among the general population of children and adolescents: a systematic review. PLoS One 12 (11), e0187668.

CHAPTER FOUR

Transport poverty and car dependence: A European perspective

Giulio Mattioli*
Transport Research Group, Department of Spatial Planning, TU Dortmund University, Dortmund, Germany
*Corresponding author: e-mail address: giulio.mattioli@tu-dortmund.de

Contents

Abstract

In the Global North, and increasingly in emerging countries, car use can be essential to access services, opportunities and social networks that are instrumental to need satisfaction. The concept of car dependence helps understanding the multiple facets of transport poverty in these societies. Building on previous research, this chapter defines transport poverty as a broad phenomenon encompassing *mobility poverty*, *accessibility poverty*, *transport affordability* and *exposure to transport externalities*. The chapter reviews evidence on each of these dimensions, drawing mainly from literature on European case studies. It is argued that a holistic consideration of the multiple facets of transport poverty is needed, in contrast with the tendency in transport policy debates to use equity arguments in a selective or opportunistic way. This point is illustrated with reference to plans to introduce urban vehicle access regulations in UK cities.

Keywords: Transport poverty, Transport equity, Car dependence, Accessibility, Air pollution, Vehicle access regulations, Time poverty, Affordability

Advances in Transport Policy and Planning, Volume 8
ISSN 2543-0009
https://doi.org/10.1016/bs.atpp.2021.06.004
Copyright © 2021 Elsevier Inc.
All rights reserved.

1. Introduction

Questions of transport poverty (Allen and Farber, 2019; Lucas et al., 2016; Mattioli et al., 2017), equity (Di Ciommo and Shiftan, 2017; Lucas et al., 2019) and justice (Martens, 2016; Mullen and Marsden, 2016; Pereira et al., 2017; Verlinghieri and Schwanen, 2020) are increasingly at the forefront of transport research. Although rarely identified as such, they are also a fixture of public and political debates, notably at the local level. While academic research increasingly recognizes that transport poverty is a multifaceted problem (e.g., Lucas et al., 2016, 2019; Mattioli et al., 2017), this is less true in the public debate, where social equity issues in transport are (too) often reduced to questions around affordability.

This chapter provides a literature review of research on transport poverty, presenting illustrative empirical evidence of its multiple dimensions as defined by Lucas et al. (2016), i.e., *mobility poverty*, *accessibility poverty*, *transport affordability* and *exposure to transport externalities*. In doing so, I focus mainly on European countries. This limits the generalizability of the arguments presented here, but a selective focus is made necessary by the large differences between world regions in terms of car dependence and other socio-economic aspects. While there is a large and growing literature on transport poverty in the Global South (e.g., Benevenuto and Caulfield, 2019; Diaz Olvera et al., 2003; Lucas and Porter, 2016), the issues that dominate this research reflect transport systems that are relatively less car-dominated, although this is changing rapidly (Gandelman et al., 2019; Pojani and Stead, 2017). Conversely, countries like the US and Australia are characterized by extremely high levels of car dependence, which leads to partly different questions and perspectives in transport poverty research (King et al., 2019). Europe presents an intermediate situation, being less car dependent than North America (as often noted), but more car dependent than many other parts of the world. As I attempt to show in the remainder of this chapter, this tends to magnify the diversity of transport poverty's manifestations.

The chapter is structured as follows. Section 2 summarizes evidence on car dependence in Europe, providing context for the remaining sections. Section 3 reviews literature for each of the four dimensions of transport poverty. In Section 4, this academic evidence is contrasted with an illustrative example of a policy controversy around Clean Air Zones in the European context, where arguments on transport inequalities have been prominent.

I use this example to show which dimensions of transport poverty are emphasized in the public and political debate, and which tend to be overlooked. Section 5 concludes the chapter.

2. Car dependence in the European context

Car dependence can be defined as a situation in which access to modes alternative to the car and/or their viability are diminished, such that car use becomes essential to access services, opportunities and social networks that are instrumental to need satisfaction (Mattioli, 2016). High levels of car dependence are typically associated with high levels of car use, although the two concepts ought to be analytically distinguished.

In the Global North, car dependence is the result of a historical process that played out in twentieth century (Pooley, 2016) consisting of several interlinked developments, including (Mattioli et al., 2020): the rise of the automotive industry; the transformation of roads into spaces where car use is prioritized, and the rapid expansion of road networks; the diffusion of car-dependent land use patterns (urban sprawl); the struggle of public transport to provide competitive services in the new conditions; the development of cultures of consumption around car use. This is sometimes referred to as the "system of automobility," to highlight the pervasive, entangled and path-dependent nature of the different elements at play (Urry, 2004). A similar process is now under way in emerging economies, where motorization levels are rapidly increasing (Pojani and Stead, 2017).

The car dependence phenomenon provides the context within which to understand the multiple facets of transport poverty, as most of them are in one way or another linked to access to cars (or lack thereof) and to the implications of living in car-dominated transport systems.

While North American and Australian research often present Europe as a sort of role model for sustainable transport (e.g., Buehler et al., 2017; Newman and Kenworthy, 1999; Pucher and Buehler, 2008), European transport systems are characterized by high and increasing levels of car dependence, although this obviously varies between countries and across the urban-rural spectrum (Fiorello et al., 2016; Jeekel, 2013). This is attested by data on levels of car use, the perceived necessity of car ownership for social inclusion, and the poor performance of modal alternatives in terms of access to essential services and opportunities.

While Europe-wide figures are scarce, a 2014 survey found that 82% of EU-28 residents had a driving license, while there were on average 1.4 cars available per household (Fiorello et al., 2016). In 16 out of 28 EU countries, more than 70% of the population uses the car at least a few times a week (either as driver or as passenger). In 13 countries, more than 50% of the population uses the car "at least once a day" (EC, 2013a). In 16 countries, cars are the mode of transport "used most often on a typical day" by at least 50% of the population. In further 10 countries, the share is over 40% (EC, 2014). Cars account for more than 80% of passenger kilometers by motorized modes on land in 21 EU countries, and for more than 66% in all of them (EC, 2019a).

When asked about the reasons for not using public transport, most car users in the EU mention lack of connections (72%), lower perceived levels of convenience (74%), low frequency of services (64%) and lack of reliability (54%) (EC, 2011). This perception is confirmed by studies showing large disparities in travel time between public transport and car in European cities. Liao et al. (2020) find that using public transport takes on average twice as long as driving a car for trips to frequently visited locations in Amsterdam (Netherlands) and Stockholm (Sweden). Public transport outperforms car use in very specific and limited circumstances such as for short trips during peak rush hour, and in the innermost parts of urban areas. Similar disparities are documented for other large EU urban areas such as Helsinki, Finland (Salonen and Toivonen, 2013), Göteborg, Sweden (Elldér et al., 2012) and Porto, Portugal (Silva and Pinho, 2010), and are likely to be even larger in periurban and rural areas. Research conducted by the UK Department for Transport shows that 82% of the working age population in England can reach seven or more large employment centers by car within 45 min, as compared to just 23% by public transport (essentially just those living in the core of large metropolitan areas) (DfT, 2017). 91% of households in England can reach the nearest hospital within 30 min by car, as compared to just 38% who are able to do so by public transport or walking (whichever is the quickest) (DfT, 2019).

It is not surprising, therefore, that 44% of Britons saw the car as "a necessity that households should not have to do without" in 2012, up from just 22% in 1983 (Mattioli, 2016; based on Poverty and Social Exclusion UK, Necessities of life survey, 1983–2012). The same question was asked in 2007 in all EU countries, and in most of them, more than 50% of the population agreed that the car is a necessity (EC, 2007). On this basis, being able to afford a car is one of nine items "considered by most people to be desirable or even necessary to lead an adequate life" included in the EU social indicator of material deprivation, alongside other necessities like being able to afford keeping home adequately warm, and a washing machine[a] (Fusco et al., 2013).

Research on "Minimum Income Standards" (MIS) explores the public perception of what is needed for minimum acceptable standard of living, based on focus groups assisted by experts. A recent report looking back on a decade of MIS focus groups in the UK (Davis et al., 2018) shows how car dependence has worsened in recent years. The report finds that "transport is the category that has seen the most widespread changes in the MIS budgets over the past decade" noting that "in 2008 a local bus pass provided for most travel needs, but since that time transport requirements in MIS have grown, due in particular to a perception of less adequate public transport" (p. 22). The 2018 focus groups found that "families with children now need cars, and other households need to spend more on taxis than in the past to meet their needs," and that "costs are also rising because of a need to travel further afield, for both work and social purposes" (p. 22). A similar exercise in France concluded that car ownership is a necessity for all social groups (Jaboeuf et al., 2016).

In recent years, car sharing services have drawn much attention as a possible alternative to private car ownership. However, in the European context at least, their diffusion remains very limited and concentrated in large urban areas that are already less car dependent (Marsden et al., 2019). In the UK, for example, just 27% of the population is aware of the existence car sharing services, and no more than 1% uses them (Birch and Bullock, 2019). As such, at present they do not seem to constitute a valid substitute to car ownership for most Europeans.

To sum up, evidence from various European countries suggest that private car use is the dominant form of passenger transport, as it accounts for the largest share of travel activity, it outperforms public transport (in terms of travel time) even in large urban areas, and is perceived by large and increasing numbers of Europeans as essential for social inclusion.[b] At the same time, car dependence is far from universal, as there is a substantial level of travel activity by alternative modes, and a sizeable minority of the population with little or no access to cars. This is particularly true in some

[a] https://ec.europa.eu/eurostat/statistics-explained/index.php/Glossary:Material_deprivation.

[b] Social inclusion is defined as "the process of improving the terms of participation in society, particularly for people who are disadvantaged, through enhancing opportunities, access to resources, voice and respect for rights" (UN, 2016).

contexts such as (certain) large urban areas, where the accessibility advantage provided by car use is less pronounced (see e.g., Buehler et al., 2017).

3. Transport poverty: A multidimensional concept

As discussed in the previous section, Europeans live in increasingly car-dependent societies. The implication of this is that most forms of transport poverty can be related in one way or another to the dominance of automobiles over other transport modes (Mattioli and Colleoni, 2016). And yet transport poverty is a much more complex and multifaceted problem than just lack of access to cars, as I shall try to illustrate.

Research on transport poverty is characterized by a confusing variety of concepts. A series of searches on abstract and citation database Scopus shows that numerous terms are used in the English-speaking literature, including but not limited to: "transport disadvantage" (105 documents), "oil vulnerability" (63), "transport poverty" (38), "transport-related social exclusion" (37), "transport affordability" (20), "transport exclusion" (14), "forced car ownership" (8), "accessibility poverty" (6), "car-related economic stress" (3).[c] While greater conceptual consistency would be desirable, the best any author can do in the present situation is to be clear about the concepts they employ, their definition, and how they relate to each other.

In this chapter, I draw on the multidimensional definition of transport poverty put forward by Lucas et al. (2016), which has been adopted by numerous studies since then. In this understanding, transport poverty is a broad overarching concept covering most inequality and distributional issues in transport, related to both the benefits and burdens of transport. Within this broad concept, there are four sub-dimensions: *mobility poverty*, *accessibility poverty*, *transport affordability* and *exposure to transport externalities*.[d] These are defined in Table 1, along with a short discussion of how they relate to car dependence. In the remainder of this section, I review literature on each of these dimensions, drawing mainly from European research.

---

[c] Document search for article title, abstracts and keywords, using the terms listed in the main text, conducted on 29 September 2020.

[d] By adopting the notion of "transport poverty," one implicitly assumes: (i) that there are disparities in the distribution of the benefits and burdens of transport, which ought be the subject of an equity analysis; (ii) that there is (at least in principle) an equity principle according to which such disparities are unfair; (iii) that there are thresholds (corresponding to the minimum of a benefit or the maximum of a burden) allowing the identification of disadvantaged groups. A fuller discussion of these normative aspects—in terms of *transport equity* and *justice*—is beyond the scope of this chapter but see Martens et al. (2019) and Pereira et al. (2017).

Table 1 The four sub-dimensions of transport poverty and their relationship with car dependence.

Sub-dimension	Definition	Relationship to car dependence
Mobility poverty	Lack of transport resources	Car dependence is defined by the reduced availability and viability of modes other than the car. In car-dependent contexts, lack of access to a car typically results in sub-par levels of accessibility
Transport affordability	Inability to meet the cost of transport	In car-dependent contexts, low-income households are under pressure to own and use cars, despite the substantial economic investment that these require
Accessibility poverty	Difficulties in reaching key activities	The expansion of activity spaces associated with car dependence can make it difficult to reach essential activities within reasonable time and cost, both for people with and without access to cars
Exposure to transport externalities	Disproportionate exposure to the negative effects of the transport system	In car-dependent societies, most negative effects in terms of, e.g., road safety, noise and air pollution are related to cars and their dominance over transport systems

Own elaboration based on Lucas, K., Mattioli, G., Verlinghieri, E., Guzman, A., 2016. Transport poverty and its adverse social consequences, Proc. Inst. Civ. Eng. Transp. 169 (6), 353–365.

While Lucas et al.'s typology is useful to frame the discussion in this chapter, it is not without limitations. The four sub-dimensions are not mutually exclusive, and there are multiple overlaps and interactions between them. As discussed in Section 3.1, *mobility poverty* points to the lack of access to more tangible transport resources, such as cars and public transport, but this is only of interest insofar as it results in reduced *accessibility*.[e] The broader notion of *accessibility poverty*, on the other hand, is used by Lucas et al. (2016) to

[e] Accessibility is one of the most important concepts in transport studies and a variety of understandings and definitions exist (Shi et al., 2020). In this chapter, the term is used "in its broadest interpretation" to point to "the degree to which people can reach the goods and services that society considers are necessary for them to live their daily lives, but with an emphasis on potential/capability rather than actual behavior" (Jones and Lucas, 2012).

emphasize that there are various other factors, besides lack of transport resources, that can result in reduced accessibility. This would include for example mobility restrictions caused by aging or physical and mental disabilities. Section 3.3 illustrates accessibility poverty with a discussion of *transport-related time poverty*, showing how even people with plenty of transport options and high levels of travel activity can experience reduced participation to social activities, for reasons that are transport-related. The concept of *transport affordability* (Section 3.2) is used to point more specifically to the implications of not being able to meet the costs of transport. It overlaps to some extent with both previous concepts, as affordability issues can limit the availability of transport resources (thus resulting in mobility poverty), but can also limit the use of those transport resources that are available (thus constituting a form of accessibility poverty).

The first three sub-dimensions of Lucas et al.'s typology ultimately refer to inequalities in the distribution of the main benefit of transport, i.e., accessibility. As such, there are multiple overlaps and interrelationships between them. The fourth sub-dimension, *exposure to transport externalities*, refers to inequalities in the distribution of the burdens of transport, which are often considered as a separate domain. As I argue in Section 3.4, there are good reasons to conceptualize them as a further sub-dimension of transport poverty.

3.1 Mobility poverty

The first and perhaps most explored dimension of transport poverty is *mobility poverty*, defined by Lucas et al. (2016) as "the lack of (usually motorized) transport." As Martens et al. (2019, pp. 15–16) argue, in transport equity analysis it is important to distinguish between more tangible *resources*—such as "ownership of various means of transport (and) access to public transport or to safe walking and cycling environments"—and *opportunities*, i.e., "a person's ease of movement (and) ability to reach important activity opportunities." The concept of mobility poverty, as defined by Lucas et al. (2016) refers to such resources, although it also implies that they are essential for the realization of opportunities. In car-dependent transport systems, access to a car is the most important resource, as a result of diminished availability and viability of alternative modes. The result is that lack of access to a car generally results in sub-par levels of accessibility and activity participation. As Lucas and Le Vine (2009) put it: "one of the most effective and immediate ways in which to identify the benefits of transport in general and car ownership in particular, is to look (at) what happens when people in predominantly car-based societies do not have regular access to a private motor vehicle" (pp. 8–9).

Unsurprisingly then, given the origins of transport poverty research in car-dominated societies, much of the literature on mobility poverty has focused on individuals without access to cars, as well as on low-income households, who are more likely to be carless. This emphasis is apparent in the covers of major books on the subject, typically depicting dispirited looking people using (or waiting for) public transport (Currie, 2011; Lucas, 2004; Martens, 2016) or walking (Currie et al., 2007). These groups account for a non-negligible share of the population in the EU-28, where 6.5% of the population reports being unable to afford a car, ranging from 1.6% in Cyprus to 27.1% in Romania.[f]

There is a growing body of evidence documenting the relationship between access to cars, accessibility to services and opportunities and activity participation. Much of it focuses on employment, given its importance for economic and social mobility. The findings tend to show that cars outperform other modes in terms of access to employment opportunities, with knock-on effects on the employment chances of persons without cars. A recent study of the Rotterdam-The Hague metropolitan region in the Netherlands (Martens and Bastiaanssen, 2019) finds that "in spite of the relatively well-developed public transport system in the region, the average weighted accessibility (to jobs) by car in morning peak hours is substantially higher than by public transport" (p. 46). Fransen et al.'s (2018) study of Flanders (Belgium) finds that "job seekers with a driver's license have a higher accessibility to job opportunities than those without." Bastiaanssen et al. (2020) review quantitative studies on the link between car ownership and employment, including from Europe, concluding that "car ownership significantly increases individual employment probabilities."

Qualitative studies confirm this picture. Villeneuve and Kaufmann's (2020) find that a substantial minority of individuals in households without cars in Strasbourg (France) feel social excluded on account of poor access to destinations related to professional, leisure, associative and medical activities. Crisp et al.'s (2018) study of transport-related barriers to employment in low-income neighborhoods in the UK finds that "the ability to drive or access private transport can significantly increase commuting options, particularly to more peripheral locations, but financial constraints rule out

[f] https://ec.europa.eu/eurostat/databrowser/view/ilc_mddu05/default/table?lang=en.

vehicle ownership for many" (p. 2). Mullen et al.'s (2020) study of low-to-middle-income households in Northern England finds that many of them cling on or aspire to car ownership, despite its substantial cost, because it guarantees continuous access to the workplace in a context of heightened housing and employment precarity.

While much research has focused on access to employment and other formal services, Cass et al. (2005) criticize "analyses of transport-related social exclusion ... based upon a model that views inclusion in terms of people being able to 'get at' pre-defined 'public' goods and services located within pre-determined 'formal' locations/destinations" (p. 551), arguing that there is a wider range of "obligations of co-presence" that ought to be considered. These include in particular access to social networks, i.e., the ability to visit friends and relatives, which people perceive as essential for social inclusion.

Evidence from Europe suggests that lack of access to cars constrains participation in social activities and contact with relatives. Rubin and Bertolini (2016) find that lack of car ownership is associated with a reduction in the frequency of face-to-face meetings with parents among Dutch adults. Based on sample of low-income individuals from the Netherlands, Canada, Spain and the UK, Morris et al. (2020a) find that lack of access to a car is associated with reduced frequency of participation in various non-work out-of-home activities such as caring for others, socializing, leisure, and volunteering and religious activities. Most of these activities are rated highly by respondents in terms of subjective well-being. Interestingly, the finding of a link between car ownership and activity participation is not universal, as the association is weaker for low-income individuals in urban areas, and is even reversed for urbanites the UK (where car ownership is associated with less activity participation, perhaps reflecting low levels of car dependence in London). While these differences might to some extent be explained by different lifestyle and preferences between car owners and non-car owners, and between residents of different types of areas, they are also suggestive of a negative impact of non-car ownership on participation in out-of-home activities, particularly outside of urban cores.

Other research findings confirm that the role played by car access in mobility poverty is highly variable across space. Mattioli (2013, 2014) uses national travel survey data for Germany and the UK to investigate how the socio-economic make-up, travel behavior and accessibility situation of households without cars change across different types of areas. He finds that, as you move from dense cities to more sparsely populated, car-dependent areas: (i) the share of households without cars decreases; (ii) the carless are more concentrated among certain social groups (older adults, single-person households, and the non-employed); (iii) there is a wider gap between households with and without cars in terms of levels of travel activity; (iv) the accessibility gap between households with and without cars widens. Overall, this suggests that who is carless and what being carless entails depends crucially on the degree of car dependence of the local area. In dense, large cities, households without cars are relatively numerous, include a greater variety of household types such as families with children, and the accessibility and activity participation penalty associated with lack of car ownership is moderate (as in Gothenburg, Sweden, see Lagrell et al., 2018). In car-dependent areas, by contrast, there are very few households without cars (mostly those who for age or other reasons are prevented from driving), but the degree of disadvantage associated with this condition is severe.

A corollary of this is that in lower-density, car dependent areas, most of those who are able and allowed to own and use cars will do so, almost regardless of the financial costs that this entails. This points to a problem of transport affordability and car-related economic stress, as discussed in the next section.

3.2 Transport affordability

Research on transport affordability investigates the implications of not being able to meet the costs of transport. This can mean being unable to afford car ownership, in contexts where this is essential for social inclusion, as discussed in the previous section. At the same time, in car-dependent contexts, lower-income households are under pressure to own and use cars, despite the substantial economic investment that these require. If they do, they then face a trade-off between: (i) curtailing travel in order to save on running expenses (e.g., fuel) and (ii) cutting expenditure in other areas (e.g., home heating). In most cases, both coping strategies will be adopted with potentially serious implications for social inclusion and well-being.

This is another area where several concepts are used: some, like "forced car ownership" (Curl et al., 2018; Currie and Senbergs, 2007; Mattioli, 2017) and "car-related economic stress" (Belton-Chevallier et al., 2018; Mattioli et al., 2018; Rock et al., 2016), look at the problem from a static perspective. Others, like "oil vulnerability" (Dodson and Sipe, 2007; Leung et al., 2018; Lovelace and Philips, 2014) and "vulnerability to fuel price increases" (Mattioli et al., 2019) stress how these groups are more likely to experience hardship when the costs of motoring increase, a question with heightened policy relevance (Creutzig et al., 2020).

Besides constraints to travel activity and household expenditure, it has been suggested that issues of transport affordability can have important impacts on personal wellbeing. Rachele et al. (2018) put forward the hypothesis that the costs of automobile ownership among lower-income households can result in financial strain, stress, and ultimately negative health outcomes. This is consistent with research on "energy poverty," showing that struggling to afford home heating is associated with mental health conditions such as anxiety and depression (Gilbertson et al., 2012; Liddell and Morris, 2010). Research from Australia has found an association between high expenditure on fuel and fuel price increases, on one hand, and reductions in subjective wellbeing and mental health on the other (Churchill and Smyth, 2019). The main channel through which this effect operates is reduced visits to friends and family (Prakash et al., 2020).

A recent research project[g] investigated British households who struggle to afford the costs of motoring, aiming to establish how many they are, who they are, where they live and what that entails in terms of economic stress and material deprivation. Mattioli et al. (2018) find that 9% of UK households have low income and high motoring costs, and that these households have rather inelastic demand for fuel, i.e., they are unable to reduce mileage when fuel prices increase. There is, however, another rather large group (10%) of low-income households with low motoring costs (mostly without a car) and these are hardly affected by changes in the cost of motoring. Similarly, Mattioli (2017) finds that 7% of UK households own a car despite being in absolute poverty, and that these are characterized by relatively high levels of social exclusion, material deprivation, economic strain and indebtedness. There is, however, a larger and even more deprived group (11%) of households who report not being able to afford a car. Both studies show that households struggling with the costs of motoring are different from the rest of the low-income population in several respects, as they are more likely to be larger, middle-aged, employed households living in owner-occupied accommodation. These are not characteristics normally associated with social disadvantage, suggesting that many of these households live "on the

[g] (t)ERES (Energy-related economic stress in the UK, at the interface between transport, housing and fuel poverty)—see https://teresproject.wordpress.com/.

edges of social exclusion": car access facilitates their access to employment, everyday activities, and home ownership, but the price to pay is (quite literally) economic stress.

Studies from France point to similar conclusions. Currently, this is the only country in the EU with an official indicator of transport affordability (referred to as "transport energy precarity"). It is estimated that 10% of households need to spend disproportionate amounts on car travel to reach the workplace and other key services (Cochez et al., 2015). These households tend to have low-to-middle incomes, to be active in the labor market, and to live in peri-urban and rural areas (Cochez et al., 2015; ONPE, 2014; Verry et al., 2017). Qualitative studies have highlighted the coping strategies adopted by periurban households facing car-related economic stress, which include giving up on activities that require too much travel, reliance on local social networks, and curtailed expenditure on domestic energy (Belton-Chevallier et al., 2018; Ortar, 2018).

From a spatial perspective most studies find that, holding other factors equal, transport affordability problems related to car use are more pronounced in car-dependent suburban, periurban and rural areas. However, this pattern can be reinforced or compounded depending on the prevailing socio-spatial configuration, i.e., how different income groups are distributed across space (Kesteloot, 2008). Such configurations can vary between countries and city-regions, which calls for a context-sensitive analysis of transport affordability.

Transport affordability issues are often linked to housing affordability issues. Early research from Australia (Currie and Delbosc, 2011; Currie and Senbergs, 2007; Dodson and Sipe, 2007) showed that low-income households are concentrated in suburban and periurban areas, where housing prices are lower but there are few alternatives to car use. This leads them to spend a high share of income on motoring, while also making them vulnerable to fuel price increases. A similar pattern has been observed in various EU regions. In Munich (Germany), for example, there is an overlap between areas of low income and areas with poor public transport accessibility to jobs (Büttner et al., 2013), due to the supply-dominated housing market pushing low-income households toward less well-connected suburban areas (Sterzer, 2017). French studies have highlighted how prudential measures in housing access contribute to this (Coulombel, 2018; Polacchini and Orfeuil, 1999): since there are limits to the share of income that households are allowed to spend on rent or mortgage, many choose to relocate to car-dependent periurban areas where they can access affordable housing.

The problem is that the extra expenditure on car use typically more than offsets the savings on housing, which increases the risk of insolvency and magnifies vulnerability to fuel price increases.

There are, however, alternative socio-spatial configurations, where low-income households are not disproportionately concentrated in car-dependent areas. This is the case for example in England, where accessibility to key services by alternative modes is on average better in low-income neighborhoods (Mattioli et al., 2019), because of the relative concentration of poverty in inner cities (Bailey and Minton, 2018). The implication for transport affordability is that in large cities there are more low-income households, but most of them are without cars, whereas in periurban and rural areas there are fewer low-income households, but most of them have cars. The two effects tend to offset each other, which explains why the incidence of car-related economic stress is relatively similar across different types of areas in the UK (Mattioli, 2017; Mattioli et al., 2018). Curl et al. (2018), for example, find a surprisingly high and increasing number of "forced car owners" in deprived urban neighborhoods in Glasgow (UK), many of which consist of "financially slipping drivers" who maintained a vehicle despite entering financial difficulties.

Overall, this suggests that transport affordability cannot be properly understood without considering similar questions of housing affordability, and the broader processes behind the sorting of income groups across different types of areas. These are likely to be country and context-specific, although there is a common trend toward the suburbanization of poverty in both the Global North and Global South (Bailey and Minton, 2018; Miraftab and Kudva, 2014). This leads to the displacement of low-income groups from accessible neighborhoods and toward car-dependent areas—as observed, e.g., in London (Cao and Hickman, 2018)—and has negative consequences on transport affordability.

While most European research on transport affordability focuses on the costs of motoring, issues of public transport affordability are also of relevance. A recent EU report argues that "the right to access to public transport—understood ... as both the physical availability of transport services within a reasonable distance and their affordability—is ... not being adequately implemented p.77" (Baptista and Marlier, 2020). Moreover, there is evidence to suggest that the affordability of public transport has deteriorated over time, both in countries with regulated and deregulated public systems. Germany's model of coordinated public transport provision (*Verkehrsverbund*) is internationally acclaimed for providing competitive service, and for accommodating increasing passenger numbers (Buehler et al., 2019). Yet comparative data shows that Germany is one of the EU countries with the highest share of low-income population that cannot afford regular use of public transport (10%) (Baptista and Marlier, 2020). Indeed, public transport fares in Germany have increased more rapidly than the price of other goods since the 1990s (Frey et al., 2020), just as *Verkehrsverbund* systems were being developed. Between 1990 and 2015 inflation-adjusted average fare change was +15% in Hamburg, +46% in Munich, +33% in the Rhine-Ruhr area (Buehler et al., 2019). Qualitative evidence suggests that price is an important barrier to public transport use for low-income people in Germany. Daubitz (2014, 2017) finds that, while there is a reduced monthly fare for the unemployed (*Sozialticket*) in Berlin, this costs more than the flat-rate amount to cover transport costs included in minimum income benefits, and the "working poor" are not eligible for reduced fares. As a result, many low-income people forego the *Sozialticket* entirely, opting for more expensive single tickets, walking and cycling, or foregoing trips entirely; others cut on necessities (e.g., clothes) in order to be able to afford the *Sozialticket*.

In the UK, the radical privatization and deregulation of local public transport (outside of London) in the 1980s has had adverse consequences for the low-income population, in terms of both reduced quality of service and increasing cost of fares (Bayliss et al., 2020). A recent study into the transport-related barriers to work that face households in poverty in low-income neighborhoods (Crisp et al., 2018) finds "a tendency to dismiss rail (train or tram) as a viable mode of for commuting because of its perceived expense" (p. 45) as well as evidence of people giving up on employment opportunities when the cost of commuting by public transport is too high relative to wages.

3.3 Accessibility poverty

According to Lucas et al. (2016) accessibility poverty "extends the concept of mobility poverty to consider in addition whether people can reach their basic daily activities within a reasonable time, ease and cost" (p. 356). A proper assessment of accessibility should consider not just the availability of transport resources (as considered under the mobility poverty sub-dimension), but also aspects such as cost and "the service quality and safety dimension of people's travel experiences (and) the temporal dimension in terms of long travel distances" (Lucas et al., 2016, p. 356).

In plain language, the idea is that one may have transport options available, and even high levels of travel activity, and still end up with a transport poverty problem. An illustration of this is the issue of car-related economic stress, whereby excessive transport costs tend to limit accessibility. Another possible mechanism is through time poverty (Giurge et al., 2020), i.e., when individuals need to spend such a long time traveling that it leads them to miss out on other important activities and/or to social isolation (Currie and Delbosc, 2010; Farber and Páez, 2011). In the remainder of this section, I will focus on this problem of transport-related time poverty, as an illustration of a broader issue of accessibility poverty.

Time poverty is an important issue in the Global South, where it is often linked to long travel times among the peripheral poor who have limited access to motorized modes (see e.g., Hernandez and Titheridge, 2016). In Europe, it is more often related to long commutes with motorized modes, including both cars and public transport. Mattioli's (2014) study of carless households in Great Britain finds a cluster of "public transport commuters" characterized by residence in large urban areas, high levels of travel activity, but also by the long amount of time spent traveling (ca. 8.5 h per week, as compared to a national average of 7.5), despite the fact that they do not travel much for reasons other than work or education. This suggests that in large urban areas, it is possible to live without a car and travel to work by public transport, but that seems to entail a considerable burden in terms of commuting time, and the risk of time poverty.

Whether by public transport, car or other modes, European studies have found an association between long commutes and a range of adverse effects. Based on UK data, Morris et al. (2020b) find an association between longer duration of commuting and less time spent on activities such as visiting others, exercise, volunteering and non-commute travel. Viry et al.'s (2009) study of Swiss metropolitan areas finds that commuting over long distances is associated with a reduced share of relatives and friends providing emotional and moral support. They argue that "increasing time spent traveling may foster a weaker involvement in the activities with significant others" (p. 131). There is also evidence of an association between long commutes, higher separation rates (Sandow, 2014) and lower fertility (Rüger and Viry, 2017), both of which are indicative of difficulties balancing commuting with family demands. Rüger et al. (2017) find that "long commutes are associated with substantially lower health-related quality of life and that this relation is well-accounted for by associated increases in stress, particularly among parents." Hansson et al. (2011) find an association between long duration of commuting in Sweden and a range of negative health outcomes, particularly for those traveling by public transport. While the direction of causality between long commutes and its correlates cannot always be firmly established, existing evidence is strongly suggestive that they have a range of negative impacts on health, wellbeing and quality of life.

The share of the population at risk of travel-related time poverty in Europe is far from negligible. Based on survey data from eight European cities, Joly and Vincent-Geslin (2016) find that 10–15% of the mobile population travels for more than 120 min a day (for all purposes combined). Based on a survey conducted in six European countries Lück and Ruppenthal (2010) estimate that 7% of the population aged 25–54 consists of "long-distance commuters" (i.e., traveling to and from work for at least 120 min at least three times a week). They are roughly evenly split between car and public transport users, and 64% of them reports that long-distance commuting is "necessary to have a job."

Broadly, the European literature suggests that the probability of spending an excessive amount of time traveling is higher for men, the full-time employed, singles and/or adults without children, as well as among people with higher income and education levels (e.g., Joly and Vincent-Geslin, 2016; Lück and Ruppenthal, 2010; Rüger et al., 2011)—i.e., groups that would not otherwise be considered at risk of social exclusion. This is consistent with research on time poverty, which stresses how some people can be "work rich but time poor" (Sullivan and Gershuny, 2004), what raises the question of what degree of priority it should be given to this dimension of transport poverty relative to the others. Perhaps for this reason, travel-related time poverty is the least explored dimension of transport poverty in European research.

3.4 Exposure to transport externalities

Up to this point in this chapter, I have focused on inequalities in the distribution of the benefits of mobility, i.e., access to services and opportunities and the resources that are required to achieve it. Traditionally, this is also what most European transport poverty research has focused on. Yet many have argued that a more holistic approach is required, i.e., one that integrates a consideration of the negative impacts of transport, and their inequitable distribution[h] (Curl et al., 2020; Lucas et al., 2016, 2019; Mattioli, 2016; Mullen and Marsden, 2016). Many of these are environmental in nature, which means that patterns of inequality have been investigated in (what is often seen as) the separate field of "environmental justice"[i] (Fuller and Brugge, 2020; Walker, 2012).

There are multiple burdens related to car-dominated transport systems, with perhaps the most dramatic being climate change. The impacts of global warming are very unequally distributed, both between and within countries, and tend to weigh most heavily on the most vulnerable nations and population groups (Alston, 2019). There is however a range of other negative impacts, many of which on health (Nieuwenhuijsen and Khreis, 2018) including, e.g., issues of road safety (Davis and Pilkington, 2019), exposure to noise (von Szombathely et al., 2018) and air pollution (Khreis et al., 2020). Across all of these areas, it is often observed that "perversely, the people who have the lowest access to vehicle ownership, less overall vehicle use, and poorer availability of other transport resources ... are most often also the worst impacted by the disbenefits of the transport system" (Martens et al., 2019, p. 3).

A thorough discussion of the distributional aspects of all the negative impacts of car-dominated transport systems is clearly beyond the scope of this chapter. For illustrative purposes, in the remainder of this section I focus on traffic-related air pollution (TARP) (Khreis et al., 2020), given its salience in the European public and political debate. TARP is associated with a range of adverse health effects, including most notably cardiovascular, cancer and respiratory diseases (Fox et al., 2020).

There is evidence of inequalities in exposure to TARP in Europe. For example, Flacke et al. (2016) find a positive correlation between exposure to PM_{10} and NO_2 and socioeconomic disadvantage at the neighborhood level in Dortmund, Germany. The Federal Environment Agency reviewed German studies on this topic, concluding that low-income individuals tend

[h] The term "externality" has a specific and technical meaning in mainstream economics and refers to both negative and positive externalities. It comes loaded with theoretical assumptions around which costs should be reflected in market prices, as well as normative assumptions derived from utilitarianism. In transport studies, however, it is sometimes used in a generic way to indicate the negative impacts of transport, notably on the environment. Lucas et al.'s (2016) use of the term, which I adopt here, reflects this more generic understanding.

[i] The term "environmental justice" originally referred to social movements contesting inequalities in the exposure to environmental hazards in the US (Fuller and Brugge, 2020). It has since developed into a broad field of research which focuses on the intertwining of environment and social difference, often adopting an explicitly normative perspective (Walker, 2012).

to be more exposed to air pollution (Frey et al., 2020). Fecht et al. (2015) find higher levels of air pollution in "ethnically mixed" neighborhoods in both England and the Netherlands. A recent systematic review of studies from Europe finds "good evidence ... that higher deprivation indices and low economic position are usually linked with higher levels of pollutants" (Fairburn et al., 2019). These associations are generally explained with reference to the tendency for socially disadvantaged groups to live in closer proximity to heavily trafficked roads, for reasons such as housing affordability (Fuller and Brugge, 2020). These patterns of exposure can be compounded by other vulnerability factors, as e.g., poorer general health and reduced ability to access good health care among low-income households (Walker, 2012).

Within this broad pattern, specific studies have yielded less straightforward results. For example, Fecht et al. (2015) find a net association between socioeconomic deprivation and TARP concentrations for neighborhoods in England, notably in London, but not in the Netherlands. Forastiere et al. (2007) find that in Rome (Italy), PM_{10} exposure is higher among persons with higher area-based income and socioeconomic status although the association between exposure and mortality is weaker for this privileged group, possibly due to less susceptibility. Temam et al. (2017) found "important heterogeneity" in the association between socioeconomic position and NO_2 exposure across 16 cities from eight Western European countries. A global systematic review (Hajat et al., 2015) has documented that while North American studies find a robust association between low socioeconomic status and exposure to TRAP, the evidence is more mixed for Europe.

The literature also points to a discrepancy between patterns of TARP generation and exposure in Europe, from both a social and spatial perspective. Barnes et al. (2019) find that in Great Britain the poorest neighborhoods are the most exposed but "emit the least NO_x and PM, while the least poor areas emitted the highest ... vehicle emissions per household through having higher vehicle ownership, owning more diesel vehicles and driving further," which highlights environmental justice issues. In the UK, there is a strong spatial dimension to this discrepancy, reflecting the concentration of poverty in urban areas, and the relative affluence of periurban and rural areas. There is a similar pattern within British urban areas, as e.g., in Leicester, where Jephcote et al. (2016) find that the "greatest polluters typically reside in affluent suburban communities located along the city's periphery, while those creating the least emissions reside in (less affluent) central locations, and most likely experience the largest associated health burdens."

This again highlights the importance of socio-spatial configurations, which vary between cities and countries. For example, in Rome the most affluent social groups tend to live in the city center and are thus more exposed to TRAP (Forastiere et al., 2007). Da Schio et al.'s (2019) study of Brussels (Belgium) finds no great overlap between the geography of air pollution (concentric, with higher levels in the city center) and that of socio-economic status (structured around a historical North-West vs South-East divide). Importantly, this suggests that patterns of inequalities in TRAP exposure might change along with structural changes in socio-spatial configurations. Bailey et al. (2019) investigate 12 UK cities where the process of "suburbanization of poverty" is most pronounced and conclude that this is likely to bring improvements in exposure to TRAP for low-income groups, particularly in cities like Leicester and Liverpool.[j]

Overall, the TRAP example suggests that exposure to transport externalities is characterized by complex socio-spatial patterns, which need to be investigated in a context-sensitive way.

4. The public and political debate on transport poverty in the EU: An illustrated example

In the EU, concerns around TRAP have led to the introduction of air quality standards, i.e., limits to the daily and annual concentrations of pollutants such as PM_{10} and NO_2. These are set at the EU level, with the threat of infringement proceedings and fines for non-compliant countries. Yet most member states systematically breach EU and World Health Organization limits (EC, 2019b), which has led to increasing pressure to implement effective policy measures. These include more stringent vehicle emission standards, but also "urban vehicle access regulations" (EC, 2013b), broadly defined as measures to regulate vehicular access to urban infrastructure (Ricci et al., 2017). This has only intensified since the "Dieselgate"

[j] Interestingly, the same process of suburbanization of poverty is likely to make problems of transport affordability and car-related economic stress worse, as discussed in Section 3.2. This highlights a conundrum for low-income households, whereby living in inner cities brings accessibility benefits, but also greater exposure to transport externalities, whereas moving to suburban areas tends to reduce such exposure, while also entailing the risk of forced car ownership and associated economic stress. This trade-off is to some extent inherent in urban agglomeration (da Schio et al., 2019; Higgins et al., 2019).

scandal of 2015 (Brand, 2016), which has highlighted the limitations of relying on technological innovation and vehicle fleet renewal for TRAP emission reductions.

In policy documents, the issue of TRAP exposure is predominantly framed as a public health and environmental issue (see e.g., DEFRA, 2019; EC, 2013c). While implications in terms of premature mortality, economic and ecosystem damage are emphasized, the distribution of the health impacts, and hence the *social* dimension of exposure to TRAP, is comparatively less prominent. This goes beyond health, including also negative impacts on wellbeing, psychological stress, and community interactions.

In the UK, the government strategy (DEFRA, 2019; DEFRA and DfT, 2017) includes a range of measures including "Clean Air Zones" (CAZ), i.e., areas where vehicles that do not meet minimum engine standards are subject to a charge or a fine (also referred to as "Low Emission Zones" in the international debate). However, many local authorities have shied away from introducing charges for private vehicles as part of CAZs due to concerns around the equity impacts of the proposed measures.

The city of Leeds (in Northern England) provides a good illustration of this dynamic. Like many urban areas in Europe, Leeds struggles with problems of air quality, with pollutant concentrations of NO_2 beyond EU thresholds, largely as a result of vehicle emissions. In 2017, the UK government identified Leeds as one of 35 local authorities with persistent exceedances required to undertake local action. Action plans ought to include the introduction of a "Clean Air Charging Zone," i.e., an area where vehicles that do not meet minimum engine standards would be subject daily charge, unless the local authorities could demonstrate that they will deliver compliance with alternative measures in the shortest time possible (DEFRA and DfT, 2017). Relatively early in the process, though, Leeds city council decided that CAZ would only affect buses, heavy goods vehicles and taxis. The option of charging private vehicles was rejected because "(it) would be likely to hit (Leeds') poorest communities the hardest as this is where many of the non-compliant cars will be based" (LCC, 2017, p. 13), as well as because of "the absence of practical transport alternatives for those affected" (p. 2). By the council's own admission, the exemption of private cars from charging limits the effectiveness of the scheme in reducing levels of air pollution (pp. 12–13).

Along with a cost-benefit analysis, Leeds City Council undertook a "distributional analysis" to investigate whether the different CAZ options would disproportionately affect low-income social groups (LCC, 2018, pp. 28–38). The results showed that the benefits of air quality improvements would be highly progressive (being greater in lower-income areas), particularly if private vehicles were charged. At the same time, it found that charging private vehicles would have a regressive impact in terms of transport affordability, as low-income households are more likely to live within the charging area and (at least those of them who own cars) to have older, non-compliant vehicles. The analysis however did not explicitly discuss the trade-offs between the various distributional impacts identified. In the end, charging private vehicles was rejected because of the negative results of the cost-benefit analysis, as well as concerns around transport affordability.

The case of Leeds parallels what happened in other British cities. In Bristol for example, the mayor has opposed the charging of private vehicles on the grounds that it "would disproportionately affect families from poorer households" (Cameron, 2020). The mayor of Manchester has similarly supported the exemption of private vehicles from the local CAZ scheme, arguing that "it would have been disproportionate to hit people with often the least ability to change their car," to which environmental local groups have countered that "dirty air disproportionately impacts the health of the poorest communities, children and the elderly"[k] (Pidd, 2019).

From the perspective of this chapter, the policy debate on CAZs in Leeds (and other British cities) illustrates a rather selective consideration of transport-related inequalities. Arguably, a more holistic approach is required, i.e., one that takes into account the multiple facets of transport poverty. A first step here is to acknowledge that policy measures have impacts on all dimensions of transport poverty, and that these can be contradictory. For illustration purposes, I discuss these below with reference to the introduction of CAZs in British cities.

Vehicle access regulations are precisely aimed at reducing *exposure to transport externalities*, namely TRAP. In a context like the UK, this would be to the benefit of lower-income and ethnic minority groups in urban areas, which are typically the most exposed to dangerous air pollution while bearing the least responsibility for it (Barnes et al., 2019; Fecht et al., 2015; Jephcote et al., 2016). At the time of writing, the COVID-19 crisis is highlighting the seriousness of this issue, with emerging epidemiological

[k] At the time of writing, CAZ plans for most English cities have been delayed (or scrapped entirely), as traffic reductions during the COVID19 crisis have ensured compliance with legal air pollution limits (Mistlin, 2020).

evidence of a net association between long-term PM2.5 exposure and higher COVID-19 mortality rates at the area level, due to the fact that both the coronavirus disease and fine particles adversely affect the respiratory and cardiovascular system[l] (Wu et al., 2020). It has been suggested that this could partly explain why people from minority ethnic groups account for a disproportionate share of critically ill Covid-19 patients in the UK (Carrington, 2020). Overall, it is likely that effective CAZs would contribute to a reduction of inequalities in TRAP exposure in the UK.

At the same time, vehicle access regulations that charge private vehicles raise issues of *transport affordability*. Research reviewed in Section 3.2 suggests that 7–9% of UK households struggle to afford car-related expenses (Mattioli, 2017; Mattioli et al., 2018), and road charging schemes could exacerbate hardship for this group. Low-income motorists are also more likely to own those older vehicles that are subject to charges (Parkhurst, 2019), and less able to afford the purchase of a new vehicle that is compliant with regulations. It must be remembered, however, than an even larger share of the low-income population, particularly in urban areas, does not rely on cars for their daily mobility and would thus be largely unaffected by a charging scheme.

Regarding *mobility poverty*, vehicle access regulations where certain types of vehicles are not permitted to enter the zone (such as the "low emission zone" scheme proposed in Edinburgh—see Morton et al., 2018) might have adverse effects on those who rely on such vehicles for traveling to destinations on the other side of the "clean air zone" boundary, and have few viable alternatives to car use. Again, it must be kept in mind that a non-negligible share of the population in UK urban areas does not own cars, particularly among low-income and ethnic minority groups.[m] If CAZ schemes are accompanied by measures to improve the viability of alternative modes (as recommended by UK national guidance), they might even mitigate mobility poverty among these groups. More broadly, CAZ schemes can result in a modal shift toward public transport, increasing patronage, revenue and thus providing the opportunity for investment in service expansion.

In terms of *accessibility poverty*, vehicle access regulations might raise issues concerning access to key services and opportunities that are located on the

[l] Pozzer et al. (2020) estimate that 15% of COVID-19 deaths worldwide could be attributed to long-term exposure to ambient fine particulate air pollution, a share that increases to 19% in Europe, 26% in Germany and 29% in the Czech Republic.

[m] In 2011 32.1% of households in Leeds and 39.9% in Edinburgh did not have a car available (ONS—Office for National Statistics, 2021; National Records of Scotland, 2013).

other side of the "clean air zone" boundary. These could arise from affordability issues, but also from travel-related time poverty. For example, if vehicle access regulations lead some commuters to shift from car to public transport, this might result in increased travel time and increased risk of time poverty for at least some of them.

Overall, this suggests that there are multiple and potentially contradictory impacts of measures such as vehicle access regulations on transport poverty, with various trade-offs between them. This certainly complicates the assessment of what an equitable policy would look like. What the British CAZ debate shows, however, is that some of these impacts are emphasized, while others are overlooked. For example, the distributional effects of improving air quality, while occasionally acknowledged, tend to be absent from the public debate. The negative impacts in terms of affordability and accessibility on specific groups (low-income motorists with older vehicles) are given much prominence, while the potentially positive impacts on other groups (carless households) tend to be neglected. This leads to a framing of the CAZ debate as a conflict between "environmental" and (certain) "social" issues. When framed in these terms, the debate is unlikely to lead to outcomes that alleviate transport poverty in any meaningful way. Also, as Lamb et al. (2020) point out, actors with vested interests (or otherwise supportive of the status quo) can use social justice issues as a pretext to oppose sustainable transport policies.

A better approach would follow the following principles. First, aim for a holistic consideration of the multiple dimensions of transport poverty, and of the diversity of social groups that are affected, avoiding the implicit prioritization of some of them over others. Second, acknowledge that there is an important social and distributional dimension to issues that are commonly seen as "environmental" or health-related. Finally, avoid framing the discussion in terms of "winners and losers" from specific policy interventions, as this tends to tacitly assume that the status quo is fair, and that there are no equity issues to address in the existing situation (as cogently argued by Martens et al., 2019).

5. Conclusions

The literature reviewed in this chapter shows that transport poverty is a multi-faceted and complex problem, which is hard to reduce to a single concept or indicator, and hard to break down into non-overlapping sub-dimensions. Taken together, the various manifestations of transport poverty affect a wide and diverse set of population groups. Lucas et al. (2016), for example, estimate that more than half of UK households are affected by issues of accessibility poverty, transport affordability, or exposure to transport externalities. This breadth makes transport poverty a highly relevant issue for research and practice, but also one that is challenging to apprehend in a comprehensive way. This author's impression is that perhaps too much effort has gone into trying to identify a single definition or metric of transport poverty, and not enough into exploring its multidimensionality and the trade-offs between the different dimensions. This remains a promising area for future research.

A key message of this chapter is that there is much to be gained from framing transport poverty in the context of car dependence. As countries transition from low to high levels of motorization, the predominant forms of transport poverty change, with the emergence of new problems such as car-related economic stress and increasing health and environmental externalities. Europe is in a somewhat peculiar position in this respect, as it is more car dependent than most other world regions, but less so than North America and Australia, where much of the early research on car dependence was conducted. This perhaps tends to magnify the diversity of transport poverty's manifestations.

These nuances notwithstanding, the empirical evidence reviewed in this chapter confirms that most forms of transport poverty in Europe are linked in one way or another to the nature of car-dominated transport systems. In such context, car use is often an essential precondition for access to services and opportunities, although not always to the same extent. This situation disadvantages those with limited access to cars, while also leading others to adopt car-dependent travel patterns that take up too much of their income, or too much of their time. Finally, car use has a range of negative environment- and health-related impacts. These have serious consequences on human well-being and are unequally distributed, often to the detriment of those who are the least responsible for them.

This situation is rife with opportunities for conflict, as illustrated in this chapter by the controversies surrounding vehicle access regulations in UK cities. These are common across Europe, as attested, e.g., by the heated discussions on measures such as road space reallocation and fuel tax increases. The example of the British Clean Air Zones discussed here illustrates a tendency to use equity arguments in a selective or opportunistic way. When this happens, transport poverty problems are unlikely to be addressed in just or fair way. Arguably, a more holistic approach is needed, i.e., one that properly takes into account the multiple dimensions of transport poverty and the trade-offs between them.

Ultimately, this also requires a willingness to recognize that transport problems, far from being a purely technical matter, are inherently political (Kębłowski and Bassens, 2018; Mattioli et al., 2020). As such, there is scope for legitimate disagreement on the normative principles to adopt when assessing patterns of inequality, and when determining what to do about them. What is essential is that the full spectrum of transport poverty issues is duly considered, and that these are subject to an informed and open societal debate.

References

Allen, J., Farber, S., 2019. Sizing up transport poverty: a national scale accounting of low-income households suffering from inaccessibility in Canada, and what to do about it. Transp. Policy 74, 214–223.

Alston, P., 2019. Climate Change and Poverty. Report of the Special Rapporteur on Extreme Poverty and Human Rights. UN, Human Rights Council, Special Rapporteur on Extreme Poverty and Human Rights, Geneva.

Bailey, N., Minton, J., 2018. The suburbanisation of poverty in British cities, 2004–16: extent, processes, and nature. Urban Geogr. 39 (6), 892–915.

Bailey, N., Stewart, J.L., Minton, J., 2019. The welfare consequences of the suburbanisation of poverty in UK cities: air pollution and school quality. Urban Dev. Issues 61 (1), 15–32.

Baptista, I., Marlier, E., 2020. Access to Essential Services for People on Low Incomes in Europe. An Analysis of Policies in 35 Countries. European Commission/European Social Policy Network, Brussels.

Barnes, J.H., Chatterton, T.J., Longhurst, J.W., 2019. Emissions vs exposure: increasing injustice from road traffic-related air pollution in the United Kingdom. Transp. Res. Part D: Transp. Environ. 73, 56–66.

Bastiaanssen, J., Johnson, D., Lucas, K., 2020. Does transport help people to gain employment? A systematic review and meta-analysis of the empirical evidence. Transp. Rev. 40 (5), 607–628.

Bayliss, K., Mattioli, G., Steinberger, J., 2020. Inequality, poverty and the privatization of essential services: a "systems of provision" study of water, energy and local buses in the UK. Compet. Change.

Belton-Chevallier, L., Motte-Baumvol, B., Fol, S., Jouffe, Y., 2018. Coping with the costs of car dependency: a system of expedients used by low-income households on the outskirts of Dijon and Paris. Transp. Policy 65, 79–88.

Benevenuto, R., Caulfield, B., 2019. Poverty and transport in the global south: an overview. Transp. Policy 79, 115–124.

Birch, D., Bullock, D., 2019. DfT evidence on public attitudes to sharing. In: Commission on Travel Demand Shared Mobility Inquiry: Evidence Session 3, 18th June 2019. (Retrieved from: https://www.creds.ac.uk/commission-on-travel-demand-shared-mobility-inquiry-evidence-session-3/, last accessed on 4 March 2021).

Brand, C., 2016. Beyond 'dieselgate': implications of unaccounted and future air pollutant emissions and energy use for cars in the United Kingdom. Energy Policy 97, 1–12.

Buehler, R., Pucher, J., Gerike, R., Götschi, T., 2017. Reducing car dependence in the heart of Europe: lessons from Germany, Austria, and Switzerland. Transp. Rev. 37 (1), 4–28.

Buehler, R., Pucher, J., Dümmler, O., 2019. Verkehrsverbund: the evolution and spread of fully integrated regional public transport in Germany, Austria, and Switzerland. Int. J. Sustain. Transp. 13 (1), 36–50.

Büttner, B., Wulfhorst, G., Crozet, Y., Mercier, A., 2013. The impact of sharp increases in mobility costs analysed by means of the vulnerability assessment. In: World Conference on Transport Research, Rio de Janeiro.

Cameron, A., 2020. Bristol clean air zone: charging may not be needed in wake of coronavirus. In: Bristol Live. 19 August 2020. [Retrieved from https://www.bristolpost.co.uk/news/bristol-news/bristol-clean-air-zone-charging-4439713, last accessed on 14 October 2020].

Cao, M., Hickman, R., 2018. Car dependence and housing affordability: an emerging social deprivation issue in London? Urban Stud. 55 (10), 2088–2105.

Carrington, D., 2020. Covid-19 impact on ethnic minorities linked to housing and air pollution. In: The Guardian. 19 July 2020. [Retrieved from https://www.theguardian.com/world/2020/jul/19/covid-19-impact-on-ethnic-minorities-linked-to-housing-and-air-pollution, last accessed on 14 October 2020].

Cass, N., Shove, E., Urry, J., 2005. Social exclusion, mobility and access. Sociol. Rev. 53 (3), 539–555.

Churchill, S.A., Smyth, R., 2019. Transport poverty and subjective wellbeing. Transp. Res. A Policy Pract. 124, 40–54.

Cochez, N., Durieux, E., Levy, D., 2015. Vulnérabilité énergétique. Loin des pôles urbains, chauffage et carburant pèsent fortement dans le budget. Insee Premiere, p. 1530.

Coulombel, N., 2018. Why housing and transport costs should always be considered together: a monocentric analysis of prudential measures in housing access. Transp. Policy 65, 89–105.

Creutzig, F., Javaid, A., Koch, N., Knopf, B., Mattioli, G., Edenhofer, O., 2020. Adjust urban and rural road pricing for fair mobility. Nat. Clim. Chang. 10 (7), 591–594.

Crisp, R., Ferrari, E., Gore, T., Green, S., McCarthy, L., Rae, A., Reeve, K., Stevens, M., 2018. Tackling Transport-Related Barriers to Employment in Low-Income Neighbourhoods. Joseph Rowntree Foundation.

Curl, A., Clark, J., Kearns, A., 2018. Household car adoption and financial distress in deprived urban communities: a case of forced car ownership? Transp. Policy 65, 61–71.

Curl, A., Watkins, A., McKerchar, C., Exeter, D., Macmillan, A., 2020. Social Impact Assessment of Mode Shift. Waka Kotahi NZ Transport Agency Research Report 666.

Currie, G. (Ed.), 2011. New Perspectives and Methods in Transport and Social Exclusion Research. Emerald.

Currie, G., Delbosc, A., 2010. Modelling the social and psychological impacts of transport disadvantage. Transportation 37 (6), 953–966.

Currie, G., Delbosc, A., 2011. Mobility vs. affordability as motivations for car-ownership choice in urban fringe, low-income Australia. In: Lucas, K., Blumenberg, E., Weinberger, R. (Eds.), Auto Motives: Understanding Car Use Behaviours. Emerald, Bingley, pp. 193–208.

Currie, G., Senbergs, Z., 2007. Exploring Forced Car Ownership in Metropolitan Melbourne. Australasian Transport Research Forum.

Currie, G., Stanley, J.R., Stanley, J. (Eds.), 2007. No Way to Go: Transport and Social Disadvantage in Australian Communities. Monash University Publishing, Clayton.

da Schio, N., Boussauw, K., Sansen, J., 2019. Accessibility versus air pollution: a geography of externalities in the Brussels agglomeration. Cities 84, 178–189.

Daubitz, S., 2014. Die "Captives" sind die eigentlichen Mobilitätspioniere. Zum Innovationspotential einer marginalisierten Bevölkerungsgruppe. In: Schwedes, O. (Ed.), Öffentliche Mobilität. Springer VS, Wiesbaden.

Daubitz, S., 2017. Mobilität und soziale Exklusion: Ein Plädoyer für ein zielgruppenspezifisches Mobilitätsmanagement. In: Wilde, et al. (Eds.), Verkehr und Mobilität zwischen Alltagspraxis und Planungstheorie. Springer VS, Wiesbaden.
Davis, A., Pilkington, P., 2019. A public health approach to assessing road safety equity—the RoSE cycle. In: Lucas, K., Martens, K., Di Ciommo, F., Dupont-Kieffer, A. (Eds.), Measuring Transport Equity. Elsevier, pp. 159–170.
Davis, A., Hirsch, D., Padley, M., Shepherd, C., 2018. A Minimum Income Standard for the UK 2008–2018: Continuity and Change. Joseph Rowntree Foundation.
DEFRA, DfT, 2017. UK Plan for Tackling Roadside Nitrogen Dioxide Concentrations. Detailed Plan. Department for Environment, Food and Rural Affairs & Department for Transport.
DEFRA—Department for Environment, Food and Rural Affairs, 2019. Clean Air Strategy 2019. DEFRA, London.
DfT—Department for Transport, 2017. Journey Time Statistics 2015 (Revised). DfT.
DfT—Department for Transport, 2019. Journey Time Statistics, England; 2017. DfT.
Di Ciommo, F., Shiftan, Y., 2017. Transport equity analysis. Transp. Rev. 37 (2), 139–151.
Diaz Olvera, L., Plat, D., Pochet, P., 2003. Transportation conditions and access to services in a context of urban sprawl and deregulation. The case of Dar es Salaam. Transp. Policy 10 (4), 287–298.
Dodson, J., Sipe, N., 2007. Oil vulnerability in the Australian city: assessing socioeconomic risks from higher urban fuel prices. Urban Stud. 44 (1), 37–62.
EC—European Commission, 2007. Special Eurobarometer 279 "Poverty and Exclusion". European Commission.
EC—European Commission, 2011. Future of Transport—Analytical Report. Flash Eurobarometer Series #312.
EC—European Commission, 2013a. Special Eurobarometer 406. Attitudes of Europeans Towards Urban Mobility. European Commission.
EC—European Commission, 2013b. A Call for Smarter Urban Vehicle Access Regulations. SWD(2013) 526 final. Brussels, 17.12.2013.
EC—European Commission, 2013c. A Clean Air Programme for Europe. COM(2013) 918 final, Brussels, 18.12.2013.
EC—European Commission, 2014. Special Eurobarometer 422a—Quality of Transport. European Commission.
EC—European Commission, 2019a. EU Transport in Figures—Statistical Pocketbook 2019. Publications Office of the European Union, Luxembourg.
EC—European Commission, 2019b. The First Clean Air Outlook. COM(2018) 446 final/2, Brussels, 30.1.2019.
Elldér, E., Solá, A.G., Larsson, A., 2012. Featured graphic. Spatial inequality and workplace accessibility: the case of a major hospital in Göteborg, Sweden. Environ. Plan A. 44 (10), 2295–2297. https://doi.org/10.1068/a44627.
Fairburn, J., Schüle, S.A., Dreger, S., Karla Hilz, L., Bolte, G., 2019. Social inequalities in exposure to ambient air pollution: a systematic review in the WHO European region. Int. J. Environ. Res. Public Health 16 (17), 3127.
Farber, S., Páez, A., 2011. Running to stay in place: the time-use implications of automobile oriented land-use and travel. J. Transp. Geogr. 19 (4), 782–793.
Fecht, D., Fischer, P., Fortunato, L., Hoek, G., de Hoogh, K., Marra, M., Hansell, A., 2015. Associations between air pollution and socioeconomic characteristics, ethnicity and age profile of neighbourhoods in England and the Netherlands. Environ. Pollut. 198, 201–210.
Fiorello, D., Martino, A., Zani, L., Christidis, P., Navajas-Cawood, E., 2016. Mobility data across the EU 28 member states: results from an extensive CAWI survey. Transp. Res. Procedia 14, 1104–1113.

Flacke, J., Schüle, S.A., Köckler, H., Bolte, G., 2016. Mapping environmental inequalities relevant for health for informing urban planning interventions—a case study in the city of Dortmund, Germany. Int. J. Environ. Res. Public Health 13 (7), 711.
Forastiere, F., Stafoggia, M., Tasco, C., Picciotto, S., Agabiti, N., Cesaroni, G., Perucci, C.A., 2007. Socioeconomic status, particulate air pollution, and daily mortality: differential exposure or differential susceptibility. Am. J. Ind. Med. 50 (3), 208–216.
Fox, M., Koehler, K., Johnson, N., 2020. Established and emerging effects of traffic-related air pollution. In: Khreis, H., Nieuwenhuijsen, M., Zietsman, J., Ramani, T. (Eds.), Traffic-Related Air Pollution. Elsevier, pp. 207–228.
Fransen, K., Deruyter, G., De Maeyer, P., 2018. The impact of driver's license ownership on unemployed job seekers' access to job openings: assessing the driver's license at school project in Flanders. Case Stud. Transp. Policy 6 (4), 695–705.
Frey, K., Burger, A., Dziekan, K., Bunge, C., Lünenbürger, B., 2020. Verkehrswende für Alle. So erreichen wir eine sozial gerechtere und umweltverträglichere Mobilität. Umweltbundesamt.
Fuller, C.H., Brugge, D., 2020. Environmental justice. Disproportionate impacts of transportation on vulnerable communities. In: Khreis, H., Nieuwenhuijsen, M., Zietsman, J., Ramani, T. (Eds.), Traffic-Related Air Pollution. Elsevier, pp. 495–510.
Fusco, A., Guio, A.C., Marlier, E., 2013. Building a material deprivation index in a multinational context: lessons from the EU experience. In: Berenger, V., Bresson, F. (Eds.), Poverty and Social Exclusion around the Mediterranean Sea. Springer, Boston, pp. 43–71.
Gandelman, N., Serebrisky, T., Suárez-Alemán, A., 2019. Household spending on transport in Latin America and the Caribbean: a dimension of transport affordability in the region. J. Transp. Geogr. 79, 102482.
Gilbertson, J., Grimsley, M., Green, G., 2012. Psychosocial routes from housing investment to health: evidence from England's home energy efficiency scheme. Energy Policy 49, 122–133.
Giurge, L.M., Whillans, A.V., West, C., 2020. Why time poverty matters for individuals, organisations and nations. Nat. Hum. Behav. 4, 993–1003. https://doi.org/10.1038/s41562-020-0920-z.
Hajat, A., Hsia, C., O'Neill, M.S., 2015. Socioeconomic disparities and air pollution exposure: a global review. Curr. Environ. Health Rep. 2 (4), 440–450.
Hansson, E., Mattisson, K., Björk, J., Östergren, P.O., Jakobsson, K., 2011. Relationship between commuting and health outcomes in a cross-sectional population survey in southern Sweden. BMC Public Health 11 (1), 834.
Hernandez, D.O., Titheridge, H., 2016. Mobilities of the periphery: informality, access and social exclusion in the urban fringe in Colombia. J. Transp. Geogr. 55, 152–164.
Higgins, C.D., Adams, M.D., Réquia, W.J., Mohamed, M., 2019. Accessibility, air pollution, and congestion: capturing spatial trade-offs from agglomeration in the property market. Land Use Policy 84, 177–191.
Jaboeuf, R., Nimal, E., Sevenet, M., 2016. The two faces of energy poverty: Can we talk about energy need in transport sector? In: DEMAND Conference 2016, Lancaster.
Jeekel, H., 2013. The Car-Dependent Society: A European Perspective. Routledge.
Jephcote, C., Chen, H., Ropkins, K., 2016. Implementation of the polluter-pays principle (PPP) in local transport policy. J. Transp. Geogr. 55, 58–71.
Joly, I., Vincent-Geslin, S., 2016. Intensive travel time: an obligation or a choice? Eur. Transp. Res. Rev. 8 (1), 10.
Jones, P., Lucas, K., 2012. The social consequences of transport decision-making: clarifying concepts, synthesising knowledge and assessing implications. J. Transp. Geogr. 21, 4–16.

Kębłowski, W., Bassens, D., 2018. "All transport problems are essentially mathematical": the uneven resonance of academic transport and mobility knowledge in Brussels. Urban Geogr. 39 (3), 413–437.
Kesteloot, C., 2008. Urban socio-spatial configurations and the future of European cities. In: Kazepov, Y. (Ed.), Cities of Europe: Changing Contexts, Local Arrangement and the Challenge to Urban Cohesion. Wiley-Blackwell, pp. 123–148.
Khreis, H., Nieuwenhuijsen, M.J., Zietsman, J., Ramani, T., 2020. Traffic-related air pollution: emissions, human exposures, and health: an introduction. In: Khreis, H., Nieuwenhuijsen, M., Zietsman, J., Ramani, T. (Eds.), Traffic-Related Air Pollution. Elsevier, pp. 1–21.
King, D.A., Smart, M.J., Manville, M., 2019. The poverty of the carless: toward universal auto access. J. Plan. Educ. Res. 0739456X18823252.
Lagrell, E., Thulin, E., Vilhelmson, B., 2018. Accessibility strategies beyond the private car: a study of voluntarily carless families with young children in Gothenburg. J. Transp. Geogr. 72, 218–227.
Lamb, W.F., Mattioli, G., Levi, S., Roberts, J.T., Capstick, S., Creutzig, F., Steinberger, J.K., 2020. Discourses of climate delay. Glob. Sustain. 3, 1–5.
LCC—Leeds City Council, 2017. Report of the Director of Resources and Housing, the Director of City Development and the Director of Public Health to Executive Board: Improving Air Quality within the City. 13th December 2017.
LCC—Leeds City Council, 2018. Clean Air Solution for Leeds. Outline Business Case—Economic Case. Leeds City Council. 17th July 2018.
Leung, A., Burke, M., Cui, J., 2018. The tale of two (very different) cities–mapping the urban transport oil vulnerability of Brisbane and Hong Kong. Transp. Res. Part D: Transp. Environ. 65, 796–816.
Liao, Y., Gil, J., Pereira, R.H., Yeh, S., Verendel, V., 2020. Disparities in travel times between car and transit: spatiotemporal patterns in cities. Sci. Rep. 10 (1), 1–12.
Liddell, C., Morris, C., 2010. Fuel poverty and human health: a review of recent evidence. Energy Policy 38, 2987–2997.
Lovelace, R., Philips, I., 2014. The 'oil vulnerability' of commuter patterns: a case study from Yorkshire and the Humber, UK. Geoforum 51, 169–182.
Lucas, K. (Ed.), 2004. Running on Empty: Transport, Social Exclusion and Environmental Justice. Policy Press.
Lucas, K., Le Vine, S., 2009. The car in British Society. In: Working Paper 2: Literature Review. RAC Foundation, London.
Lucas, K., Porter, G., 2016. Mobilities and livelihoods in urban development contexts: introduction. J. Transp. Geogr. 55, 129–131.
Lucas, K., Mattioli, G., Verlinghieri, E., Guzman, A., 2016. Transport poverty and its adverse social consequences. Proc. Inst. Civ. Eng. Transp. 169 (6), 353–365.
Lucas, K., Martens, K., Di Ciommo, F., Dupont-Kieffer, A. (Eds.), 2019. Measuring Transport Equity. Elsevier.
Lück, D., Ruppenthal, S., 2010. Insights into mobile living: spread, appearances and characteristics. In: Schneider, N.F., Collet, B. (Eds.), Mobile Living Across Europe II: Causes and Consequences of Job-Related Spatial Mobility in Cross-National Comparison. Verlag Barbara Budrich, pp. 37–68.
Marsden, G., Anable, J., Bray, J., Seagriff, E., Spurling, N., 2019. Shared Mobility: Where Now? Where Next? The Second Report of the Commission on Travel Demand. Centre for Research into Energy Demand Solutions, Oxford.
Martens, K., 2016. Transport Justice: Designing Fair Transportation Systems. Routledge.
Martens, K., Bastiaanssen, J., 2019. An index to measure accessibility poverty risk. In: Lucas, K., Martens, K., Di Ciommo, F., Dupont-Kieffer, A. (Eds.), Measuring Transport Equity. Elsevier, pp. 39–55.

Martens, K., Bastiaanssen, J., Lucas, K., 2019. Measuring transport equity: key components, framings and metrics. In: Lucas, K., Martens, K., Di Ciommo, F., Dupont-Kieffer, A. (Eds.), Measuring Transport Equity. Elsevier, pp. 13–36.
Mattioli, G., 2013. Where Sustainable Transport and Social Exclusion Meet: Households Without Cars and Car Dependence in Germany and Great Britain (Doctoral dissertation, PhD thesis). University of Milan-Bicocca.
Mattioli, G., 2014. Where sustainable transport and social exclusion meet: households without cars and car dependence in Great Britain. J. Environ. Policy Plan. 16 (3), 379–400.
Mattioli, G., 2016. Transport needs in a climate-constrained world. A novel framework to reconcile social and environmental sustainability in transport. Energy Res. Soc. Sci. 18, 118–128.
Mattioli, G., 2017. "Forced car ownership" in the UK and Germany: socio-spatial patterns and potential economic stress impacts. Soc. Incl. 5 (4), 147–160.
Mattioli, G., Colleoni, M., 2016. Transport disadvantage, car dependence and urban form. In: Pucci, P., Colleoni, M. (Eds.), Understanding Mobilities for Designing Contemporary Cities. Springer, Cham, pp. 171–190.
Mattioli, G., Lucas, K., Marsden, G., 2017. Transport poverty and fuel poverty in the UK: from analogy to comparison. Transp. Policy 59, 93–105.
Mattioli, G., Wadud, Z., Lucas, K., 2018. Vulnerability to fuel price increases in the UK: a household level analysis. Transp. Res. A Policy Pract. 113, 227–242.
Mattioli, G., Philips, I., Anable, J., Chatterton, T., 2019. Vulnerability to motor fuel price increases: socio-spatial patterns in England. J. Transp. Geogr. 78, 98–114.
Mattioli, G., Roberts, C., Steinberger, J.K., Brown, A., 2020. The political economy of car dependence: a systems of provision approach. Energy Res. Soc. Sci. 66, 101486.
Miraftab, F., Kudva, N. (Eds.), 2014. Cities of the Global South Reader. Routledge.
Mistlin, A., 2020. Delays to clean air zones in English cities 'put wellbeing at risk. In: The Guardian. 18 September 2020. [Retrieved from https://www.theguardian.com/environment/2020/sep/18/delays-clean-air-zones-english-cities-wellbeing-risk-birmingham-leeds-manchester-covid?CMP=share_btn_tw, last accessed on 14 October 2020].
Morris, E.A., Blumenberg, E., Guerra, E., 2020a. Does lacking a car put the brakes on activity participation? Private vehicle access and access to opportunities among low-income adults. Transp. Res. A Policy Pract. 136, 375–397.
Morris, E.A., Ettema, D., Zhou, Y., 2020b. Which activities do those with long commutes forego, and should we care? Transp. Res. Interdiscip. Perspect. 5, 100119.
Morton, C., Mattioli, G., Anable, J., 2018. A framework for assessing spatial vulnerability to the introduction of low emission zones: a case study of Edinburgh, Scotland. In: 50th Annual Universities' Transport Study Group.
Mullen, C., Marsden, G., 2016. Mobility justice in low carbon energy transitions. Energy Res. Soc. Sci. 18, 109–117.
Mullen, C., Marsden, G., Philips, I., 2020. Seeking protection from precarity? Relationships between transport needs and insecurity in housing and employment. Geoforum 109, 4–13.
National Records of Scotland, 2013. Figure 22: Households With Access to One or More Cars or Vans by Council Area, Scotland, 2001 and 2011. Scotland's Census. [Retrieved from: https://www.scotlandscensus.gov.uk/documents/censusresults/release2a/rel2asbfigure22.pdf, last accessed on 15 October 2020].
Newman, P., Kenworthy, J., 1999. Sustainability and Cities: Overcoming Automobile Dependence. Island Press.
Nieuwenhuijsen, M., Khreis, H., 2018. Integrating Human Health into Urban and Transport Planning. Springer, Cham, Switzerland.

ONPE, 2014. Premier rapport de l'ONPE. Définitions, indicateurs, premiers résultats et recommendations. Observatoire National de la Precarité énergétique.

ONS—Office for National Statistics, 2021. Table KS404EW—2011 Census: Car or Van Availability, Local Authorities in England and Wales. (undated). [Retrieved from https://www.ons.gov.uk/file?uri=/peoplepopulationandcommunity/populationandmigration/populationestimates/datasets/2011censuskeystatisticsforlocalauthoritiesinenglandandwales/r21ewrttableks404ewladv1_tcm77-290721.xls, last accessed on 15 October 2020].

Ortar, N., 2018. Dealing with energy crises: working and living arrangements in peri-urban France. Transp. Policy 65, 72–78.

Parkhurst, G., 2019. The in(justice) of clean air zones. In: 51th Annual Universities' Transport Study Group, Leeds.

Pereira, R.H., Schwanen, T., Banister, D., 2017. Distributive justice and equity in transportation. Transp. Rev. 37 (2), 170–191.

Pidd, H., 2019. Burnham criticised over exemption for private cars from clean air charge. In: The Guardian. 26 February 2019 [Retrieved from https://www.theguardian.com/environment/2019/feb/26/andy-burnham-manchester-cop-out-exempting-private-cars-from-clean-air-zone-charge, last accessed on 14 October 2020].

Pojani, D., Stead, D., 2017. The Urban Transport Crisis in Emerging Economies. Springer, Cham.

Polacchini, A., Orfeuil, J.-P., 1999. Les dépenses des ménages franciliens pour le logement et les transports. Recherche Transp. Sécur. 63, 31–46.

Pooley, C., 2016. Mobility, transport and social inclusion: lessons from history. Soc. Incl. 4 (3), 100–109.

Pozzer, A., Dominici, F., Haines, A., Witt, C., Münzel, T., Lelieveld, J., 2020. Regional and global contributions of air pollution to risk of death from COVID-19. Cardiovasc. Res. 116 (14), 2247–2253.

Prakash, K., Churchill, S.A., Smyth, R., 2020. Petrol prices and subjective wellbeing. Energy Econ. 90, 104867.

Pucher, J., Buehler, R., 2008. Making cycling irresistible: lessons from the Netherlands, Denmark and Germany. Transp. Rev. 28 (4), 495–528.

Rachele, J.N., Sugiyama, T., Turrell, G., Healy, A.M., Sallis, J.F., 2018. Automobile dependence: a contributing factor to poorer health among lower-income households. J. Transp. Health 8, 123–128.

Ricci, A., Gaggi, S., Enei, R., Tamassini, M., Fioretto, M., 2017. Study on Urban Vehicle Access Regulations. (Retrieved from: https://ec.europa.eu/transport/sites/transport/files/uvar_final_report_august_28.pdf, last accessed on 16 October 2020).

Rock, S., Ahern, A., Caulfield, B., 2016. The economic boom, bust and transport inequity in suburban Dublin, Ireland. Res. Transp. Econ. 57, 32–43.

Rubin, O., Bertolini, L., 2016. Social and environmental sustainability of travelling within family networks. Transp. Policy 52, 72–80.

Rüger, H., Viry, G., 2017. Work-related travel over the life course and its link to fertility: a comparison between four European countries. Eur. Sociol. Rev. 33 (5), 645–660.

Rüger, H., Feldhaus, M., Becker, K.S., Schlegel, M., 2011. Circular job-related spatial mobility in Germany: comparative analyses of two representative surveys on the forms, prevalence and relevance in the context of partnership and family development. Comp. Popul. Stud. 36 (1).

Rüger, H., Pfaff, S., Weishaar, H., Wiernik, B.M., 2017. Does perceived stress mediate the relationship between commuting and health-related quality of life? Transp. Res. F 50, 100–108.

Salonen, M., Toivonen, T., 2013. Modelling travel time in urban networks: comparable measures for private car and public transport. J. Transp. Geogr. 31, 143–153.

Sandow, E., 2014. Til work do us part: the social fallacy of long-distance commuting. Urban Stud. 51 (3), 526–543.
Shi, Y., Blainey, S., Sun, C., Jing, P., 2020. A literature review on accessibility using bibliometric analysis techniques. J. Transp. Geogr. 87, 102810.
Silva, C., Pinho, P., 2010. The structural accessibility layer (SAL): revealing how urban structure constrains travel choice. Environ Plan A 42 (11), 2735–2752.
Sterzer, L., 2017. Does competition in the housing market cause transport poverty? Interrelations of residential location choice and mobility. Eur. Transp. Res. Rev. 9 (3), 45.
Sullivan, O., Gershuny, J., 2004. Inconspicuous consumption: work-rich, time-poor in the liberal market economy. J. Consum. Cult. 4 (1), 79–100.
von Szombathely, M., Albrecht, M., Augustin, J., Bechtel, B., Dwinger, I., Gaffron, P., Strüver, A., 2018. Relation between observed and perceived traffic noise and socio-economic status in urban blocks of different characteristics. Urban Sci. 2 (1), 20.
Temam, S., Burte, E., Adam, M., Antó, J.M., Basagaña, X., Bousquet, J., Le Moual, N., 2017. Socioeconomic position and outdoor nitrogen dioxide (NO2) exposure in Western Europe: a multi-city analysis. Environ. Int. 101, 117–124.
UN, 2016. Leaving No One Behind: The Imperative of Inclusive Development. Report on the World Social Situation 2016. United Nations, Department of Economic & Social Affairs, New York.
Urry, J., 2004. The 'system'of automobility. Theory Cult. Soc. 21 (4–5), 25–39.
Verlinghieri, E., Schwanen, T., 2020. Transport and mobility justice: evolving discussions. J. Transp. Geogr. 87, 102798.
Verry, D., Dy, K., Nicolas, J.P., 2017. Vulnérabilité énergétique et mobilité quotidiennes: quelle mesure? In: Dussud, F.-X., Lepoittevin, D., Riedinger, N. (Eds.), Les ménages et la consummation d'énergie. Ministère de l'Environnement, de l'Énergie et de la Mer, en Charge des Relations Internationales sur le Climat.
Villeneuve, D., Kaufmann, V., 2020. Exploring the causes of social exclusion related to mobility for non-motorized households. Transp. Res. Rec. 2674 (8), 911–920.
Viry, G., Kaufmann, V., Widmer, E.D., 2009. Social integration faced with commuting: more widespread and less dense support networks. In: Ohnmacht, T., Maksim, H., Bergman, M.M. (Eds.), Mobilities and Inequality. Ashgate, pp. 121–144.
Walker, G., 2012. Environmental Justice. Concepts, Evidence and Politics. Routledge.
Wu, X., Nethery, R.C., Sabath, B.M., Braun, D., Dominici, F., 2020. Air pollution and COVID-19 mortality in the United States: strengths and limitations of an ecological regression analysis. Sci. Adv. 6 (45), eabd4049.

CHAPTER FIVE

Making the links between accessibility, social and spatial inequality, and social exclusion: A framework for cities in Latin America

Daniel Oviedo*
Development Planning Unit, University College London, London, United Kingdom
*Corresponding author: e-mail address: daniel.oviedo@ucl.ac.uk

Contents

Abstract

This chapter presents a literature review of key concepts and connections that serve as a framework for understanding the conditions of access inequalities of socially disadvantaged residents of cities of Latin America: accessibility, social and spatual inequality, and transport-related social exclusion. The review seeks to identify conditions that underpin the ability of low-income, peripheral and other marginal population groups to access essential services and opportunities for their well-being. Building on such a review, the paper proposes a framework that identifies relevant connections between transport and urban configurations and inequalities that may affect socially vulnerable groups such as low-income groups, people with disabilities, elderly, women, and ethnic minorities. This review proposes a integrated framework linking splintering urbanism and social exclusion, placing accessibility—or the lack thereof—as a core issue bringing the two concepts together while considering their translation into the context of urban transport inequalities and inequities in cities in Latin America. The review contends

Advances in Transport Policy and Planning, Volume 8
ISSN 2543-0009
https://doi.org/10.1016/bs.atpp.2021.07.001
Copyright © 2021 Elsevier Inc.
All rights reserved.

that fragmentations stemming from splintered urbanism lead to inaccessibility that leads to exclusion in mutually reinforcing processes. Such processes reflect the limitations of mainstream approaches to urban and transport planning to address the needs of socially disadvantaged populations in Latin America.

Keywords: Transport, Social exclusion, Splintering urbanism, Latin America

1. Introduction

This chapter presents a thorough literature review of key concepts and connections that serve as a framework for understanding the conditions of access inequalities and inequities of socially disadvantaged populations in the Global South cities. The review explores the role of access and connectivity as both enablers and hinderers of participation in the everyday activities of urban society in the Global South under specific spatial, social and economic conditions. Building on previous research from transport, development and urban studies, the review explores the underlying causes of fragmentation in providing urban infrastructure and services for transport to socially and spatially disadvantaged populations, and the social consequences fragmented access and connectivity have on such populations. The review's primary objective is to inform conditions that may underpin the ability of socially vulnerable groups such as low-income groups, people with disabilities, elderly, women and ethnic minorities to access essential services and opportunities for their well-being.

The review builds on three core concepts to structure a framework applicable to access-related inequalities in rapidly developing cities. First, it approaches the issue of fragmentation in the provision of urban infrastructure and services for transport from the perspective of Splintering Urbanism (Light, 2002), which is defined as the differentiated provision of infrastructure (which can be extended to public transport services) to social groups depending on their power, wealth and influence. According to Graham and Marvin (2001), such patterns of infrastructure and networks of transport and communications tend to produce "premium networked spaces" for the wealthy while bypassing less-powerful groups (Graham & Marvin, 2001). In this process of production and reproduction of urban spaces, certain social groups and geographic areas experience "poverty of connections," as a result of continuous improvement of connectivity of central areas, while less profitable areas and groups "tend to get increasingly disconnected, (being) bypassed by infrastructure and socio-cultural investment" (Ohnmacht et al., 2009 p. 31). The review explores the fragmented provision concerning networks of transport infrastructure and services and the potential fragmentations present in urban and metropolitan governance and planning.

Second, the research explores the social consequences of a fragmented transport provision using a framework of transport-related social exclusion. The term social exclusion refers to the decline in participation in normal processes of society and increasing deprivation among particular social groups (Burchardt et al., 2002; Colleoni, 2016). An individual is socially excluded when he or she resides geographically in society but cannot be involved in its regular activities (Cass et al., 2005). In this regard, transport-related social exclusion is defined as the process by which, due to an insufficiency or lack of adequate means of travel, people are prevented from reaching opportunities (i.e. facilities, services, activities or interactions) that enable them to participate in the economic, political and social life of the community (Kenyon et al., 2002). This represents a complex concept that involves several dimensions such as economic, spatial, political, societal, personal, and temporal disadvantages, which can be exacerbated by poverty (Delbosc and Currie, 2018; Kenyon et al., 2002; Stanley and Vella-Brodrick, 2011).

The third core concept, which mediates the relationship between splintering urbanism and social exclusion is accessibility. In a seminal paper on transport-related social exclusion, Lucas (2012) argues that social exclusion emerges from inaccessibility to jobs, education, social and cultural opportunities available at specific destinations (i.e. locations in the city). Therefore accessibility emerges as a central issue in the transition from a fragmented provision of urban services and infrastructures to the conditions of limited participation in society. Accessibility is approached in this review as "the ease of reaching desired destinations given many available opportunities and intrinsic impedance to the resources used to travel from the origin to the destination" (Bocarejo and Oviedo, 2012).

This chapter's ultimate objective is to propose a conceptual structure to frame and understand the structural drivers of inaccessibility for socially disadvantaged groups and their social consequences, approached through the social exclusion definition.

This review proposes a integrated framework linking splintering urbanism and social exclusion, placing accessibility—or the lack thereof—as a core issue bringing the two concepts together while considering their translation into the context of urban transport inequalities and inequities in cities in Latin America.

The review contributes to theoretical bodies addressing the links between urban form and transport networks and social and physical marginalization in global south cities. One the one hand, the paper makes a proposition on the links between the fragmentation of networked infrastructure and services for transport and the potential social exclusion of people in conditions of social and spatial disadvantage. On the other hand, the paper adopts Western approaches to urban fragmentation and transport-related social exclusion to explore these dynamics, testing their applicability in contexts of strong physical marginalization of socially disadvantaged populations emerging for historical imbalances in governance structures, planning and physical infrastructure in the global south. The use of the concepts defined above is not frequent in the academic literature related to transport in Latin America. Combining the two concepts to analyze of the social consequences of urban fragmentation serves as a critique of Western approaches to transport planning. Furthermore, it illustrates the implications for social development and inequality of differentiated delivery of transport infrastructure and services and its in cities in the Global South.

2. Transport, urban development and cumulative disconnection in Latin America

According to the United Nations' Economic Commission for Latin America and the Caribbean –ECLAC-, the region has experienced unprecedented urban growth in the past four decades, increasing from 56.4% of the population living in cities over 100,000 inhabitants in the late 1970s to 79.5% in the second decade of the 2000s (ECLAC, 2015). In the decades between 1950 and 1980, Latin American countries experienced large migrations from the countryside to rising urban agglomerations. Although far more stable nowadays than in the period before the structural reforms of the 1990s, the rapid increase in urban population had severe implications concerning social exclusion, vulnerability, and disorganized urban growth (Rodríguez-Vignoli and Rowe, 2018).

Urban expansion in the last decades of the twentieth century and the more moderate but still substantial urban growth after 2000, led to an increase in socio-economic segregation as well as growing spatial segregation between wealthier and poorer households in cities where jobs and services tended to be physically concentrated close or in city business districts (Andreano et al., 2020; Inostroza et al., 2013). Economic disparities led to the marginality of specific social groups, which translated into a lack of public amenities, security, and conditions that worsened dependency on motorized transport (Coatsworth, 2008; Smets and Salman, 2016). Deficits in urban infrastructure and public services that confront citizens with increasing insecurity levels, both in relation to crime and road-related hazards, and decreasing quality of the environment due to noise and air pollution characterize the Latin American city. This aggravates spatial polarization between high and low-income groups has more recently led to intensification in the development of gated communities for the elite and increase in the vulnerability of the poor in informal neighborhoods (Caldeira (2000); Caldeira, 2017).

Inappropriate land regulations, unclear institutional arrangements, inadequate enforcement, political corruption, changes in levels of poverty and extreme poverty, and largely variable approaches to social housing from many Latin-American governments between the 1970s and 2000s increased the rhythm of development of informal housing in the region (Gilbert, 2009; Vinet and Zhedanov, 2011). These developments were often located in the outskirts of already large cities, sometimes in neighboring municipalities, generating conurbation and urban expansion processes. Given conditions of higher affordability of informal settlements, the region witnessed an increase in illegal or unregulated developers that divided large areas of private land into plots that local migrants and new in-migrants to the cities bought and developed through self-help construction (Caldeira, 2017; Habitat, 2012; Watson, 2009). Occupation of informal developments and low-cost housing in emergent neighborhoods in growing cities has also been incentivized by a growing demand for rental housing, particularly from poorest in-migrants and the more recent vulnerable migrants, unable to locate in the city centers (Dávila et al., 2006; Gilbert, 2005; Guzman and Bocarejo, 2017). Renters frequently accounted for up to half of the total families in several low-income informal settlements in large cities in Latin America in the late 1970s, a phenomenon that persists in many informal neighborhoods in the region today (Habitat, 2012). The rapid increase in informal neighborhoods' population resulted in worsening of urban poverty and vulnerability as informal housing for low-income communities is often characterized by generalized lack of infrastructure and sanitary facilities, and precariousness in construction materials and techniques (Abramo, 2012; Yunda and Sletto, 2017).

In combination with a relatively weak local industry and specialized job markets in large cities, migration patterns have another unintended effect on social inequalities and differences in access to opportunities for both low-income citizens and new migrants. The majority of the poor in large cities of Latin America resort to work in activities with variable or centralized locations, becoming inextricably reliant on motorized transport (Boisjoly et al., 2017; Portes and Schauffler, 1993; Vinet and Zhedanov, 2011). Activities like street-vending, occasional service provision, domestic services and construction work take place at multiple or variable locations, which in turn translates in more considerable travel expenditure from low-income areas, usually located in the city outskirts (Suárez et al., 2016; UN, 2020).

Economic activities of low-income populations are commonly managed informally and are primarily dependent on the unqualified labor force. The International Labor Organization (ILO) estimates that at least 2 billion people worldwide work informally. Turner (2009) defines the informal economy as part of the economy where activities occur beyond official recognition and record. Everyday informal economic activities may include small-scale enterprises and trade, self-employment, street vending, garbage recycling ventures, subcontracting, and unregistered home-based work, all of which are often localized. In 2012, the informal economy in Latin America was distributed in 38% in wage employment, 10.9% in household wage employment, and 41.4% in self-employment (Abramo, 2012). These informal economy activities commonly share a lack of job security, access to social protection, and fair wages (Günther and Launov, 2012). In Latin America and the Caribbean, 53% of the employed population works in the informal economy, while in Colombia, this figure is over 45% of the economically active urban population (ILO, 2019).

2.1 Linking Latin American urban form and social and transport disadvantage

The distribution of activities in cities and transport supply characteristics can lead to socially disadvantaged groups becoming transport disadvantaged. As argued by Gleeson and Randolph (2002), social disadvantage is a multidimensional construct that arises from a variety of causes that have social and spatial manifestations and refers to the combination of social characteristics and conditions that may impair the ability of people to participate in social and economic life (Gleeson and Randolph, 2002; Newburn, 2016). Social groups that may be socially disadvantaged include, among others, impoverished populations, women, people with disabilities, ethnic minorities, or even people belonging to some cultural, religious or age group depending on the context. As many migrants, including rural-urban migrants and immigrants from neighboring countries, share the intersection of more than one of such forms of disadvantage, they have been identified as groups at a particular social disadvantage, particularly about health, resilience and the ability to build and maintain social and human capital (Brockerhoff, 1995; Daniels, 2020; Malmusi et al., 2010; Newburn, 2016). Arguably, there is an overlap between social disadvantage and social exclusion. However, while the first focuses on the individual factors that may place individuals at a disadvantaged position, the second has a normative dimension that governs the definition of disadvantages and its consequences, placing more focus on the processes by which people at social disadvantage are prevented from normal participation in social life and on the consequences of such exclusion.

Analogous to the definition of social disadvantage, people marginalized due to the interaction between land use patterns, transport systems and individual characteristics and circumstances can experience transport disadvantage (Currie and Delbosc, 2011). Transport disadvantage is a multidimensional construct that focuses on the effects of lack of transport and other external factors on individuals, which limit their ability to reach and be reached from places, thus having limited participation in social, economic and cultural life (Hurni, 2007; Murray and Davis, 2001). From this perspective, factors such as residential location choice, the spatial distribution of opportunities and inadequate transport can lead to specific individuals becoming transport disadvantaged (Combs et al., 2016; Murray and Davis, 2001). Revisiting the definition of transport-related social exclusion introduced in Section 1, the intersection between social and transport disadvantage leads to insufficient resources to travel and reach opportunities for employment, education, leisure and social interactions, thus leading to transport-related social exclusion (Lucas, 2012).

2.1.1 Transport disadvantages in Latin American cities and their link with urban development

In urban Latin America, transport disadvantages, inequalities, and inequities are reflected in restricted travel capacity and increasing distances and travel time for socially disadvantaged groups such as the poor, people with disabilities, the unemployed, women, and migrants. Most cities in the region show spatial concentration patterns that increase travel distances for some social groups. Thibert and Osorio (2014) argue that most cities in the region have strong tendencies toward spatial segregation, defined as the concentration of social groups (determined by income, ethnicity, and status, among others) in specific areas of a city or metropolitan region (Thibert and Osorio, 2014). In Latin America, such segregation is heightened by the development of gated communities and suburban settlements of high value and connectivity by the elites, who seek larger spaces, security and a reduced 'social burden' by living farther from the city center. By the same token, the development and consolidation of both formal and informal settlements of low-cost housing for the poor in areas where land is still affordable, which tends to be in the periphery or less attractive suburban areas (Gilbert, 1981; Mclafferty, 2015; Sabatini, 2006; Tarazona, 2015; Thibert and Osorio, 2014; Vignoli, 2008).

This situation is aggravated by the tendency for the concentration of economic activities in the city centers, where there is an accumulation of wealth and opportunities that lead to a self-reinforcing cycle of investment and development which in turn pushes for greater connectivity, and that reinforces its attractiveness, keeping most economic activities circumscribed to specific areas of cities. In other words, spatial mismatch describes an ample range of geographical barriers to employment that originate from a disparity, or mismatch, between where people live and where they work (McLafferty, 2015). This concept finds its origins in the North American literature, where the spatial mismatch hypothesis was developed to explain geographical barriers for accessing jobs for African-American communities (Jocoy and Del Casino, 2010). In Latin America, racial housing segregation is not the dominant feature. However, areas of economic activity tend to be far from where most of the middle and low-income population lives, leading to its own form of spatial mismatch (Blumenberg and Manville, 2004; Fan, 2012; Mclafferty, 2015; Ong and Blumenberg, 1998).

One of the main consequences of such spatial mismatch is high transport costs and time required to travel in most cities. Data from CAF (2011), shows that in the largest 15 metropolitan areas in Latin America people consume 1.1 hours/trip/day, which adds to over 118 million hours per day. The distribution of such travel times is not uniform across social groups and transport users. Data from the same source for 2009 indicates that while bus users spend 58.8 minutes per trip, car users in the region spend 25.5 min/trip (Montoya et al., 2011). Today, in many cities across the region, travel by public transport can imply spending between 1.5 and 2 times the average travel times in private vehicles (Vecchio et al., 2020). This can be related to the previous arguments related to spatial mismatch and long travel distances. By being farther from the city center, lower-income citizens, who are the social group that uses public transport the most, is forced to experience long travel times as a consequence of longer distances, congestion, and often inadequate local coverage of public transport that requires long walking times to bus and train stations (Benevenuto and Caulfield, 2019; Hidalgo and Huizenga, 2013; Vecchio et al., 2020). Long travel times and distances are added to economic expenditure, which in some cases can be disproportionately high. People in large cities in the region spend in total 82 million US$ per day in transport, of which 78% are spent in the use of private vehicles. Average expenditure per trip in public transport is 0.7 US$, while in private vehicles this average is 4 US$ (UNCRD-IDB, 2011). However, as argued by different studies, this lower cost compared to the car can become a heavy burden for low-income households. People buying up to 50 tickets per month can spend up to 20% of their income, while car users tend to spend on average below 10% (Bocarejo and Oviedo, 2012; Falavigna and Hernandez, 2016; (Yañez-Pagans et al., 2019).

Gómez and Acevedo (2013) argue that car and motorcycle ownership rates in Latin America can be explained mainly by income and population distribution Gómez and Acevedo (2013). A regional analysis of household transport expenditure across 12 countries in Latin America and the Caribbean (LAC) found that out of the total, private transport accounts for 76% and public transport accounts for the remaining 24% (Gandelman et al., 2019). Despite comparatively lower total expenditure on public than private transport, public transport is often a necessity for poor and middle-income households, while higher-income Latin American and Caribbean citizens perceive it as an inferior good (Gandelman et al., 2019).

With the rise of the middle classes and the transition from low to middle-income levels, there is an expected increase in automobiles and motorcycles in cities of the region. Nonetheless, motorization rates in Latin America are still low compared to industrialized countries. The number of cars per 1,000 inhabitants varies from 55 in Ecuador to 185 vehicles in Mexico (UNCRD-IDB, 2011). As a reference, car ownership rates in countries such as the United States and Australia is 797 and 717 cars per 1,000 inhabitants, respectively (Our World in Data, 2021). Countries in the lower range of motorization rates such as Peru and Bolivia are between 51 and 56 cars per 1,000 inhabitants. The same figures in Venezuela, Chile and Argentina are between 135 and 165 cars/1,000 inhabitants. Evolution of the personal vehicles industry has led to increasingly affordable cars and motorcycles. In particular, the latter has a much lower income threshold for purchasing and daily operation, which has led to rapid growth in motorcycle ownership (Gómez & Acevedo, 2013). In Uruguay, the number of motorcycles per 1,000 inhabitants reaches 141 vehicles, while this figure is 81 and 68 in Brazil and Colombia (Hidalgo and Huizenga, 2013). These figures show a tendency to increase in the following years due to economic growth and a reduction in the price of vehicles being distributed. The number of motorcycles in Brazil increased by 38% annually between 2000 and 2010, while Colombia and Mexico's growth rates have been between 15% and 16% per year, respectively. On average, cars have increased by about 6% annually in the region (Hidalgo and Huizenga, 2013; UNCRD-IDB, 2011).

This increase in motorization rates has consequences on environmental sustainability as a result of externalities such as congestion and air and noise pollution. However, in most cities, private vehicles' rates of usage (cars and motorcycles) are still relatively low (Vasconcellos, 2014). In cities like La Paz, Rio de Janeiro and Montevideo, less than 20% of daily trips are made by private vehicles. In other cities, such as Bogotá, Belo Horizonte, Porto Alegre, Santiago, Caracas and Guadalajara, this percentage is still below 30%. These figures contrast with increasing percentages of journeys made by public transport and non-motorized modes. In Rio de Janeiro, Belo Horizonte, Santiago, León, Guadalajara and Curitiba, non-motorized travel represents between 32% and 42% daily trips. This is complemented by at least 40% of public transport trips (Hidalgo and Huizenga, 2013).

2.1.2 Poverty and informality: A cycle of reinforcing disadvantage

The rapid growth of cities and lack or inadequate regulations and enforcement of land-use plans have led to the development of unsuitable land for housing by informal developers in most large cities in Latin America (Gilbert, 2009). Informal housing has become the receptacles par excellence of internal and external migrants with limited to no social links within the city, or with preceding social connections that ease their transition to the settlement. Such neighborhoods are generally marked by lack of access to suitable land, severe conditions of lack of infrastructure and services, illegality and generalized precariousness in construction materials and techniques. With the eventual recognition of these settlements as a non-temporary phenomenon, housing policy has shifted from repressive strategies that sought relocation as a primary objective, to processes of improvement of local environments through self-help and eventually upgrading interventions aiming to the provision of services and security of tenure (Abramo, 2012; Inostroza, 2017).

The constant evolution of housing policies related to either formal or informal developments of low-cost housing for the urban poor has often been a central issue in local governments' agendas worldwide, international development agencies and donors. The number of people living in informal housing by 2001 was about 924 million people, representing more than 30% of the global urban population. This number was projected to increase to 2 billion people in 30 years (Marx et al., 2013). Informal settlements have been the only large-scale solution to providing housing for low-income people as they respond to needs of affordability and accessibility, within a context of limited available options, competitive land markets and scarce supply of cheap land (Hernandez-Garcia, 2013; Kamalipour and Dovey, 2019; Watson, 2015). A limited supply of local employment in informal and low-income settlements and urban economies centered on the services sector (Montoya et al., 2011) also leads low-income and other socially disadvantaged populations to work in the informal economy.

Principles of economic rationality underpinning transport and infrastructure provision lead to precarious coverage of roads, utilities and essential social services in 'less-profitable' areas of the city (Samuels, 2001). As shown earlier, these conditions feed upon a continuous cycle of spatial segregation and poverty that reshape city boundaries through informal settlements in the peripheries (Thibert and Osorio, 2014). Consequently, the mobility of peripheral populations differs significantly from those living in more attractive and better-served areas of the city due to imposed gaps of connectivity (Oviedo Hernandez and Dávila, 2016).

Lack of adequate connectivity imposes high financial loads on poor households, especially in areas where integrated transport systems are not available, increasing transfer costs to reach employment and economic activities (Scholl and Gray, 2016; Suárez et al., 2016). In most cases the demand in peripheral and low-income areas is not fully covered by the formal system, opening gaps for the operation of small-scale, informal transport operators and leading to a complex interplay of formal and informal transport alternatives in the definition of travel choices (Blanco and Apaolaza, 2018; Cervero and Golub, 2007). Transport informality is interpreted in terms of the conjunction of services that operate outside formal regulations for collective transport supply, which works on a small scale and responds to specific transport needs. These informal alternatives are mainly characterized by low-capacity vehicles and flexible tariff schemes that usually complement regular public transport, entering neighborhoods poorly served by formal operators and addressing undersupplied demand segments, particularly in lower-income groups. However, informal mechanisms have a limited effect in giving low-income families access to large cities' opportunities and generally entail higher externalities -such as higher pollution, noise, and traffic accidents- than formal supply (Behrens et al., 2020; Heinrichs et al., 2017).

The review builds on the hypothesis that the interrelation between transport and urban planning and social exclusion of the poor in urban peripheries is shaped by (i) the spatial and physical structure of urban environments in Latin America, (ii) the governance and formal and informal practices of transport and urban planning, which reconfigure the availability and nature of transport networks, and (iii) systematic inequities at different scales (metropolitan, municipal and local) that underpin household and individual strategies for addressing the multiple dimensions of social exclusion for socially vulnerable populations.

3. A splintering urbanism interpretation for spatial inequalities in access and connectivity in Latin American cities

The notion of a networked society developed by Castells (2000) is a good starting point for introducing the splintering urbanism framework (Castells, 2012; Light, 2002) to analyse transport provision in low-income urban areas. From a geographical perspective, modern urban societies can be interpreted in a comprehensive, yet very simplified manner, as a set of flows and networks (Caprotti et al., 2019; Castells, 2012; Lussault, 2007). In these networked spaces, flows can be understood as the movements and exchanges of people, goods, services and information between spatial, social and economic positions within different social systems. At the same time, networks correspond to such flows' material base (Castells, 2001). For these movements and exchanges to occur, a series of conduits comprised of networks of communication and transport is required, making uneven access to transport networks a source of disparities between social groups (Manderscheid, 2009, 2016). This definition of urban spaces as networks gives social relevance to the unequal distribution of material infrastructures for transport and communication. These contribute to the definition of patterns of movement of people, goods and information (Ohnmacht et al., 2009). Urban planning and provision of transport networks translate into forces that can either moderate or aggravate social inequalities and inequities by enhancing or restricting accessibility (Manderscheid and Bergman, 2008). Travel expenditure depends on the availability of travel alternative and mechanisms needed to access relevant opportunities, which are reliant on infrastructure, communications, and technology networks.

Graham and Marvin (2001) interpret these networks as techno-economic constructs arising from social and historical processes and highlight the mutual relationship between the development of networks and urban spaces (Zérah, 2008). As urban structures develop and become more complex, transport infrastructure's supply tends to follow the concentration of activities, wealth and power within urban spaces. The splintering urbanism thesis (SU) responds to what Graham and Marvin describe as an urgent need for developing a more robust, comprehensive approach to the understanding of "the changing relations between contemporary cities, infrastructure networks and technological mobilities" (2001, p. 33).

In rapidly growing cities, utility and communication infrastructures can become instruments of production and reproduction of social and spatial inequalities. As urban areas grow and develop and capital seeks more advantageous conditions for its reproduction, processes of structuring and re-structuring of networks of opportunities arise. In this context, wealthier groups can segregate themselves in premium nodes of well-connected networks, access information, interact socially, and improve their welfare levels. In contrast, more remote nodes, often concentrating low-income and other socially disadvantaged populations, are simultaneously excluded due to the discontinuity of links and services and a restricted capacity to interact with the city. This suggests a central role of material infrastructures for mobility in enabling physical access to the city by the poor and helping reduce social exclusion.

The core of the SU argument is that this dialectical relationship is currently undergoing structural changes through a "(...) process of 'unbundling' and 'splintering' the diverse political and regulatory regimes that supported the roll-out of power, transport, communications, street and transport networks towards the rhetorical goal of standardized ubiquity" (Graham and Marvin, 2001). In other words, a fragmentation of the systems for delivery of networks for transport and communications under a banner of universal coverage and access that is often driven by economic objectives. Unbundling processes arising from the infrastructure sector reforms sought economic efficiency instead of a reduction in social and spatial inequalities (Graham & Marvin, 2001). Moreover, through constant creation of premium developments that include gated communities, commercial complexes, and high-tech economic clusters, the production of urban spaces is modified along with infrastructure provision, leading to an increasing separation between socio-economic groups (Zérah, 2008). As termed in

Graham and Marvin's narrative, Premium networked spaces allow higher income groups to segregate themselves from the rest of the urban fabric while, paradoxically, remaining firmly connected to other premium spaces (Graham & Marvin, 2001). Differentiated mechanisms of infrastructure development not only allow the segregation of wealthier groups. They bypass less powerful groups generating inequalities concerning the capacity to interact with the city's economic and social structure (Graham & Marvin, 2001). For instance, better road infrastructures and public spaces are provided in wealthier neighborhoods, contributing to a cycle of growing connectivity. By contrast, low-income and informal neighborhoods tend to receive lesser levels of investment in road connectivity, walking and cycling infrastructure, often impairing the provision of public transport services and reducing connectivity. Bypassed social groups lack the necessary resources and choose to move away from interacting with the whole extent of society's opportunities (Anand and Tiwari, 2006; Stoekl and Musiol, 2015).

The production of bypassing strategies in infrastructure provision makes SU a potentially useful framework for studying transport planning and delivery in segregated nodes of the networked society. Increasing gaps between connected and disconnected people lead to the "poverty of connections" (Graham & Marvin, 2001, p. 288), or transport poverty, described earlier in this chapter. In this process of production and reproduction of urban spaces, "whereas the connectivities of central nodes in space continue to increase, less profitable areas and groups between the nodes and hubs tend to get increasingly disconnected, bypassed by infrastructure and socio-cultural investment" (Ohnmacht et al., 2009, p. 31). Thus, the cycle of segregation and spatial concentration of opportunities is strengthened, increasingly representing a barrier for less powerful groups to interact with society. Understanding the causes and consequences of this type of exclusion becomes central to transport planning. Limited provision of infrastructure to specific groups in society has severe implications in terms of transport-related social exclusion, which involves spatial, political, personal and societal disadvantages that can be aggravated by poverty and in turn, helps deepen it (Blair et al., 2013; Bostock, 2001; Kenyon et al., 2002).

Transport-related social exclusion derives from the insufficiency or inexistence of adequate means to travel (Kenyon et al., 2002). People who experience exclusion conditions see their travel choice removed as a consequence of an urban environment built around the notion of high mobility (Macdonald and Grieco, 2007). If the social exclusion is understood as the combination of a set of social problems related to social fragmentation, limited access to networks of connectivity can be interpreted as one of such social problems, which limits participation in normal processes of society (Burchardt et al., 2002; Curran, 2016).

Graham and Marvin's framework is useful in approaching limited connectivity in urban contexts marked by centralization and spatial segregation such as that of Latin American cities. It relates to relevant transport paradigms and provides a socially-informed interpretation of infrastructure networks, identifying on-going processes in dynamic cities. Graham and Marvin's interpretation relates well to the weakness of regulation and policies of privatization and the provision of infrastructure and services that may increase inequalities and exclude specific socio-demographic groups (Fernández-Maldonado, 2008). When approached from a perspective of access to essential opportunities and facilities for socially vulnerable populations, the strength of the SU framework lays in its applicability to other essential infrastructure such as water, sanitation and electricity, which also tends to be unavailable for the most socially vulnerable groups in Latin-American urban societies.

Some limitations of Graham and Marvin's paper become apparent when testing its claims in the context of (1) cities in developing countries, and (2) groups who are spatially segregated based on their poverty instead of their wealth. As Coutard (2008) highlights, this theory does not apply to each infrastructure sector (Coutard, 2008). Furthermore, assumes that observable changes produce a similar mismatch between connected spaces and bypassed areas. There is a symmetry hypothesis that needs to be controlled for. However, considering the social and spatial stratification and segregation of many cities in Latin America in the present research, the SU paper would seem to help explain the consolidation of networks in the most profitable areas and the lack of investment in less-attractive and influential neighborhoods.

One of the main critiques of recent developments regarding splintering urbanism is that it cannot be considered a general, universal, thesis (Coutard, 2008). Recent research suggests that some of the principles related to the drivers of discriminatory and socially regressive patterns of the provision of networks of services and infrastructure have value as a framework for understanding contemporary urban issues (Coutard, 2008; Furlong, 2014; Odendaal, 2011; Zérah, 2008). In most cases, research on urban networks and their fragmentation adopt case study methodologies to confront the principles of the SU theory with local realities to provide a critique on the main drivers of differentiation in the delivery of infrastructure and services in different urban contexts such as Jakarta, Mumbai, Cape Town and eastern Germany, among others (see Jaglin, 2008; Kooy and Bakker, 2008; Moss, 2008). The main contribution of these research is to reinforce the need for reinterpreting the principles outlined by Graham and Marvin (2001) and question the validity of postcolonial assumptions and neoliberal thinking, emphasizing structural inequalities and the fragmentation of urban networks.

Other research such as Frith's (2012) paper on the links between physical and virtual mobility and the splintering of space, seeks to bring some of the ideas of Graham and Marvin (2001) into contemporary concerns related to information and communication technologies and their role in the networked society (Frith, 2012). Something similar happens with other recent studies focusing on critical urban theory (see Brenner et al., 2011; McFarlane, 2011; McFarlane et al., 2017), where a shift from splintering urbanism to assemblage urbanism is proposed. In this interpretation, urban spaces are conceptualized as a continuous, mobile, unequal, and changing dwelling process, constituting an alternative to the idea of fragmenting networks to propose one of continuous construction. These theorizations reflect an evolving field of debate where researchers from different disciplines are continuously devising new ways to understand complex urban phenomena. However, they are also a reflection of the validity of many of the postulates of influential theories such as splintering urbanism and a need for flexibility and recognition of local realities in their interpretation. This context gives appeal to reviewing and translating Graham and Marvin's (2001) concept of SU,as it constitutes an opportunity to contribute to current international debates in disciplines such as urban geography, urban studies and planning, while also testing the applicability of this framework in the traditionally isolationist transport sector and transport studies.

The State has the responsibility to provide ubiquitous coverage of infrastructure and connectivity, which aligns with the 'modern infrastructure ideal' in the SU Theory. In the Global South, transport infrastructure and services are still mainly within the remit of government, with the responsibility of design, planning, and -in no small extent- delivering infrastructure. As it has the responsibility of steering and sustaining development, the State ultimately determines the distribution of (primary) connectivity networks. Graham and Marvin (2001) also refer to a set of influential factors that challenge this 'modern infrastructure ideal', which include changes in the political economies of urban infrastructure development and its governance; neoliberalism; economic integration, open competition and imperatives of global-local connectivity; the development of infrastructural consumerism; the collapse of the comprehensive ideal number planning; new urban landscapes; and new structures of feeling (Graham and Marvin, 2001; Coutard, 2008). It ought to be recognized that not all these changes apply to cities in the global south, where some authors have challenged the idea of this universalization of infrastructure provision (Coutard, 2008; Furlong, 2014; Parnell, 2014). However, one of the central governance and political economy challenges in many contexts in the global south was the decentralization of power and transference of responsibilities for urban infrastructure development, including transport, to the local government (Prud'homme, 1995; Rahman and Barter, 1998). What splintering urbanism refers to as the "unbundling" of infrastructure that results from the influence of powerful actors and structural drivers such as privatization and the concentration of wealth (Graham and Marvin, 2001) is observed in the context of transport infrastructure and services. Both the "bypassing strategies" and production of "premium networked spaces" in the SU theory is a result not only of the unequal distribution of wealth and power and space but of a traditional planning process that prioritizes the connectivity of areas with higher attractiveness as a result of the deeply rooted principles of utilitarianism, efficiency and economic growth in mainstream planning approaches (Levy, 2013). The combination of cumulative and self-reinforcing social, economic, and spatial inequalities with a planning system underpinned by "neoclassical economic concepts, focusing upon the representation of people as rational choice-makers" (Avineri, 2012, p. 513) creates a self-reinforcing cycle of accumulation of attractiveness and improvements in connectivity, while simultaneously -if not entirely-, bypassing or giving less priority to areas of low-power and attractiveness.

Explicit social and spatial inequalities in many cities of Latin America are partly a consequence of a traditional approach to transport infrastructure planning, the concentration of attractiveness at the city center and other areas of concentration of high-income population, and the clash of jurisdictions and mismatches in governance between adjacent municipalities that constrained the seamless integration of infrastructure networks. This has been explored in detail in an analysis of SU's manifestation in the context of Soacha, Colombia (Oviedo Hernandez and Dávila, 2016). Splintering urbanism also introduces a relevant discussion regarding power and influence, and the emergence of forms of resistance from communities and public authorities confronted with these splintering processes (Graham and Marvin, 2001). Splintering urbanism can also become a theoretical lens that understands the emergence of informal ways of connectivity in bypassed nodes

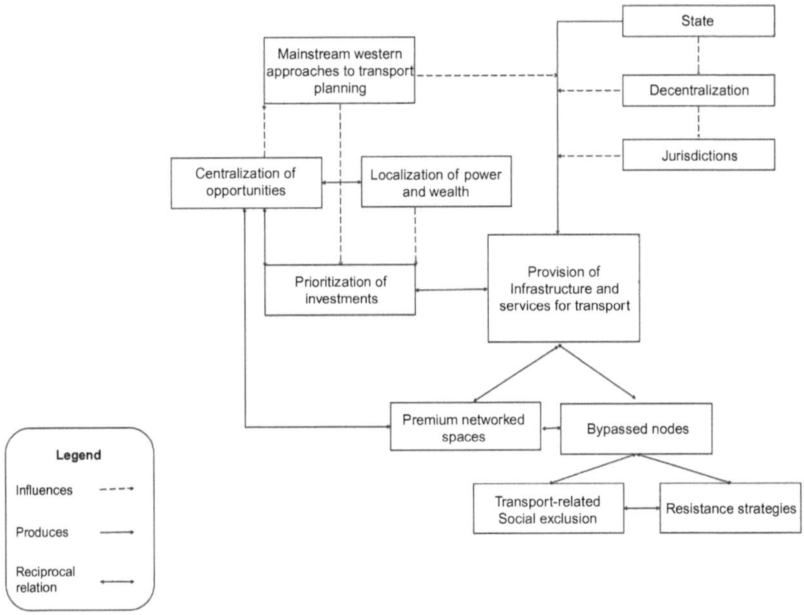

Fig. 1 The splintering urbanism process related to transport. *Oviedo Hernandez, D.R., 2017. Mobilities at the edge: splintering urbanism and transport- related social exclusion in Soacha, Colombia, 2000-2013. In: Bull. Am. Assoc. Univ. Prof. (vol. 13, Issue 3, p. 163). UCL (University College London).*

concentrating socially vulnerable populations. Fig. 1 shows the main elements involved in the interpretation of splintering urbanism adopted in this chapter. The framework reads SU as a self-reinforcing process of differentiated provision of transport networks influenced by structures of government and systems of planning in place and the configuration of the city simplified in terms of centralization of opportunities and localization of power and wealth. The framework presented in Fig. 1 also connects social exclusion as both a product and a contributing factor to splintering urbanism related to transport, supporting the selection of a framework for a social exclusion that interprets it as a set of more considerable consequences of transport and social disadvantages.

The delivery of transport infrastructure and services and their social consequences are closely connected with the discussions about the limitations of mainstream Western transport planning. It has been argued that social exclusion can either be interpreted from the literature as the process that leads to people not being able to fully participate in society or as the resulting constraints to interact with the opportunities and connections in an urban space (Lucas, 2012). This is the entry point to link the theory of splintering urbanism with the interpretation of Church et al. (2000) interpretation of social exclusion. In their study in London, Church et al. (2000), construct a framework that identifies the structuring factors behind potential exclusion stemming for transport, while discussing some of the consequences of such factors. This framework has been reinterpreted in subsequent studies and sparked research focusing on one or more specific dimensions. However, similarly to splintering urbanism, the literature has consistently maintained the framework's most general principles unchallenged. This is one of the strongest appeals of both frameworks. It becomes an opportunity to test the "universality" of such frameworks while pushing forward existing knowledge on how they can be used to understand transport-related inequities and weaknesses in its delivery planning (Church et al., 2000).

(Church et al., 2000) framework for transport-related social exclusion deconstructs the links between the dynamics of the splintering of networks of connectivity and the different dimensions in which people at bypassed nodes experience and confront social exclusion. Relationships between transport and social exclusion have been explored by several studies in the UK and the European community where survey methodologies have been used to identify specific conditions related to the influence of transport in social exclusion (Lucas and Currie, 2012 ; Social Exclusion Unit, 2003). Other work has expanded these analyses in the Australian context, where the concept of social exclusion has occupied a relevant normative role as well as sparked various research related to transport, which explore its links with wellbeing, social disadvantage and social capital (Delbosc and Currie, 2011; Engels and Liu, 2011; Nansen et al., 2015; Stanley (2011a); Stanley et al., 2011). However, as Stanley (2011, p. 33) argued, this has constrained the development of the concept as most research has been developed in contexts "where those being excluded are in the minority." Therefore, further consideration is required in research regarding the usefulness of the concept of social exclusion in cities and regions where a larger share of the population (sometimes the majority) can be said to be, at least partially, excluded.

From a social exclusion perspective, inequalities and inequities related to transport, such as those described for the Latin American context and which are often a consequence of mainstream transport planning, can disproportionally affect people experiencing social and transport disadvantage. From earlier studies, it has been identified that poor transport contributes to social exclusion in various ways beyond its role as a constraint for accessibility (Delbosc and Currie, 2011; Preston and Rajé, 2007).

Communities experiencing social disadvantage can suffer disproportionately from the externalities associated with the inequitable distribution of urban transport such as pedestrian deaths because of limited or no facilities for walking, air and noise pollution that contribute to poor health, and the fragmentation and isolation that can result from the development of large and busy roads in proximity to low-income communities (Social Exclusion Unit (United Kingdom), 2003).

For people experiencing exclusion conditions, access to goods and services and the ability to travel to activities relevant for normal participation in society are removed. These conditions are often reinforced by poverty in its multiple dimensions, and low quality of public transport services in neighborhoods with low car ownership. As argued by Stanley et al. (2011), although the concept of social exclusion finds its origins in work that sought to improve our understanding and representation of poverty, it has since evolved to describe barriers that can prevent full participation in society. Like conditions of poverty, these barriers can include low income and unemployment and the less discussed condition of lack of familiarity and social capital associated with migration. Other barriers are more closely related to structural issues such as poor health, limited or no education, or to social identities such as ethnic background and age, among others (Stanley et al., 2011). In this regard, research has found that although social exclusion and poverty are closely related conditions, neither all people that experience transport-related social exclusion live in poor neighborhoods nor that all people experiencing poverty are excluded (Lyons, 2003; Macdonald and Grieco, 2007; Schwanen et al., 2015). There is a tendency to define and operationalize social exclusion "through the nomination of specific dimensions of exclusion, researchers tending to use four or five dimensions" (Stanley, 2011, p. 31). Lyons (2003) points to several inter-related accessibility factors which govern the understanding and influencing of exclusion such as mobility, use of ICTs, land use and (de)concentration of public services, time use, management and constraints, and availability of and entitlement to use public space. Church et al. (2000) identify seven instances in which social exclusion can be detected concerning the configuration of urban spaces and urban transport systems and their interactions with individual characteristics. While earlier research has suggested adding a dimension of social identities to such a framework (Benevenuto and Caulfield, 2019), the original framework of seven dimensions is maintained as it has been empirically tested in socially disadvantaged areas in the context of Latin America (Oviedo Hernandez and Titheridge, 2016). Such dimensions are as follows:

1. Physical exclusion: physical features of the built environment and systems for mobility can constrain accessibility for social groups and individuals who may experience physical and/or psychological difficulties using transport systems. Such barriers can affect different groups of people, including people with learning difficulties, children and the elderly, impaired mobility, and limited sight and hear (Church et al., 2000; Hine, 2003). The combination of different physical features of the transport systems and the built environment might lead to various exclusion levels and be cumulative. For example, inadequate facilities for pedestrians at the local level can prevent specific groups from travel even if there is appropriate coverage of public transport and other infrastructure and vice versa (Mackett and Thoreau, 2015).
2. Geographical exclusion: while Church et al. (2000) argued at the time their paper was published that there were no systematic evidence of the relationship between inaccessibility related to geographical and urban segregation factors, more recent research has proven that peripherality, inadequate transport provision at the home end and spatial mismatches between housing and opportunities contributes to exclusion and deprivation (Combs and Rodríguez, 2014; Giuliano et al., 2015; Halás et al., 2014; Litchenberger, *2015*; Mclafferty, 2015; Oviedo and Guzman, 2020; Willis, 2009). In Latin America, cities tend to be more spatially and socially segregated, and whilst peripheral gated communities of high income can be as far or more from centers of employment as informal settlements of low-income populations, the first are well-connected to the transport systems while the second are often bypassed in the processes of infrastructure and services provision (Graham, 2009; Irazábal, 2004; Light, 2002; Oviedo Hernandez and Dávila, 2016; Thibert and Osorio, 2014). These areas also tend to have a very poor local supply of employment and other opportunities, which might reinforce urban geography's adverse effects in their accessibility and inclusion (Bocarejo et al., 2014; Crankshaw, 2014; Heinrichsa and Bernet, 2014).
3. Exclusion from facilities: Urban geographies' configuration negatively affects poor populations and other socially disadvantaged groups.

People living in areas with high levels of social exclusion, as identified by Church et al. (2000), have limited access to jobs and opportunities for shopping, financial services, health and education facilities, and spaces for leisure and cultural activities. Land-use policies and market trends can lead to areas being increasingly attractive for certain facilities, which tend to be farther away from where the poor and the disadvantaged live. This dimension differs from geographical exclusion as it considers more than distance to opportunities, focusing on the structural drivers of provision of services, facilities and amenities in different parts of the city. In some cases, social issues in poor neighborhoods such as crime and insecurity, or fear by business owners, can drive away local opportunities, increasing deprivation (Smeeding, 2015; Valenzuela Aguilera, 2013; Wegelin and Borgman, 1995). Policies and strategies for distributing facilities for health and education are other potential factors of exclusion. Increasing distances and inaccessibility to different opportunities, including those that do not generate income, are clear factors of inequity in urban societies, and conditions that make prohibitive to participate in social and cultural opportunities, as well as facilities for health and education are factors of exclusion as relevant as not being able to secure income for the family (Grengs, 2015; Oviedo and Guzman, 2020).

4. Economic exclusion: as argued earlier, social exclusion is closely related to poverty and insufficient income to address needs. Church et al. (2000) identify that affordability constraints of the transport network reduces accessibility to different opportunities, emphasizing employment. Prohibitive monetary costs of travel prevent low-income people from travelling or restricts the geographical extent of their search for potential destinations (Church et al., 2000; Schwanen et al., 2015). In cities of Latin America, evidence suggests that transport costs, even in public transport can take a considerable portion of disposable income in middle-low and low-incom,e populations (Bocarejo and Oviedo, 2012; Falavigna and Hernandez, 2016; Santana Palacios et al., 2020; Serebrisky et al., 2009; Vecchio et al., 2020; Welch, 2013).
5. Time-based exclusion: Church et al. (2000) point at difficulties for allocating time to different commitments and the constraints of the transport network to play a role in social exclusion of specific social groups and individuals, such as carers. Research exploring the issues of time availability as a factor of social inequities suggest the existence of 'time poverty', which might disproportionally affect specific individuals, with particular gaps related to gender and the distribution of domestic

work ((Anand and Tiwari, 2006); Harvey and Mukhopadhyay, 2007; Levy, 2013; Montoya-Robledo et al., 2020; Turner and Grieco, 2000; Warren, 2003). Social conventions and traditionally defined roles in households that impose caring for children, domestic work, distribution of paid and unpaid labor and other commitments lead to people having limited time to travel, which is compounded by restricted availability of transport services at certain times, such as nights (Montoya-Robledo et al., 2020; Rest and Hirsch, 2016; Salonen and Toivonen, 2013). Household structure, availability of social and support networks, and jobs' nature are factors influencing time exclusion (Church et al., 2000).

6. Fear-based exclusion: the definition of social exclusion related to transport includes factors beyond geographies and the economy, incorporating issues such as fear of crime and perceived insecurity as factors that can prevent people from accessing certain places (i.e. a specific neighborhood, public transport stops, facilities, etc.) and modes of transport (Church et al., 2000). Fear of crime is closely related to social characteristics. Recent research argues that one of the more robust determinants of fear of crime is gender. However, other characteristics such as ethnic background and religious identities can also influence the interaction with public spaces and transport facilities related to fear of crime, victimization and abuse (Altman and Zube, 1989; Casas and Delmelle, 2014; Day, 2001; Levy, 2013; Whitzman, 2007). In Latin America, factors such as conflict and forced displacement, high presence of gangs and street crime, and localized poverty in specific areas of the city, contribute to high perceptions of crime and insecurity that can prevent different population groups from travelling to certain areas or to use public transport (Gutiérrez et al., 2020; Romero, 2014; Sánchez and Palau, 2006; Torres, 2011).
7. Space-based exclusion: this dimension of social exclusion is associated by Church et al. (2000) with the design, security and management strategies of different public spaces, which might impair the sense of ownership if certain social groups from accessing them. This can also be extended to semi-public spaces (e.g. open areas of private property enabled for public use), common in cities of the UK, and be related to groups at risk of prejudice and discrimination (Schwanen et al., 2015). In contexts where marked divides between the elites and the poor produce splintering urbanism (Graham and Marvin, 2001), spaces tailored for access opportunities and mobility by the elites become exclusive and disempowering

other social groups leading to exclusion. In other contexts, where power relations are defined and exercised informally, and where illegality and crime can have a higher influence on the rules for interacting with public space (Levy, 2013), Space-based exclusion can be more severe or involve a broader range of social groups and individuals.

The seven dimensions of exclusion outlined by Church et al. (2000), which have been explored and redefined by subsequent studies, including applications in the global south (Benevenuto and Caulfield, 2019; Lucas, 2019; Lucas et al., 2016; Oviedo Hernandez and Titheridge, 2016; Schwanen et al., 2015; Vecchio et al., 2020; Venter et al., 2018), are interrelated, intersecting for certain groups, at different scales and changing over time. This poses challenges for the analysis of social exclusion and the allocation of resources and design of actions for tackling different dimensions of social exclusion for different social groups. As argued by Stanley (2011b), another clear issue of research on social exclusion is that the concept is used in a circular sense. Social exclusion is treated as "both a cause and driver of a lack of personal opportunities and the outcome of a lack of opportunities" (Stanley, 2011b, p. 32). This requires careful interpretation of the conceptual definitions of different social exclusion dimensions and available evidence concerning each dimension. It is essential to acknowledge the cumulative nature of factors of exclusion, which can reinforce each other and change over time (i.e. low education and skills influence income, political and social participation, which can, in turn, be related to housing choice and security) (Schwanen et al., 2015). Social exclusion is relative, to other individuals, social groups, communities and neighborhoods, which also marks the concept as a non-discrete issue, not a binary one. It has been argued that although the definition of social exclusion has evolved since its first developments in the area of transport studies, there is still lack of consensus between researchers on the definition of social exclusion, and even more of its opposite, inclusion (Lucas, 2019).

The various dimensions of social exclusion in the work of Church et al. (2000) engage with transport-related constraints for participation in society that span from location to social identities and positions. When linked with the patterns of urban development of cities in Latin America in other similar contexts in the developing world, it can be argued that social exclusion related to transport being mainly a consequence from, and reinforces the main drivers of, the localization of splintering urbanism. Fig. 2 summarizes some of the links between the two frameworks building on the previously discussed literature.

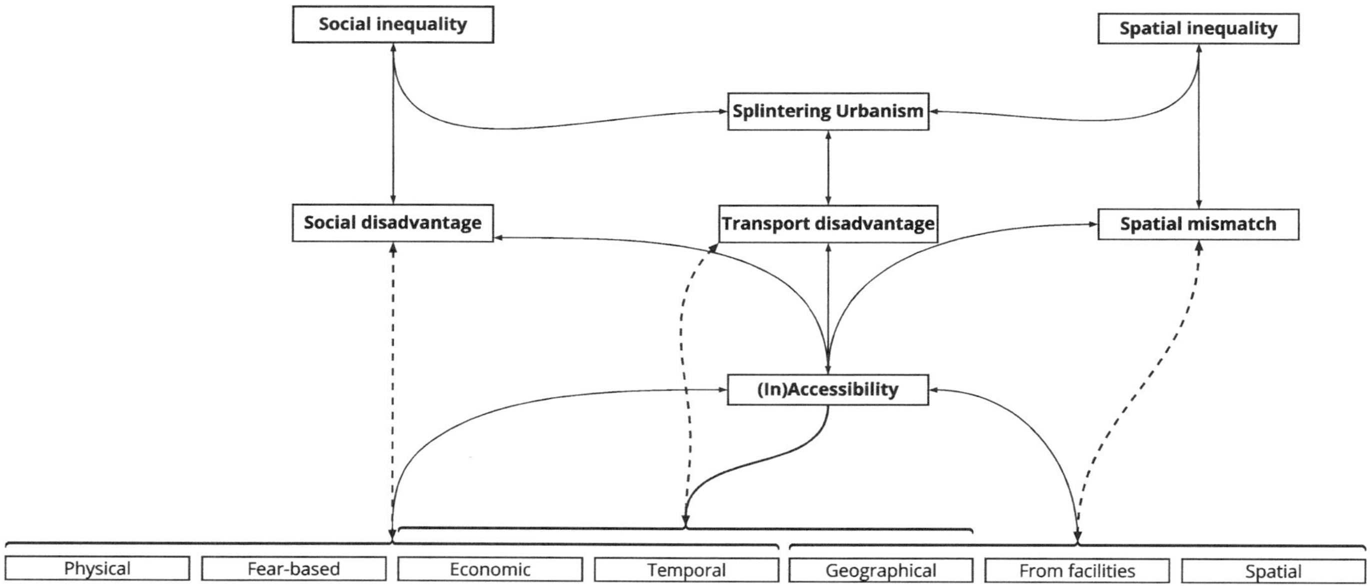

Fig. 2 Drawing the links between splintering urbanism and transport-related social exclusion *Own elaboration.*

This review argues that there is a strong interrelation between splintering urbanism and social exclusion. As shown in Fig. 2, some of the dimensions of social exclusion identified by Church, Frost, and Sullivan, have a direct bidirectional relationship with the practices of splintering urbanism related to transport and issues of transport disadvantage, social disadvantage and spatial mismatch. In contrast, others have either a unidirectional or indirect relationship with it. Dimensions such as the geographical are directly linked with peripherality, poor transport provision, and the resulting inaccessibility as primary factors of transport-related social exclusion (Church et al., 2000). From a splintering urbanism perspective, it can be argued that this dimension is a direct consequence of both the concentration of wealth in attractiveness in specific areas that make unaffordable for the poor to locate near employment centers and the technocratic approach of mainstream transport planning that gives precedence to the connectivity of this high-value areas.

In contrast, bypassed areas where socially disadvantaged population concentrate, contribute to spatial mismatch. The reinforcing cycle of spatial concentration of wealth and attractiveness and the development of high-quality transport networks and services supplying these areas produce barriers for affordability for low-income groups. As a consequence, such groups resort to informal dwellings in the periphery, low-cost rental, or even homelessness near the city center to have access to the opportunities in the city. In this regard, splintering becomes an explanatory factor of geographical exclusion. The peripheral location of socially and transport disadvantaged populations in the periphery reinforces its position as a low-power and influential node in the network, leading to further bypassing. Other dimensions that can be interrelated with splintering urbanism in the framework of Church et al. (2000) are exclusion from facilities, economic, physical, and space exclusion. The above dimensions can be argued to be either a by-product of the larger dynamics that involve splintering urbanism or a direct consequence of the disconnection from the networks of connectivity that come out of it.

It can be argued that infrastructure provision bypassing specific areas of the city can have a direct influence on levels of investment in local urban amenities, facilities, and services. This is particularly the case for informal settlements, but it can also be extended to other marginalized parts of the city, which tend to be forgotten from mainstream planning perspectives. One the other hand, despite being also a responsibility of the State, privatization of services such as health and education can lead to limited local provision of the services in socially vulnerable neighborhoods. The connection between splintering urbanism and most dimensions of social exclusion is accessibility or the lack thereof. In the case of economic and physical exclusion, the combined effect of social and spatial segregation and the bypassing and lack of integration with the rest of the transport network increases costs of travel. It reduces available alternatives to travel for people with physical or cognitive disabilities via an increasing number of transfers to reach the core city due to inadequate supply, coverage, and integration of transport services. In this regard, another connection between the two frameworks is the notion of informality as a strategy of resistance to splintering, where self-help provision of informal transport and community-based initiatives for building infrastructure help bypassed population overcoming physical obstacles for local mobility.

The fear and spatial dimensions of transport-related social exclusion have a reciprocal relation with splintering urbanism. First, segregation and disconnection facilitate the localization and concentration of crime and insecurity. These social tensions and vulnerabilities, in turn, reinforce social stigmas and negative external perceptions that decrease further the attractiveness of bypassed areas. This has direct implications for exclusion related to the fear of crime, which is mediated by the notion of social disadvantage. It also facilitates the devolution of power and control of spaces. The limited State presence materialized in the lack of investment, connectivity, and availability of government facilities in peripheral neighborhoods leads to the reconfiguration of structures of power to local leaders, civil society organizations, and criminal groups, which may produce exclusion from spaces of the local scale. These elements are usually overlooked by standard quantitative approaches to the analysis of accessibility and transport disadvantage. It is an added justification to the adoption of a qualitative approach. Finally, dimensions such as time deprivation and physical exclusion which tend to manifest on the most socially disadvantaged, become a cumulative consequence of all the direct products and by-products of splintering urbanism and its interaction with other dimensions of social exclusion. Exclusion experienced by single-parent households, women not at work, the elderly and people with disabilities as suggested by (Church et al., 2000), is expected to be more severe in contexts where social tensions, informality, adverse topography and geographies compound levels of exclusion for different social groups and individuals.

4. Conclusions

This chapter discusses some of the main drivers of splintering urbanism, providing a localized interpretation of the theory and giving more weight to governance issues and their role in planning and delivery. The chapter reviewed empirical research in a diversity of urban contexts where constraints related to the geographies, lack of transport provision, poverty, and social tensions limit accessibility for socially vulnerable urban residents across a major region of the Global South. The analysis presented provides learnings for transport researchers and planners concerning access and production of information exploring multiple transport-related social exclusion dimensions in similar contexts. The chapter also provides arguments for the need for multi-disciplinary frameworks for transport studies about access and connectivity.

Beyond the analysis of literature and the translation of frameworks such as splintering urbanism and social exclusion, the chapter finds relevant connections between practices of the differentiated provision of transport networks to different population groups and informal mechanisms to resist social exclusion. The unique combination of theoretical frameworks for transport-related social exclusion presented allows identifying the high relevance of informal transport for disadvantaged groups such as the elderly and people with disabilities residing in already marginalized urban areas. This framework and the evidence used to illustrate it allow to de-construct structural drivers involved in the production and experiences of social exclusion and to reflect on the notion of informality as a flexible and adaptable practice of resistance from selective marginalization and disconnection.

The splintering urbanism thesis of Graham and Marvin (2001) suggests that processes of development of infrastructure are influenced by power and wealth and that while the elites are increasingly improving their living conditions in well-connected premium spaces, those areas without sufficient power and influence are bypassed in the processes of urban and infrastructure development. The network resulting from such patterns of development, planning and governance is a splintered one, as shown in Oviedo Hernandez and Dávila (2016). When such limited connections are not improved, the cycle of transport disadvantage is reinforced by limiting the available supply of public transport, safe pedestrian and cycling circulation and integration with the rest of the transport system. Although this fragmentation is partially addressed through informal mechanisms, these are insufficient in both scale and quality for the multiplicity of needs for the mobility and access to services and opportunities of disadvantaged populations, thus reinforcing the conditions of geographic and social peripherality, adding to already severe cycles of spatial and social segregation.

This chapter engaged with concepts such as splintering urbanism and transport-related social exclusion in Latin America as a region marked by wide gaps between advantaged and disadvantaged urban citizens. Such an exercise seeks to entice a necessary reflection on the multidimensional, multi-scalar, relative and cumulative nature of the cycles that drive the fragmentation of urban transport networks in specific urban contexts and the resulting exclusion of vulnerable population groups. The framework in Fig. 2 builds on the multiple dimensions of social exclusion to expand on our understanding of social disadvantage, spatial mismatch and transport disadvantage. Each dimension reflects the need to examine different forms of disadvantage considering, among other issues, the role of the person in the household, power relations at different scales, and the availability of structural conditions for connectivity and social support (Oviedo Hernandez and Titheridge, 2016). While this has been one of the main contributions of the social exclusion approach, the integrated framework also posits that these cannot be examined in isolation from city-scale processes of planning and delivery of transport networks that determine social and spatial inequalities underpinning splintering urbanism in transport networks.

To engage with social exclusion in a context of splintering urbanism is to connect issues of insecurity, crime and unattractiveness with the physical connectivity produced by networks of transport and other urban services. Linking the two frameworks makes it possible to recognize the general conditions that place residents of marginalized neighborhoods in a disadvantaged position for experiencing social exclusion while acknowledging that such exclusion is individually and collectively experienced. The translation of such frameworks to the Latin American context gives a new perspective on the resistance strategies in the SU theory, reframing informal transport, housing and employment as ways for individuals and communities to challenge structural processes of bypassing and exclusion.

Future applied research can build on the proposed framework for analyzing the drivers of splintering urbanism, and both the experience of and strategies for addressing dimensions of transport-related social exclusion by disadvantaged populations. Further research can test the above framework in specific policy contexts to assert the potential of the various links identified in this review to inform actions to reduce the gaps between the advantaged and disadvantaged in LAC. The proposed framework also can expand on the often narrow definition of disadvantage as a synonym of poverty and deprivation. By introducing a multi-dimensional and multiscalar understanding of the links between provision of transport networks and exclusion, the chapter hopes to inform further reflections about the considerable risks of falling into severe disconnection from modern urban society by people in conditions of social and economic vulnerability beyond poverty and peripherality, which becomes a priority for reducing urban inequalities in contexts experiencing rapid demographic, social and economic change such as many Latin American cities.

References

Abramo, P., 2012. La ciudad com-fusa: Mercado y producción de la estructura urbana en las grandes metrópolis latinoamericanas. Eure 38 (114), 35–69. https://doi.org/10.4067/S0250-71612012000200002.

Altman, I., Zube, E.H., 1989. Public places and spaces. In: Public Places and Spaces, vol. 10. Springer Science & Business Media. https://doi.org/10.1007/978-1-4684-5601-1.

Anand, A., Tiwari, G., 2006. A gendered perspective of the shelter-transport-livelihood link: the case of poor women in Delhi. Trans. Rev. 26 (1), 63–80. https://doi.org/10.1080/01441640500175615.

Andreano, M.S., Benedetti, R., Piersimoni, F., Savio, G., 2020. Mapping poverty of latin American and Caribbean Countries from heaven through night-light satellite images. Soc. Indic. Res., 1–30. https://doi.org/10.1007/s11205-020-02267-1.

Avineri, E., 2012. On the use and potential of behavioural economics from the perspective of transport and climate change. J. Trans. Geogr. 24, 512–521. https://doi.org/10.1016/j.jtrangeo.2012.03.003.

Behrens, R., Chalermpong, S., Oviedo Hernandez, D., 2020. Informal paratransit in the Global South. In: Ison, S., Nelson, J., Mulley, C. (Eds.), Routledge Handbook of Public Transport. Routledge.

Benevenuto, R., Caulfield, B., 2019. Poverty and transport in the global south: an overview. Trans. Policy 79, 115–124. https://doi.org/10.1016/j.tranpol.2019.04.018.

Blair, N., Hine, J., Bukhari, S.M.A., 2013. Analysing the impact of network change on transport disadvantage: a GIS-based case study of Belfast. J. Trans. Geogr. 31, 192–200. https://doi.org/10.1016/j.jtrangeo.2013.06.015.

Blanco, J., Apaolaza, R., 2018. Socio-territorial inequality and differential mobility. Three key issues in the Buenos Aires Metropolitan Region. J. Trans. Geogr. 67, 76–84. https://doi.org/10.1016/j.jtrangeo.2017.07.008.

Blumenberg, E., Manville, M., 2004. Beyond the spatial mismatch: welfare recipients and transportation policy. J. Plan. Lit. 19 (2), 182–205. https://doi.org/10.1177/0885412204269103.

Bocarejo, S.J.P., Oviedo, H.D.R., 2012. Transport accessibility and social inequities: a tool for identification of mobility needs and evaluation of transport investments. J. Trans. Geogr. 24, 142–154. https://doi.org/10.1016/j.jtrangeo.2011.12.004.

Bocarejo, J.P., Portilla, I.J., Velásquez, J.M., Cruz, M.N., Peña, A., Oviedo, D.R., 2014. An innovative transit system and its impact on low income users: the case of the metrocable in Medellín. J. Trans. Geogr. 39, 49–61. https://doi.org/10.1016/j.jtrangeo.2014.06.018.

Boisjoly, G., Moreno-Monroy, A.I., El-Geneidy, A., 2017. Informality and accessibility to jobs by public transit: evidence from the São Paulo Metropolitan Region. J. Trans. Geogr. 64, 89–96. https://doi.org/10.1016/j.jtrangeo.2017.08.005.

Bostock, L., 2001. Pathways of disadvantage? Walking as a mode of transport among low-income mothers. Health Soc. Care Commun. 9 (1), 11–18. https://doi.org/10.1046/j.1365-2524.2001.00275.x.

Brenner, N., Madden, D.J., Wachsmuth, D., 2011. Assemblage urbanism and the challenges of critical urban theory. City 15 (2), 225–240. https://doi.org/10.1080/13604813.2011.568717.

Brockerhoff, M., 1995. Child survival in big cities: the disadvantages of migrants. Soc. Sci. Med. 40 (10), 1371–1383. https://doi.org/10.1016/0277-9536(94)00268-X.

Burchardt, T., Le Grand, J., Piachaud, D., 2002. Degrees of Social Exclusion: Developing a dynamic measure. Understanding Social Exclusion. Oxford University Press, Oxford.

CAF, (2011). Desarrollo urbano y movilidad en America Latina. Panama. Retrieved from https://www.caf.com/media/4203/desarrollourbano_y_movilidad_americalatina.pdf.

Caldeira, T.P.R., 2000. City of Walls. Crime, Segregation and Citizenship in São Paulo. University of California Press, Berkeley, CA.

Caldeira, T.P.R., 2017. Peripheral urbanization: autoconstruction, transversal logics, and politics in cities of the global south. Environ. Plan. D Soc. Space 35 (1), 3–20. https://doi.org/10.1177/0263775816658479.

Caprotti, F., Yu, L., Levy, C., Allen, A., Castán Broto, V., Westman, L., 2019. Unlocking urban trajectories. In: Sustainable Cities in Asia, pp. 7–22. Routledge https://doi.org/10.4324/9781315643069-1.

Casas, I., Delmelle, E.C., 2014. Identifying dimensions of exclusion from a BRT system in a developing country: a content analysis approach. J. Trans. Geogr. 39, 228–237. https://doi.org/10.1016/j.jtrangeo.2014.07.013.

Cass, N., Shove, E., Urry, J., 2005. Social exclusion, mobility and access. Soc. Rev. 53 (3), 539–555. https://doi.org/10.1111/j.1467-954X.2005.00565.x.

Castells, M., 2000. The Rise of the Network Society, Second Edition. Blackwell Publishing, U.S.

Castells, M., 2001. Space of flows, space of places: Materials for a theory of urbanism in the information age. The City Reader. Retrieved from https://books.google.co.uk/books?hl=en&lr=&id=hAItCgAAQBAJ&oi=fnd&pg=PA229&dq=Castells,+2001&ots=ON16I83aXj&sig=mirpTlD0ArWl0NNTWV-GuJvHU8k.

Castells, M., 2012. Space of flows, space of places: materials for a theory of urbanism in the information age. Comp. Plan. Cult., 45–63. https://doi.org/10.4324/9780203826508.

Cervero, R., Golub, A., 2007. Informal transport: a global perspective. Trans. Policy 14 (6), 445–457. https://doi.org/10.1016/j.tranpol.2007.04.011.

Church, A., Frost, M., Sullivan, K., 2000. Transport and social exclusion in London. Trans. Policy 7 (3), 195–205. https://doi.org/10.1016/S0967-070X(00)00024-X.

Coatsworth, J.H., 2008. Inequality, institutions and economic growth in latin America. J. Latin Am. Stud. 40 (3), 545–569. https://doi.org/10.1017/S0022216X08004689.

Colleoni, M., 2016. A social science approach to the study of mobility: an introduction. In: Research for Development. Springer, pp. 23–33. https://doi.org/10.1007/978-3-319-22578-4_2.

Combs, T.S., Rodríguez, D.A., 2014. Joint impacts of bus rapid transit and urban form on vehicle ownership: new evidence from a quasi-longitudinal analysis in Bogotá, Colombia. Trans. Res. Part A Policy Pract. 69, 272–285. https://doi.org/10.1016/j.tra.2014.08.025.

Combs, T.S., Shay, E., Salvesen, D., Kolosna, C., Madeley, M., 2016. Understanding the multiple dimensions of transportation disadvantage: the case of rural North Carolina. Case Stud. Trans. Policy 4 (2), 68–77. https://doi.org/10.1016/j.cstp.2016.02.004.

Coutard, O., 2008. Placing splintering urbanism: introduction. Geoforum 39 (6), 1815–1820. https://doi.org/10.1016/j.geoforum.2008.10.008.

Crankshaw, O., 2014. Causal mechanisms, job search and the labour market spatial mismatch: a realist criticism of the neo-positivist method. J. Crit. Realism 13 (5), 498–519. https://doi.org/10.1179/1476743014Z.00000000041.

Curran, D., 2016. Social exclusion. In: Currie, G. (Ed.), Work, Employment and Society, vol. 30. Emerald Group Publishing, pp. 894–896. Issue 5 https://doi.org/10.1177/0950017016644417.
Currie, G., Delbosc, A., 2011. Transport disadvantage: a review. In: New Perspectives and Methods in Transport and Social Exclusion Research. Emerald Group Publishing Limited, pp. 15–25. https://doi.org/10.1108/9781780522012-002.
Daniels, J.P., 2020. Venezuelan migrants "struggling to survive" amid COVID-19. Lancet (London, England) 395 (10229), 1023. https://doi.org/10.1016/S0140-6736(20)30718-2.
Dávila, J.D., Gilbert, A., Brand, P., Rueda, N., Coupe, F., 2006. Housing and Land for the Urban Poor. Case studies of Bogotá–Soacha and Medellín. Unpublished Report for World Bank Cities Alliance & Departamento Nacional de Planeacion.
Day, K., 2001. Constructing masculinity and women's fear in public space in Irvine, California. Gender Place Cult. 8 (2), 109–127. https://doi.org/10.1080/09663690120050742.
Delbosc, A., Currie, G., 2011. Exploring the relative influences of transport disadvantage and social exclusion on well-being. Trans. Policy 18 (4), 555–562. https://doi.org/10.1016/j.tranpol.2011.01.011.
Delbosc, A., Currie, G., 2018. Accessibility and Exclusion Related to Well Being. pp. 57–69. https://doi.org/10.1007/978-3-319-76623-2_4.
ECLAC, 2015. Social Panorama of Latin America 2015. Briefing paper | Publication | Economic Commission for Latin America and the Caribbean. http://www.cepal.org/en/publications/39964-social-panorama-latin-america-2015-briefing-paper.
Engels, B., Liu, G.-J.J., 2011. Social exclusion, location and transport disadvantage amongst non-driving seniors in a Melbourne municipality, Australia. J. Trans. Geogr. 19 (4), 984–996. https://doi.org/10.1016/j.jtrangeo.2011.03.007.
Falavigna, C., Hernandez, D., 2016. Assessing inequalities on public transport affordability in two latin American cities: Montevideo (Uruguay) and Córdoba (Argentina). Trans. Policy 45, 145–155. https://doi.org/10.1016/j.tranpol.2015.09.011.
Fan, Y., 2012. The Planners' War against spatial mismatch: lessons learned and ways forward. J. Plan. Lit. 27 (2), 153–169. https://doi.org/10.1177/0885412211431984.
Fernández-Maldonado, A.M., 2008. Expanding networks for the urban poor: water and telecommunications services in Lima, Peru. Geoforum 39 (6), 1884–1896. https://doi.org/10.1016/j.geoforum.2007.11.007.
Frith, J., 2012. Splintered space: hybrid spaces and differential mobility. Mobilities 7 (1), 131–149. https://doi.org/10.1080/17450101.2012.631815.
Furlong, K., 2014. STS beyond the "modern infrastructure ideal": extending theory by engaging with infrastructure challenges in the South. Technol. Soc. 38, 139–147. https://doi.org/10.1016/j.techsoc.2014.04.001.
Gandelman, N., Serebrisky, T., Suárez-Alemán, A., 2019. Household spending on transport in Latin America and the Caribbean: a dimension of transport affordability in the region. J. Trans. Geogr. 79, 102482. https://doi.org/10.1016/j.jtrangeo.2019.102482.
Gilbert, A., 1981. Pirates and invaders: Land acquisition in urban Colombia and Venezuela. World Dev. 9 (7), 657–678. https://doi.org/10.1016/0305-750X(81)90069-3.
Gilbert, A., 2005. Sustaining urban development in Latin America in an unpredictable world. In: Managing Urban Futures. Sustainability and Urban Growth in Developing Countries, pp. 53–62. https://doi.org/10.4324/9781315249827-13.
Gilbert, A., 2009. The rise (and fall?) of a state land bank. Habit. Int. 33 (4), 425–435. https://doi.org/10.1016/j.habitatint.2009.01.003.
Giuliano, G., Chakrabarti, S., Rhoads, M., 2015. Transportation geography. In: International Encyclopedia of the Social & Behavioral Sciences, second ed, pp. 607–615. https://doi.org/10.1016/B978-0-08-097086-8.72071-X.
Gleeson, B., Randolph, B., 2002. Social disadvantage and planning in the sydney context. Urban Policy Res. 20 (1), 101–107. https://doi.org/10.1080/08111140220131636.

Gómez, J., Acevedo, J., 2013. Studying Car and Motorcycle Ownership Levels in Developing Countries Using Individual Income Distributions. In: 13th World Congress on Transport Research, Rio de Janeiro, Brazil. CONF.
Graham, S., 2009. Disrupted cities: when infrastructure fails. In: Disrupted Cities: When Infrastructure Fails. https://doi.org/10.4324/9780203894484.
Graham, S., Marvin, S., 2001. Splintering Urbanism: Networked Infrastructures, Technological Mobilities and the Urban Condition. Routledge, London.
Grengs, J., 2015. Nonwork accessibility as a social equity indicator. Int. J. Sustain. Transport. 9 (1), 1–14. https://doi.org/10.1080/15568318.2012.719582.
Günther, I., Launov, A., 2012. Informal employment in developing countries: opportunity or last resort? J. Dev. Econ. 97 (1), 88–98. https://doi.org/10.1016/j.jdeveco.2011.01.001.
Gutiérrez, M., Cantillo, V., Arellana, J., Ortúzar, J.d.D., 2020. Estimating bicycle demand in an aggressive environment. Int. J. Sustain. Transport. https://doi.org/10.1080/15568318.2020.1734886.
Guzman, L.A., Bocarejo, J.P., 2017. Urban form and spatial urban equity in Bogota, Colombia. Transport. Res. Proc. 25, 4491–4506. https://doi.org/10.1016/j.trpro.2017.05.345.
Habitat, O., 2012. Estado de las Ciudades de América Latina y el Caribe 2012, Rumbo a una nueva transición urbana. In: Exit imagen y cultura. Issue 17. https://doi.org/HS/053/12S ISBN Serie 978-92-1-133397-8.
Halás, M., Klapka, P., Kladivo, P., 2014. Distance-decay functions for daily travel-to-work flows. J. Trans. Geogr. 35, 107–119. https://doi.org/10.1016/j.jtrangeo.2014.02.001.
Harvey, A.S., Mukhopadhyay, A.K., 2007. When twenty-four hours is not enough: time poverty of working parents. Soc. Indic. Res. 82 (1), 57–77. https://doi.org/10.1007/s11205-006-9002-5.
Heinrichs, D., Goletz, M., Lenz, B., 2017. Negotiating territory: strategies of informal transport operators to access public space in urban Africa and Latin America. Transport. Res. Proc. 25, 4507–4517. https://doi.org/10.1016/j.trpro.2017.05.346.
Heinrichsa, D., Bernet, J.S., 2014. Public transport and accessibility in informal settlements: aerial cable cars in Medellín, Colombia. Transport. Res. Proc. 4, 55. https://doi.org/10.1016/j.trpro.2014.11.005.
Hernandez-Garcia, J., 2013. Slum tourism, city branding and social urbanism: the case of Medellin, Colombia. J. Place Manage. Dev. 6 (1), 43–51. https://doi.org/10.1108/17538331311306122.
Hidalgo, D., Huizenga, C., 2013. Implementation of sustainable urban transport in Latin America. Res. Transport. Econ. 40 (1), 66–77. https://doi.org/10.1016/j.retrec.2012.06.034.
Hine, J., 2003. Social exclusion and transport systems. Transport Policy 10 (4). https://doi.org/10.1016/j.tranpol.2003.08.003.
Hurni, A., 2007. Marginalised groups in Western Sydney: the experience of sole parents and unemployed young people. In: No Way To Go: Transport and Social Disadvantage in Australian Communities, pp. 10.01–10.11.
ILO, 2019. The future of work in Latin America and the Caribbean: old and new forms of employment and challenges for labour regulation (Issue 20). ILO. http://www.ilo.org/santiago/publicaciones/coyuntura-laboral-américa-latina-caribe/WCMS_701409/lang- -es/index.htm.
Inostroza, L., 2017. Informal urban development in Latin American urban peripheries. Spatial assessment in Bogotá, Lima and Santiago de Chile. Landscape Urban Plan. 165, 267–279. https://doi.org/10.1016/j.landurbplan.2016.03.021.
Inostroza, L., Baur, R., Csaplovics, E., 2013. Urban sprawl and fragmentation in Latin America: a dynamic quantification and characterization of spatial patterns. J. Environ. Manage. 115, 87–97. https://doi.org/10.1016/j.jenvman.2012.11.007.

Irazábal, C., 2004. Models of Urban Governance and Planning in Latin America and the United States: Associationism, Regime Theory, and Communicative Action. Planning Models Cult. Cities 1–19.

Jaglin, S., 2008. Differentiating networked services in Cape Town: echoes of splintering urbanism? Geoforum 39 (6), 1897–1906. https://doi.org/10.1016/j.geoforum.2008.04.010.

Jocoy, C.., Del Casino Jr., V.J., 2010. Homelessness, travel behavior, and the politics of transportation mobilities in Long Beach, California. Environ. Plan A. 42 (8), 1943–1963. http://doi.org/10.1068/a42341.

Kamalipour, H., Dovey, K., 2019. Mapping the visibility of informal settlements. Habitat Int. 85, 63–75. https://doi.org/10.1016/j.habitatint.2019.01.002.

Kenyon, S., Lyons, G., Rafferty, J., 2002. Transport and social exclusion: investigating the possibility of promoting inclusion through virtual mobility. J. Trans. Geogr. 10 (3), 207–219. https://doi.org/10.1016/S0966-6923(02)00012-1.

Kooy, M., Bakker, K., 2008. Splintered networks: the colonial and contemporary waters of Jakarta. Geoforum 39 (6), 1843–1858. https://doi.org/10.1016/j.geoforum.2008.07.012.

Levy, C., 2013. Travel choice reframed: "deep distribution" and gender in urban transport. Environ. Urban. 25 (1), 47–63. https://doi.org/10.1177/0956247813477810.

Light, J.S., 2002. Splintering urbanism: networked infrastructures, technological mobilities, and the urban condition (review). Technol. Cult. 43 (3). https://doi.org/10.1353/tech.2002.0124.

Litchenberger, E., 2015. Cities: Internal structure, International Encyclopedia of the Social & Behavioral Sciences, second ed., p. 593. https://doi.org/10.1016/B978-0-08-097086-8.72083-6.

Lucas, K., 2012. Transport and social exclusion: where are we now? Transport Policy 20, 105–113. https://doi.org/10.1016/j.tranpol.2012.01.013.

Lucas, K., 2019. A new evolution for transport-related social exclusion research? J. Transport Geogr. 81, 102529. https://doi.org/10.1016/j.jtrangeo.2019.102529.

Lucas, K., Currie, G., 2012. Developing socially inclusive transportation policy: transferring the United Kingdom policy approach to the State of Victoria? Transportation 39 (1), 151–173. https://doi.org/10.1007/s11116-011-9324-2.

Lucas, K., Mattioli, G., Verlinghieri, E., Guzman, A., 2016. Transport poverty and its adverse social consequences. Proc. Inst. Civil Eng. Transport 169 (6), 353–365. https://doi.org/10.1680/jtran.15.00073.

Lussault, M., 2007. L'homme spatial: la construction sociale de l'espace humain. vol. 363 Seuil Paris.

Lyons, G., 2003. The introduction of social exclusion into the field of travel behaviour. Transport Policy 10 (4), 339–342. https://doi.org/10.1016/j.tranpol.2003.09.001.

Macdonald, K., Grieco, M., 2007. Accessibility, mobility and connectivity: the changing frontiers of everyday routine. Mobilities 2 (1), 1–14. https://doi.org/10.1080/17450100601106153.

Mackett, R.L., Thoreau, R., 2015. Transport, social exclusion and health. J. Transport Health 2 (4), 610–617. https://doi.org/10.1016/j.jth.2015.07.006.

Malmusi, D., Borrell, C., Benach, J., 2010. Migration-related health inequalities: showing the complex interactions between gender, social class and place of origin. Soc. Sci. Med. 71 (9), 1610–1619. https://doi.org/10.1016/j.socscimed.2010.07.043.

Manderscheid, K., 2009. Integrating space and mobilities into the analysis of social inequality. Distinktion 10 (1), 7–27. https://doi.org/10.1080/1600910X.2009.9672739.

Manderscheid, K., 2016. Unequal mobilities. Mobilities Inequality, pp. 27–50. https://books.google.co.uk/books?hl=en&lr=&id=fikHDAAAQBAJ&oi=fnd&pg=PA27&dq=manderscheid+2009+mobilities&ots=TWSr1pbJRr&sig=NzmE3tGbmq3GvUF8uQwkW9TpG-c.

Manderscheid, K., Bergman, M.M., 2008. Spatial patterns and social inequality in Switzerland–modern or post-modern. In: The Social Fabric of the Networked City, pp. 41–65.
Marx, B., Stoker, T., Suri, T., 2013. The economics of slums in the developing world. J. Econ. Perspect. 27 (4), 187–210. https://doi.org/10.1257/jep.27.4.187.
McFarlane, C., 2011. One assemblage and critical urbanism. City 15 (2), 204–224. https://doi.org/10.1080/13604813.2011.568715.
McFarlane, C., Silver, J., Truelove, Y., 2017. Cities within cities: intra-urban comparison of infrastructure in Mumbai, Delhi and Cape Town. Urban Geogr. 38 (9), 1393–1417. https://doi.org/10.1080/02723638.2016.1243386.
Mclafferty, S., 2015. Spatial mismatch. In: International Encyclopedia of the Social & Behavioral Sciences, second ed, pp. 157–160. https://doi.org/10.1016/B978-0-08-097086-8.32193-6.
Montoya, C.C., Dirección de Análisis y Programación, & CAF., S. de la V. de I. de, 2011. Desarrollo urbano y movilidad en América Latina. In: Banco de desarrollo de America Latina CAF. https://www.caf.com/media/4203/desarrollourbano_y_movilidad_americalatina.pdf.
Montoya-Robledo, V., Montes Calero, L., Bernal Carvajal, V., Galarza Molina, D.C., Pipicano, W., Peña, A.J., Pipicano, C., López Valderrama, J.S., Fernández, M.A., Porras, I., Arias, N., Miranda, L., 2020. Gender stereotypes affecting active mobility of care in Bogotá. Transport. Res. D Transport Environ. 86, 102470. https://doi.org/10.1016/j.trd.2020.102470.
Moss, T., 2008. "Cold spots" of urban infrastructure: "Shrinking" processes in Eastern Germany and the modern infrastructural ideal. Int. J. Urban Regional Res. 32 (2), 436–451. https://doi.org/10.1111/j.1468-2427.2008.00790.x.
Murray, A.T., Davis, R., 2001. Equity in regional service provision. J. Regional Sci. 41 (4), 557–600. https://doi.org/10.1111/0022-4146.00233.
Nansen, B., Gibbs, L., MacDougall, C., Vetere, F., Ross, N.J., McKendrick, J., 2015. Children's interdependent mobility: compositions, collaborations and compromises. Children's Geogr. 13 (4), 467–481. https://doi.org/10.1080/14733285.2014.887813.
Newburn, T., 2016. Social disadvantage: crime and punishment. In: Social Advantage and Disadvantage, pp. 322–340.
Odendaal, N., 2011. Splintering urbanism or split agendas? examining the spatial distribution of technology access in relation to ICT policy in Durban, South Africa. Urban Stud. 48 (11), 2375–2397. https://doi.org/10.1177/0042098010388951.
Ohnmacht, T., Maksim, H., Bergman, M.M., 2009. Mobilities and inequality—making connections. Mobilities Inequality, 7–25. https://books.google.co.uk/books?hl=en&lr=&id=iByaNpTiCR4C&oi=fnd&pg=PA7&dq=Ohnmacht+et+al.+2008+transport&ots=h92MBN2xX1&sig=VQvEek58OwDzszGU3fnphv1Yn00.
Ong, P., Blumenberg, E., 1998. Job access, commute and travel burden among welfare recipients. Urban Stud. 35 (1), 77–93. https://doi.org/10.1080/0042098985087.
Our World in Data, 2021. Motor vehicles per 1000 inhabitants vs GDP per capita, 2014. https://ourworldindata.org/grapher/road-vehicles-per-1000-inhabitants-vs-gdp-per-capita?tab=table.
Oviedo, D., Guzman, L.A., 2020. Revisiting accessibility in a context of sustainable transport: capabilities and inequalities in Bogota. Sustain. (Switzerland) 12 (11), 4464. https://doi.org/10.3390/su12114464.
Oviedo Hernandez, D., Dávila, J.D., 2016. Transport, urban development and the peripheral poor in Colombia—placing splintering urbanism in the context of transport networks. J. Transport Geogr. 51, 180–192. https://doi.org/10.1016/j.jtrangeo.2016.01.003.
Oviedo Hernandez, D., Titheridge, H., 2016. Mobilities of the periphery: informality, access and social exclusion in the urban fringe in Colombia. J. Transp. Geogr. 55, 152–164. https://doi.org/10.1016/j.jtrangeo.2015.12.004.

Parnell, S., 2014. Poverty and 'The City'. pp. 16–18.
Portes, A., Schauffler, R., 1993. Competing perspectives on the Latin American informal sector. Popul. Dev. Rev. 19 (1), 33–60. https://doi.org/10.2307/2938384.
Preston, J., Rajé, F., 2007. Accessibility, mobility and transport-related social exclusion. J. Transp. Geogr. 15 (3), 151–160.
Prud'homme, R., 1995. The dangers of decentralization. World Bank Res. Observ. 10 (2), 201–220. https://doi.org/10.1093/wbro/10.2.201.
Rahman, A., Barter, P., 1998. UNCHS (Habitat) Regional Symposium on Urban Poverty in Asia Fukuoka, 27-29 October 1998 Transport and Urban Poverty in Asia : A Brief Introduction to the Key Issues. UNCHS, October 1998. 27–29 http://www.fukuoka.unhabitat.org/docs/occasional_papers/project_a/06/transport-barter-e.html.
Rest, K.D., Hirsch, P., 2016. Daily scheduling of home health care services using time-dependent public transport. Flex. Serv. Manuf. J. 28 (3), 495–525. https://doi.org/10.1007/s10696-015-9227-1.
Rodríguez-Vignoli, J., Rowe, F., 2018. How is internal migration reshaping metropolitan populations in Latin America? A new method and new evidence. Popul. Stud. 72 (2), 253–273. https://doi.org/10.1080/00324728.2017.1416155.
Romero, D., 2014. Insecurity or perception of insecurity? Urban crime and dissatisfaction with life: evidence from the case of Bogotá. Peace Econ. Peace Sci. Publ. Policy 20 (1), 169–208. https://doi.org/10.1515/peps-2013-0057.
Sabatini, F., 2006. The Social Spatial Segregation in the Cities of Latin America. Publications https://publications.iadb.org/publications/english/document/The-Social-Spatial-Segregation-in-the-Cities-of-Latin-America.pdf.
Salonen, M., Toivonen, T., 2013. Modelling travel time in urban networks: comparable measures for private car and public transport. J. Transport Geogr. 31, 143–153. https://doi.org/10.1016/j.jtrangeo.2013.06.011.
Samuels, I., 2001. Achieving sustainable urban form'. compact cities: sustainable urban forms for developing countries. Urban Design Int. 6 (3–4). Taylor & Francis https://doi.org/10.1057/palgrave.udi.9000039.
Sánchez, F., Palau, M.D.M., 2006. Conflict, decentralisation and local governance in Colombia, 1974-2004. Document. CEDE 20.
Santana Palacios, M., Cochran, A., Bell, C., Hernández Jiménez, U., Leshner, E., Trejo Morales, F., Chatman, D.G., 2020. Bus rapid transit arrives in Barranquilla, Colombia: understanding a changing landscape through residents' travel experiences. Travel Behav. Soc. 21, 131–139. https://doi.org/10.1016/j.tbs.2020.06.003.
Scholl, L., Gray, C., 2016. Urban Transport and Poverty: Mobility and Accessibility Effects of IDB-Supported BRT Systems in Cali and Lima. Inter-American Development Bank. https://publications.iadb.org/.../Urban-Transport-and-Poverty-Mobility-and-Accessibility-Effects-of-IDB-supported-BRT-Systems-in-Cali-and-Lima.pdf.
Schwanen, T., Lucas, K., Akyelken, N., Cisternas Solsona, D., Carrasco, J.A., Neutens, T., 2015. Rethinking the links between social exclusion and transport disadvantage through the lens of social capital. Transport. Res. Part A Policy Pract. 74, 123–135. https://doi.org/10.1016/j.tra.2015.02.012.
Serebrisky, T., Gómez-Lobo, A., Estupiñán, N., Muñoz-raskin, R., Gómez-Lobo, A., Estupiñán, N., Muñoz-Raskin, R., Gómez-Lobo, A., Estupiñán, N., Muñoz-raskin, R., Gómez-Lobo, A., Estupiñán, N., Muñoz-Raskin, R., 2009. Affordability and subsidies in public urban transport: what do we mean, what can be done? Transport Rev. 29 (6), 715–739. https://doi.org/10.1080/01441640902786415.
Smeeding, T., 2015. Poverty, sociology of. Int. Encycl. Soc. Behav. Sci., 753–759. https://doi.org/10.1016/B978-0-08-097086-8.32113-4.
Smets, P., Salman, T., 2016. The multi-layered-ness of urban segregation. On the simultaneous inclusion and exclusion in Latin American cities. Habitat Int. 54, 80–87. https://doi.org/10.1016/j.habitatint.2015.08.013.

Stanley, J.R., Vella-Brodrick, D.A., 2011. What leads to social inclusion? An examination of trips, social capital and well-being. In: New Perspectives and Methods in Transport and Social Exclusion Research. Emerald Group Publishing Limited, pp. 187–200. https://doi.org/10.1108/9781780522012-013.

Social Exclusion Unit, 2003. Making the Connections: Final report on Transport and Social Exclusion. Office of the Deputy Prime Minister, London.

Stanley, J.R., 2011b. Social Exclusion. In: Currie, G. (Ed.), New Perspectives and Methods in Transport and Social Exclusion Research. Emerald Group Publishing, Bingley, UK, pp. 15–26.

Stanley, J. R. (2011a). Measuring Social Exclusion. In New Perspectives and Methods in Transport and Social Exclusion Research (pp. 77–90). Book Section. Retrieved from <Go to ISI>://WOS:000304367800006.

Stanley, J., Hensher, D.A., Stanley, J., Currie, G., Greene, W.H., Vella-Brodrick, D., 2011. Social exclusion and the value of mobility. J. Transport Econ. Policy 45 (2), 197–222.

Stoekl, A., Musiol, H., 2015. Liquid modernity. Oil Cult. https://doi.org/10.5749/minnesota/9780816689682.003.0007.

Suárez, M., Murata, M., Delgado Campos, J., 2016. Why do the poor travel less? Urban structure, commuting and economic informality in Mexico city. Urban Stud. 53 (12), 2548–2566. https://doi.org/10.1177/0042098015596925.

Tarazona, A.H., 2015. From utopian planning to lived experience in a suburban social housing community: the case of Ciudad Verde, Colombia. In: C21 International Conference on "The Ideal City: Between Myth and Reality. Representations, Policies, Contradictions and Challenges for Tomorrow's Urban Life" Urbino (Italy) 27–29 August 2015, 127, p. 10.

Thibert, J., Osorio, G.A., 2014. Urban segregation and metropolitics in Latin America: the Case of Bogotá, Colombia. Int. J. Urban Regional Res. 38 (4), 1319–1343. https://doi.org/10.1111/1468-2427.12021.

Torres, A.I.A., 2011. Conflicto armado, crimen organizado y disputas por la hegemonía en Soacha y el sur de Bogotá. Pontificia Universidad Javeriana.

Turner, S., 2009. Economy, informal. In: International Encyclopedia of Human Geography. Elsevier, pp. 367–371. http://doi.org/10.1016/B978-008044910-4.00179-6.

Turner, J., Grieco, M., 2000. Gender and time poverty: the neglected social policy implications of gendered time, transport and travel. Time Soc. 9 (1), 129–136. https://doi.org/10.1177/0961463X00009001007.

UN, 2020. Employment Situation in Latin America and the Caribbean: Work in times of pandemic: the challenges of the coronovirus disease (COVID-19) (Serie: ECLAC-ILO Bulletin No.22). United Nations. https://repositorio.cepal.org/handle/11362/45582.

UNCRD-IDB, 2011. Sustainable Transport Survey FTS Latin America. http://www.uncrdlac.org/fts/.

Valenzuela Aguilera, A., 2013. Urban surges: power, territory, and the social control of space in Latin America. Latin Am. Perspect. 40 (2), 21–34. https://doi.org/10.1177/0094582X12466834.

Vasconcellos, E.A., 2014. Urban transport environment and equity: the case for developing countries. In: Urban Transport Environment and Equity: The Case for Developing Countries. Routledge. https://doi.org/10.4324/9781315071756.

Vecchio, G., Tiznado-Aitken, I., Hurtubia, R., 2020. Transport and equity in Latin America: a critical review of socially oriented accessibility assessments. Transport Rev. 40 (3), 354–381. https://doi.org/10.1080/01441647.2020.1711828.

Venter, C., Jennings, G., Hidalgo, D., Valderrama Pineda, A.F., 2018. The equity impacts of bus rapid transit: a review of the evidence and implications for sustainable transport. Int. J. Sustain. Transport. 12 (2), 140–152. Taylor and Francis Ltd. https://doi.org/10.1080/15568318.2017.1340528.

Vignoli, J.R., 2008. Movilidad cotidiana, desigualdad social y segregacíón residencial en cuatro metrópolis de América Latina. Eure 34 (103), 49–71. https://doi.org/10.4067/s0250-71612008000300003.

Vinet, L., Zhedanov, A., 2011. A “missing” family of classical orthogonal polynomials. J. Phys. A Math. Theor. 44 (8). Cepal https://doi.org/10.1088/1751-8113/44/8/085201.

Warren, T., 2003. Class- and gender-based working time?: time poverty and the division of domestic labour. Sociology 37 (4), 733–752. https://doi.org/10.1177/00380385030374006.

Watson, V., 2009. “The planned city sweeps the poor away...”: urban planning and 21st century urbanisation. Progr. Plan. 72 (3), 151–193. https://doi.org/10.1016/j.progress.2009.06.002.

Watson, V., 2015. Planning and development. In: International Encyclopedia of the Social & Behavioral Sciences, second ed, pp. 180–186. https://doi.org/10.1016/B978-0-08-097086-8.74023-2.

Wegelin, E.A., Borgman, K.M., 1995. Options for municipal interventions in urban poverty alleviation. Environ. Urban. 7 (2), 131–151. https://doi.org/10.1177/095624789500700219.

Welch, T.F., 2013. Equity in transport: the distribution of transit access and connectivity among affordable housing units. Transport Policy 30, 283–293. https://doi.org/10.1016/j.tranpol.2013.09.020.

Whitzman, C., 2007. Stuck at the front door: gender, fear of crime and the challenge of creating safer space. Environ. Plan. A 39 (11), 2715–2732. https://doi.org/10.1068/a38449.

Willis, K.D., 2009. Squatter settlements. In: International Encyclopedia of Human Geography, pp. 403–408. https://doi.org/10.1016/B978-008044910-4.00122-X.

Yañez-Pagans, P., Martinez, D., Mitnik, O.A., Scholl, L., Vazquez, A., 2019. Urban transport systems in Latin America and the Caribbean: lessons and challenges. Lat. Am. Econ. Rev. 28 (1), 1–25.

Yunda, J.G., Sletto, B., 2017. Property rights, urban land markets and the contradictions of redevelopment in centrally located informal settlements in Bogotá, Colombia, and Buenos Aires, Argentina. Plan. Perspect. 32 (4), 601–621. https://doi.org/10.1080/02665433.2017.1314792.

Zérah, M.H., 2008. Splintering urbanism in Mumbai: contrasting trends in a multilayered society. Geoforum 39 (6), 1922–1932. https://doi.org/10.1016/j.geoforum.2008.02.001.

CHAPTER SIX

Transit-induced gentrification and displacement: The state of the debate

Elizabeth C. Delmelle*
Department of Geography and Earth Sciences, University of North Carolina at Charlotte, Charlotte, NC, United States
*Corresponding author: e-mail address: edelmell@uncc.edu

Contents

Abstract

Investments in new transportation infrastructure hold the potential to transform the urban socioeconomic landscape by reshaping accessibility and by encouraging new developments around these investments. This chapter outlines the theoretical arguments for why and how transport, specifically rail transit, is expected to impact the socioeconomic composition of neighborhoods and reviews the relevant empirical literature on the subject. Neighborhood socioeconomic change, including gentrification, can be viewed as the product of shifts in residential sorting of residents reacting to the placement of a new (transit) amenity which may place increased demand for living in a particular area. This demand may place an upward pressure on nearby housing values and rents, affecting the socioeconomic composition of those willing and able to afford these price premiums, thus spurring or accelerating gentrification. Rising land values may also lead to the disproportionate exit of lower-income residents unable to keep up with elevated rents or property taxes. To date, the empirical evidence on the link between transport investments and gentrification has mixed findings, very often underscoring the importance of local context in directing a neighborhood's path. Research has overwhelmingly centered on aggregate neighborhood changes, but several studies have recently emerged that center on individual movements that give rise to these neighborhood-scale outcomes.

Keywords: Transit, Gentrification, Neighborhood change

Advances in Transport Policy and Planning, Volume 8
ISSN 2543-0009
https://doi.org/10.1016/bs.atpp.2021.06.005
Copyright © 2021 Elsevier Inc.
All rights reserved.

1. Introduction

Investments in transport often have multiple, sometime conflicting goals. For instance, new transport infrastructure offers mobility solutions to residents while also impacting land-use changes or encouraging or re-directing economic development. These goals may come into conflict when considering the impacts of transport, and in particular, new rail stations, on neighborhood outcomes. When new fixed rail stations are placed in lower-income neighborhoods, they may increase accessibility to opportunities that could lift the economic prospects of residents given that access has been directly linked to positive labor market outcomes (Andersson et al., 2017; Jin and Paulsen, 2018). However, this increase in accessibility may increase demand for property nearby stations, placing an upward pressure on housing values and rents, potentially leading to the disproportionate exodus of those residents who could benefit the most from the mobility improvements. This transit-induced displacement and gentrification scenario has raised concerns from social equity advocates who contend that the economic development goals associated with transit, especially in the case of transit-oriented developments (TODs)—the intentional design considerations around fixed-rail transit stations that promote dense, mixed-use, walkable developments (Calthorpe, 1993)—have become a priority at the expense of vulnerable residents (Rayle, 2015; Revington, 2015).

Over the past several decades, cities across the United States have placed a renewed emphasis on investing in rail transit systems as a means for promoting urban redevelopment or city branding (Ferbrache and Knowles, 2017). The impacts that these investments have had on the urban socioeconomic landscape and in potentially exacerbating gentrification, segregation, and inequalities, have generated a growing body of scholarly inquiry. In some instances, these concerns have led to protests of new transit plans as residents or advocacy groups have concluded that the potential negative impacts to neighborhoods outweigh the positives of transit expansion (Rayle, 2015). Contrary to the expected hypothesis, much of the empirical research on the subject has found the impacts of transit to be rather small, or at a minimum, challenging to quantify. In this chapter, I review the current state of knowledge on the topic, tracing the empirical and theoretical links between transit's impact on land values, residential mobility, and neighborhood outcomes. Given the breadth of research on the topic, and heterogeneity across modes and geographic contexts (Efthymiou and Antoniou,

2013; Eliasson et al., 2020), I focus on fixed rail transit from a North American perspective. I close with future research directions at gaps in this state of knowledge.

2. Theoretical background

The theoretical connection from investments in transport to neighborhood changes can be understood by tracing the impacts from land values to residential mobility decisions to neighborhood outcomes. Transport investments can alter nearby land values via two pathways: (1) it changes the accessibility landscape and (2) it provides new amenities near stations (especially in the case of TOD). In either case, these changes result in an increased demand for locations near transit stations, elevating property values and rents, which in turn impacts who moves into and out of a neighborhood. Those willing and able to pay a premium for transit proximity can outbid lower-income residents who may be priced out of these locations. Furthermore, as a neighborhood's socioeconomic or demographic composition begins to change, some existing residents may also decide to relocate due to the changing fabric of the neighborhood. Even if lower-income residents are not disproportionately displaced, rising rents may reduce the overall supply of affordable housing in a metropolitan area and may therefore indirectly exacerbate inequalities in sorting patterns (Newman and Wyly, 2006). In this respect, transit may serve to exclude lower-income residents from moving in to the newly invested-in neighborhood.

The first pathway to neighborhood change describes traditional urban location theory's connection between transportation and land use where accessibility plays a key role. According to this well-documented theory, as a result of the increased accessibility brought about by a new transport investment, transportation costs decline closer to the new infrastructure, resulting in a shift in demand, leading to increased land values (Huang, 1996). Per this perspective, households make a tradeoff between commuting costs and larger lot and home sizes; those with higher incomes are expected to pay higher transportation costs while opting to reside in larger, suburban homes on the outskirts of cities (Alonso, 1964; Muth, 1969). In the case of urban rail transit investments, the accessibility improvements are usually marginal at the regional level, given that there is already an existing automotive infrastructure network. Accessibility improvements may be felt more acutely by those without automobile access or the ability to drive, in regions with higher levels of traffic congestion, and with larger and more well-connected the transit system. Overall, the impacts on development are thought to be more redistributive, directing growth that would have likely occurred already toward new stations where accessibility improvements are greatest (Cervero et al., 2002; Huang, 1996).

The second pathway to change is based on the increasingly important role that urban amenities are thought to play in influencing where residents choose to live, or sorting patterns, as many US cities are in the process of undergoing a reversal in the center-city poor/suburban-rich dichotomy that traditional urban location theory describes. Over the past several decades, younger, more educated, and higher-income residents have increasingly re-populated urban centers. Creative-cultural amenities that establish vibrant neighborhoods are attributed with helping to attract this population back to cities (Bereitschaft, 2014; Culver, 2017). Rail transit stations and their associated developments and design principles can be viewed as one such amenity (Bartholomew and Ewing, 2011; Culver, 2017). As acknowledged in a review by Bartholomew and Ewing (2011), the amenity-based design elements of TOD alone play a crucial role in reshaping land markets independent of the accessibility benefits provided by the system. Higgins and Kanaroglou (2018) demonstrate that the combined bundle of accessibility and TOD amenities establish distinct submarkets surrounding stations that generate heterogenous effects along a transit line. While differing from urban economic sorting models centered on accessibility, this amenity-based perspective does align with the longstanding sorting process described by Tiebout (1956) where households make residential location choice decisions based on the availability of local public goods. Sorting outcomes are a byproduct of the willingness and ability of households to pay for these goods. In the context of transit, a new station and associated developments serve to shift the demand toward these new amenities.

Both the accessibility and amenity-based pathway from transit investment to neighborhood outcomes rest on neoclassical economic theories of urban land values and residential sorting. Revington (2015) argues that there is a place for Marxist theory in explaining transit's role in perpetuating gentrification. According to this perspective, within a Capitalist system, the capitalist class' objective is to preserve its domination over labor through a process of capital accumulation. Rather than viewing all residents as having uniform preferences and levels of agency, a typical critique of the underlying assumptions behind neoclassical economic models, in a Marxist perspective, households do not react uniformly to urban spatial changes. As capital investments in infrastructure alters the locational advantage landscape (by impacting the placement of transportation, housing, and employment), households with the monetary and educational resources to act most swiftly to these changes are most poised to reap their benefits, furthering their self-interests. Those without these resources are left with locations of disinvestment and at a locational disadvantage (Revington, 2015). Investments in the built environment may therefore serve to reinforce spatial inequalities and may open new markets for the re-entry of capital by the most advantaged class, resulting in gentrification (Rérat, 2018).

Regardless of the theoretical lens, both neoclassical and Marxist explanations provide a framework for understanding that new rail transit stations are expected to contribute to rising land values through increased accessibility, amenities, or both, and that these changes should then precipitate down to impact who is willing or able to move into out of a nearby neighborhood, thus perpetuating gentrification. Given these theoretical considerations, I now turn to the empirical evidence that has evaluated how transit has impacted housing values and rents, residential mobility, and location choices, and finally neighborhood changes.

3. Housing values and rents

The body of literature that has investigated the impacts of new transit investments on property values and rents is vast and while some meta-analyses have drawn the conclusion that proximity to new stations generally leads to price premiums (Debrezion et al., 2007; Hamidi et al., 2016), the broader consensus of this work is that impacts vary significantly depending on several factors. First, the type of station and development around the station appear to be an important precursor in determining price premiums. Walk-and-ride and stations with stronger TOD design principles such as mixed land-uses and walkability appear to generate higher premiums than park-and-ride stations which in some cases lead to price declines (Atkinson-Palombo, 2010; Hamidi et al., 2016; Zhong and Li, 2016). In the case of San Diego, Duncan (2011a) found price premiums to be strongest when paired with pedestrian-friendly environments while condominiums in auto-dominated landscapes sold at a discount. Digging further into disentangling the impacts of rail stations and the surrounding land use and street design, Duncan (2011b) concluded that price premiums were contingent upon the permissive zoning regulations that enabled TOD, but that this type of zoning had a negative impact on home values beyond the area immediately surrounding the stations.

Second, the initial characteristics of a neighborhood may determine whether property values increase. At least two studies suggested that larger capitalization effects were experienced in higher-income neighborhoods (Bowes and Ihlanfeldt, 2001; Hess and Almeida, 2007). However, Mathur (2020) found positive price impacts across the entire spectrum of properties in the case of the San Francisco BART heavy rail system. Redfearn (2009) makes an important point with respect to modeling efforts that attempt to capture price premiums and fail to recognize the significant variations across time and neighborhood types. In the case of light rail in Los Angeles, Redfearn (2009) shows that a global model yielded significant omitted variable biases, producing a wide range of coefficients. However, when a local regression was used, a more stable set of estimates was produced, all pointing to no impact of transit on local house prices. The differences in these two studies may stem from differences in metropolitan-level factors or in the type of rail system under investigation (light vs heavy) or due to different modeling approaches (global vs local).

Distance from a station is another factor with varying and sometimes contradictory evidence. Some studies have suggested that properties closest to a station will experience negative externalities such as noise and therefore undergo price declines (Golub et al., 2012; Ke and Gkritza, 2019). In the case of Atlanta, Bowes and Ihlanfeldt (2001) found negative home value impacts for higher-income neighborhoods located close to downtown and within one quarter mile of a station. The largest, positive impacts were found one quarter to one half mile of a station, away from the central business district. The authors attributed these benefits primarily to the presence of retail clusters near stations that appear to be valued by homeowners, supporting the amenity draw argument of TOD. Negative impacts were also found for properties in lower-income neighborhoods beyond a quarter of a mile from a station in the case of Atlanta.

The timing of price premium effects is another factor that can cause variations across studies. Many of the earlier studies on the transit-home value connection were cross-sectional in nature which prohibited an in-depth examination onto when capitalization effects may begin and end. A more recent study by Pilgram and West (2018) for the case of a new transit line in Minneapolis, MN used repeat sales data found for single family homes, price premiums were present only in the years immediately following the opening of the line and dissipated to zero seven years after service began. The authors controlled for station heterogeneity and tested the robustness of their results on several sets of control groups—limitations present in earlier studies. An additional analysis on housing prices in Minneapolis showed single family home prices increasing following the announcement of the line, but then stabilizing once it actually opened (Cao and Lou, 2018).

Finally, metropolitan-level factors are a likely determinant in property price premiums. Case studies in varying metropolitan areas have ranged from positive impacts of greater than 10% in the case of condominiums in Charlotte, North Carolina (Billings, 2011) to negative impacts along the new light rail line in Norfolk, Virginia (Wagner et al., 2017). Given the strong effects of TOD, as opposed to auto-dominated landscapes on generating price increases described above, the survey of nation-wide TOD projects by Hess and Lombardi (2004) offers one explanation behind these metropolitan-level variations. According to their analysis, TODs that are successful at attracting new developments are in rapidly growing places with a strong local economy such as San Diego and absent from older cities like Buffalo or St. Louis. Within growing cities, the most successful stations are then found outside of struggling neighborhoods (Hess and Lombardi, 2004). This aligns with the notion that transit redirects growth toward stations rather than generates it and so, there must be growth to direct (Cervero et al., 2002).

Many of these empirical findings are consistent with the preconditions for station-area development to occur stipulated by Huang (1996). These include a healthy and growing metropolitan economic climate—as discussed previously, in the case of rail investments, stations are more likely to guide developments toward them rather than generating a substantial amount of new growth. This is also the case with residential properties—with a growing population and healthy demand for housing, this demand may be redirected toward new or existing properties near stations, but absent of growth, it is unlikely to prompt enough existing residents to move within the metropolitan area near a station. In addition, there needs to be coordinate local government policies to enact zoning changes to enable higher density uses and there must be a willing residential base to accept these density changes or mixed land uses. This point was emphasized in the findings from (Duncan, 2011a,b). Finally, there needs to be enough available land for developments to take place on. Areas that are already extensively built up are unlikely to experience drastically new developments as the costs of acquisition and demolition, for example, would be prohibitive.

4. Residential mobility

Given that in some cases, the combined effects of accessibility and, perhaps, more importantly, associated TOD characteristics surrounding new rail stations do generate price premiums, shifts in sorting behaviors might be expected in those areas. The residential mobility impacts may include a change in those moving into new developments or an out-bidding of higher-income residents for existing properties. It might involve a change in those moving out as a reaction to higher rents or property taxes, or it might be some combination of both. Studies on residential mobility responses to transit have been rather limited, especially compared to those on property value effects or neighborhood outcomes. This is primarily due to an absence of a convenient data sources to capture movements or displacement, a conundrum that has hindered the gentrification literature more broadly from quantifying displacement (Rayle, 2015).

Several studies have attempted to capture characteristics of those moving into new transit or TOD neighborhoods based on surveys. There is some evidence that those moving into TODs or near new stations are more likely to be younger or child-less couples, consistent with the creative-cultural amenity theory discussed above (Cao and Schoner, 2013; Cervero, 2007; Liu et al., 2016). However, the similarities across cities and studies seem to stop there. Some suggest that residents in TODs and near new stations have lower-incomes and are more likely to be Hispanic or Asian (Cervero, 2007; Liu et al., 2016) while others show the opposite: that they tend to have higher-incomes and are less likely to be Hispanic (Lund, 2006).

Studies employing residential mobility data in the context of transit stations are much scarcer. Two studies use the Panel Study on Income Dynamics (PSID), the longest running social survey of residents throughout the United States, to track movements out of new transit neighborhoods nationwide from 1970 to 2014 (Delmelle and Nilsson, 2020; Nilsson and Delmelle, 2020). The first study tests the displacement hypothesis, which posits that lower-income residents have disproportionately moved out in the time just before a station opened or just afterwards. The results showed that while lower-income residents were more likely to move overall, those in new transit neighborhoods were not significantly more likely to move, thus providing no supporting evidence at a national scale for the displacement hypothesis. This null finding was the case for renters and homebuyers, when differentiated by decade, and for varying definitions of what constituted a "transit neighborhood" (Delmelle and Nilsson, 2020). In a follow-up analysis, the authors examined the neighborhood relocation choices of those moving out of new transit neighborhoods—testing more generally the role of stations on metropolitan sorting patterns. In that analysis, there was some evidence of unequal sorting outcomes: of those moving out, middle and higher-income homeowners were more likely to move to a neighborhood of a higher income composition whereas lower-income homeowners and renters did not see an increased probability of neighborhood upgrading by income (Nilsson and Delmelle, 2020). One hypothesis behind this finding is that middle- and higher-income homeowners are better able to capitalize on the price premiums that transit placed on their properties. This would be consistent with the studies identifying greater price impacts in middle- and higher-income neighborhoods or with Marxists notions that those with greater resources can more quickly react and benefit from changes in the housing market.

National-scale studies such as the ones mentioned above capture very broad changes, or averages, but may mask local nuances where displacement may have occurred. Rodnyansky (2018) used a local dataset of tax records in Los Angeles to test the transit-induced displacement hypothesis and reached the same conclusion: that lower-income residents did not disproportionately leave transit neighborhoods. In fact, they were less likely to move. This finding does align with the null capitalization impacts reported by Redfearn (2009) in Los Angeles. Despite the lack of empirical support, however, narratives surrounding Los Angeles' transit system continue to suggest that it is responsible for gentrification and displacement within the city (Rosenthal, 2018).

The use of residential mobility data to measure displacement has received some criticism when applied in the broader gentrification literature—it was not designed for that purpose and reduces a complex process into a single data point in time. As an alternate, Delmelle et al. (2021) used eviction filing rates to test the transit-induced displacement hypothesis in a study of four US cities: Newark, New Jersey; San Diego, California; Seattle, Washington; and St. Louis, Missouri. Evictions represent a form of direct displacement, or an involuntary move, that occurs when a tenant is unable to afford rent increases, for instance. The use of eviction data to study displacement therefore has some theoretical advantages as compared to residential mobility data, but limitations remain. For example, not all evictions result in formal court filings, many are settled informally, and these are not captured in official statistics. In the case of rising rents, many renters will simply opt to relocate once their lease expires rather than going through an eviction process. Nonetheless, it represents an alternative vantage point from which to investigate the problem. According to the four-city study, Delmelle et al. (2021) compared eviction filing rates in gentrifiable neighborhoods close to new rail stations with those in similar gentrifiable neighborhoods away from the stations in each city. No significant differences were found between the two suggesting that the new stations in these four contrasting cities did not lead to different eviction rates.

Overall, the limited studies that have attempted to capture transit's impact on residential sorting have provided very minimal support that it plays a significant role in reshaping sorting trends. However, more research is certainly needed in this area, especially those that emphasize the nuances that the house price capitalization has revealed—focusing on changes in the immediate vicinity of stations with strong TOD principles.

5. Neighborhood change

The net result of changes in land and housing values, residential mobility, and location choices is a change to the aggregate characteristics of a neighborhood. While gentrification is typically the outcome under investigation in studies examining a link between transit and neighborhood change (Padeiro et al., 2019), that is just one pathway in which a neighborhood's composition may change. Gentrification represents a particular type of change characterized by an influx of new, younger, highly educated with professional, highly paid jobs and mostly White population. This new population replaces an older, working-class, lower-income, and minority population in neighborhoods close to the urban core that had undergone disinvestment and physical deterioration (Marcuse, 1985). Other types of neighborhood changes may include improvements or declines to the socioeconomic circumstances of existing residents (incumbent upgrading/downgrading), or other pathways that lead to a shift in the racial, socioeconomic, or housing characteristics composition of the neighborhoods (Delmelle, 2017).

The evidence pertaining to transit's impact on neighborhoods is very consistent with the variations revealed in the land/home value and residential mobility literature. As the number of studies on the topic has increased, it is increasingly evident that gentrification is not the typical outcome that follows the placement of a new station. Rather, in some circumstances, when the existing pre-conditions are prime, transit may act as an accelerator to changes, but in many instances, does little to alter the trajectory of the neighborhood.

While many neighborhoods do not change in the time after a station is built, of those that do, there are some similarities in the ways in which they change. For instance, there is evidence that the share of college educated residents (Deka, 2017; Kahn, 2007; Nilsson and Delmelle, 2018) and multifamily housing (Dong, 2017; Nilsson and Delmelle, 2018) increased in Census tracts near stations. Consistent with the prior house value literature, changes have been found to occur more often in neighborhoods close to a walk-and-ride or TOD station and in faster growing metropolitan areas (Baker and Lee, 2019; Nilsson and Delmelle, 2018)—though there are some exceptions to this as well. Two studies examined changes around stations in Portland, Oregon, a city heralded for its progressive land-use policies, located in the fast-growing Western United States and neither found evidence that new stations led to an increase in gentrification-type chances or reduced affordability in nearby neighborhoods (Baker and Lee, 2019; Dong, 2017). Dong (2017) found that densification and the share of rental units increased—this increased supply may serve to offset rising demand.

Two studies found that incomes and housing values or rents increased in new transit neighborhoods (Bardaka et al., 2018; Pollack et al., 2010), however, both of these analyses compared transit neighborhoods to the city or metro-area as a whole. Other research has pointed out that city-wide comparisons tend to inflate price capitalization impacts (Pilgram and West, 2018). The use of a set of control neighborhoods that closely match the "treatment" or transit neighborhoods is the more desirable method. The lack of inclusion of appropriate counterfactuals is one limitation of much of the neighborhood change research and has been attributed to some of the discrepancies in their findings (Padeiro et al., 2019). Echoing the price capitalization literature, Heilmann (2018) found neighborhood-level income changes to be contingent upon its initial income composition—strongest for the most well-off, and weakest or negative for poorer.

With respect to changes in the racial makeup of neighborhoods, a number of studies found it to be unchanged—even when other characteristics did change in a direction that pointed to gentrification (Barton and Gibbons, 2017; Deka, 2017; Nilsson and Delmelle, 2018; Pollack et al., 2010)—this is an effect that has previously been identified in the neighborhood change literature and is not necessarily unique to transit neighborhoods (Delmelle, 2016). Of course, deviations from this null effect on racial changes exist. For instance, Hess (2020) reported on a rising share of Whites corresponding to the start of construction in neighborhoods in Seattle, but a growth in racial and ethnic diversity in more peripheral locations. Delmelle et al. (2021) used mortgage lending applications from the Home Mortgage Disclosure Act (HMDA) to examine changes in the income and racial composition of those applying for loans along a new transit corridor in Charlotte, North Carolina.

By comparing lending rates over time between transit neighborhoods and a set of controls, the authors showed that there was a significant decline in the share of Black loan applicants in transit neighborhoods and an increase in White applicants following the announcement of the opening of the new line. They did not find a significant difference in the income profile of applicants. A further scrutiny of the data unveiled significant heterogeneity along the rail line with the most significant changes occurring in neighborhoods closest to the city center. A complementary analysis of property advertisement text illustrated that the light rail was advertised most often in neighborhoods closest to the core and in proximity to a previously gentrified neighborhood. Overall, the analysis helped to underscore the importance of the contextual circumstances that may shape changes in residential location decisions. Coupled with existing amenities serving to attract a younger and Whiter population—proximity to the urban core, walkability, the presence of breweries, and importantly, proximity to an established, gentrified neighborhood—the opening of the new rail line likely served to exacerbate the speed of changes in those neighborhoods. However, further from that core, in more suburban, and largely minority neighborhoods, changes were much less apparent.

6. Discussion and conclusions

The current state of the literature increasingly suggests that the impacts of transit on neighborhoods is either marginal or very difficult to quantify. In the review of existing empirical studies beginning with transit's impact on land and property values, the evolution of this work suggests that more sophisticated modeling efforts that correct for spatial heterogeneity, differentiate impacts between types of neighborhoods, and that utilize a proper set of controls, find more muted impacts than earlier research that did not do these things. If the impacts on housing values and rents is less than originally thought, then the subsequent negligible impacts on residential sorting and neighborhood change studies are not tremendously surprising. Collectively, this body of work suggests that changes associated with new stations are not automatic and are likely only when certain contextual circumstances accompany these stations. These include presence of other cultural amenities, strong TOD design principles around stations, and economically vibrant metropolitan climate. After more than two decades of empirical research, many of the findings reiterate the original stated preconditions for successful TOD (Hess and Lombardi, 2004; Huang, 1996).

Nonetheless, as reported in the recent article by Carlton (2019), many transit planners have unrealistic expectations on the development potential surrounding TOD, placing prospects above what would be expected given the current state of knowledge on the subject. Thus, many transit projects have likely been pushed through based on unachievable promises—and thus academics have continued to capture these null effects.

Limitations in the body of work that have investigated neighborhood outcomes stemming from transit investments remain. As reported in the review by Padeiro et al. (2019), many of the neighborhood-scale analyses fail to utilize a proper set of control neighborhoods to test whether trends differ from other similar neighborhoods in a metropolitan area. As the price capitalization literature has increasingly shown, this can have a significant impact on results and needs to become the norm in the neighborhood studies (Pilgram and West, 2018). Likewise, controlling for heterogeneity and isolating transit from other confounding factors remains a challenge. Finally, the sensitivity of results to their spatial and temporal scales needs further scrutiny. Most neighborhood-scale studies use Census tracts which may be too large to capture changes that may only occur in the area immediately surrounding a station. Census data are also typically restricted to examining changes at a decennial time-frame, or use notoriously unreliable estimates in between. Recent price capitalization literature has suggested that price increases are felt only in the years immediately preceding and following a station opening (Cao and Lou, 2018; Pilgram and West, 2018). It could be that the course temporal granularity of Census data does not enable changes to be capture. These limitations could be addressed by the use of alternate datasets.

Despite the limitations that exist in the state of the transit-induced gentrification literature, there are other plausible explanations for the lack of consistent evidence supporting the hypothesis. The first is the fact that many new rail lines are placed through previously underutilized industrial or commercially zoned land uses. Coordinating higher-density residential construction around stations increases the supply of housing and does not physically displace anyone in doing so. Many studies have agreed that a hallmark of changes around stations is an increase in density or multifamily housing (Bhattacharjee and Goetz, 2016; Dong, 2017; Nilsson and Delmelle, 2018) as it is one of the very essences of TOD principles. Some may argue that many of these new developments are higher-end luxury apartment units unaffordable to lower-income residents, and thus represent a form of exclusionary displacement (Rayle, 2015). This may certainly be the case in areas immediately surrounding a station, however, it is also relevant to acknowledge current debates on the role of increasing housing supply more generally on increasing overall affordability (Been et al., 2019). As summarized nicely their recent review article, Been et al. (2019) suggest that building new market rate housing does provide a moderating effect on the affordability landscape for low- and moderate-income families, but that this is not a sufficient way of addressing housing affordability in a competitive market. Government intervention is likely necessary for increasing the supply of affordable housing. Coordinating these efforts in TODs would seem to be a prime opportunity to do so and the mechanisms for successfully achieving this is a welcome area of research.

A second potential explanation behind the null displacement findings surrounds the notion of locational affordability—that the transportation savings enabled by residing in highly accessible locations will offset higher housing costs (Renne et al., 2016). In this scenario, displacement may not occur given that residents experience a new cost savings on transportation even though rents may have risen. The literature is far from settled on whether residing close to transit provides enough residual income to overcome a rent premium. Two recent studies offer to contrasting conclusions on the matter—Smart and Klein (2018) suggest that the cost savings provided by living in transit-rich neighborhoods in the United States have been overstated while Makarewicz et al. (2020) take a more granular approach and do find evidence of significant savings for several income groups, but not the lowest.

Finally, this review focused on quantitative analyses of neighborhood changes and an argument can be made that transit changes neighborhoods in ways that are unquantifiable—removing or possibly improving their sense of place or community. The influx of newer residents to TOD locations, even if they do not displace residents in nearby neighborhoods, may change the cultural preferences and make established residents feel out of place (Hyra, 2015). There have been far fewer qualitative studies on the impacts of transit neighborhoods—though the few that exist do note that residents generally tend to view transit favorably (Jackson and Buckman, 2020; Lung-Amam et al., 2019; Nilsson et al., 2020), but that this sentiment is stronger for newer residents, as skepticism by poorer and minority residents remain regarding large public investments. Longer-term studies on the impacts felt by residents remains a welcome area of future research.

Literature debates surrounding transit-induced gentrification and displacement have followed broader public debates as fears about planned transit systems' impact on communities has caused resistance by residents (Rayle, 2015). This speaks to a broader need to reconcile investments in underserved communities and subsequent fears of gentrification—or a "catch-22" (Danley and Weaver, 2018). For historically marginalized communities, a sudden influx of capital in the form of a new transit station can be accompanied by a sense of distrust that the investment is not for current residents, but for newcomers. Based on the empirical evidence thus far, transit alone is unlikely to dramatically transform a neighborhood, but in locations where gentrification pressure is already strong—in growing cities and in neighborhoods close to other urban amenities, the additional investment in transit may accelerate this pressure. In these neighborhoods, cities need to have a plan for helping residents stay in their homes and to maintain their sense of community. In other places where disinvestment remains except for a new station, sudden change is unlikely, but in those places, plans for the station need to take residents' needs seriously and include their voices in the planning process. Forcing a particular type of station or style of development that does not have the buy-in of residents is not going to help ameliorate years of distrust between the planners and marginalized communities (Danley and Weaver, 2018). This needs to be more than an "empty ritual" of public participation in the planning process, but one that prioritizes the needs and interests of the community (Silverman et al., 2020).

References

Alonso, W., 1964. Location and Land Use. Toward a General Theory of Land Rent. Harvard University Press.

Andersson, F., Haltiwanger, J.C., Kutzbach, M.J., Pollakowski, H.O., Weinberg, D.H., 2017. Job displacement and the duration of joblessness: the role of spatial mismatch. Rev. Econ. Stat. 100 (2), 203–218.

Atkinson-Palombo, C., 2010. Comparing the capitalisation benefits of light-rail transit and overlay zoning for single-family houses and condos by neighbourhood type in metropolitan Phoenix, Arizona. Urban Stud. 47 (11), 2409–2426.

Baker, D.M., Lee, B., 2019. How does light rail transit (LRT) impact gentrification? Evidence from fourteen US urbanized areas. J. Plan. Educ. Res. 39 (1), 35–49.

Bardaka, E., Delgado, M.S., Florax, R.J., 2018. Causal identification of transit-induced gentrification and spatial spillover effects: the case of the Denver light rail. J. Transp. Geogr. 71, 15–31.

Bartholomew, K., Ewing, R., 2011. Hedonic price effects of pedestrian-and transit-oriented development. J. Plan. Lit. 26 (1), 18–34.

Barton, M.S., Gibbons, J., 2017. A stop too far: how does public transportation concentration influence neighbourhood median household income? Urban Stud. 54 (2), 538–554.

Been, V., Ellen, I.G., O'Regan, K., 2019. Supply skepticism: housing supply and affordability. Hous. Policy Debate 29 (1), 25–40.

Bereitschaft, B., 2014. Neighbourhood change among creative–cultural districts in mid-sized US metropolitan areas, 2000–10. Reg. Stud. Reg. Sci. 1 (1), 158–183.

Bhattacharjee, S., Goetz, A.R., 2016. The rail transit system and land use change in the Denver metro region. J. Transp. Geogr. 54, 440–450.
Billings, S.B., 2011. Estimating the value of a new transit option. Reg. Sci. Urban Econ. 41 (6), 525–536.
Bowes, D.R., Ihlanfeldt, K.R., 2001. Identifying the impacts of rail transit stations on residential property values. J. Urban Econ. 50 (1), 1–25.
Calthorpe, P., 1993. The Next American Metropolis: Ecology, Community, and the American Dream. Princeton Architectural Press.
Cao, X., Lou, S., 2018. When and how much did the green line LRT increase single-family housing values in St. Paul, Minnesota? J. Plan. Educ. Res. 38 (4), 427–436.
Cao, J., Schoner, J., 2013. Transportation Impact of Transitways: A Case Study of Hiawatha Light Rail Transit in Minneapolis. Center for Transportation Studies, University of Minnesota.
Carlton, I., 2019. Transit Planners' transit-oriented development-related practices and theories. J. Plan. Educ. Res. 39 (4), 508–519.
Cervero, R., 2007. Transit-oriented development's ridership bonus: a product of self-selection and public policies. Environ. Plan. A 39 (9), 2068–2085.
Cervero, R., Ferrell, C., Murphy, S., 2002. Transit-Oriented Development and Joint Development in the United States: A Literature Review. TCRP Research Results Digest (52).
Culver, G., 2017. Mobility and the making of the neoliberal "creative city": the streetcar as a creative city project? J. Transp. Geogr. 58, 22–30.
Danley, S., Weaver, R., 2018. "They're not building it for us": displacement pressure, unwelcomeness, and protesting neighborhood investment. Societies 8 (3), 74.
Debrezion, G., Pels, E., Rietveld, P., 2007. The impact of railway stations on residential and commercial property value: a meta-analysis. J. Real Estate Financ. Econ. 35 (2), 161–180.
Deka, D., 2017. Benchmarking gentrification near commuter rail stations in New Jersey. Urban Stud. 54 (13), 2955–2972.
Delmelle, E.C., 2016. Mapping the DNA of urban neighborhoods: clustering longitudinal sequences of neighborhood socioeconomic change. Ann. Am. Assoc. Geogr. 106 (1), 36–56.
Delmelle, E.C., 2017. Differentiating pathways of neighborhood change in 50 US metropolitan areas. Environ. Plan. A 49 (10), 2402–2424.
Delmelle, E., Nilsson, I., 2020. New rail transit stations and the out-migration of low-income residents. Urban Stud. 57 (1), 134–151.
Delmelle, E.C., Nilsson, I., Bryant, A., 2021. Investigating transit-induced displacement using eviction data. Hous. Policy Debate 31 (2), 326–341.
Dong, H., 2017. Rail-transit-induced gentrification and the affordability paradox of TOD. J. Transp. Geogr. 63, 1–10.
Duncan, M., 2011a. The impact of transit-oriented development on housing prices in San Diego, CA. Urban Stud. 48 (1), 101–127.
Duncan, M., 2011b. The synergistic influence of light rail stations and zoning on home prices. Environ. Plan. A 43 (9), 2125–2142.
Efthymiou, D., Antoniou, C., 2013. How do transport infrastructure and policies affect house prices and rents? Evidence from Athens, Greece. Transp. Res. Part A Policy Pract. 52, 1–22.
Eliasson, J., Kopsch, F., Mandell, S., Wilhelmsson, M., 2020. Transport mode and the value of accessibility–a potential input for sustainable investment analysis. Sustainability 12 (5), 2143.
Ferbrache, F., Knowles, R.D., 2017. City boosterism and place-making with light rail transit: a critical review of light rail impacts on city image and quality. Geoforum 80, 103–113.

Golub, A., Guhathakurta, S., Sollapuram, B., 2012. Spatial and temporal capitalization effects of light rail in phoenix: from conception, planning, and construction to operation. J. Plan. Educ. Res. 32 (4), 415–429.
Hamidi, S., Kittrell, K., Ewing, R., 2016. Value of transit as reflected in US single-family home premiums: a meta-analysis. Transp. Res. Rec. 2543 (1), 108–115.
Heilmann, K., 2018. Transit access and neighborhood segregation. Evidence from the Dallas light rail system. Reg. Sci. Urban Econ. 73, 237–250.
Hess, C.L., 2020. Light-rail Investment in Seattle: gentrification pressures and trends in neighborhood ethnoracial composition. Urban Aff. Rev. 56 (1), 154–187. 1078087418758959.
Hess, D.B., Almeida, T.M., 2007. Impact of proximity to light rail rapid transit on station-area property values in Buffalo, New York. Urban Stud. 44 (5–6), 1041–1068.
Hess, D.B., Lombardi, P.A., 2004. Policy support for and barriers to transit-oriented development in the inner city: literature review. Transp. Res. Rec. 1887 (1), 26–33.
Higgins, C., Kanaroglou, P., 2018. Rapid transit, transit-oriented development, and the contextual sensitivity of land value uplift in Toronto. Urban Stud. 55 (10), 2197–2225. https://doi.org/10.1177/0042098017712680.
Huang, H., 1996. The land-use impacts of urban rail transit systems. J. Plan. Lit. 11 (1), 17–30.
Hyra, D., 2015. The back-to-the-city movement: neighbourhood redevelopment and processes of political and cultural displacement. Urban Stud. 52 (10), 1753–1773.
Jackson, S.L., Buckman, J., 2020. Light rail development with or without gentrification?: neighborhood perspectives on changing sense of place in Denver, Colorado. J. Transp. Geogr. 84, 102678.
Jin, J., Paulsen, K., 2018. Does accessibility matter? Understanding the effect of job accessibility on labour market outcomes. Urban Stud. 55 (1), 91–115.
Kahn, M.E., 2007. Gentrification trends in new transit-oriented communities: evidence from 14 cities that expanded and built rail transit systems. Real Estate Econ. 35 (2), 155–182.
Ke, Y., Gkritza, K., 2019. Light rail transit and housing markets in Charlotte-Mecklenburg County, North Carolina: announcement and operations effects using quasi-experimental methods. J. Transp. Geogr. 76, 212–220.
Liu, X., Deng, Y., Le Vine, S., 2016. Residential relocation in response to light rail transit investment: case study of the Hudson–Bergen light rail system. J. Mod. Transp. 24 (2), 139–144.
Lund, H., 2006. Reasons for living in a transit-oriented development, and associated transit use. J. Am. Plan. Assoc. 72 (3), 357–366.
Lung-Amam, W., Pendall, R., Knaap, E., 2019. Mi casa no es su casa: the fight for equitable transit-oriented development in an inner-ring suburb. J. Plan. Educ. Res. 39 (4), 442–455.
Makarewicz, C., Dantzler, P., Adkins, A., 2020. Another look at location affordability: understanding the detailed effects of income and urban form on housing and transportation expenditures. Hous. Policy Debate 30 (6), 1033–1055.
Marcuse, P., 1985. Gentrification, abandonment, and displacement: connections, causes, and policy responses in New York City. Wash. U. J. Urb. Contemp. L. 28, 195.
Mathur, S., 2020. Impact of transit stations on house prices across entire price spectrum: a quantile regression approach. Land Use Policy 99, 104828.
Muth, R.F., 1969. Cities and Housing; The Spatial Pattern of Urban Residential Land Use. University of Chicago Press.
Newman, K., Wyly, E.K., 2006. The right to stay put, revisited: gentrification and resistance to displacement in New York City. Urban Stud. 43 (1), 23–57.
Nilsson, I., Delmelle, E., 2018. Transit investments and neighborhood change: on the likelihood of change. J. Transp. Geogr. 66, 167–179.

Nilsson, I., Delmelle, E.C., 2020. Impact of new rail transit stations on neighborhood destination choices and income segregation. Cities 102, 102737.

Nilsson, I., Schuch, J.C., Delmelle, E.C., Canales, K.L., 2020. Should I stay or should I go? A survey analysis of neighborhood change and residential mobility concerns around new light rail stations in Charlotte, NC. J. Transp. Geogr. 86, 102790.

Padeiro, M., Louro, A., da Costa, N.M., 2019. Transit-oriented development and gentrification: a systematic review. Transp. Rev. 39 (6), 733–754.

Pilgram, C.A., West, S.E., 2018. Fading premiums: the effect of light rail on residential property values in Minneapolis, Minnesota. Reg. Sci. Urban Econ. 69, 1–10.

Pollack, S., Bluestone, B., Billingham, C., 2010. Maintaining Diversity in America's Transit-Rich Neighborhoods: Tools for Equitable Neighborhood Change. Dukakis Center for Urban and Regional Policy.

Rayle, L., 2015. Investigating the connection between transit-oriented development and displacement: four hypotheses. Hous. Policy Debate 25 (3), 531–548.

Redfearn, C.L., 2009. How informative are average effects? Hedonic regression and amenity capitalization in complex urban housing markets. Reg. Sci. Urban Econ. 39 (3), 297–306.

Renne, J.L., Tolford, T., Hamidi, S., Ewing, R., 2016. The cost and affordability paradox of transit-oriented development: a comparison of housing and transportation costs across transit-oriented development, hybrid and transit-adjacent development station typologies. Hous. Policy Debate 26 (4–5), 819–834.

Rérat, P., 2018. Spatial capital and planetary gentrification: residential location, mobility and social inequalities. In: Handbook of Gentrification Studies. Edward Elgar Publishing.

Revington, N., 2015. Gentrification, transit, and land use: moving beyond neoclassical theory. Geogr. Compass 9 (3), 152–163.

Rodnyansky, S., 2018. Household Mobility and Neighborhood Impacts. University of Southern California.

Rosenthal, T.J., 2018. Transit-Oriented Development? More like Transit Rider Displacement. Los Angeles Times. Retrieved from https://www.latimes.com/opinion/op-ed/la-oe-rosenthal-transit-gentrification-metro-ridership-20180220-story.html.

Silverman, R.M., Taylor Jr., H.L., Yin, L., Miller, C., Buggs, P., 2020. Are we still going through the empty ritual of participation? Inner-city residents' and other grassroots stakeholders' perceptions of public input and neighborhood revitalization. Crit. Sociol. 46 (3), 413–428.

Smart, M.J., Klein, N.J., 2018. Complicating the story of location affordability. Hous. Policy Debate 28 (3), 393–410.

Tiebout, C.M., 1956. A pure theory of local expenditures. J. Polit. Econ. 64 (5), 416–424.

Wagner, G.A., Komarek, T., Martin, J., 2017. Is the light rail "tide" lifting property values? Evidence from Hampton Roads, VA. Reg. Sci. Urban Econ. 65, 25–37.

Zhong, H., Li, W., 2016. Rail transit investment and property values: an old tale retold. Transp. Policy 51, 33–48.

CHAPTER SEVEN

From "para-transit" to transit? Power, politics and popular transport

Jacqueline M. Klopp*
Center for Sustainable Urban Development, Earth Institute, Columbia University, New York, NY, United States
*Corresponding author: e-mail address: jk2002@columbia.edu

Contents

Abstract

This chapter reviews shifting evidence, understandings and debates around the politics of privately or cooperatively owned minibus and taxi systems often called paratransit or informal transport. These systems tend to run unscheduled mobility services that cater to the majority of residents in many of the world's cities. Until recently, these forms of transit have been under-scrutinized and relatively absent from transportation planning. The assumption has been that they would eventually be replaced. Yet except in a few cases, this has not occurred. Challenges for planners include addressing diverse informalities associated with these systems, the politics around change, poor data and understanding of operations, as well as attitudes among policymakers who often tend to vilify or marginalize these systems in planning. As transportation planning increasingly recognizes the role of diverse forms of shared mobility and last mile options, para or informal transit comes to the fore as playing a key integrating role across other modes. Hence, a paradigm shift from paratransit to transit is under way with more scholars embracing these neglected modes as a critical form of *popular* transport that needs to be thoughtfully integrated into transportation planning-especially in cities where popular modes are dominant. In order to move forward with improvements and reforms, we need a better understanding of the politics that produced these popular transport systems in the first place and the social injustices underlying them including often severe labor exploitation, disregard of passenger needs and lack of subsidies

Advances in Transport Policy and Planning, Volume 8
ISSN 2543-0009
https://doi.org/10.1016/bs.atpp.2021.07.002
Copyright © 2021 Elsevier Inc.
All rights reserved.

and investment in these systems that serve the poor and middle class. Overall, an examination of paratransit and informal transport as popular transport reveals complex threads of power that reproduce persistent spatial, environmental and social injustices. This suggests the need for more nuanced, inclusive and holistic approaches to transportation planning and reform for them to be effective, equitable and just.

Keywords: Paratransit, Informal transport, Planning, Power, Social justice

1. Introduction

"Paratransit" is a term commonly used to describe the diverse kinds of shared vehicles used for public transport across the globe.[a] Varied in their operations and ownership structures and ranging in size from regular buses and minibuses to smaller tuktuks, motorcycles or shared taxis, these mobility services are ubiquitous in most of the world's cities, serving the majority of residents- including the poor. Yet "para" in para-transit tends to connote something that is "alongside of, beside, near, resembling, beyond, apart from, or abnormal"[b] transit, but not actual transit defined as public mass transit operating fixed routes and scheduled service (Orski, 1975). "Paratransit" is indeed often viewed as problematic, a barrier to reform and the development of more regulated and publicly managed mass transit (Wilkinson, 2010).

From this perspective, these systems are not to be planned for but instead, displaced and replaced by properly managed or "modern" public transport. As a result of this overall thinking, these services are typically neither invested in nor planned for which in turn, fosters the image of chaos surrounding these transport modes (Klopp and Cavoli, 2019; Thet et al., 2020). This also has meant that, until recently, they were poorly studied with little data collected on them; hence, no maps, apps or passenger information services as well as models and associated metrics were developed for them. This means that while these modes are critical to public transport in most cities across the globe, they tend to be very poorly understood by planners creating problems for reform and public transport and access improvements.

[a] In North America, para-transit is used to refer to a form of public or community transport that provides individualized, on demand, flexible trips that serve the elderly and others who face mobility challenges. This kind of public transport in North America can share some characteristics of the more general concept of paratransit used here including service to those with mobility challenges (Kariuki, 2015).

[b] This is the definition of "para" taken from Mednet accessed at https://www.medicinenet.com/para-_prefix/definition.htm.

After years of often troubled transport reform, these kinds of mobility services, with some important exceptions, show no sign of decline especially as demand for these services intensifies with growing urbanization and deepening inequalities (Nijman and Wei, 2020; UN-Habitat, 2020). In addition, the climate crisis is leading to stronger demands for shifts to integrated multi-modal public transport systems (Sims et al., 2014). Related concerns about air pollution from transport emissions in cities is also drawing attention to upgrading and even electrifying popular transport which often involves highly polluting vehicles such as motorcycles or old vehicles (Colville et al., 2001). Many of the vehicles used for popular transport are recycled from Europe, the United States or Japan, transferring emissions from one location to another (Environment, 2020).

Overall, a paradigm shift is now underway that involves taking "paratransit" or informal transport seriously and integrating these services into investment and planning strategies around improving integrated multi-modal public transport—a task that is gaining urgency with the need to address poverty, public health and inequality along with the climate crisis. However, debate continues around whether to replace and displace or embrace and engage these modes (Schalekamp and Klopp, 2018). As more and more planners and policymakers engage with these systems of popular transport as important modes to integrate into city planning, the question increasingly becomes focused on *how to engage and work to improve and integrate these modes*. At the same time, we see experimentation around popular transport improvements, often occurring from within the sector itself—which can help answer how to plan with and for popular transport. This chapter reviews this journey in thinking around popular transport modes as transit rather than paratransit. We scan the landscape of popular transport, explore social issues associated with these modes and look at the new data and innovation around them, all the while discussing implications for transport planning.

2. Diverse informalities: The landscape of popular transport

Popular transport systems involve shared mobility using a wide variety of vehicle types from large buses and minibuses to tuktuks and shared cars to motorcycle or bicycle taxis. Owned by private actors or cooperatives and emerging to meet demand unmet from within "formal" or mass public transport systems, these mobility services tend to have flexible schedules, stops and routes as well as diverse operations and business models (Behrens et al., 2016; Cervero and Golub, 2007). Popular transport operators often show considerable creativity and entrepreneurship (Khayesi et al., 2016) from combining micro-freight and passenger services to personalized drop off service and adoption of ride hailing to using music and colorful art as well as messages on the vehicle body to draw in customers (Ference, 2019; Hart, 2016; Mungai, 2013; Mutongi, 2017).

These services often generate significant access in cities and provide services to poorer and middle class populations. For example, minibuses called matatus in Nairobi, Kenya serve 70% of the adult population every day and extensively cover the city; evidence shows they generate most of the access to health facilities, parks and job opportunities (Avner and Lall, 2016; Babijes, 2016; Campbell et al., 2019; Fried et al., 2020). Another critical social aspect involves the fact that popular transport systems not only provide access to jobs, services and amenities, but also generate many jobs and livelihoods through their supply chains and operations (Global Labour Institute, Manchester, 2019; Rizzo, 2017). Such jobs range from cooks, drivers, touts, mechanics, terminal managers, to artists among others. Not only do these poorly paid workers support transport systems across the globe, but their wages uphold the survival of those living in poor communities in these cities. In contrast, some of the owners and financiers of the sector can be extremely wealthy, and the sector as a whole can have substantial bargaining power with its ability to paralyze economic activity with strikes (Klopp and Mitullah, 2016; Mutongi, 2017; Sopranzetti, 2018).

It is worth emphasizing why the term "informal transport" can be misleading. Transport modes commonly called "informal" tend to be widely used, recognized and registered or licensed. The informality we need to focus on emerges out of governance processes and power dynamics. These dynamics give rise to informal *government, business and labor practices* that demand more scrutiny. Many of these practices, like police extraction and harassment, skewed and inequitable transport investment or violation of labor laws, victimize workers.

Detailed studies into labor conditions in the sector show low wages, long hours and overall precarious, stressful, and unhealthy working conditions (International Transport Workers Federation, 2017; Ramukumba and Mathikhi, 2016; Rizzo, 2017). As the most public facing people in the system, the drivers and conductors face stigma and are most often blamed for the real problems passengers face (Boateng, 2020; Rizzo, 2017). In most cases, popular transport operators pay for vehicle and route licenses and other fees. In this sense, these modes are, in fact, formally recognized. Further, to call an essential part of the transportation system that people use daily "informal" is problematic; the word "informal" in planning in practice often connotes reduced legal status, legitimacy or rights. Hence the "informal" within planning often seems to implicitly rationalize marginalization of certain groups within formal planning processes. It is thus important to scrutinize more deeply how informalities are produced and work within the transportation sector including who benefits and who loses out. Informalities are not just a characteristic of popular modes but, in fact, emerge out of how actors in the state and popular transport sector more generally cooperate and compete, with both sides of this relationship acting inside and outside the law (Agbiboa, 2018; Klopp and Mitullah, 2016).

From this perspective, the institutional landscapes that popular transport must navigate are full of unwritten rules and diverse informalities involving politicians, police, bureaucrats, varied vehicle owners, insurance companies, umbrella and route associations, drivers, touts, route managers, mechanics and, of course, the users. Characteristics associated with popular transport emerge out of this institutional context: no fixed schedules, fluctuating fares, stops and sometimes routes, formation of cartels and violence, poor working conditions for labor which is heavily skewed toward men and—on the positive side—flexibility, demand responsiveness and ubiquity—for those who can pay. These features emerge out of the ways diverse actors relate and jockey for benefits, as well as navigate—and often undermine—the institutional environment set up (often poorly) to regulate public transport (Cervero, 2000; Cervero and Golub, 2007; Klopp and Mitullah, 2016). It is thus critical to unpack diverse, interwoven formal and informal processes around how popular transport works, conceptualize informality not as a "setting, sector or outcome" but rather as a site of critical analysis that unveils how informal strategies work for both powerful actors and those with little power (Banks et al., 2020).

3. A focus on labor conditions

One key feature of operating without much regulation and generally without subsidies is that popular transport operators face intense competition which in turn feeds into poor labor conditions. Pressure to compete combined with poor wages incentivize speeding, overloading, overcharging, surge pricing and other practices that create serious passenger discomfort and safety issues as drivers of vehicles try to maximize fare intake

(Cervero and Golub, 2007; Gwilliam, 2001). These practices along with the crashes and human suffering associated with them are often highlighted in the social media and press giving popular transport a bad reputation. Unfortunately, this often leads to blame being unfairly placed on "rogue" drivers (Boateng, 2020) even though evidence suggests that these problems are structural and could be reduced if workers were paid properly and given training and support (Kelly et al., 2018). Labor exploitation within popular transport modes is one critical social issue that requires more attention in order to improve safety and quality of service and to draw on labor as valuable allies in the agenda of public transport improvements (Attoh, 2019).

Drivers, conductors and other workers in popular transport are often stigmatized and easily victimized as less powerful actors in a wider ecosystem. Yet this exploited labor is what makes these systems feasible. Low wages act as a subsidy to the operators and the transportation system as a whole, while workers and passengers often pay the price. In the minibus sector in Tanzania, for example, 90% of the workers are casual laborers who do not own buses and work for long hours and low wages and with high levels of precarity (Rizzo, 2017) and a vast array of workers in the minibus system in Nairobi work long hours for little pay (Global Labour Institute, Manchester, 2019). Similarly, rickshaw drivers in India face very poor conditions and economic hardship (Harding et al., 2016) as do motorcycle taxi operators and minibus drivers in Ho Chi Minh City (Ames et al., 2014). To add to low wages are health concerns; workers in the sector are at serious risk of respiratory and cardiovascular illness as well as stress from the continuous exposure to noise and air pollution on the roads and in traffic (Gupta and Elumalai, 2019; Ngo et al., 2015; Omm-e-Hany et al., 2015). Sitting for long hours and eating poorly can also lead to serious health problems, as was found for minibus taxi drivers in South Africa (Ramukumba and Mathikhi, 2016).

Within this challenging context, workers develop strategies to address wage shortfalls and costs. This includes trying to organize for social welfare and advocacy as well as exploiting the cash economy to take a little extra from the day's proceeds, driving quickly to increase their takings and paying bribes to avoid often exorbitant fines and police harassment. These strategies of the exploited must be contrasted to the strategies of the more powerful including owners who shirk formal labor laws and the police and other government officials who engage in high levels of extraction from the popular transport system for their personal use. Matatu workers in Nairobi, for example, often express anger at arbitrary extraction from the police, and extensive research has shown that the traffic police in many countries have a bribe quota system; they are expected to extract at least so much each day to redistribute upward to the highest levels of the traffic police (Foltz and Opoku-Agyemang, 2015; Klopp and Mitullah, 2016). In addition, many senior police officers and politicians are also minibus owners benefitting from both extraction and labor exploitation. This is in part why recommendations to make it illegal for police to own minibuses in Kenya goes nowhere (Klopp and Mitullah, 2016).

In an important randomized control study on the labor contract between matatu owners and drivers in Nairobi, tracking devices were placed on matatus and the owners were given dashboards to track their vehicles (Kelly et al., 2018). Hence, they were able to see the number of trips, estimate revenue and watch driving. While this transparency led drivers to decrease risky behavior that damages the vehicle and to less under-reporting revenue, as well as to owners asking for less, it was only when drivers were directly paid more did they slow down. This suggests a strong need to address wages and reduce police extraction, which makes workers drive faster and engage in other risky behaviors to make up lost income. Despite the centrality of labor conditions to improving safety within the popular sector, this is rarely the focus of reforms.

4. Reform processes

Reform processes tend to focus on a particular vision of modernization that involves investment in technological change such as Bus Rapid Transit (BRT) systems, bigger buses, mobile payments or ride hailing apps. Rarely does reform involve a look at labor behind these systems and where transforming labor conditions might play a profound role in improving transport across the city as a whole. Labor is more conceptualized as something that will be disrupted by reforms, rather than a central part of reforms. Most often when labor is addressed, it is as an afterthought to achieve a vision of technological transformation. Venter in his analysis of BRT in South Africa, for example, suggests that if the BRT is implemented as planned no jobs would be lost (Venter, 2016) but of course, labor dislocation will occur with impacts on vulnerable people (Global Labour Institute, Manchester, 2019; Rizzo, 2017). Fortunately, South Africa is one place that does try to address these issues. Overall, the high potential for labor disruption and suffering is one reason why the Global Labor Institute is arguing for formalization and inclusion of workers in discussions around BRT and other reform processes to mitigate these impacts (Global Labour Institute, Manchester, 2019; Spooner et al., 2020).

Another reason exists for inclusion of popular transport workers in transportation planning and reform processes. Popular transport sector actors hold invaluable knowledge and are de facto planners as they devise routes, stops, fares and other key features of the public transport system to address needs that are not being met by existing services and plans. In some cities, popular transport operators and workers in this sector are bottom-up or "regenerative" planners of a remarkably large part of the transport system (Uzzell, 1987). Hence, their granular, detailed knowledge of local routes and passengers should be taken seriously in planning processes. Currently, much of the discussion around these systems in relation to planning does not focus on how to leverage this knowledge, but instead on how to displace these systems with alternatives like Bus Rapid Transit or higher capacity buses and, increasingly and more positively, how to integrate them into "hybrid systems" and leverage their existing services for better functioning multi-modal systems (Ferro et al., 2013; Jennings and Behrens, 2017; Spooner et al., 2020).

Popular transport, in fact, reveals where the planned public transport system is failing. Inadequate investment in public transport and planning for poor populations as well as for last-mile connections creates demand for the popular transport sector services. A very good example of this involves the dollar vans in New York City. Serving more than 120,000 riders per day, these vans or jitneys are licensed by the Taxi and Limousine Commission, but are not governed by the city's Metropolitan Transportation Authority (MTA). They very clearly step in when MTA bus routes are discontinued or unreliable and provide critical service to lower income, immigrant communities that are underserved by the current system (Goldwyn, 2017; Reiss and Lavey, 2014). Like in other cities, this is one of the reasons why popular transport is tolerated and accepted by the authorities and like popular transport elsewhere, dollar vans can have a complex relationship with the police they often respond to demand by stopping along routes and are deeply connected to the communities they serve, sometimes offering service to the door of a passenger (Reiss and Lavey, 2014).

5. Recognizing popular transport: The rise of data, integrated planning and "hybrid" systems: A Nairobi case study

Until recently, little data was collected on popular transport systems for reform or planning. Of course, operators collect data for business purposes, but given the fragmented nature of ownership and the exclusion of these systems from planning, basic, holistic data for these modes tends to be missing, making it even more likely that these modes get sidelined in formal planning processes. With the growing involvement of "civic hackers" or "transit techies," dedicated mappers using GPS enabled cell phones and big data, more systematic data gathering of basic characteristics for the purposes of understanding, planning and improving popular transport systems has been growing as a practice (Berlingerio et al., 2013; Klopp et al., 2020). A push exists as well to make this data standardized and open to support research, technology and innovation ecosystems centered around supporting better planning and service delivery including passenger information for these modes (Klopp et al., 2020; Klopp and Cavoli, 2019; Williams et al., 2015). In this section, we will demonstrate the power of data collection by looking at the relatively well-studied case of matatus in Nairobi.

One of the simplest kinds of data involves looking at stops and route structures to see the network and its characteristics. This also gives a remarkable view of the extent of some of these popular transport systems as seen in Fig. 1 which is the map of minibus (matatu) routes in Nairobi created by the DigitalMatatus project (Williams et al., 2015). The routes stretch throughout the city giving extensive coverage to residents.

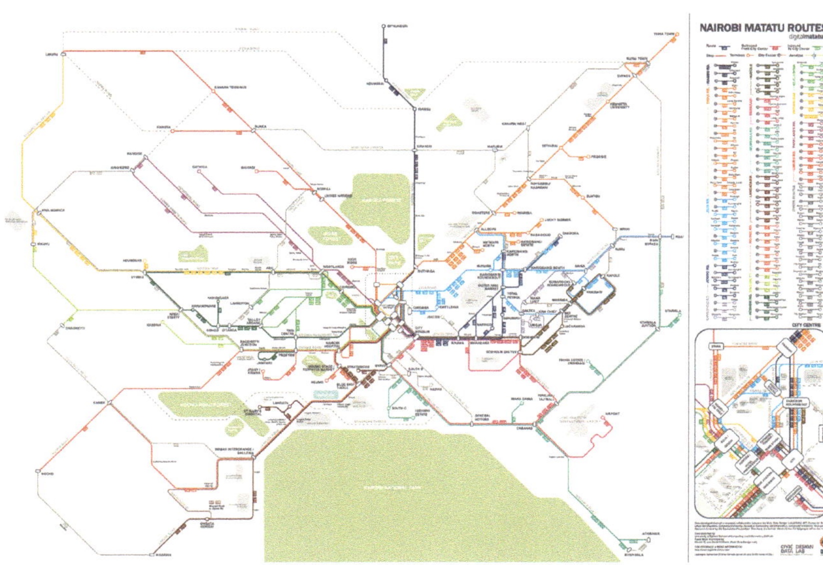

Fig. 1 Map of matatu routes in Nairobi. Source: *DigitalMatatus.com.*

The flexible nature of some of the routes and stops in popular transport present challenges for data collecting which might involve tracing routes and stops many times to get the full picture and degree of variability. The maps created out of this data give a stylized and somewhat probabilistic view of the system. Areas where popular modes like motorcycle taxis pick up passengers on demand might be best represented as shaded regions of operation rather than a route map. Data standards like the General Transit Feed Specification (GTFS) which have been designed for scheduled, fixed route transport modes like subways or buses also need transformation and a strong effort is underway to revise or build a new standard (MobilityData.org, 2021) in order to include popular modes as well as other shared mobility modes like Uber or Bolt coming out of the technology sector. These forms of new shared mobilities, in fact, behave like popular modes such as shared taxis or dollar vans but with the addition of ride hailing technologies. Interestingly, these technologies are also increasingly being used by operators of popular transport. Examples include the Jetty app in Mexico City which allows pre-booking of minibuses and improved service for a small premium (Flores, 2019) and the safeboda app in Uganda which allows a passenger to hail a motorcycle taxi with a driver who is vetted and trained to drive safely (SafeBoda—Your City Ride, 2021).

Improved data on popular transport allows exploration on how well these systems work and hence also where they could be improved (Orski, 1975). To illustrate this we will draw on the case of matatus in Nairobi. For example, with data, we can examine the network of stops and routes which can allow us to see the access generated by these systems and where there are exclusions. In Fig. 2 we can see the matatu stop coverage by income group in Nairobi.

The lowest income communities living in poor quality rental housing in the slums and very high income communities living in large houses surrounded by vast yards tend to have less access to matatu stops (see also Fig. 3). This makes sense as the lowest income individuals live in slum conditions that often do not even have access roads for minibuses to enter; whereas very high income neighborhoods often discourage public service vehicles which they see as nuisances even though they carry labor in and out of these neighborhoods. Further, low income residents can often not afford fares and the very poorest continue to live in slum neighborhoods closer to the center of the city and hence to work and services. Estimates suggest that those living in slums constitute around 60% of Nairobi's

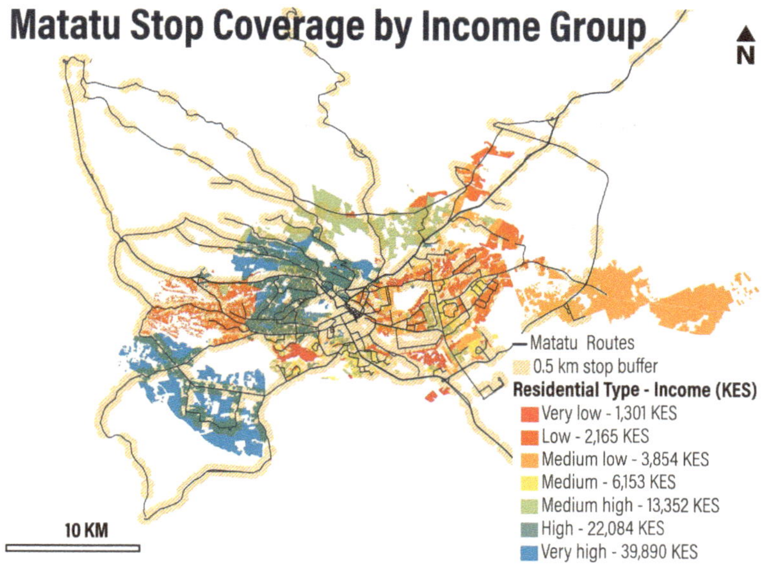

Fig. 2 Matatu stop coverage by income group for Nairobi. Source: *Fried, T., Tun, T.H., Klopp, J.M., Welle, B., 2020. Measuring the Sustainable Development Goal (SDG) transport target and accessibility of Nairobi's matatus. Transp. Res. Rec. 2674, 196–207. doi: https://doi.org/10.1177/0361198120914620.*

population of 4.4 million people (APHRC, 2012). This shows that, despite the fact that popular modes cater to lower or middle income residents, many exclusions remain.

This is not to detract from the very large amount of access that popular transport modes generate; it is clear that if these systems were not in place, many cities would fare very poorly on accessibility metrics. For example, analysis shows that key amenities like medical facilities and parks are within a 30 min matatu ride for large proportions of the Nairobi population (Campbell et al., 2019; Fried et al., 2020; World Bank, 2016). Clear inequalities exist: residents on average can access fewer than 10% of existing jobs by walking for an hour and about a quarter of jobs by taking a matatu for the same amount of time; these are far fewer jobs than those with a private car can access (Nakamura and Avner, 2021).

Matatus, by far carry the bulk of the public transport passengers every day to all corners of the city. In December 2018, a misguided anti-congestion measure in the form of a ban on matatus accessing the Central Business District (CBD) resulted in widespread suffering and economic disruption.

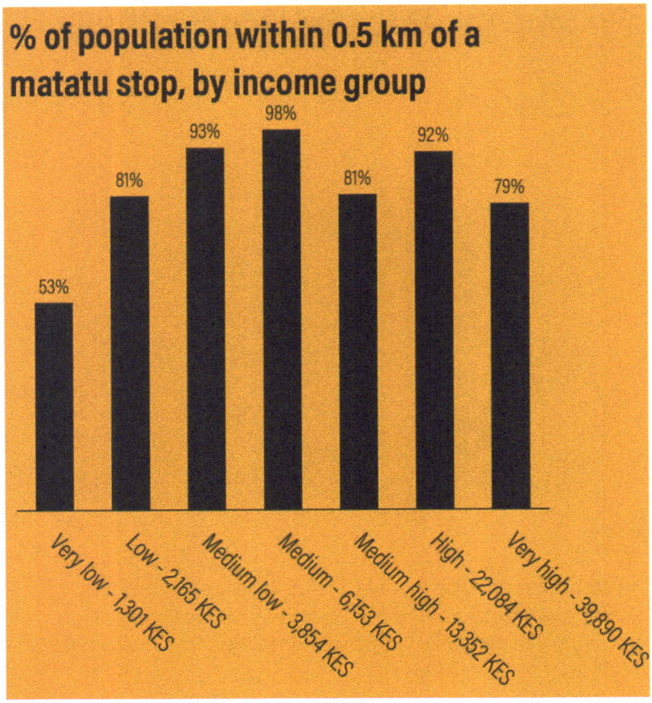

Fig. 3 Percentage of population by income within a 0.5 km of a matatu stop in Nairobi. Source: *Fried, T., Tun, T.H., Klopp, J.M., Welle, B., 2020. Measuring the Sustainable Development Goal (SDG) transport target and accessibility of Nairobi's matatus. Transp. Res. Rec. 2674, 196–207. doi: https://doi.org/10.1177/0361198120914620.*

As a result, it lasted 1 day. A close up look at the DigitalMatatus map (Fig. 4) shows the main matatu terminals are in the city center, and this is where all the main matatus routes converge. During the ban, cutting off access to the terminals where transfers take place disrupted the entire system and also forced people to walk long distances. Being able to see the network structure in this way, thus helps better understand the system dynamics, and the results of the ban were in fact quite predictable. Further, banning matatus instead of private cars from the CBD is highly regressive.

Another important observation about the matatus network is that it is not optimal from an efficiency point of view. As transport planner Jarrett Walker commented, "every matatu wants to go downtown because it's the biggest market, and a matatu driver doesn't have to be coordinated with anyone else to fill a bus going to and from there. This geometry problem bedevils privately routed [...] operations everywhere" (Walker, 2014). A more

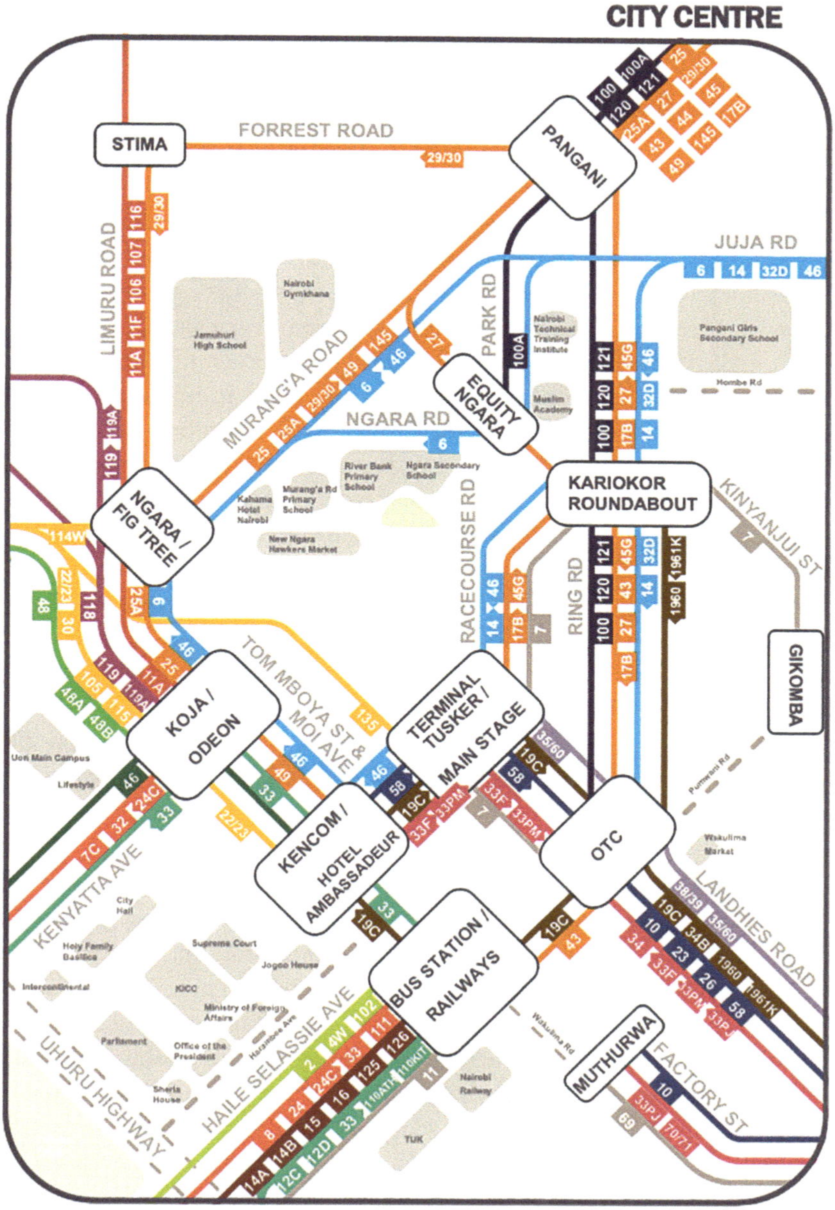

Fig. 4 Map of main matatu terminals in Nairobi in 2019. Source: *DigitalMatatus.com*.

efficient configuration would involve rationalized crosstown routes, much like those the original Kenya Bus Services ran before it was deliberately run down (Klopp and Mitullah, 2016). Overall, one way to improve this system would then be to engage in a network redesign, which has been shown in other contexts to work to improve service (Higashide, 2019).

This approach would require good data and a negotiation process with the operators with the aim of replacing the default profit maximizing network with one that replaces many transfers and walking with a safer, more convenient and efficient network. This approach would be more effective in improving a complex minibus system compared to bans and punishment. This would require long term and respectful engagement including capacity building and transparency within the sector and within the institutions responsible for managing and regulating road transport (Schalekamp, 2017). Resources would also be needed to incentivize minibus services to better integrate with mass transit modes, providing off peak feeder service where it does not exist and operating on less profitable but important routes (du Preez et al., 2019; Plano et al., 2018). Other important interventions involve finding ways to reduce and stabilize fares as well as funnel investment into innovation in passenger information, operations and basic infrastructure such as proper shelters, dedicated lanes and better organized terminals (Schalekamp and Klopp, 2018). Many possible avenues exist for upgrading these services, but they all require finance, data, patience, innovation and, most critically, careful approaches that build trust, which is often missing given the contentious historical relations between popular transport and local and national government.

Data that can be used for better understanding these popular transport systems is increasing with on board surveys that include passenger counts and waiting times or frequencies (head ways), reliability, passenger perceptions and views across gender, age, physical abilities and other demographics along with rich ethnographic understandings of how these "vernacular" systems work. As Saddier et al. note in their study of minibus (trotro) operations in Ghana, "the body of work on paratransit and the work that characterizes paratransit as unreliable are almost exclusively based on self-reported or indirect data" (Saddier and Johnson, 2018). This is true for many features of popular transport systems more generally, demanding more empirically grounded and rigorous work.

Fortunately, more detailed empirical work is growing and increasingly involves careful historically informed ethnographies and data gathering from those who know these systems best-workers and passengers (Agbiboa, 2016;

Ference, 2021; Hart, 2016; Mungai, 2013; Mutongi, 2017; Rizzo, 2017; Uzzell, 1987; Vargas, 2021). This growing body of empirical work also helps planners to identify opportunities to build on what currently works with these systems and support changing what does not. It is important to note that even if the planning aim is to eliminate these systems and replace them, it is critical to understand which services are being taken away when these systems are banned or partially replaced by new systems like Bus Rapid Transit and what this means in practice for people. For example, the introduction of a new BRT system along with changes to popular transport services in Barranquilla, Colombia in 2010 evoked mixed reactions in passengers. When queried about the transition, they noted positive changes such as reductions in travel time, air conditioning and an increased sense of personal safety but those interviewed also noted "significant problems from overcrowding, the insufficiency and complexity of BRT feeder routes, and the elimination of several private transit bus routes along with loss of the ability to bargain over fares" (Santana Palacios et al., 2020, p. 131). It is hard to escape the conclusion that proper understanding of and engagement with the popular transport system are critical to address within transportation planning if we seek to improve equity and address the needs of the majority as well as poorer populations facing challenges of access, service quality and poor labor conditions if they work in the sector.

6. Conclusions

Despite the importance of popular transport modes to the wellbeing of most people in the world and the functioning of most cities, for too long transportation planners have neglected understanding how these modes operate and why. Their service qualities, drawbacks and impacts are often assumed rather than measured and studied carefully; further the equity implications of marginalizing these critical services in planning are simply ignored. Fortunately, we are now moving away from this problematic paradigm of popular transport as "paratransit" and toward a more empirical and empathetic approach that sees these modes as transit. More and more researchers are gathering diverse kinds of data to understand these systems better. This work to collect and share improved and standardized data needs to be accelerated along with using this data to better understand these systems including how to decarbonize them (Collett and Hirmer, 2021); the next phase is to leverage this foundation to develop thoughtful engagement, finance and investment strategies and to explore and test new approaches to improving service, working conditions and integration of popular transport with mass transit to create high quality seamless multi-modal public transport systems and equitable access to the city (Kumar et al., 2021; Thet et al., 2020). To do this we need to recognize that popular transport modes emerge out of unmet demand for mobility services, poor and unequal land-use, and profound underinvestment in equitable, high quality and affordable public transport. Now as we confront the fact that our current transportation and land-use systems are not only highly inequitable, but are also leading to serious inter-related problems of climate change, air pollution, traffic fatalities and gridlock, the need for more nuanced, inclusive, empirical and holistic approaches to transportation planning and reform has never been greater.

References

Agbiboa, D.E., 2016. No condition is permanent': informal transport workers and labour precarity in Africa's largest city: 'no condition is permanent. Int. J. Urban Reg. Res. 40, 936–957. https://doi.org/10.1111/1468-2427.12440.

Agbiboa, D.E. (Ed.), 2018. Introduction: transport, transgression and politics in African cities: an introduction. In: Transport, Transgression and Politics in African Cities: The Rhythm of Chaos, Cities and Society. Routledge, Abingdon, Oxon, New York, NY.

Ames, A., Mateo-Babiano, I.B., Susilo, Y.O., 2014. Transport workers' perspective on indigenous transport and climate change adaptation. Transp. Res. Rec. 2451, 1–9. https://doi.org/10.3141/2451-01.

APHRC, 2012. Population and Health Dynamics in Nairobi's Informal Settlements: Report of the Nairobi Cross-Sectional Slums Survey (NCSS). https://aphrc.org/publication/population-and-health-dynamics-in-nairobis-informal-settlements-report-of-the-nairobi-cross-sectional-slums-survey-ncss-2012-2/.

Attoh, K.A., 2019. Rights in Transit: Public Transportation and the Right to the City in California's East Bay. University of Georgia Press, https://doi.org/10.2307/j.ctt22nmc4p.

Avner, P., Lall, S., 2016. Matchmaking in Nairobi: The Role of Land Use, Policy Research Working Papers. The World Bank, https://doi.org/10.1596/1813-9450-7904.

Babijes, R.M., 2016. Kenya Urbanization Review.

Banks, N., Lombard, M., Mitlin, D., 2020. Urban informality as a site of critical analysis. J. Dev. Stud. 56, 223–238. https://doi.org/10.1080/00220388.2019.1577384.

Behrens, R., McCormick, D., Mfinanga, D. (Eds.), 2016. Paratransit in African Cities: Operations, Regulation and Reform.

Berlingerio, M., Calabrese, F., Di Lorenzo, G., Nair, R., Pinelli, F., Sbodio, M.L., 2013. AllAboard: a system for exploring urban mobility and optimizing public transport using cellphone data. In: Blockeel, H., Kersting, K., Nijssen, S., Železný, F. (Eds.), Machine Learning and Knowledge Discovery in Databases. Springer, pp. 663–666, https://doi.org/10.1007/978-3-642-40994-3_50.

Boateng, F.G., 2020. "Indiscipline" in context: a political-economic grounding for dangerous driving behaviors among Tro-Tro drivers in Ghana. Humanit. Soc. Sci. Commun. 7, 1–5. https://doi.org/10.1057/s41599-020-0502-8.

Campbell, K.B., Rising, J.A., Klopp, J.M., Mbilo, J.M., 2019. Accessibility across transport modes and residential developments in Nairobi. J. Transp. Geogr. 74, 77–90. https://doi.org/10.1016/j.jtrangeo.2018.08.002.

Cervero, R., 2000. Informal Transport in the Developing World | UN-Habitat. [WWW Document]. URL https://unhabitat.org/informal-transport-in-the-developing-world. (accessed 2.28.21).

Cervero, R., Golub, A., 2007. Informal transport: a global perspective. Transp. Policy 14, 445–457. https://doi.org/10.1016/j.tranpol.2007.04.011.

Collett, K.A., Hirmer, S.A., 2021. Data needed to decarbonize paratransit in Sub-Saharan Africa. Nat. Sustain., 1–3. https://doi.org/10.1038/s41893-021-00721-7.

Colville, R.N., Hutchinson, E.J., Mindell, J.S., Warren, R.F., 2001. The transport sector as a source of air pollution. Atmos. Environ. 35, 1537–1565. https://doi.org/10.1016/S1352-2310(00)00551-3.

du Preez, D., Zuidgeest, M., Behrens, R., 2019. A quantitative clustering analysis of paratransit route typology and operating attributes in Cape Town. J. Transp. Geogr. 80. https://doi.org/10.1016/j.jtrangeo.2019.102493.

Ference, M.E., 2019. Joyriding: making place in Nairobi's Matatu sector. City Soc. 31, 188–207. https://doi.org/10.1111/ciso.12226.

Ference, M.E., 2021. 'You will build me': fiscal disobedience, reciprocity and the dangerous negotiations of redistribution on Nairobi's matatu. Africa 91, 16–34. https://doi.org/10.1017/S0001972020000820.

Ferro, P., Behrens, R., Wilkinson, P., 2013. Hybrid urban transport systems in developing countries: portents and prospects. Res. Transp. Econ. 39, 121–132. https://doi.org/10.1016/j.retrec.2012.06.004.

Flores, O., 2019. App-Based Collective Transport Service in Mexico City ITF Paper. Accessed at https://www.itf-oecd.org/app-based-collective-transport-service-mexico-city.

Foltz, J.D., Opoku-Agyemang, K.A., 2015. Do Higher Salaries Lower Petty Corruption? A Policy Experiment on West Africa's Highways. International Growth Center. https://www.theigc.org/wp-content/uploads/2016/02/Foltz-Opoku-Agyemang-2016 Working-paper.pdf.

Fried, T., Tun, T.H., Klopp, J.M., Welle, B., 2020. Measuring the sustainable development goal (SDG) transport target and accessibility of Nairobi's Matatus. Transp. Res. Rec. 2674, 196–207. https://doi.org/10.1177/0361198120914620.

Global Labour Institute, Manchester, 2019. Nairobi Bus Rapid Transit: Labour Impact Assessment Research Report. Accessed at https://www.itfglobal.org/en/reports-publications/power-informal-transport-workers.

Goldwyn, E.L., 2017. An Informal Transit System Hiding in Plain Sight: Brooklyn's Dollar Vans and Transportation Planning and Policy in New York City. Columbia University, https://doi.org/10.7916/D8W959RP.

Gupta, S.K., Elumalai, S.P., 2019. Exposure to traffic-related particulate matter and deposition dose to auto rickshaw driver in Dhanbad, India. Atmos. Pollut. Res. 10, 1128–1139. https://doi.org/10.1016/j.apr.2019.01.018.

Gwilliam, K.M., 2001. Competition in urban passenger transport in the developing world. J. Transp. Econ. Policy 35, 99–118.

Harding, S.E., Madhav, B.G., Reynolds, C.C., Kandlikar, M., 2016. Auto-rickshaws in Indian cities: public perceptions and operational realities. Transp. Policy 52, 143–152. https://doi.org/10.1016/j.tranpol.2016.07.013.

Hart, J.A., 2016. Ghana on the go: African Mobility in the Age of Motor Transportation. Indiana University Press, Bloomington, Indianapolis.

Higashide, S., 2019. Better Buses, Better Cities: How to Plan, Run, and Win the Fight for Effective Transit. Island Press, Washington, DC.

International Transport Workers Federation, 2017. The Power of Informal Transport Workers.

Jennings, G., Behrens, R., 2017. The Case for Investing in Paratransit Strategies for Regulation and Reform. Volvo Research and Educational Foundations (VREF).

Kariuki, D., 2015. Matatu Crew That Helps People With Disabilities at no Extra Fee. Kenyans.co.ke.

Kelly, E., Lane, G., Schonholzer, D., 2018. The Impact of Monitoring Technologies on Contracts and Employee Behavior: Experimental Evidence From Kenya's Transit Industry.

Khayesi, M., Nafukho, F.M., Kemuma, J., 2016. Informal Public Transport in Practice: Matatu Entrepreneurship.

Klopp, J.M., Cavoli, C., 2019. Mapping minibuses in Maputo and Nairobi: engaging paratransit in transportation planning in African cities. Transplant. Rev. 39, 657–676. https://doi.org/10.1080/01441647.2019.1598513.

Klopp, J., Mitullah, W., 2016. Politics, policy and paratransit: a view from Nairobi. In: Behrens, R., McCormick, D., Mfinanga, D. (Eds.), Paratransit in African Cities: Operations, Regulation and Reform.

Klopp, J., Delattre, F., Chevre, A., 2020. Open Data for Inclusive Urban Public Transport Globally. French Development Agency.

Kumar, A., Zimmerman, S., Arroyo-Arroyo, F., 2021. Myths and Realities of "Informal" Public Transport in Developing Countries: Approaches for Improving the Sector. The World Bank.

MobilityData.org, 2021. MobilityData. [WWW Document] URL https://mobilitydata.org/. (accessed 4.24.21).

Mungai, M.W., 2013. Nairobi's "Matatu" Men: Portrait of a Subculture, Contact Zones NRB. Twaweza Communications: Goethe-Institut Kenya: Native Intelligence: Jomo Kenyatta Foundation, Nairobi.

Mutongi, K., 2017. Matatu: A History of Popular Transportation in Nairobi. The University of Chicago Press, Chicago.

Nakamura, S., Avner, P., 2021. Spatial distributions of job accessibility, housing rents, and poverty: the case of Nairobi. J. Hous. Econ. 51, 101743.

Ngo, N.S., Gatari, M., Yan, B., Chillrud, S.N., Bouhamam, K., Kinney, P.L., 2015. Occupational exposure to roadway emissions and inside informal settlements in sub-Saharan Africa: a pilot study in Nairobi, Kenya. Atmos. Environ. 111, 179–184. https://doi.org/10.1016/j.atmosenv.2015.04.008.

Nijman, J., Wei, Y.D., 2020. Urban inequalities in the 21st century economy. Appl. Geogr. Sevenoaks Engl. 117, 102188. https://doi.org/10.1016/j.apgeog.2020.102188.

Omm-e-Hany, Sarang, M., Asia, N., Aamir, A., Kanza, A., 2015. Epidemiological study of rickshaw drivers health status and accident encounters in towns of Karachi. Bull. Environ. Pharmacol. Life Sci. 3, 55–59.

Orski, C.K., 1975. Paratransit: the coming of age of a transportation concept. Transportation 4 (4), 329–334.

Plano, C., Behrens, R., Zuidgeest, M., 2018. Towards a Stated Choice Methodology to Determine Minibus-Taxi Driver Willingness to Provide off-Peak Feeder Service.

Ramukumba, T.S., Mathikhi, M.S., 2016. Health assessment of taxi drivers in the city of Tshwane. Curationis 39, 1–7. https://doi.org/10.4102/curationis.v39i1.1671.

Reiss, A., Lavey, N., 2014. New York's Shadow Transit. The New Yorker. http://projects.newyorker.com/story/nyc-dollar-vans.

Rizzo, M., 2017. Taken for a Ride: Grounding Neoliberalism, Precarious Labour, and Public Transport in an African Metropolis, Critical Frontiers of Theory, Research, and Policy in International Development Studies. Oxford University Press, Oxford.

Saddier, S., Johnson, A., 2018. Understanding the operational characteristics of paratransit services in Accra, Ghana: a case study. In: Presented at the Transportation Research Board 97th Annual Meeting. Transportation Research Board.

SafeBoda, 2021. SafeBoda—Your City Ride. https://safeboda.com/ug/.

Santana Palacios, M., Cochran, A., Bell, C., Hernández Jiménez, U., Leshner, E., Trejo Morales, F., Chatman, D.G., 2020. Bus rapid transit arrives in Barranquilla, Colombia: understanding a changing landscape through residents' travel experiences. Travel Behav. Soc. 21, 131–139. https://doi.org/10.1016/j.tbs.2020.06.003.

Schalekamp, H., 2017. Lessons from building paratransit operators' capacity to be partners in Cape Town's public transport reform process. Transp. Res. Part Policy Pract. 104, 58–66. https://doi.org/10.1016/j.tra.2017.08.002.

Schalekamp, H., Klopp, J., 2018. Beyond BRT: innovation in minibus-taxi reform in South African cities. In: Presented at the Southern African Transport Conference, Pretoria.

Sims, R., Schaeffer, R., Creutzig, F., Cruz-Núñez, X., D'Agosto, M., Dimitriu, D., Figueroa Meza, M.J., Fulton, L., Kobayashi, S., Lah, O., McKinnon, A., Newman, P., Ouyang, M., Schauer, J.J., Sperling, D., Tiwari, G., 2014. In: Edenhofer, O., Pichs-Madruga, R., Sokona, Y., Farahani, E., Kadner, S., Seyboth, K., Minx, J.C. (Eds.), Mitigation of Climate Change. Contribution of Working Group III to the Fifth Assessment Report of the Intergovernmental Panel on Climate Change. Cambridge University Press, Cambridge, United Kingdom and New York, NY, USA.

Sopranzetti, C., 2018. Owners of the Map: Motorcycle Taxi Drivers, Mobility, and Politics in Bangkok, first ed. University of California Press.

Spooner, D., Mwanika, J.M., Matamba, S., Manga, E.O., 2020. Kampala Bus Rapid Transit: Understanding Kampala's Paratransit Market Structure. Global Labor Institute.

The United Nations Environment Programme, 2020. Global Trade in Used Vehicles Report.

Thet, H.T., Welle, B., Hidalgo, D., Castellanos, S., Sclar, R., Escalante, D., 2020. Informal and Semiformal Services in Latin America: An Overview of Public Transportation Reforms. Publications.

UN-Habitat, 2020. World Cities Report 2020: The Value of Sustainable Urbanization | UN-Habitat. Nairobi.

Uzzell, D., 1987. A homegrown mass transit system in Lima, Peru: a case of generative planning. City Soc. 1, 6–34. https://doi.org/10.1525/city.1987.1.1.6.

Vargas, A.M., 2021. Organising everyday resistance: an ethnographic study of rickshaw drivers in Bogotá. Bull. Lat. Am. Res. https://doi.org/10.1111/blar.13148. n/a.

Venter, C., 2016. Assessing the potential of bus rapid transit-led network restructuring for enhancing affordable access to employment—the case of Johannesburg's corridors of freedom. Res. Transp. Econ. 59, 441–449. https://doi.org/10.1016/j.retrec.2016.05.006.

Walker, J., 2014. The evolution of logic in privately planned transit. Hum. Transit. URL https://humantransit.org/2014/02/the-evolution-of-logic-in-developing-world-transit.html. (accessed 2.11.19).

Wilkinson, P., 2010. The regulatory cycle stalled? An assessment of current institutional obstacles to regulatory reform in the provision of road-based public transport in Cape Town, South Africa. Res. Transp. Econ. 29, 387–394. https://doi.org/10.1016/j.retrec.2010.07.049.

Williams, S., White, A., Waiganjo, P., Orwa, D., Klopp, J., 2015. The digital matatu project: using cell phones to create an open source data for Nairobi's semi-formal bus system. J. Transp. Geogr. 49, 39–51. https://doi.org/10.1016/j.jtrangeo.2015.10.005.

World Bank, 2016. Kenya Urbanisation Review. World Bank, Washington DC.

CHAPTER EIGHT

What are we doing with all that satisfaction data? Evaluating Public Transport customer satisfaction data collection and analysis techniques

Cherise Roberts[a], Emily Grisé[a,*], and Dea van Lierop[b]
[a]School of Urban and Regional Planning, University of Alberta, Edmonton, AB, Canada
[b]Department of Human Geography & Spatial Planning, Utrecht University, Utrecht, The Netherlands
*Corresponding author: e-mail address: egrise@ualberta.ca

Contents

Abstract

Emphasis on measuring and understanding public transport (PT) users' satisfaction is driven by research that has found that passengers who are satisfied with PT services also often report the intention and desire to use PT in the future. The relationship between overall satisfaction and long-term loyalty is not straightforward and is often indirectly influenced by many factors related to both PT services as well as the characteristics, opinions, and previous experiences of PT users. To increase retention of existing riders requires an understanding of the customer's needs and perspectives of service quality, both for the overall service and for attribute-specific items (e.g., reliability and safety). For that reason, several PT agencies have adopted marketing strategies to elicit knowledge on users to identify the relative influence of these service attributes on a users' overall service assessment. However, the methodologies used to collect and

Advances in Transport Policy and Planning, Volume 8
ISSN 2543-0009
https://doi.org/10.1016/bs.atpp.2021.06.003
Copyright © 2021 Elsevier Inc.
All rights reserved.

analyze satisfaction data can limit the ability of decision makers to create policies which are not only representative of a population, but also benefit all segments of a population, impacting their effectiveness. This chapter provides a review of the most common practices and approaches to analyzing passenger satisfaction with PT, focusing on prevalent techniques to estimate the relative importance of service quality attributes on overall satisfaction. It critically assesses the advantages and limitations of each method with regards to its ability to be put into practice by PT professionals and translated into policy effective for stimulating loyalty across population segments.

Keywords: Public transport, Customer satisfaction, Loyalty, Data collection, Data analysis, Market segmentation

1. Introduction

Urban regions and public transport (PT) agencies around the world aspire to increase PT mode share in order to increase PT revenues, reduce road congestion and improve environmental sustainability. However, the propensity for people to choose PT as their main mode of transport, when other modes are available to them, often depends on how satisfied they are with the available services.

As a means of attracting new riders to PT and retaining existing riders, PT agencies are focused on providing a level of service quality that, at a minimum, meets the expectations of users. Service quality is related to a series of attributes describing the different elements of PT service, such as reliability, accessibility, safety, and travel time. While most PT agencies have internal operational performance measurements, such as on-time performance and ridership, the customer's point of view is particularly relevant for evaluating perceived performance as these subjective experiences are key for evaluating how satisfied riders are with service quality (Berry et al., 1990). Moreover, how satisfied a customer is, and has been, with a service has an impact on the likelihood that they will continue using PT in the future (Lai and Chen, 2011; Thøgersen, 2006; van Lierop and El-Geneidy, 2016).

Related to the concept of satisfaction, and just as elusive in nature, customer loyalty is highly sought after by PT agencies. A commonly-accepted operational definition of loyalty to PT is a based on a rider's intended future use, willingness to recommend PT to others, and high overall satisfaction ratings (van Lierop et al., 2018). Research has also found that satisfaction and future intentions of using PT are positively correlated with a user's image of PT, suggesting that image is also a key component of loyalty (van Lierop and El-Geneidy, 2017). Loyal riders are more likely to encourage others to use PT and are less likely to make a switch from using PT to alternative modes of transport, such as using a personal car or ridesharing service. Loyal and satisfied customers enable PT agencies to build a dedicated rider base helping to support ongoing farebox revenues, as well as helping meet regional environmental goals related to mode use.

Fare revenue, which is largely determined by the number of riders, is a significant component of the operating budget and financial viability of most PT agencies. However, while attaining ridership targets is considered a measure of success for most PT agencies, (European Metropolitan Transport Authorities, 2020; National Academies of Sciences, Engineering, and Medicine, 2009; Transportation Research Board, and Price Waterhouse Company, 1998; Verbich et al., 2017), ridership is by no means the only goal commonly considered by agencies when assessing the overall success, or "health," of a service. Rather, PT is an essential service that keeps society moving. A recent example of the essential role that PT plays in cities was experienced during the COVID-19 pandemic in 2020. While dramatic declines in ridership occurred around the world due to stay-at-home provisions, PT agencies continued to provide limited or amended services for individuals who relied on PT to meet their needs (DeWeese et al., 2020; Gkiotsalitis and Cats, 2020; Hu and Chen, 2021; Jenelius and Cebecauer, 2020). In this example, in most cases fares were not adjusted to make-up for lost ridership revenues, but instead significant emergency funding was made available in many cities to keep services running and minimize the long-term implications of the pandemic on PT operations. The COVID-19 pandemic is an example of an external factor that had a devastating impact on PT ridership. Internal factors impacting PT ridership, including assets of an agency, its operations and its fare policy (Boisjoly et al., 2018), can be effectively managed with customer expectations in mind.

The intangibility, heterogeneity and inseparability inherent to customer satisfaction makes it notoriously difficult to measure and apply satisfaction research findings to develop policies (Parasuraman et al., 1985). There are many characteristics of service quality that are intangible by nature, such as subjective experiences of safety and comfort, which are difficult for agencies to monitor and deliver consistently for all users. Services are heterogeneous, particularly those with a high dependency on personnel labor, resulting in service performance that is highly variable, from day to day and operator to operator. Finally, delivery of service and user participation of the service are also inseparable, meaning that participation of the individual, for example, arriving for the train on time, can impact the users' experience of the service.

Yet, despite these difficulties, it is important for PT agencies and policymakers to measure how satisfied their customers are with the PT services provided to assess how services can be improved in the quest to increasing overall customer loyalty.

Marketing research strategies focusing on increasing customer satisfaction, have been applied by PT agencies across the globe to determine which service attributes and policy interventions would be the most likely to increase overall customer satisfaction, loyalty, and ridership. This information enables PT agencies to engage in benchmarking activities related to assessing customer satisfaction over time and across service attributes, thereby effectively using their limited resources to implement targeted policies, interventions, and marketing campaigns to attract and retain riders.

Satisfaction data collection methods play a key role in acquiring representative and usable information from a given population, which is of crucial importance to help decision makers design policies that address the diverse needs of an agency's customer base. Moreover, methods used by decision makers to analyze this data across key sociodemographic groups and needs can result in the development of transport policies that fail to recognize the diverse preferences and desires of public transport users, challenging transport agencies from achieving transportation equity. This chapter critically examines several prominent data collection and analysis methods used for assessing PT customers' overall satisfaction and loyalty. It focuses on how commonly used methods influence the policies that can be derived from satisfaction data and provides a discussion about the importance of analyzing customer satisfaction among different population segments. Rather than conducting a systematic literature review that covers all methods used by researchers and transport agencies, this chapter instead focuses on the primary data collection and analysis methods used in PT satisfaction research in recent years. The chapter concludes with recommendations and future considerations for PT customer satisfaction research.

2. How agencies collect satisfaction data

The concept of satisfaction with travel originated from customer satisfaction research, which has been a popular field of study in domains such as marketing (Fornell et al., 1996). Given that trip satisfaction can be considered a type of customer satisfaction, it often results from a commuter's reaction to his or her experience with the service and to what extent it meets their needs and/or expectations (Grigoroudis and Siskos, 2009), which can vary depending on an individual's attitudes, personality, and predispositions (Beirão and Cabral, 2007). Public transport agencies regularly engage with their riders to better understand how customers perceive elements of service quality and to learn more about their riders. The design of customer satisfaction surveys varies significantly between transport agencies, with respect to the frequency of data collection, questions asked, target populations, and use of survey collection tools.

2.1 Commonly asked questions

Satisfaction surveys commonly begin by asking respondents to rate their overall satisfaction, typically on a 5-, 7-, or 10-point rating scale ranging from very unsatisfied to very satisfied, over a stated period of time. The time span used as a reference point can vary widely between surveys, sometimes narrowly asking about overall satisfaction with their last trip while other times asking about satisfaction over a specific time frame (i.e., past month or year). De Vos and Witlox (2017) explain that satisfaction with a specific trip (trip satisfaction) refers to emotions and a cognitive evaluation of this one trip, whereas satisfaction with daily travel using this mode is a measure of how satisfied people are with their daily travel habits. Respondents are then typically asked to rate their satisfaction with specific service attributes, such as reliability, frequency, and safety. This information is used by agencies to understand where service improvements can be made, and also potentially assess touch points of a customer journey with the goal of improving the customer experience (van Lierop et al., 2019). To measure passenger loyalty, satisfaction surveys are commonly designed to ask customers to state their future intentions to continue using PT using a 5-, 7-, or 10-point rating scale (Carrel et al., 2016) and whether or not they would be willing to recommend PT to other people (Ingvardson and Nielsen, 2019; van Lierop et al., 2018), since these are two commonly-accepted components of loyalty to PT.

To better understand their customers and the sample of users in the dataset, PT agencies use surveys to collect demographic information on riders, such as age, gender, ethnicity, and income level. The size and composition of a household, employment status, and whether or not the respondent has access to other modes of transportation and a valid driver's license are often also commonly asked (e.g., Grisé and El-Geneidy, 2020). Although less common, psychological factors, such as perceptions, attitudes, and habits can be collected in satisfaction surveys to better understand different motivations and constraints of the survey population (e.g., (Diez-Mesa et al., 2016)). Collecting this data is important as the attributes of PT service appreciated by each user are highly dependent on the users' social and demographic characteristics, context (i.e., geographical area and type of transport services available), reason for travel, and modes of transport used (de Oña and de Oña, 2015).

2.2 Location characteristics and benchmarking activities

Satisfaction data is typically gathered at the local level, within the boundaries of municipal or regional PT networks. Some satisfaction surveys, however, are conducted at the national level. For example, Sweden has been surveying people on an ongoing basis since 2001 through the Public Transport Barometer (Abenoza et al., 2017). In the Netherlands, a panel is used to assess rail commuters' levels of satisfaction (Nederlandse Spoorwegen, 2020). Furthermore, on an international scale, benchmarking exercises can be conducted between cities nationally or worldwide for PT operators to better understand their relative performance across various key performance indicators. The International Bus Benchmarking Group (IBBG) developed a survey tool in, 2009 to overcome key challenges associated with comparing satisfaction of customers in different cities and countries, namely differences in questionnaires used, sample frames, response collection methods, and potential cultural bias (Trompet et al., 2013). As Trompet et al. (2013) describe, for public transport agencies to achieve the true benefit of a benchmarking exercise, distinct areas of improvement need to be identified alongside related best practices by peer organizations. Inter-organizational sharing of knowledge and best practices through benchmarking can increase quality and efficiency in the sector (Geerlings et al., 2006). Nonetheless, benchmarking activities remain relatively rare, particularly at the national level, largely because of the key challenges associated with comparing customer satisfaction in different cities and countries, as outlined above.

2.3 Data collection methods

How PT agencies approach collecting and analyzing customer data has changed significantly over the years due to technological advances. While in-person and telephone surveys were common during the last half of the twentieth century, the increasing prevalence of online information and communications technology (ICT) in the 21st century, including personal communication devices, have changed how people communicate.

Similar changes are expected in the future as it is important that the survey mode is adapted to the changing preferences of the general population in order to encourage participation in survey research (Dillman, 2016, 2017).

Today, there are several different data collection modes commonly used in PT satisfaction research, each presenting their own advantages and drawbacks to achieving a sample that is representative of a given population and also allows for gaining insight into customer satisfaction. However, the requirement to achieve a representative sample often needs to be balanced with the cost of conducting the research.

Intercept surveys conducted in-person with PT riders either at stops or on-board buses or trains (as demonstrated in Allen et al., 2019; Echaniz et al., 2019), have been and continue to be one of the most used methods for collecting PT satisfaction data. Data from intercept surveys are useful to gain a snapshot of who an agency's PT riders are at a particular time and location, and is often used for determining the sociodemographic characteristics, motivations, and preferences of existing riders (Transportation Research Board, and National Academies of Sciences, Engineering, and Medicine, 2005). Intercept surveys are particularly useful to understand a riders' emotions and cognitive evaluation of a specific trip since this method is less susceptible to memory bias, compared to other questionnaire-based survey methods where data is collected after the completion of the trip (Transportation Research Board, and National Academies of Sciences, Engineering, and Medicine, 2005). The sooner a rider has a chance to report his or her level of satisfaction with their most recent trip, the more accurate the reported information (Kahneman et al., 2004). This kind of sampling strategy can also effectively account for weather variations (i.e., trips during summer and winter), temporal variations (i.e., during different times of day which can capture different trip purposes), variations in operational performance (which can be observed through linking satisfaction data with automatically collected vehicle location (AVL) data and automatic passenger count (APC) data), and can effectively capture individuals who would otherwise be difficult to survey (i.e., those on a no-call list). Intercept surveys are also commonly designed in such a way to ensure that the user population is surveyed proportionally to the actual usage and frequency of service per route. However, by design, intercept surveys exclude individuals who do not use PT. They also generally also exclude those with very short PT trips and waiting times. To capture the perspective of non-riders, transport agencies would need to invest additional resources to sample individuals who do not use PT. Without such additional investment, transport agencies will systematically fail at understanding the reasons why certain individuals or populations do not use public transport. Moreover, intercept surveys are very resource-intensive, often requiring multiple interviewers to collect data over the span of several months in order to acquire a sample that is large enough and representative of PT users (Agrawal et al., 2016).

Telephone surveys are another commonly used survey method and have the potential to collect information from both riders and non-riders. Compared to intercept surveys, phone surveys are typically less expensive and can be conducted over a shorter time frame (Stern et al., 2014). While it is possible, in theory, to obtain a representative sample using random digit dialing (RDD), telephone survey response rates in recent years have dropped drastically (Dillman, 2017). For instance, the Pew Research Center found that telephone survey response rates decreased from 36% in 1997 to 9% in 2012, with response rates remaining at 9% between 2012 and 2016 (Keeter et al., 2017). Moreover, this decrease in telephone survey response rates is evident for both landlines and cellphones (Dutwin and Lavrakas, 2016). A low response rate increases the likelihood of non-response bias, thus threatening the representativeness of the sample.

Online questionnaires have grown in popularity in recent years due to changing communication preferences and the opportunity to reach a wide audience at a relatively low cost. Online questionnaires allow respondents to interact and complete a survey when it is convenient for them (Chang and Krosnick, 2009), and, like phone surveys, can potentially reach both PT riders and non-riders. Further, self-administered surveys greatly reduce the amount of resources needed to conduct the survey and virtually eliminate the need for data entry (Campbell et al., 2018), resulting in significant cost savings. Engaging with customers through online questionnaires allows PT agencies to effectively build panels of their customers for future satisfaction questionnaires and other forms of engagement. However, research has shown that obtaining a representative sample through online surveys is often difficult since they tend to be biased toward younger people with higher education and income levels. These groups are more likely to own a computer, have access to the internet or cell phone data (Dillman, 2016), and be tech-savvy enough to be inclined to interact with online survey software. Moreover, it is nearly impossible to create a representative sampling frame using email addresses (Dillman, 2017), leading to many researchers resorting to non-probability sampling methods, such as quota or snowball sampling. To overcome this issue, Dillman (2017) suggests using a mixed-mode sampling method, such as mailing notices to randomly selected households to participate in an online survey.

Over the last several years *smartphone survey applications* have emerged as a promising new data collection method for collecting PT satisfaction data from particular population segments. Surveys conducted through smartphone applications are already gaining in popularity in other areas of travel research, taking advantage of the devices' existing GPS technology and other sensing devices, such as accelerometers (Cottrill et al., 2013; Gadziński, 2018). Mobile applications such as the Advance Travel Logging Application for Smartphones II (ATLAS II) (part of the National Household Travel survey of New Zealand) have been used in several recent travel behavior studies (Roddis et al., 2019; Safi et al., 2017), and involve tracking respondents' movements, then prompting individuals to validate their travel data.

Although smartphone applications have only been used in a few PT satisfaction and loyalty studies to date (for example, Carrel et al., 2016; Carrel and Li, 2019), this technology could be used on a wider basis in the future to not only collect satisfaction data, but to also incorporate performance measures and spatial data into the analysis. This technology also has the potential to be used in longitudinal studies, for instance comparing predicted versus actual future PT use (Carrel and Li, 2019). Due to cost, time, and the availability of personnel, most surveys conducted in PT research are single-wave surveys. Nevertheless, longitudinal surveys provide researchers with valuable insights into how satisfaction-improvement measures are working. Longitudinal surveys also allow researchers or PT agencies to passively measure customers' behavior over time. One such study conducted over the course of a year in San Francisco was able to measure respondents' initial predicted frequency of PT use against their actual frequency of PT use, finding that those who intended to decrease PT use had a higher accuracy rate compared to those who intended to increase their frequency of PT use (Carrel and Li, 2019).

One limitation to using smart phone applications to collect data is that many individuals only interact with either Apple or Android smartphones, thus biasing the results toward one type of smartphone user if both operating systems are not accounted for. Moreover, a poor user interface can have a significant impact on survey participation, potentially affecting data quality (Roddis et al., 2019; Safi et al., 2017). Also, as continuous sampling with GPS has been found to drain a smartphone battery very quickly (Zhuang et al., 2010), smartphone applications need to be designed to impose little inconvenience to participants while providing high quality data (Harding et al., 2017). In a trial of bringing new data collection methods to the National Household Travel Survey in New Zealand, Safi et al. (2017) found that younger people tended to be more interested in smartphone application-based surveys while people over the age of 55 tended to gravitate toward web-based and hand-held GPS methods. If an agency uses multiple methods for data collection, this might mean that the time between when a trip and survey are taken may vary significantly between population segments, with younger individuals feeling more comfortable engaging with smart phone surveys during a trip, and older participants participating once they are able to interact with a personal computer.

Intercept, telephone, online, and smartphone surveys, all of which use quantitative data collection techniques, continue to be the dominant form of data collection in PT satisfaction research. Yet, the sampling strategies required by these methods can greatly limit their representativeness both because of the ways in which potential participants are engaged and due to the threat of non-response bias. Since surveys tend to be composed primarily of closed-ended questions, respondents are constrained by the types of responses they can give.

An alternative is to use qualitative methods such as *focus groups*, *semi-structured personal interviews*, and *ride-along interviews*. While these methods are not commonly used, they tend to be flexible in nature and can often be used to shine a light on issues or concerns not previously captured by quantitative methods, expose more nuances, and highlight the unique experiences of specific groups of PT users. Qualitative methods are, however, rarely representative of the population (Shay et al., 2016). Oftentimes, without attractive incentives or compensation for participation, only people with the time and desire typically participate in focus groups or panel discussions, limiting the generalizability of their findings and thus the policies that can be developed.

To conclude this section, a summary table of data collection methods described above is presented in Table 1. The benefits and drawbacks of each data collection method are also summarized in Table 1, as each survey method offers unique advantages and disadvantages that should be carefully considered by public transport agencies when selecting the optimal data collection method for their needs.

3. Common methods of analyzing data

3.1 Stated and derived importance

Following data collection, there are several different approaches that can be used to analyze and report satisfaction data and inform policy. PT agencies commonly report average levels of satisfaction, but academia has introduced several more statistically advanced methods to derive findings from satisfaction data. These methods, however, described below, have had limited diffusion within PT agencies due to a lack of available resources, in-house expertise, or desire to do so. As we mentioned in the introduction, this

Table 1 Summary of data collection methods.

Data collection method	Description	Benefits	Drawbacks
Intercept survey	Conducted in-person either at stops or on-board buses or trains	Gain a snapshot of the characteristics, motivations, and preferences of existing PT riders	Excludes non-riders
		Surveys conducted during or immediately after a trip reduce memory bias and provide insight into riders' emotions and cognitive evaluation of a specific trip	Acquiring a representative sample is resource and time-intensive
		Can effectively account for weather, temporal, and operational performance variations	
Telephone survey	Survey is conducted over the telephone (landline or cellphone)	Potential to collect data from both riders and non-riders	Declining response rates for both landline and cellphones are low
	Responses are typically closed-ended. Interviewer is required to ask questions and record responses		

Continued

Table 1 Summary of data collection methods.—cont'd

Data collection method	Description	Benefits	Drawbacks
Online questionnaire	Questionnaire is accessed and completed by the respondent over the internet	Respondents can complete at a time that is convenient for them	Difficult to create a representative sampling frame using email addresses
		Opportunity to reach a wide audience at a relatively low cost	Online surveys require internet access, technical skills and the ability to operate a computer, which may result in biases toward younger respondents with higher education and income levels
		Data entry is automatic, and few personnel and physical resources are required, resulting in significant cost savings	
		Potential to collect data from both riders and non-riders	
		Opportunity to build a panel of customers for future satisfaction questionnaires and other forms of engagement	
Smartphone survey application	Satisfaction data is recorded and collected by a smartphone application downloaded to the respondent's phone	Potential to incorporate performance measures and spatial data into analysis	Poor user interface can significantly impact participation, affecting data quality
		Can easily facilitate longitudinal analysis	Continuous use of GPS can drain battery more quickly
			Common over-representation of younger respondents

Table 1 Summary of data collection methods.—cont'd

Data collection method	Description	Benefits	Drawbacks
Qualitative research methods	Approaches include focus groups, semi-structured personal interviews, ride-along interviews, etc.	Can identify issues or concerns not captured through quantitative methods and expose more nuances in people's responses	Without incentives, only people with the time and/or desire participate, limiting the generalizability of findings and the policies that can be developed
		Can effectively highlight the unique experiences of specific groups of PT users	Rarely representative of the population

chapter focuses on understanding the relative importance of possible attributes to PT customers and does not provide an all-encompassing review.

Many different service attributes influence overall satisfaction, namely on-board cleanliness and comfort, courteous and helpful behavior from operators, safety, as well as punctuality and frequency of service are commonly associated with satisfaction (van Lierop et al., 2018). However, with limited operating budgets PT agencies commonly aim to determine the level of importance of each attribute in relation to overall customer satisfaction. Attribute importance can either be determined through a questionnaire designed to ask users to report the importance of several attributes (stated importance) or through statistical analyses that determine the relative importance of each attribute (derived importance).

Stated importance involves asking respondents to rank the importance of each listed service attribute in addition to indicating how satisfied they are with each. Although it has been noted that this method is more intuitive and easier for general practitioners to implement (Chu, 2002), asking respondents to indicate both their level of importance and satisfaction of each attribute can significantly increase the length of a questionnaire, increasing non-response and dropout rates (Chu, 2002). Some methods have been developed to shorten surveys, such as a combination of rating and choice through a conjoint analysis (Eboli and Mazzulla, 2010) or the best-worst case method, which involves asking respondents to select the most and least important attributes from a list of service attributes (Echaniz et al., 2019). An additional limitation of stated importance is that respondents may rate nearly all attributes as important when in reality they are less important than other service attributes (de Oña and de Oña, 2015; Weinstein, 2000).

These shortcomings have led researchers to measure derived importance, which uses statistical methods to infer how satisfaction with each attribute affects overall evaluations of service quality. The different types of statistical analyses employed for assessing the relative importance among service attributes can vary considerably in complexity (Stuart et al., 2000). A *bivariate model* (Fig. 1) uses methods such as a Pearson's correlation coefficient or a Cramer's V to measure the strength (and depending on variable type, the direction) of the relationship between two variables, such as satisfaction with service frequency and overall customer satisfaction. However, this method cannot indicate whether there is a causal relationship, it can only determine if the is an association between the variables. Moreover, this method does not allow for the impact of more than one variable to be considered at a time and can provide an overly simplistic view of the relationship between variables (Stuart et al., 2000), and therefore provide limited information about how agencies can best increase satisfaction.

A potential improvement on the bivariate model is *multivariable regression analysis*, which permits more than one variable to have direct association with another by modeling the impact that two or more independent variables, such as opinions about safety or frequency of usage, have on a dependent variable, such as overall satisfaction or agency loyalty. In PT satisfaction research, the independent variables are typically attribute-specific satisfaction scores, while the dependent variable is typically overall satisfaction with PT. This allows analysts to measure the relative strengths of variables in relation to one another, thereby providing insight into the drivers of satisfaction (Fig. 2). Multivariable regression analysis is commonly preceded by a *factor analysis*, which extracts a small number of factors or dimensions from a larger set of intercorrelated scale variables, which are often derived from questions about stated importance, preference and agreement. Factor analysis is often used to reduce large datasets (for example: Anable, 2005), as it helps researchers to evaluate and identify patterns of how different variables relate

Fig. 1 Hypothetical bivariate model (correlation analysis).

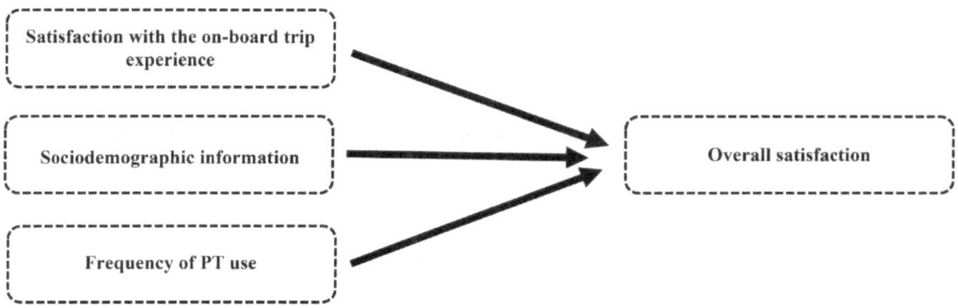

Fig. 2 Hypothetical multivariable regression analysis.

to one another, and these dimensions reduce multicollinearity in the data. The derived factors are then used in a regression analysis to determine the relative importance of each factor with respect to overall satisfaction.

There are several models of multivariable regression analysis that have been applied in customer satisfaction research. Most notably, *logistic* or *logit*, modeling is commonly used, considering that the dependent variable is categorical and binary. Also, *ordered logit* and *ordered probit* models have been proposed allowing for more than two (ordered) response categories. Since satisfaction data are commonly collected using scale data, and is therefore an ordinal variable, ordered logit models (e.g., Abenoza et al., 2017; Tyrinopoulos and Antoniou, 2008) as well as ordered probit models (e.g., dell'Olio et al. (2010)) are preferable to model the relationship between overall satisfaction and selected service attributes. However, satisfaction variables are oftentimes transformed to a binary term as it often fails to meet the parallel regression assumption, indicating that the relationship between each pair of outcome groups is not the same (Carrel and Li, 2019; Grisé et al., 2019). While both logit and probit models are similar, logit regression is likely more widely used by researchers for the ability to calculate and easily interpret an odds ratio. Also, probit models assume a cumulative standard normal distribution (Fiorio et al., 2013) and are more computationally demanding (Clark and Watling, 2000). Satisfaction scale data presents well-noted challenges to researchers, as for instance, respondents tend to choose central response options rather than options at the extremes of a scale, and the impact of the number of scale points used and the influence of the format and verbal labeling of the scale points often result in the need to transform ordinal satisfaction data to cardinal data (de Oña and de Oña, 2015). Examples include a study by Diab et al. (2017) who used a binary logit model to calculate the probability of respondents in Montreal, Canada recommending PT service to others. In a study of satisfaction among riders with physical disabilities and riders with encumbrances in London, UK, Verbich and El-Geneidy (2016) used logit models to explore how satisfaction with different service attributes predicted the odds of whether a rider would have been satisfied with the overall PT experience of their last trip or not. By converting overall satisfaction into a discrete binary variable (0 being dissatisfied and 1 being satisfied), the authors were able to find that bus stop conditions and access to information were significant predictors of overall satisfaction among these populations. In Wong et al. (2017), ordered probit models, coupled with an importance-satisfaction analysis, were used to conclude that improvements to bus stops or stations and attitudes among bus drivers would have the largest impact on improving overall customer satisfaction among elderly PT riders in Hong Kong.

Weinstein (2000) compared using a bivariate correlation analysis and a combined factor and multivariable regression analysis (factor-regression) approach using satisfaction data from the San Francisco Bay Area. The bivariate correlation approach offered key advantages over the factor-regression analysis, for reasons related to the derivation of factors included in the regression model. Specifically, the loss of detail of specific attributes within a factor that might be of high interest for a PT agency and the exclusion of attributes that did not neatly factor with other variables were identified as weaknesses of this approach. However, bivariate analyses can be misleading as a result of the complex nature of customer satisfaction often requiring consideration of more than one variable simultaneously.

An important weakness of both the bivariate and multivariable regression methods discussed above is the need to define relationships between dependent and independent variables. There are two issues associated with this modeling technique. First, no variable can be both dependent and independent. Second, incorrectly identifying underlying relationships between dependent and independent variables could lead to erroneous estimations from the model. Customer satisfaction is likely derived by a complex set of relationships where some variables influence each other, which can in turn affect other measures (Stuart et al., 2000). Accordingly, a more complex approach to regression analysis, structural equation modeling (SEM), is becoming more commonly used in academia to evaluate customer satisfaction and loyalty (and the important relationships between satisfaction and loyalty). SEM can be used to examine a network of interrelated variables, where both direct and indirect relationships can be evaluated, allowing select variables to function as both dependent and independent. A structural equation model is constructed according to hypothesized causal relationships

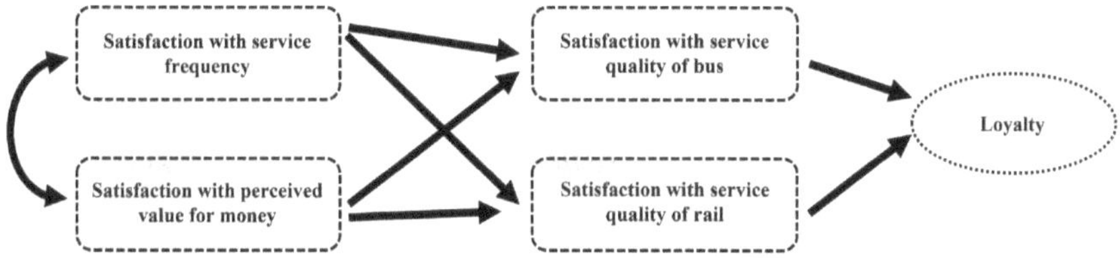

Fig. 3 Hypothetical structural equation model.

postulated from previous literature and theory, and these hypotheses are then tested. For statistically significant findings, the strength of the relationship indicates their importance.

For example, as shown in the hypothetical SEM model in Fig. 3, PT users' satisfaction with service frequency and perceived value for money are directly associated with overall mode specific satisfaction and indirectly with loyalty. This conceptualization has been established in previous SEM studies (van Lierop and El-Geneidy, 2016; Zhao et al., 2014).

Although SEM has been demonstrated in the literature as a very important technique for understanding customer satisfaction and loyalty, SEM is a complex method that is less intuitive to interpret and communicate and only provides information about correlation, not causation. Moreover, PT agencies often do not have the in-house capacity or desire to perform this kind of advanced modeling.

To overcome the requirement of pre-defining underlying relationships between dependent and independent variables as is needed in the methods described above, de Oña et al. (2012) used a classification and regression tree (CART) method using customer satisfaction data collected in the Metropolitan Area of Granada (Spain). Although less commonly used in the PT literature, this modeling technique provides "if-then" rules that make the model practical and easy to interpret for PT operators and managers (de Oña et al., 2012). For example, de Oña et al. (2012) observed that if users rate punctuality as poor or fair, frequency as poor and perception of bus space is rated poor, then the overall evaluation of service is likely to be poor. Data mining techniques such as this CART method demonstrate an alternative way to assess and determine the importance of various service factors on overall satisfaction and loyalty.

3.2 Market segmentation

Not all PT riders use and experience PT in the same way; for example, people of different genders, life stages, and abilities all use and experience PT differently. Riders also differ with regard to their trip purpose, trip frequency, and reliance on PT as their main mode of transportation. Performing a PT user segmentation analysis can help practitioners uncover groups of riders with similar behavioral and attitudinal patterns. These groups then serve as a base for future marketing strategies that suit the motivations, needs, and desires of these different groups. However, while marketing strategies allow transport agencies to better understand their riders, they might not directly serve to address equity concerns. Yet, to develop effective policy for addressing specific equity concerns, it is essential for agencies to understand who their riders are, and what their needs and desires are.

Commonly used approaches to segment the market stem from the field of consumer behavior and marketing, and are related to factors which impact decision making, including demographics, motivations or needs, or purchasing habits. Two key approaches to market segmentation include: (i) a priori, whereby groups are selected from a population in advance based on characteristics of interest (e.g., socio-demographic characteristics or car access), and (ii) post hoc, whereby empirical investigation using some form of multivariate statistical analysis (e.g., K-means cluster analysis) is used to segment a study population.

3.2.1 A priori segmentation

A priori segmentation method is driven by theory or assumptions that predefined segments (e.g., women, seniors, irregular commuters, etc.) have different needs (Tyrinopoulos and Antoniou, 2008; Verbich and El-Geneidy, 2016). Several studies have highlighted significant differences between demographic groups using a priori segmentation. For instance, in Scotland, Morton et al. (2016) found that women tend to be less satisfied than men with on board experience. The authors concluded that policies which work to improve attributes like cleanliness, comfort, and safety will most likely increase women's overall satisfaction. Analysis of an intercept survey conducted in Santiago, Chile, found that as age increases, overall satisfaction with PT tends to decrease, suggesting that more needs to be done by the PT agency to improve the satisfaction of their older riders (Allen et al., 2018). However, the relationship between age and satisfaction levels is not consistent in the literature. For example, van Lierop and El-Geneidy (2017), observed that younger (students, etc.) and older (retirees, etc.) users tend to be more satisfied relative to users between 35 and 54 years thus, increasing satisfaction of this group could be important to motivate continued ridership as transit use tends to decrease with age and lifestyle changes (Grimsrud and El-Geneidy, 2014). Meanwhile, Allen et al. (2020) found that as users age they are more satisfied with the system. Further research should explore the relationship between age and satisfaction with transit service further to identify how age potentially interacts with other variables to predict satisfaction levels. For example, the relationship between age and satisfaction levels can be context-specific and is not straight-forward. Furthermore, there might be intersectionality to note between age and income, or age and gender, age and time of travel, as well as age and major life events that needs to be explored in further research.

Segmentation of riders as either *captive* or *choice* users has been widely accepted in both academic literature and professional transport planning practice (Beimborn et al., 2003; Krizek and El-Geneidy, 2007; Polzin et al., 2000; Zhao et al., 2014). Captive riders are typically defined as being relatively lower income and without access to a car or those who cannot drive, and therefore are PT-dependent. Choice users do have access to a car but for certain purposes choose to take PT. The proportion of choice and captive riders that comprise the ridership of a PT system can vary significantly across regions (Krizek and El-Geneidy, 2007). More recently, van Lierop and El-Geneidy (2016) identified a new group of PT users, *captive by choice* users, to reflect users who are captive to PT because they do not have access to a car, but whose income level does not appear to be a barrier to car ownership compared to captive users.

Losses in PT ridership are often attributed to choice riders, as these users are more sensitive to service factors such as fares and service quality, and negative experiences with PT can encourage choice riders to choose alternative mobility options that are available to them (Krizek and El-Geneidy, 2007). Alternatively, captive riders are often perceived by PT agencies as a key source of base ridership (Polzin et al., 2000). As a consequence, efforts are commonly focused on increasing the retention of choice riders and attracting new riders to the system, as it is assumed that captive riders will always use PT despite the quality of the service provided (Beimborn et al., 2003). These tend to be short-sighted policies, as captive users will potentially transition away from PT captivity, either with age and life-cycle changes or by acquiring the resources to purchase an automobile. In addition, overlooking the needs and preferences of captive PT riders brings important equity concerns as these riders rely on PT and potentially have the most to gain with respect to policies aiming to increase their satisfaction levels. In addition, many captive riders are not captive to transit throughout their entire life, which means that investing in their preferences in the short term could motivate their loyalty to transit in the medium- to long-term, even in cases where alternatives to transit become available to them.

3.2.2 Post hoc segmentation

Post hoc segmentation is performed using statistical analyses with the intent to uncover how a combination of variables can be used to identify unique segments from the sample population. Selection of these variables is driven by previous research and the objective at hand, and may include attitudinal, behavioral, or socio-demographic characteristics. Eldeeb and Mohamed (2020) used mixed logit and latent class choice models to segment riders in Hamilton, Ontario based on their desired PT service quality. Three distinct segments were found using the latent class choice model. The first, *Direct Trip Enthusiasts* tended to be middle-aged females with a negative attitude toward PT and who prefer shorter, direct trips and a higher frequency of PT service. *Cost-Sensitive Riders* were more likely to be middle-aged with a positive attitude toward PT and were mostly concerned with the cost of PT and total travel time. The third group, *Real-time Information Supporters*, were more likely to be middle-aged males who have a positive attitude toward PT and exhibited a significant preference for real-time information in comparison to other clusters.

Post hoc segmentation analyses can help overcome notable limitations to a priori market segmentation exercises. For example, while the a priori categories of captive, choice, and captive-by-choice typology of PT riders has been effectively applied in both academic research and practice, such a typology might not be generalizable to other urban contexts as most riders cannot be categorized as entirely PT captive or a choice rider. A lack of homogeneity of users within a segment can mean that strategies designed for these riders do not suit the diverse needs, motivations, and desires of users in the group. Post hoc segmentation techniques can offer a solution to this issue as researchers or practitioners can uncover distinct groups of PT riders in a region using empirical techniques such as factor-cluster analysis and can also assess when individuals should be associated with more than one population segment. Nonetheless, this segmentation technique is not without limitations. Namely, researchers play an important role in the selection of data that are applied to identify the unique segments and apply discretion for selecting the optimal number of segments. Furthermore, this method requires more advanced training and software which may not be possible for PT agencies to apply in-house.

4. Demographic representativeness

Policy and insight generated through statistical analyses is not only influenced by the analysis techniques applied but also by the quality of data collected. Specifically, in order for policies and service interventions designed to increase customer satisfaction and loyalty to be effective across the broad spectrum of PT users, it is necessary to collect a representative sample, which both represents the population of the region and includes the many voices from across the transit community. Certain data collection methods are more likely to engage specific populations. For instance, as mentioned earlier, internet surveys often oversample younger people with higher education and incomes (Dillman, 2016).

Marginalized groups might not easily be captured using general intercept, phone, or internet survey data collection methods that are designed to collect information from the general population. For example, to effectively collect information about users' paratransit experience a sampling strategy should focus on how to best engage with these PT customers. As individual needs and abilities vary greatly among paratransit riders, using a variety of qualitative and quantitative data collection methods may have the most effective results (see for example: van Lierop et al. (2019)). Also, without the use of segmentation techniques, the needs and concerns of marginalized groups are likely to be lost in the averages of large quantitative samples.

As in any form of public engagement, acquiring a representative sample is challenging but essential to limit bias in your study and policy recommendations. To draw valid generalizations requires a clear understanding of the sample (age, gender, ethnicity, employment status, etc.) and how it relates to the population it represents. With that said, PT users are dynamic and enumerating the population is challenging. In academic papers, clear information on the study sample is expected for readers to assess the sample representativeness. For example, a study by Allen et al. (2019) on the effect of critical incidents on satisfaction and loyalty conducted in Madrid, Spain clearly outlined the demographic and trip characteristics of the sample. The authors then compared the sample characteristics to those of Madrid's Metro system users, demonstrating that the gender breakdown and age characteristics of the sample aligned with the population. However, since most of the (intercept) surveys were conducted during peak hours, trips for work and study in the sample were slightly higher than that which would have been expected when assessing all trips made by the population.

Several recent studies highlight the difficulties in obtaining representative samples of the population. As referenced in Carrel et al. (2017), only 1% of the respondents in the 2013–15 San Francisco Travel Quality Study were over the age of 65, even though this age group comprises 15.1% of the population (United States Census Bureau, 2018). The authors explain that this can be in part explained by the requirement to have a smartphone and the selected recruitment methods (multiple recruitment channels were used, including postcards and emails sent out to a variety of address lists maintained by the San Francisco Municipal Transportation Agency and several universities in San Francisco, and fliers handed out in person at one university). The gender split in a recent satisfaction survey conducted in Santander, Spain was dramatically skewed, with two thirds (67%) of respondents identifying as female and only one third (33%) identifying as male (Echaniz et al., 2019). While it is expected that for the oldest populations more data from females would be collected, to develop good policy better efforts should be made to collect data that is representative of both male and female populations. Moreover, in the same study, when asked about monthly income, 42% of respondents provided no answer. Without this information, researchers are unable to segment the data by income level, leaving an important piece of the puzzle missing. Missing data from satisfaction surveys is a common challenge faced by analysts, as respondents are commonly given the choice of responding "prefer not to answer," which greatly limits analysis possibilities. While limiting the option of "prefer not to answer" in a survey may increase the drop-out rate of participants or result in falsely reported income levels, little is known about how sensitive respondents are to such survey design strategies. Online surveys track if and when a respondent quits the survey, and therefore researchers and transit agencies can monitor how the removal of a "prefer not to answer" option impacts respondents.

In many regions, understudied populations include people with disabilities, seniors, persons who are unemployed or have lower education or income levels, non-local language speakers, youth, and immigrants, as well as race and ethnic minorities. Without adequately and purposefully sampling these individuals, little policy can be developed that is specifically tailored to these groups, which often tend to be more PT-dependent compared to the average population (Lucas, 2012). Moreover, even if these individuals are sampled, the type of data collected needs careful thought, for example, data on physical limitations or the need to travel with a caretaker. Despite the underrepresentation of populations mentioned above, research has found that select determinants of satisfaction can be distinct among marginalized populations. For example, information available at a bus stop heavily influences PT satisfaction for riders with disabilities while it had little influence on satisfaction for regular riders (Verbich and El-Geneidy, 2016). Or, occasional riders and those with low-incomes were less concerned with daytime safety than higher-income earners (Iseki and Smart, 2012). Beyond specific determinants of satisfaction, research also suggests that overall satisfaction with PT service can vary substantially between ethnic groups. For instance, Iseki and Smart (2012) found that African-American and Hispanic-Latino transit riders in Southern California were much more likely to indicate they were very satisfied with overall PT service than White or Asian respondents. These studies highlight the unique needs of certain marginalized populations and provide policymakers with pertinent information to make targeted interventions.

5. Recommendations

Understanding how individuals experience PT service is critical, given that previous experience with PT largely determines future travel behavior (Thøgersen, 2006). With growing competition in the transport market, due to the presence of privately operated on-demand mobility services, PT agencies need to be market-oriented to maintain and/or increase ridership, which can be achieved through continued development of methodologies and strategies to understand customer satisfaction and loyalty. This review has critically discussed common data collection techniques and analysis methodologies within the field of PT customer satisfaction, and recommendations for future directions are discussed below.

As presented in our review of data collection methods, over time we have seen these methods evolve as technology has advanced. Yet, technology has not eradicated traditional satisfaction survey methods, in particular face-to-face surveys, intercept surveys and phone-based surveys. Each survey method continues to offer unique advantages and disadvantages. For example, although intercept surveys limit memory bias, they are also a resource intensive form of data collection. While online questionnaires can be answered at a respondent's convenience and remove the need for manual data entry, it is difficult to invite a random sample of users to respond.

Aside from financial trade-offs between the various methods used for survey collection, a major consideration for PT agencies to consider is how distinct segments of the population can be reached and respond to different surveying methods. For this reason, Dillman (2017) suggests offering a mix of methods in order to accommodate the generational and socioeconomic differences among respondents to increase participation. The focus across segments is essential to equitably improve access to high quality transportation. Finally, it is important that PT agencies keep up to date with modern data collection techniques and consider adopting innovative strategies to foster an engaging and inclusive survey environment whereby all PT users are willing to offer their time to provide information about their opinions, experiences, and suggestions regardless of their age, gender, (dis) ability and other personal characteristics.

As technology evolves, researchers and PT agencies can explore novel options for longitudinal data collection. Knowledge about the relationship between satisfaction and future PT use is most often derived from cross-sectional survey data, where customers are asked to state their desired future PT usage (e.g., van Lierop and El-Geneidy (2016)). While this approach to customer loyalty research provides valuable insight on users' behavioral intentions, measuring customer loyalty on stated future usage rather than revealed behavior can be problematic, as predictions of future use has been shown to be unreliable (Carrel and Li, 2019). Accordingly, it is essential to develop a better understanding about the relationship between overall satisfaction and future mode choice through robust longitudinal customer satisfaction surveys, which capture revealed mode choice rather than stated intentions of PT use.

Market segmentation is an effective analysis technique for understanding how satisfaction varies across diverse segments of the population. An important limitation of predominant segmentation techniques is that we assume that people fit neatly into segments, yet it is very possible that individuals exhibit traits of more than one segment group. For that reason, a probabilistic approach to segmentation should be considered, such as latent class clustering, to account for the likely probability that an individual behaves like a given segment, but that there remains a probability that an individual behaves similarly to other identified segments. To increase the uptake of advanced market segmentation techniques by public transport professionals, academics should consider developing open-source tools that could allow for user-friendly application of these analysis techniques in practice. Also, it is important to consider that after segments are generated, individuals' membership in a segment can change over time. Accordingly, an individual's membership in a segment should not be viewed as static since individuals can move between categories for many reasons, including life changes such as switching jobs and having children, as well as changes in personal attitudes toward PT.

The traditional segmentation of riders as either "captive," "choice," or "captive by choice" is commonly used to understand the different preferences, needs, experiences, and perceptions of riders. However, further research should be conducted to better understand how satisfaction with

PT service differently affects these different groups of riders in terms of their respective loyalty to PT over the course of their lives. Recent research has started to explore the relationship between travel satisfaction and individuals' subjective wellbeing (Ettema et al., 2011), however, little is known about how PT related subjective wellbeing differs across population segments. Presumably, choice or captive-by-choice riders will be more sensitive to changes in their experienced satisfaction levels as these riders have the ability to switch modes if service quality does not meet their expectations. Captive riders, on the other hand, may be impacted differently by satisfaction levels as these riders are presumed to have limited ability to change modes of travel. Furthermore, segmentation exercises should more closely examine a riders' usage of shared mobility services such as ride-hailing and bicycle sharing. Riders who regularly use shared mobility services should be studied to explore opportunities to promote increased integration between mobility-as-a-service and PT, such as integration of these modes at PT stations and fare policies.

Directing service improvement strategies along specific bus routes, PT corridors, or geographic areas can help PT agencies focus resources where they will be most impactful for customers. This can be done through integrating key performance measures with customer's assessment of service. While a few studies have demonstrated the utility of integrating satisfaction and performance data (Allen et al., 2020; Eboli and Mazzulla, 2011; Grisé and El-Geneidy, 2020; Nathanail, 2008; van Lierop and El-Geneidy, 2017) satisfaction survey data is not commonly designed with such a practice in mind. More specifically, detailed trip information, such as trip origin and destination, and the date and time of the customer's trip are necessary details to link satisfaction surveys and performance data. Alternatively, collecting geographic data on what routes were used for the trip surveyed or types of services users typically use can allow PT agencies to evaluate how satisfaction levels vary across the network (Grisé and El-Geneidy, 2017, 2018). This geographic understanding of customer satisfaction data can effectively direct service interventions along specific routes/corridors in the PT network.

Finally, a critical evaluation of questions or data that are collected in customer satisfaction surveys is essential to contextualize the value of methods to analyze satisfaction data. For example, market segmentation exercises are most effective when satisfaction and attitudinal questions are included (Ettema et al., 2011). In addition, collecting or not collecting specific socio-demographic information can have major consequences for understanding population inequities. For example, a lack of information related to ethnicity, race, or income prevents researchers or transport agencies to investigate whether there are systematic racial or income differences in travel behavior patterns or whether service attributes are more relevant to the travel experience of one group relative to others. To help guide the design of policies, it is important that data are collected and analyzed in such a way that the heterogeneity of passengers' characteristics and needs can be adequately considered. It is recommended that public transport agencies critically reflect on the determinants of customer satisfaction and consider data that are rarely asked in surveys but have an important influence on people's travel satisfaction and experience with travel. Note, the authors acknowledge that survey design needs to be conscientious of the number of questions asked within a survey. With that said, to develop a more holistic understanding of the passenger experience may require PT agencies to balance the number of questions related to service attributes (e.g., service reliability, journey time, and ride comfort) with questions related to personal travel characteristics, including whether passengers have a physical disability or whether they were traveling alone, encumbered, or with children. Including these factors in models predicting overall satisfaction may dilute the importance of service factors in a riders overall assessment of service. This is an important knowledge gap that should be addressed in future research.

6. Conclusions

Cities worldwide need efficient and accessible PT services for all to prosper sustainably, both economically and environmentally. Emerging and new modes of transport present PT agencies with growing modal competition. To meet these challenges and promote the retention of existing users, innovative marketing strategies (including customer satisfaction research) are needed to better address the needs and expectations of PT riders in a timely and economically efficient manner. The study of satisfaction data is theoretically motivated by the notion that improvements in satisfaction will influence an individual's likelihood of future PT use, will increase one's spending on PT, or encourage one to speak positively of the service to friends or family.

This chapter has reviewed the literature and best practices as it pertains to satisfaction survey data collection and analysis techniques. Technological advancements have expanded the available types of survey collection modes, and we expect to see significant growth in the options for data collection in the future. Namely, we are seeing impressive advancements in smart-phone applications for the collection of travel behavior. While these applications show tremendous potential for collecting a rich dataset of personnel travel behavior, research regarding the best way to incorporate and collect user perception data, and details on travel behavior are needed. For example, GPS-enabled smart phones can provide PT agencies with key details of the user's trip, such as origin and destination, in-vehicle travel time, and waiting time, and by effectively designing a survey to link to trip data can enable researchers to effectively evaluate customer perceptions of service quality in parallel with performance indicators. However, we must proceed cautiously in this direction as the available evidence suggests that in order to effectively capture the perceptions of marginalized populations a mix of survey methods should be considered by PT agencies to effectively capture the engagement preferences of a diverse population. Researchers and transport professionals need to practice flexibility and participate in innovative survey design and sampling schemes which capture the various voices in cities.

Regarding satisfaction data analysis techniques, market segmentation (in combination with correlation and regression analyses to derive importance of attribute-specific service attributes) remains an essential tool in order to account for the heterogeneity of PT riders. Reporting average satisfaction levels for the sample population can be ineffective for understanding a diverse rider base and developing policies aimed at increasing satisfaction and loyalty across all segments of a population. Nonetheless, it is important that insight on riders generated through market segmentation can be translated to practice and incorporated in planning for more equitable, socially inclusive, and environmentally sustainable urban regions.

References

Abenoza, R.F., Cats, O., Susilo, Y.O., 2017. Travel satisfaction with public transport: determinants, user classes, regional disparities and their evolution. Transp. Res. Part A Policy Pract. 95, 64–84. https://doi.org/10.1016/j.tra.2016.11.011.

Agrawal, A., Granger-Bevan, S., Newmark, G., Nixon, H., 2016. Comparing data quality and cost from three modes of on-board transit surveys. Transp. Policy 54, 70–79. https://doi.org/10.1016/j.tranpol.2016.06.010.

Allen, J., Muñoz, J., Ortúzar, J., 2018. Modelling service-specific and global transit satisfaction under travel and user heterogeneity. Transp. Res. Part A Policy Pract. 113, 509–528. https://doi.org/10.1016/j.tra.2018.05.009.

Allen, J., Eboli, L., Forciniti, C., Mazzulla, G., Ortúzar, J., 2019. The role of critical incidents and involvement in transit satisfaction and loyalty. Transp. Policy 75, 57–69. https://doi.org/10.1016/j.tranpol.2019.01.005.

Allen, J., Muñoz, J., Ortúzar, J., 2020. On the effect of operational service attributes on transit satisfaction. Transportation 47, 2307–2336. https://doi.org/10.1007/s11116-019-10016-8.

Anable, J., 2005. 'Complacent Car addicts' or 'aspiring environmentalists'? Identifying travel behaviour segments using attitude theory. Transp. Policy 12 (1), 65–78. https://doi.org/10.1016/j.tranpol.2004.11.004.

Beimborn, E., Greenwald, M., Jin, X., 2003. Accessibility, connectivity, and captivity: impacts on transit choice. Transp. Res. Rec. 1835, 1–9. https://doi.org/10.3141/1835-01.

Beirão, G., Cabral, J., 2007. Understanding attitudes towards public transport and private car: A qualitative study. Transp. Policy 14 (6), 478–489.

Berry, L.L., Zeithaml, V.A., Parasuraman, A., 1990. Five imperatives for improving service quality. Sloan Manage. Rev. 31 (4), 9–38.

Boisjoly, G., Grisé, E., Maguire, M., Veillette, M.-P., Deboosere, R., Berrebi, E., El-Geneidy, A., 2018. Invest in the ride: a 14 year longitudinal analysis of the determinants of public transport ridership in 25 North American cities. Transp. Res. Part A Policy Pract. 116, 434–445. https://doi.org/10.1016/j.tra.2018.07.005.

Campbell, R.M., Venn, T.J., Anderson, N.M., 2018. Cost and performance tradeoffs between mail and internet survey modes in a nonmarket valuation study. J. Environ. Manage. 210, 316–327. https://doi.org/10.1016/j.jenvman.2018.01.034.

Carrel, A., Li, M., 2019. Survey-based measurement of transit customer loyalty: evaluation of measures and systematic biases. Travel Behav. Soc. 15, 102–112. https://doi.org/10.1016/j.tbs.2019.01.003.

Carrel, A., Mishalani, R., Sengupta, R., Walker, J., 2016. In pursuit of the happy transit rider: dissecting satisfaction using daily surveys and tracking data. J. Intell. Transp. Syst. 20 (4), 345–362. https://doi.org/10.1080/15472450.2016.1149699.

Carrel, A., Sengupta, R., Walker, J., 2017. The San Francisco travel quality study: tracking trials and tribulations of a transit taker. Transportation 44 (4), 643–679. https://doi.org/10.1007/s11116-016-9732-4.

Chang, L., Krosnick, J.A., 2009. National surveys via RDD telephone interviewing versus the internet: comparing sample representativeness and response quality. Public Opin. Q. 73 (4), 641–678.

Chu, R., 2002. Stated-importance versus derived-importance customer satisfaction measurement. J. Serv. Mark. 16, 285–301. https://doi.org/10.1108/08876040210433202.

Clark, S.D., Watling, D.P., 2000. Probit-based sensitivity analysis for general traffic networks. Transp. Res. Rec. 1733 (1), 88–95. https://doi.org/10.3141/1733-12.

Cottrill, C.D., Pereira, F.C., Zhao, F., Dias, I.F., Lim, H.B., Ben-Akiva, M.E., Zegras, P.C., 2013. Future mobility survey: experience in developing a smartphone-based travel survey in Singapore. Transp. Res. Rec. 2354 (1), 59–67. https://doi.org/10.3141/2354-07.

de Oña, J., de Oña, R., 2015. Quality of service in public transport based on customer satisfaction surveys: a review and assessment of methodological approaches. Transp. Sci. 49 (3), 605–622. https://doi.org/10.1287/trsc.2014.0544.

de Oña, J., de Oña, R., Calvo, F.J., 2012. A classification tree approach to identify key factors of transit service quality. Expert Syst. Appl. 39 (12), 11164–11171. https://doi.org/10.1016/j.eswa.2012.03.037.

De Vos, J., Witlox, F., 2017. Travel satisfaction revisited. On the pivotal role of travel satisfaction in conceptualising a travel behaviour process. Transp. Res. Part A: Policy Pract. 106, 364–373. https://doi.org/10.1016/j.tra.2017.10.009.

dell'Olio, L., Ibeas, A., Cecín, P., 2010. Modelling user perception of bus transit quality. Transp. Policy 17 (6), 388–397. https://doi.org/10.1016/j.tranpol.2010.04.006.

DeWeese, J., Hawa, L., Demyk, H., Davey, Z., Belikow, A., El-geneidy, A., 2020. A tale of 40 cities: a preliminary analysis of equity impacts of COVID-19 service adjustments across North America. Transp. Findings, 13395. https://doi.org/10.32866/001c.13395.

Diab, E., van Lierop, D., El-Geneidy, A., 2017. Recommending transit: disentangling users' willingness to recommend transit and their intended continued use. Travel Behav. Soc. 6, 1–9. https://doi-org.login.ezproxy.library.ualberta.ca/10.1016/j.tbs.2016.03.001.

Diez-Mesa, F., de Oña, R., de Oña, J., 2016. The effect of service attributes' hierarchy on passengers' segmentation. A light rail transit service case study. Transp. Res. Procedia 18, 234–241. https://doi.org/10.1016/j.trpro.2016.12.032.
Dillman, D.A., 2016. Moving survey methodology forward in our rapidly changing world: a commentary. J. Rural Soc. Sci. 31 (3), 160–174. Retrieved from https://egrove.olemiss.edu/jrss/vol31/iss3/8.
Dillman, D.A., 2017. The promise and challenge of pushing respondents to the web in mixed-mode surveys. Surv. Methodol. 43, 3. Statistics Canada. Retrieved from statistics Canada website http://www.statcan.gc.ca/pub/12-001-x/2017001/article/14836-eng.htm.
Dutwin, D., Lavrakas, P., 2016. Trends in telephone outcomes, 2008—2015. Surv. Pract. 9 (3), 1–9. https://doi.org/10.29115/SP-2016-0017.
Eboli, L., Mazzulla, G., 2010. How to capture the Passengers' point of view on a transit service through rating and choice options. Transp. Rev. 30 (4), 435–450. https://doi.org/10.1080/01441640903068441.
Eboli, L., Mazzulla, G., 2011. A methodology for evaluating transit service quality based on subjective and objective measures from the passenger's point of view. Transp. Policy 18 (1), 172–181. https://doi.org/10.1016/j.tranpol.2010.07.007.
Echaniz, E., Ho, C.Q., Rodriguez, A., dell'Olio, L., 2019. Comparing best-worst and ordered logit approaches for user satisfaction in transit services. Transp. Res. Part A 130, 752–769. https://doi.org/10.1016/j.tra.2019.10.012.
Eldeeb, G., Mohamed, M., 2020. Quantifying preference heterogeneity in transit service desired quality using a latent class choice model. Transp. Res. Part A: Policy Pract. 139, 119–133. https://doi.org/10.1016/j.tra.2020.07.006.
Ettema, D., Gärling, T., Eriksson, L., Friman, M., Olsson, L., Fujii, S., 2011. Satisfaction with travel and subjective well-being: development and test of a measurement tool. Transp. Res. Part F: Traffic Psychol. Behav. 14 (3), 167–175. https://doi.org/10.1016/j.trf.2010.11.002.
European Metropolitan Transport Authorities, 2020. EMTA Barometer 2020-Based on 2018 Data. Retrieved from https://www.emta.com/IMG/pdf/2018_emta_barometer-200526.pdf?4014/.
Fiorio, C.V., Florio, M., Perucca, G., 2013. User satisfaction and the organization of local public transport: evidence from European cities. Transp. Policy 29, 209–218. https://doi-org.login.ezproxy.library.ualberta.ca/10.1016/j.tranpol.2013.06.004.
Fornell, C., Johnson, M., Anderson, E., Cha, J., Bryant, B., 1996. The American customer satisfaction index: nature, purpose, and findings. J. Market. 60 (4), 7–18. https://doi.org/10.1177/002224299606000403.
Gadziński, J., 2018. Perspectives of the use of smartphones in travel behaviour studies: findings from a literature review and a pilot study. Transp. Res. Part C Emerg. Technol. 88, 74–86. https://doi.org/10.1016/j.trc.2018.01.011.
Geerlings, H., Klementschitz, R., Mulley, C., 2006. Development of a methodology for benchmarking public transportation organisations: a practical tool based on an industry sound methodology. J. Clean. Prod. 14 (2), 113–123. https://doi.org/10.1016/j.jclepro.2005.03.021.
Gkiotsalitis, K., Cats, O., 2020. Public transport planning adaption under the COVID-19 pandemic crisis: literature review of research needs and directions. Transp. Rev. 41 (3), 374–392. https://doi.org/10.1080/01441647.2020.1857886.
Grigoroudis, E., Siskos, Y., 2009. Customer Satisfaction Evaluation: Methods for Measuring and Implementing Service Quality. Springer Science & Business Media.
Grimsrud, M., El-Geneidy, A., 2014. Transit to eternal youth: lifecycle and generational trends in greater Montreal public transport mode share. Transportation 41 (1), 1–19. https://doi.org/10.1007/s11116-013-9454-9.

Grisé, E., El-Geneidy, A., 2017. Evaluating the relationship between socially (dis) advantaged neighbourhoods and customer satisfaction of bus service in London, UK. J. Transp. Geogr. 58, 166–175.
Grisé, E., El-Geneidy, A., 2018. Where is the happy transit rider? Evaluating satisfaction with regional rail service using a spatial segmentation approach. Transp. Res. Part A Policy Pract. 114, 84–96.
Grisé, E., El-Geneidy, A., 2020. Assessing operation and customer perception characteristics of high frequency local and limited-stop bus Service in Vancouver, Canada. Public Transp. 12, 519–534.
Grisé, E., Cui, B., Turim, A., Manaugh, K., El-Geneidy, A., 2019. The impacts of varying survey design on reported trip satisfaction. Transp. Res. F: Traffic Psychol. Behav. 60, 761–769. https://doi.org/10.1016/j.trf.2018.12.003.
Harding, C., Srikukenthiran, S., Habib, K., Miller, E., 2017. On the User Experience and Performance of Smartphone Apps as Personalized Travel Survey Instruments: Results from an Experiment in Toronto, p. 2.
Hu, S., Chen, P., 2021. Who left riding transit? Examining socioeconomic disparities in the impact of COVID-19 on ridership. Transp. Res. D Transp. Environ. 90, 102654. https://doi.org/10.1016/j.trd.2020.102654.
Ingvardson, J.B., Nielsen, O.A., 2019. The relationship between norms, satisfaction and public transport use: a comparison across six European cities using structural equation modelling. Transp. Res. A Policy Pract. 126, 37–57. https://doi.org/10.1016/j.tra.2019.05.016.
Iseki, H., Smart, M.J., 2012. How do people perceive service attributes at transit facilities?: examination of perceptions of transit service by transit user demographics and trip characteristics. Transp. Res. Rec. 2274 (1), 164–174. https://doi.org/10.3141/2274-18.
Jenelius, E., Cebecauer, M., 2020. Impacts of COVID-19 on public transport ridership in Sweden: analysis of ticket validations, sales and passenger counts. Transp. Res. Interdiscip. Perspect. 8, 100242. https://doi.org/10.1016/j.trip.2020.100242.
Kahneman, D., Krueger, A.B., Schkade, D.A., Schwarz, N., Stone, A.A., 2004. A survey method for characterizing daily life experience: the day reconstruction method. Science 306 (5702), 1776–1780. https://doi.org/10.1126/science.1103572.
Keeter, S., Hatley, N., Kennedy, C., Lau, A., 2017. What Low Response Rates Mean for Telephone Surveys. Pew Research Center. Retrieved from Pew Research Center website https://assets.pewresearch.org/wp-content/uploads/sites/12/2017/05/12154630/RDD-Non-response-Full-Report.pdf.
Krizek, K., El-Geneidy, A., 2007. Segmenting preferences and habits of transit users and non-users. J. Public Transp. 10, 71–94. https://doi.org/10.5038/2375-0901.10.3.5.
Lai, W.-T., Chen, C.-F., 2011. Behavioral intentions of public transit passengers—the roles of service quality, perceived value, satisfaction and involvement. Transp. Policy 18 (2), 318–325. https://doi.org/10.1016/j.tranpol.2010.09.003.
Lucas, K., 2012. Transport and social exclusion: where are we now? Transp. Policy 20, 105–113. https://doi.org/10.1016/j.tranpol.2012.01.013.
Morton, C., Caulfield, B., Anable, J., 2016. Customer perceptions of quality of service in public transport: evidence for bus transit in Scotland. Case Stud. Transp. Policy 4 (3), 199–207. https://doi.org/10.1016/j.cstp.2016.03.002.
Nathanail, E., 2008. Measuring the quality of service for passengers on the hellenic railways. Transp. Res. A Policy Pract. 42 (1), 48–66. https://doi.org/10.1016/j.tra.2007.06.006.
National Academies of Sciences, Engineering, and Medicine, 2009. Local and Regional Funding Mechanisms for Public Transportation. The National Academies Press, Washington, DC. Retrieved from The National Academies Press website. https://doi.org/10.17226/14187.
Nederlandse Spoorwegen, 2020. International Benchmark 2014–2018. Retrieved from https://www.rijksoverheid.nl/binaries/rijksoverheid/documenten/rapporten/2020/06/11/bijlage-8-internationale-benchmark-ns/bijlage-8-internationale-benchmark-ns.pdf.

Parasuraman, A., Zeithaml, V.A., Berry, L.L., 1985. A conceptual model of service quality and its implications for future research. J. Market. 49 (4), 41. https://doi.org/10.2307/1251430.
Polzin, S.E., Chu, X., Rey, J.R., 2000. Density and captivity in public transit success: observations from the 1995 Nationwide personal transportation study. Transp. Res. Rec. 1735 (1), 10–18. https://doi.org/10.3141/1735-02.
Roddis, S., Winter, S., Zhao, F., Kutadinata, R., 2019. Respondent preferences in travel survey design: an initial comparison of narrative, structured and technology-based travel survey instruments. Travel Behav. Soc. 16, 1–12. https://doi.org/10.1016/j.tbs.2019.03.003.
Safi, H., Assemi, B., Mesbah, M., Ferreira, L., 2017. An empirical comparison of four technology-mediated travel survey methods. J. Traffic Transp. Eng. (Engl. Ed.) 4 (1), 80–87. https://doi.org/10.1016/j.jtte.2015.12.003.
Shay, E., Combs, T.S., Findley, D., Kolosna, C., Madeley, M., Salvesen, D., 2016. Identifying transportation disadvantage: mixed-methods analysis combining GIS mapping with qualitative data. Transp. Policy 48, 129–138.
Stern, M.J., Bilgen, I., Dillman, D.A., 2014. The state of survey methodology. Field Methods 26 (3), 284–301. https://doi.org/10.1177/1525822X13519561.
Stuart, K., Mednick, M., Bockman, J., 2000. Structural equation model of customer satisfaction for the new York City Subway system. Transp. Res. Rec. 1735, 133–137. https://doi.org/10.3141/1735-16.
Thøgersen, J., 2006. Understanding repetitive travel mode choices in a stable context: a panel study approach. Transp. Res. Part A: Policy Pract. 40, 621–638. https://doi.org/10.1016/j.tra.2005.11.004.
Transportation Research Board & National Academies of Sciences, Engineering, and Medicine, 2005. On-Board and Intercept Transit Survey Techniques. The National Academies Press, Washington, DC. https://doi.org/10.17226/13866.
Transportation Research Board, & Price Waterhouse Company, 1998. Funding Strategies for Public Transportation, 2 Volumes. Transportation Research Board.
Trompet, M., Parasram, R., Anderson, R.J., 2013. Benchmarking disaggregate customer satisfaction scores of bus operators in different cities and countries. Transp. Res. Rec. 126, 37–57. https://doi.org/10.3141/2351-02.
Tyrinopoulos, Y., Antoniou, C., 2008. Public transit user satisfaction: variability and policy implications. Transp. Policy 15, 260–272. https://doi.org/10.1016/j.tranpol.2008.06.002.
United States Census Bureau, 2018. ACS Demographic and Housing Estimates: San Francisco County. vol. 2020. Retrieved from https://data.census.gov/cedsci/table?q=san%20francisco&g=0500000US06075&tid=ACSDP1Y2018.DP05.
van Lierop, D., El-Geneidy, A., 2016. Enjoying loyalty: the relationship between service quality, customer satisfaction, and behavioral intentions in public transit. Res. Transp. Econ. 59, 50–59. https://doi.org/10.1016/j.retrec.2016.04.001.
van Lierop, D., El-Geneidy, A., 2017. Perceived reality: understanding the relationship between customer perceptions and operational characteristics. Transp. Res. Rec. 2652 (1), 87–97. https://doi.org/10.3141/2652-10.
van Lierop, D., Badami, M., El-Geneidy, A., 2018. What influences satisfaction and loyalty in public transport? A review of the literature. Transp. Rev. 38 (1), 52–72. https://doi.org/10.1080/01441647.2017.1298683.
van Lierop, D., Eftekhari, J., O'Hara, A., Grinspun, Y., 2019. Humanizing transit data: connecting customer experience statistics to Individuals' unique transit stories. Transp. Res. Rec. 2673 (1), 388–402. https://doi.org/10.1177/0361198118823196.
Verbich, D., El-Geneidy, A., 2016. The pursuit of satisfaction: variation in satisfaction with bus transit service among riders with encumbrances and riders with disabilities using a large-scale survey from London, UK. Transp. Policy 47, 64–71. https://doi-org.login.ezproxy.library.ualberta.ca/10.1016/j.tranpol.2015.12.009.

Verbich, D., Badami, M.G., El-Geneidy, A.M., 2017. Bang for the buck: toward a rapid assessment of urban public transit from multiple perspectives in North America. Transp. Policy 55, 51–61. https://doi.org/10.1016/j.tranpol.2016.12.002.

Weinstein, A., 2000. Customer satisfaction among transit riders: how customers rank the relative importance of various service attributes. Transp. Res. Rec. 1735 (1), 123–132. https://doi.org/10.3141/1735-15.

Wong, R., Szeto, W., Yang, L., Li, Y., Wong, S., 2017. Elderly users' level of satisfaction with public transport services in a high-density and transit-oriented city. J. Transp. Health 7, 209–217. https://doi.org/10.1016/j.jth.2017.10.004.

Zhao, J., Webb, V., Shah, P., 2014. Customer loyalty differences between captive and choice transit riders. Transp. Res. Rec. 2415, 80–88. https://doi.org/10.3141/2415-09.

Zhuang, Z., Kim, K., Singh, J., 2010. Improving energy efficiency of location sensing on smartphones. In: *Proceedings of the 8th International Conference on Mobile Systems, Applications, and Services.* Association for Computing Machinery, New York, NY, USA, pp. 315–330. https://doi.org/10.1145/1814433.1814464.

CHAPTER NINE

Social and distributional impacts in transport project appraisals

Ruth Shortall and Niek Mouter*
Delft University of Technology, Faculty of Technology, Policy and Management, Transport and Logistics Group, Delft, The Netherlands
*Corresponding author: e-mail address: n.mouter@tudelft.nl

Contents

Abstract

Governments are involved in transport policy and planning in many ways. Quite often, policy makers want to make decisions that are informed by the expected positive and negative impacts of transport policy options. Cost-Benefit Analysis (CBA) is the most widely used appraisal method to inform policy makers about impacts of transport policies and projects. CBA is grounded in welfare economics, which provides strict procedures guiding the criteria/impacts to be considered in the analysis and the weighting of impacts. The rigor of CBA is considered to be a strength of the method, but both academics and practitioners find it problematic that CBAs degrade or ignore social, ethical (and to a lesser extent, environmental) dimensions of transport policies. The purpose of this chapter is to provide a review of the literature with regard to: (1) critiques of the way that social and ethical dimensions of transport are (not) included in CBA; (2) developments in the literature aiming to better include such dimensions in CBA or related

Advances in Transport Policy and Planning, Volume 8
ISSN 2543-0009
https://doi.org/10.1016/bs.atpp.2021.07.003
Copyright © 2021 Elsevier Inc.
All rights reserved.

appraisal methods grounded in welfare economics; (3) discussion of the way that social and ethical dimensions of transport are included in other appraisal methods such as Sustainability Assessment, Multicriteria Analysis (MCA) and Social Impact Assessment (SIA).

Keywords: Social impacts, Transport appraisal, Distributional impacts, Cost-benefit analysis, Multicriteria analysis, Deliberative methods, Participatory value evaluation

1. Introduction

Transport policy appraisals have been dominated by quantitative approaches (Mackie et al., 2014). Scholars argue that, as a result, difficult to quantify impacts have a weak position in such analyses (Mottee et al., 2020; Mouter et al., 2015). However, there is an increasing realization that such appraisals need to reflect a more complex policy environment and include social concerns (Handy, 2008). The disconnect between urban transport policy making and other policy areas, such as public health or spatial planning, for instance, is said to be causing serious negative social impacts such as chronic disease, premature mortality (Khreis et al., 2016), or community severance (Anciaes et al., 2016).

Cost-Benefit Analysis (CBA) is one of the most commonly used transport appraisal methods in the developed world (Berechman, 2018). CBA uses monetary market values to appraise transport policy. This provides a simple and efficient way to compare between policy options. Policy makers and politicians mention different reasons why they are positive about the institutionalization of CBA in the planning process of transport projects (e.g., Mouter, 2017; Mouter et al., 2013). For instance, politicians experience that a CBA informs them about all the effects of a project, which results in better informed debates and decisions, they think that a CBA can lead to the optimization of projects and in their view, the instrument serves as a countervailing power against projects which are purely pursued to foster the prestige of a politician (Mouter, 2017). However, CBA is also criticized for its capacity to adequately deal with the social impacts of transport policies and there are concerns about its narrow scope (Bellamy et al., 2014; Cass, 2006; Næss, 2006). According to Geurs et al. (2009), social impacts in transport projects are broadly defined as: "*changes in transport sources that (might) positively or negatively influence the preferences, well-being, behavior or perception of individuals, groups, social categories and society in general (in the future).*" While economic and, to a lesser extent, environmental impacts of transport projects have been integrated into transport policy appraisal, the social aspects are less recognized, even though transport systems are themselves part of social systems.

This chapter reviews the literature which criticizes CBA's ability to include social impacts and ethical concerns that may arise in transport policies or planning. After reviewing the critiques brought forward in the literature, we survey developments in welfare economics that seek to overcome the asserted shortcomings of CBA. Finally, other appraisal methods such as Sustainability Assessment, Multicriteria Analysis (MCA) and Social Impact Assessment (SIA) that may be used to account for the social and ethical concerns of transport policies are discussed.

2. Critique on the incorporation of social impacts of transport projects in CBA

According to Geurs et al. (2009), social impacts in transport projects are broadly defined as: "*changes in transport sources that (might) positively or negatively influence the preferences, well-being, behavior or perception of individuals, groups, social categories and society in general (in the future).*"

Social impacts are diverse and may arise from the construction or presence of transport infrastructure, the presence of parked vehicles or transport facilities, or traffic or travel, which may impact on (for instance) health, safety, cultural heritage, cultural diversity, social cohesion, visual quality or access to transport (Geurs et al., 2009). Social impacts have different timeframes and levels of impact and some may be cumulative. Short-run social impact categories as related to accessibility, movement and activities, health, finance and community, whereas longer-run impacts may include health condition (e.g., obesity or fitness), social exclusion or inclusion, social capital, general well-being (physical and mental), and regeneration and gentrification effects (Jones and Lucas, 2012).

An overarching fundamental critique raised against neoclassical economics, the theory which undergirds CBA, is that the inherent social nature of humans is ignored (e.g., De Waal, 2006). The representative agent in neoclassical economics—also known as homo economicus, is best pictured as a Robinson Crusoe interacting through the market exclusively with other Robinson Crusoes. In this view, the government's main economic role is enhancing the performance of the market economy (Tresch, 2014). Scholars argue that this conceptualization ignores that humans are "social creatures" who live in a group with other humans and can feel empathy with group members. De Waal (2008) observes that (reciprocal) altruism and fairness are important products of empathy and although social considerations such as sympathy appear in the writings of Adam Smith, the father of economics, these bedrocks of social interaction have historically received only marginal attention from mainstream economics. The fundamental critique on neoclassical economics and homo economicus is translated in several specific ways to conducting CBAs for government projects. We discuss three topics as these relate to the issue of how social impacts are included in the appraisal of transport projects.

In this section, we focus on the literature concerning fundamental critiques on the inclusion of social impacts of transport projects in CBA. We do not focus on the issues that are caused by lack of available data or analytical models. These pragmatic issues are important in practice, but they might differ too much across countries and contexts which limits the extent to which we can draw general conclusions in this chapter.

2.1 CBA ignores that preference formation is a social process

First, CBA has been criticized for ignoring that the formation of preferences is inherently a social process. CBA implicitly or explicitly assumes that homo economicus has preformed preferences for intangible impacts of transport projects such as social cohesion and social equality even when they do not have any experience in real life with the valuation of these impacts (Czajkowski et al., 2015). This conflicts with ample evidence in other disciplines such as psychology that certain preferences and values, e.g., those relating to socio-cultural impacts of a policy (Kenter et al., 2015), are not preformed and instead constructed through a process of inter-personal communication or deliberation (Kenter, 2014). Hence, various scholars argue that a core limitation of CBA is that the method ignores that discussions with others and the opportunity to ask questions are decisive for preference formation as the formation of preferences is an inherently social, dynamic process (e.g., Bartkowski and Lienhoop, 2017; Dietz et al., 2009). Examples of impacts of transport projects for which valuation is likely collectively formed include impacts such as community severance, which affects social cohesion (the state of togetherness and unity within a community or society) (Geurs et al., 2009) or social connectedness (presence of social interactions, relationships and networks) (Quigley and Thornley, 2011) or cultural impacts such as impacts on townscape or historic environment (Hickman and Dean, 2018).

2.2 CBA ignores equity considerations

A second critique on CBA focuses on the use of one particular ethical theory when aggregating preferences of individuals and drawing policy recommendations. CBA imposes a utilitarian framework which postulates that the consequences of an action are morally right if, as a result of this action, the total amount of good for all outweighs the total amount of bad for all (Harsanyi, 1975). However, utilitarianism has been widely disputed in the literature since human well-being can be conceived in a much broader sense than utility alone and is shown to encompass numerous dimensions, its key components being: having the basic material needs for a good life, freedom, health, good social relations, and personal security (Millennium Ecosystem Assestment, 2005). In addition, social, environmental and intergenerational equity are now also regarded as key components of human well-being (Klasen, 2008; Summers and Smith, 2014). Various scholars assert that utilitarianism, a consequentialist theory, may not be suitable for certain moral dimensions of transport policies, for example, freedom of choice or alleviating inequality (van Wee et al., 2014). They claim that alternative ethical theories like deontology or rule-based ethics (van Wee, 2012) may be more useful for assessing transport policies.

In conventional CBAs the moral theory utilitarianism is operationalized in a very specific way through the Kaldor-Hicks criterion which asserts that a policy (or other change) can be considered as welfare-increasing if those who benefit can compensate those who suffer from it, creating a Pareto improvement after compensation (Hicks, 1939; Kaldor, 1939). According to the Kaldor-Hicks criterion, the compensation does not actually have to take place: it is enough that it is theoretically possible (Koopmans and Mouter, 2020). One problem with this way of measuring the social welfare effect of a transport project is that equity concerns or distribution effects, which often arise in transport policies, are ignored even though fairness considerations are very important in social interactions (van Wee, 2012). Hence, aspects such as social exclusion or accessibility tend to be inadequately addressed in transport appraisal (Geurs and Van Wee, 2011).

The issue of transport equity is much discussed in the literature (Aparicio, 2018; Bills and Walker, 2017; Ferreira et al., 2012; Lucas and Jones, 2012; Nahmias-Biran et al., 2017; Pereira et al., 2017). Equity, or justice, refers to the distribution of impacts (benefits and costs) and whether that distribution is considered fair and appropriate. Equity concerns are cited as the most neglected (and difficult to measure) in transport policy (Berechman, 2018). For instance, CBA has been criticized for placing too much value on increasing mobility overall, rather than ensuring equitable access to transport services for different age-groups, genders, or ethnic groups at risk of social exclusion (Ferreira et al., 2012). Some argue that as well as the need to ensure the fair distribution of impacts, equity also means that the people impacted by policy should have the right to be represented in decision-making by means of participation or collaboration (Aparicio, 2018). Transport-related inequalities that tend to be neglected in the literature relate to affordability, proximity to services, inclusivity (e.g., for the disabled), agency, freedom of choice, and transport accessibility levels (Pereira et al., 2017). This is because there are various ways to understand equity and categorize people in an analysis, numerous impacts to consider and ways to measure them (Geurs and Van Wee, 2011).

2.3 CBA ignores that private preferences of individuals may not be a good proxy for their public preferences

A third critique concerns how CBA does not distinguish between private and public preferences. CBA's monetization of the impacts of government projects is based on how much affected individuals are willing to pay from their private income (Persky, 2001), but CBA fails to consider that private choices may not fully reflect citizens' preferences about public goods and means (Mouter et al., 2021). In a transport CBA, analysts use monetary metrics that are directly derived from individuals' market behavior (Mouter, 2021c). For example, impacts of transport projects on landscape, nature and noise pollution are evaluated by investigating the private decisions people make in the real estate market (e.g. Allen et al., 2015; Seo et al., 2014). When market behavior is absent, monetary values are usually derived from hypothetical consumer choices. For example, the standard approach used to empirically infer the value of travel time savings and the value of traffic safety improvements accruing from government projects relies on (hypothetical) route choice experiments (e.g., Abrantes and Wardman, 2011; Bahamonde-Birke et al., 2015). In these experiments, respondents are asked to make a series of private choices between routes which differ in terms of travel time, travel costs and accident risk. This approach has been criticized by scholars who assert that the way that individuals balance their own after-tax incomes against the attributes of government projects when making private choices may be a poor proxy for showing what individuals believe how their government should trade-off public budgets and impacts of public projects (Mouter et al., 2018). Many of these limitations of CBA arise due to individuals' perception that the government should allocate public resources in a different way then they allocate their own private income.

2.3.1 General critiques on the private willingness to pay paradigm

The literature discusses various problems with using individual private willingness-to-pay to infer the welfare of a government policy in the context of public choices. A first reason is that private choices may be distorted through collective action problems (e.g. Lusk and Norwood, 2011; Sen, 1995; Wegner and Pascual, 2011). For instance, people may not be willing to contribute individually to a public good (e.g., air pollution) because the impact of their individual contribution is negligible, but people may be willing to contribute when the whole community is forced to contribute through a new law or a tax increase because the impact of this coordinated contribution can be substantial (Lusk and Norwood, 2011; Sen, 1995).

A second reason for a distinction between private preferences and public preferences concerns how individuals value the same impact differently in a private sphere (the real estate market) and the public sphere (ballot box), as moral considerations might be more relevant in the latter context (e.g., Mouter et al., 2019; Sagoff, 1988). The idea that individuals can entertain different kinds of valuations in different spheres is, among others, covered in the contributions of Sunstein (1994). For instance, Sunstein (1994, p. 784) states: distinctions among kinds of valuation are highly sensitive to the particular setting in which they operate. People do not value goods acontextually. In one setting—say, the workplace—the prevailing kinds of valuation might be quite different from what they are elsewhere—say, the home or the ballot box. Furthermore, Sunstein (1994) asserts that because of the highly contextual nature of choice it is incorrect to assume that an individuals' private choices can be simply adaptable for policy use. Although transport economists already recognize the importance of context by valuing travel time savings for business trips in a different way from the value of time for commuting and leisure trips, they ignore the fact that these travel time savings materialize in the context of a government decision and not in the context of a private route choice (Mouter and Chorus, 2016).

A third reason why scholars criticize the private willingness to pay paradigm in CBA is that they think that this is an inappropriate way to value impacts of government projects that are not possible to measure with private income (Aldred, 2006; Clark et al., 2000). For instance, Sunstein (1994) asserts that values which are not traded in a real-life market setting, such as biodiversity and landscape might be valued incorrectly when they are expressed in private income. Raz (1986) asserts that values such as friendship and our relationship with the natural world cannot be valued in terms of private income without somehow corroding or degrading them. In short, a plurality of values, many of which are nonmonetizable, exist in our complex society. Social or shared values that are qualitative or subjective nature and collectively formed via a discursive group process (e.g., cultural, societal, communal or group values (Kenter et al., 2015)) may be particularly problematic to measure and compare (Geurs et al., 2009; Hickman and Dean, 2018).

A fourth critique on the private choice approach in CBA is cited by Jara-Díaz (2007). He argues that a reason for the divergences of people's preferences in a private context and a public context is that proportionally more tax money will end up allocated to high income groups when social appraisal is based on private willingness to pay, which deviates from people's public preferences to give a higher weight to the interests of low income groups in social appraisal. Specifically, CBA may result in solutions that are biased toward higher income groups. For example, when car drivers have a higher capacity to pay than public transport users, the people who wish to continue using cars rather than public transport may have more influence in a CBA because of their higher willingness to pay (WTP), leading to less healthy and less sustainable policy choices (Khreis et al., 2016). As well as many theoretical arguments about why individuals entertain different preferences in a private and public setting, the literature also includes empirical insights showing that individuals value impacts of transport projects such as travel time savings and accident risk differently when they trade these impacts against their own budget or the public budget (Mouter et al., 2017, 2018).

2.3.2 Critiques on the private willingness to pay paradigm in the transport literature

Various urban planners who criticize CBA do not explicitly use the four lines of reasoning outlined above, but they do implicitly assert that individuals' past consumer choices are not necessarily a good reflection of their normative ideas concerning a future mobility system (Hickman and Dean, 2018; Nicolaisen et al., 2017). The first critique of assessing urban transport projects through a CBA brought forward by planners is that the instrument degrades the forward-looking nature of the planning proficiency (e.g., Banister, 2008; Hajer and Pelzer, 2018; Handy, 2008). For instance, Nicolaisen et al. (2017) observe that policy makers' normative aspiration to reduce car traffic in the urban core through discouraging car use is not sufficiently reflected in a CBA, even though this is their key rationale for championing projects such as Light Rail Transit (LRT), removing roads/car lanes and lowering travel speed. Many scholars argue that the main objective of transport planning is to define the desired future of a place and how to obtain it. For instance, (Banister, 2008) asserts that transport planning requires clear, innovative and strategic thinking about city futures in terms of desirability, and the role that transport can (and should) play in achieving these objectives. Hajer and Pelzer (2018) assert that planning and evaluation need to refocus from a tradition of "expected futures" to an approach centering on "desirable futures" and ways to get there.

The notion of anticipating the (uncertain) future by setting goals goes beyond the conventional private WTP-based elicitation approach, which determines the value of impacts of (future) government projects through observing people's (hypothetical) consumer choices (e.g., hypothetical route choices and behavior in the housing market). Planners argue that the misalignment between people's private choice behavior and their preferences regarding the allocation of government budget toward transport policies is amplified due to the broadening of goals of transport planning in the last decades. Manaugh et al. (2015), for instance, observe that throughout most of the 20th century the goals of transport were almost entirely mobility-based, with a focus on congestion reduction, travel time savings and safety improvements for motorists. These effects are relatively easy to value through observing people's (hypothetical) private consumer choices. (Manaugh et al. 2015) state that in this era, CBA captured all the important goals of transport planning identified by policy makers at that time. However, prompted by concerns regarding climate change, social inequality and the scarcity of public space in urban areas, the focus of transport planning shifted more and more to other (more normative and/or future-oriented) goals, such as long-run sustainability, quality of life, social equity and resilience (e.g., Banister, 2008; Ferreira et al., 2012; Handy, 2008; Manaugh et al., 2015). (Banister, 2008), for instance, asserts that in urban areas a much wider notion of the street has been created, as it is no longer only being considered as a road but also as a space where people meet. Transport projects have become more complex as they are seen as part of a larger socio-technical system. Therefore, nowadays, urban transport projects pursue both traditional goals (e.g., costs, travel time savings, safety and reduction of noise pollution) as well as a diverse set of nontraditional goals such as long-run sustainability, townscape, social inclusion, cultural heritage, city image, social capital, improving the quality of urban spaces and regeneration and gentrification effects (e.g., De Bruijn and Veeneman, 2009; Geurs et al., 2009; Hickman and Dean, 2018; Jones and Lucas, 2012; Nicolaisen et al., 2017). However, several authors argue that CBA does not sufficiently appreciate many of these nontraditional goals as they are generally not included in the CBA, or are under-valued because they are not quantified or monetized (Beukers, 2015; Handy, 2008; Hickman and Dean, 2018; Nicolaisen et al., 2017). For instance, various scholars assert that CBAs for cycling projects have difficulty with including the impacts of a modal shift from car to bicycle such as the positive health impacts of increased physical activity and a reduction of road congestion and emissions, even though realizing these impacts are often a key goal of cycling projects (Adam et al., 2018; De Hartog et al., 2010; Heinen et al., 2015; Jones and Lucas, 2012; Van Wee and Börjesson, 2015). Moreover, various planning scholars argue that goals of cycling policies such as improvement of urban quality, space efficiency, social inclusion, improved mobility for children and social interaction potential often have a minor role in CBA (De Hartog et al., 2010; Te Brömmelstroet et al., 2017; Van Wee and Börjesson, 2015).

3. Scientific innovations to overcome critiques of CBA

In the past decades, scholars have developed methodologies to address the shortcomings that were discussed in the previous section. Two of these methodologies are Deliberative Monetary Valuation (DMV), a method to explicitly recognize the importance of social interaction in preference formation, and Participatory Value Evaluation (PVE), a method designed to ensure that the assessment of government projects is based on people's preferences regarding the allocation of scarce public resources. Both methods can be considered as amendments to standard welfare economics as they each adopt the essence of this theory underlying CBA.

Scholars developed so-called Deliberative Monetary Valuation (DMV) experiments in which individuals express their preferences after being exposed to one or more deliberative treatments (e.g., group discussion, consulting expert witnesses or a forum) which may facilitate them to develop well-formed preferences in the case of unfamiliar and complex public goods (e.g., Bartkowski and Lienhoop, 2017; Dietz et al., 2009; Szabó, 2011; Vatn, 2009). Augmenting preference elicitation with deliberative elements will allow participating citizens to learn from each other, to form reasoned opinions and to evaluate positions thereby ironing out critiques on the individual approach to preference formation (Kenter et al., 2016). Apart from DMV, scholars developed other deliberative approaches that are not grounded in welfare economics. We discuss these approaches in Section 4.4.

Participatory Value Evaluation (PVE) (codeveloped by the authors of this chapter) is a new method to assess the desirability of government projects based on individuals' preferences regarding the allocation of scarce public resource (Mouter et al., 2021). In a PVE, individuals are offered several possible public projects, information about the impacts of these projects (e.g., travel time savings, noise pollution and number of trees that have to be cut) and a constrained public budget in an (online) experiment. Next, individuals are asked to choose the public projects they like to see implemented while respecting the public budget constraint. The trade-offs made in selecting their preferred portfolio can be used to establish individuals' preferences for (the impacts of) the public projects and to rank these projects in terms of their desirability (Dekker et al., 2019; Mouter et al., 2021). In a PVE, it is assumed that part of the desirability of an individual project is defined by the impacts that are explicitly presented to participants for each of the transport projects (e.g., travel time savings, improvement of traffic safety) and preference parameters are estimated to determine the importance of these explicit impacts on the individual's decision (Mouter et al., 2021). On the other hand, it is assumed that the (un)attractiveness of an individual project can also be defined by other considerations than the level of the impacts that are explicitly presented to the participants (e.g., the ethical and social dimensions of a transport project or people's normative views concerning the future urban mobility system). For these aspects project specific parameters are estimated.

The main difference between CBA and PVE is that PVE establishes the desirability of government projects based on people's advises regarding the allocation of the public budget toward (impacts of) government projects, whereas CBA establishes the desirability of government projects through analyzing people's trade-offs between their private income and impacts of government projects (Mouter et al., 2021). Mouter et al. (2021) investigated whether CBA and PVE lead to different policy recommendations in the context of urban mobility investments by conducting CBAs and a PVE for 16 urban mobility investment projects. They find that projects which focus on improving traffic safety and improvements for cyclists/pedestrians rank higher in the PVE, whereas car projects rank higher in the CBA analysis.

A PVE aims to address the four lines of critique that were raised against the private willingness to pay paradigm adopted in CBA (discussed in Section 2.3). A key characteristic of PVE is that impacts of a proposed government project are considered in the context of a future government decision (and not in the context of a consumer choice). This elicitation context potentially allows individuals to express preferences that line up with their preferred future perspectives regarding the (local) urban mobility system, broader goals of transport planning as well as their ethical considerations. Moreover, it allows them to express altruistic preferences that they inhibit in a public context as well as preferences toward solving collective actions problems. Finally, PVE does not require translation of government project impacts into private income. Instead, an impact of a government project is valued through the extent to which individuals are willing to sacrifice other impacts of government projects. For instance, in a PVE, individuals are asked to trade-off environmental impacts against other impacts of governmental policy (e.g., reduction of mortality risk) which contrasts the WTP valuation approach in which individuals are asked to trade-off environmental impacts against private income.

4. How other appraisal methods include social and ethical dimensions

Apart from CBA, and other approaches grounded in welfare-economics described in the previous section, still more appraisal methods exist that attempt to include social and ethical aspects of transport policy. These include sustainability assessment, which encompasses a broad range of methods, including multicriteria analysis (MCA), which can also be used as a standalone appraisal tool. Other approaches include social impact assessment (SIA), an umbrella framework of various methods, including participative or deliberative approaches (also used in their own right for appraisals), which are especially geared at capturing social impacts. Next, we present a brief review of how these methods have been applied in transport planning. A more thorough discussion of these methods can be found in two recent textbooks (Mouter, 2021a,b).

4.1 Sustainability assessment

The purpose of sustainability assessment is, according to Kates et al. (2001) *to provide decision-makers with an evaluation of global to local integrated nature–society systems in short and long term perspectives in order to assist them to determine which actions should or should not be taken in an attempt to make society sustainable.*

A large number of tools have been developed in recent decades, which can be categorized according to their temporal characteristics, coverage areas and how they integrate environmental, social and economic aspects. Ness et al. (2007) identify three general types of sustainability assessment: indicators and indices, product-related assessment tools (e.g., life-cycle assessment (LCA)) and integrated assessments, which are collections of tools focused on policy change or project implementation. Fig. 1 shows the tools arranged on a time continuum, according to whether they are retrospective or prospective/forecasting tools.

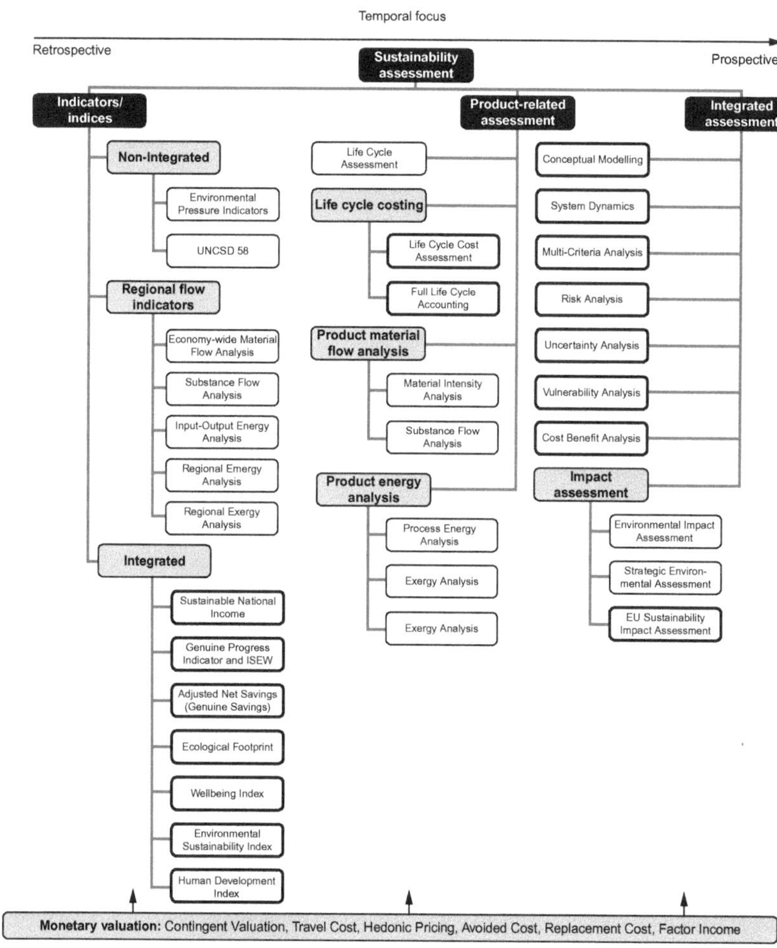

Fig. 1 Classification of sustainability assessments. *From Ness, B., Urbel-Piirsalu, E., Anderberg, S., & Olsson, L. (2007). Categorising tools for sustainability assessment. Ecol. Econ., 60(3), 498–508. https://doi.org/10.1016/j.ecolecon.2006.07.023.*

In transport policy and planning, Bueno et al. (2015) found the main approaches being used for sustainability assessment to be "traditional" appraisal methods (e.g., CBA, MCA or LCA), sustainability rating systems (specific rating schemes for evaluating sustainability of buildings, road construction projects and civil engineering works, e.g., LEED or CEEQUAL) and sustainability frameworks, guidelines, or models (e.g., WebTag or STAG). However, they found that since the concept of sustainability is fuzzy, there is currently no common methodology to reliably measure sustainability when appraising and evaluating transport projects. They also acknowledge that traditional approaches like CBA or MCA neglect some key components of the three sustainability dimensions (economic, social, and environmental). While MCA is often used as a component of sustainability appraisal, e.g., (Vassallo and Bueno, 2021), or alongside other methods, it may also be used in its own right as an appraisal method.

4.2 Multicriteria assessment

Multicriteria analysis (MCA) is a family of methods and its application in the transport field commonly includes multiattribute theory approaches (e.g., AHP) to arrive at comparable measures of different outcomes and outranking methods (e.g., PROMETHEE) to rank the preferences for alternative projects with multiattributed characteristics (Macharis and Bernardini, 2015). Types of MCA methods differ from each other in the design of the process, how stakeholders are involved and facilitated and how results are presented (Saarikoski et al., 2016). MCA is seen as methodologically suitable for dealing with multiple viewpoints and value dimensions and hence a more effective approach than CBA for appraising transport policy (e.g.,Saarikoski et al., 2016; van Wee, 2012; Vatn, 2009). Going beyond cost-effectiveness, MCA allows the inclusion of social, environmental or incommensurable values that are difficult to translate into monetary terms, such as multiple dimensions of well-being, or the cultural and moral aspects of a policy (Saarikoski et al., 2016).

Multiple examples of the use of MCA in transport appraisal exist. For example, Macharis and Bernardini (2015) review the use of MCA for transport appraisal and find that it has been applied in various forms to a wide range of policy analysis decisions, including decisions on passenger or freight transport, infrastructure and transport technology. In addition, Mardani

use methods that engage stakeholders and communities in the decision-making process through the creation of deliberative spaces (Esteves et al., 2012).

4.4 Deliberative appraisal methods

We have already had a glimpse of how deliberative interventions can be incorporated into existing transport appraisal methods, with the examples of Deliberative Monetary Valuation in Section 3 and deliberative MCA in Section 4.1. To elaborate further, deliberative methods represent a subset of participatory methods. The main distinguishing factors relate to how people participate and how they are selected. In general, participatory methods can involve large numbers of often self-selected participants, whereas deliberative methods tend toward smaller, but representative, groups (Shortall, 2020). Deliberative methods involve reasoned discussion between participants, whereas other participatory methods may not require any interaction between participants, e.g., think of surveys or consultations. Deliberative approaches conceptualize value from a pluralistic perspective and aim for the construction of societal values in a particular social context, making them suited to valuing public goods. They offer a way to address the complexities inherent in transport policy appraisal (Murray, 2011).

The basic reasoning behind deliberative approaches is that a diverse group of citizens, if given adequate information, resources and time to deliberate on a given topic can produce a rational, informed judgment. Deliberation can in theory be carried out with any group of people and is usually carried out in small groups of maximum 15 people, within an organized setting. Total attendance for one such event can range from 15 to 1000 participants. Most of the well-known deliberative methods have as their basis a step-by-step process that can be largely described as (1) learning (2) discussion or deliberation (3) reaching a collective decision and providing recommendations.

Deliberative methods offer unique insights and outputs. Analytical or technical-rational appraisal methods like CBA place an emphasis on factual perspectives and ensuring that these are based on valid methods and procedures. Their outputs may involve monetizing, ranking or rating. Deliberative appraisal methods, on the other hand, emphasize diverse values, communication, argumentation and combining expert and lay knowledge (Raymond et al., 2014). Because each type of appraisal offers its own distinct insights and benefits, many scholars now advocate for the integration of deliberative methods with analytical technical-rational approaches in order to have the best of both worlds (Chilvers, 2008; Nyerges and Aguirre, 2011; Raymond et al., 2014). Deliberative methods may hence be categorized into (purely) deliberative or analytic-deliberative.

The best-known deliberative methods are based on mini-publics and include citizen's juries, consensus conferences or deliberative polling. A mini-public is intended to provide a demographically representative sample of the greater public. Normally, citizens are recruited via stratified random sampling or sortition. Groups are usually provided with information or submissions from interest groups providing arguments for or against various options. They may also have access to experts which hold different points of view (Fishkin and Mansbridge, 2017). Purely deliberative methods involve reflection on exchanged information and points of view, with a view to collectively constructing the views of participants. Outcomes of purely deliberative approaches tend to be qualitative and be expressed in the form of recommendations or verdicts.

Various examples of how deliberative approaches have been used in transport policy appraisal are given in Shortall (2021) and include citizen's juries and citizen's assemblies. Citizen's juries have been used for providing citizen verdicts on transportation policy, e.g., relating to traffic limitation in Italy, bypass roads in Germany or highway extensions in Australia (Baumann and White, 2010). Citizen's assemblies are a relatively novel democratic innovation and have been used in various countries such as Ireland, Canada, Estonia, France and Belgium. The cross-cutting 2017 Irish citizen's assembly on climate change[a] requested 99 citizens to explicitly focus on the transport sector (among others) in their deliberations and various recommendations to the government were made, including increasing spending on public transport and increasing support for electric vehicles.

Analytic-deliberative methods remain somewhat experimental and may take on a variety of forms. The term "analytic-deliberative" describes processes that aim to balance traditional scientific or technical analysis with deliberation involving a diverse group of participants (Chilvers, 2008). Incorporating deliberation into appraisal can help participants express their preferences in various ways, for instance, in terms of moral values as well as in monetary terms. Analytic-deliberative methods therefore have combined or

[a] https://www.citizensassembly.ie/en/how-the-state-can-make-ireland-a-leader-in-tackling-climate-change/

quantitative outcomes which may include rankings or ratings (Kenter, 2014). Examples of applications in transport appraisal include deliberative monetary valuation (DMV) (Miccoli et al., 2014), the deliberative method embedded in welfare economics discussed in Section 3, deliberative polling or deliberative MCA.

An example of the use of deliberative polling (Schweigert, 2010) concerned the collapse of the Interstate 35 W Bridge in Minneapolis, Minnesota in 2007. Researchers involved a random sample of 1003 residents of the seven-county metropolitan area of Saint Paul and Minneapolis to discover their level of support for a variety of transport priorities and funding options. Examples of integrating deliberation into MCA in transport appraisal include "participatory MCA" (Dean et al., 2019), used for choosing between potential project options for the South Fylde railway line in North West England. This involved "multiactors" in two middle stages of the process, i.e., criteria weighting and impact assessment. For mega transport infrastructure appraisal, Ward et al. (2016) propose what they term "policy-led multicriteria analysis," in which stakeholder groups may get involved at various stages of the process. In general, deliberative methods are said to be best used when the issue in question involves complexity, uncertainty or conflicting values or viewpoints (Kenter, 2014), when there is a high plurality of values (Frame and O'Connor, 2011), or when socio-cultural or values related to human well-being are at stake (Kelemen and Saarikoski, 2015). Many transport infrastructure projects exhibit such characteristics, and the planning process involves overlaps with the economic, social, environmental and spatial planning domains (Beukers et al., 2015). Socio-cultural or well-being values may be connected to landscapes, recreational or cultural heritage sites, for example, which may be impacted by transport projects. Planners must take account of a great diversity of perspectives and goals, especially when assessing the sustainability of transportation policy (Lindenau and Böhler-Baedeker, 2014; Sagaris, 2018; Whitmarsh et al., 2007). The design of the method (deliberative or analytic deliberative) will depend on the goal of the process, or the type of outputs required.

4.5 Summary

Various approaches for appraising the social and ethical dimensions of transport policies have been presented in this chapter. Table 1 provides a summary of these approaches, along with their main characteristics and advantages and disadvantages in comparison with using CBA.

Table 1 Alternative appraisal methods and their (dis)advantages compared to CBA.

Approach	Description	Advantages compared to CBA	Disadvantages compared to CBA
Sustainability assessment	A broad array of tools that provide decision-makers with an evaluation of global to local integrated nature–society systems in short and long-term perspectives in order to assist them to determine which actions should or should not be taken in an attempt to make society sustainable	Tools are available to assess multiple types of impacts: environmental, economic and social, with a temporal range from retrospective to prospective. Transferring these impacts into monetary terms is not required	No common methodology available for appraising the sustainability of transport projects
Social impact assessment (SIA)	A broad framework of processes for analyzing, monitoring and managing the intended and unintended social consequences, both positive and negative, of planned interventions (policies, programs, plans, projects) and any social change processes invoked by those interventions	Uses methods that pay specific attention to social impacts, including equity concerns, which may not be adequately captured by other appraisal methods Methods are designed to elicit plural, shared or social values	While governed by international standards, SIA is not always consistently implemented. A clear theoretical framework is lacking Involves a process of multiple steps which may take several weeks or months Must be complemented with other appraisal methods to measure economic or environmental impacts of a project

5. Conclusion and future research

In this chapter, we looked at critiques of one of the most popular transport policy appraisal methods, CBA and how it falls short when it comes to including the social and ethical dimensions of appraisal. We looked at some developments in the literature that aim to better include these dimensions, including some developments in welfare economics.

While certain advances in welfare economics have been made, for instance the development Deliberative Monetary Valuation (DMV), very few examples of its application in the transportation sector exist and further research is required to determine its suitability for including social and ethical dimensions. Another promising method grounded in welfare economics is Participatory Value Evaluation (PVE), which addresses certain critiques of CBA related to the private willingness to pay paradigm, in the context of the allocation of government funding, and the possibility to express preferences based on future perspectives or altruistic interests. Nonetheless, the remaining critiques regarding methods like CBA, which is underpinned by utilitarianism, still need to be addressed. In particular: taking account of fairness, dealing with a plurality of values, or capturing values that are socially formed. We looked at how social and ethical dimensions may be included in other appraisal methods like Sustainability Assessment, Multicriteria Analysis (MCA), Social Impact Assessment (SIA) and deliberative methods. However, we see that while each method may address one or more critiques of CBA, no method alone will counter all critiques, nor will any method be able to include all aspects of policy appraisal (environmental, economic, social, ethical). Deliberative methods, for example, are a relatively recent addition to the transport policy appraisal toolbox and may be of particular benefit in complex policy situations with multiple actors, but research is still needed about the best way to combine deliberative processes with technical analyses. In general, further research into how different methods can be effectively combined and harness their individual strengths is needed.

References

Abrantes, P.A.L., Wardman, M., 2011. Meta-analysis of the UK values of time: an update. TransportationTransport research part a: policy and. Practice 45, 1–17.

Adam, L., Jones, T., Te Brömmelstroet, M.C.G., (2018). Planning for cycling in the dispersed city: establishing a hierarchy of effectiveness of municipal cycling policies. TransportationTransport, 1–25.

Aldred, J., 2006. Incommensurability and monetary valuation. Land Econ. 82 (2), 141–161.
Allen, M.T., Austin, G.W., Swaleheen, M., 2015. Measuring highway impacts on house prices using spatial regression. The Journal of Sustainable Real Estate 7 (1), 83–98.
Anciaes, P.R., Jones, P., Mindell, J.S., 2016. Community severance: where is it found and at what cost? Transport Reviews 36 (3), 293–317. https://doi.org/10.1080/01441647.2015.1077286.
Annema, J.A., Mouter, N., Razaei, J., 2015. Cost-benefit analysis (CBA), or multi-criteria decision-making (MCDM) or both: Politicians' perspective in transport policy appraisal. Transportation Research Procedia 10 (July), 788–797. https://doi.org/10.1016/j.trpro.2015.09.032.
Antonson, H., Levin, L., 2020. A crack in the Swedish welfare façade? A review of assessing social impacts in transport infrastructure planning. Progress in Planning 138 (December 2018), 100428. https://doi.org/https://doi.org/10.1016/j.progress.2018.11.001.
Aparicio, Á., 2018. Equity challenges in major transport plans. Transportation Research Procedia 31, 121–135. https://doi.org/10.1016/j.trpro.2018.09.054.
Bahamonde-Birke, F.J., Kunert, U., Link, H., 2015. The value of a statistical life in a road safety context — A review of the current literature. Transport Reviews 35 (4), 488–511.
Banister, D., 2008. The sustainable mobility paradigm. Transport Policy 15 (2), 73–80.
Barfod, M.B., Salling, K.B., Leleur, S., 2011. Composite decision support by combining cost-benefit and multi-criteria decision analysis. Decision Support Systems 51 (1), 167–175. https://doi.org/10.1016/J.DSS.2010.12.005.
Bartkowski, B., Lienhoop, N., (2017). Democracy and valuation: A reply to Schläpfer (2016). Ecological Economics 131, 557–560.
Baudry, G., Macharis, C., Vallée, T., 2018. Range-based multi-actor multi-criteria analysis: a combined method of multi-actor multi-criteria analysis and Monte Carlo simulation to support participatory decision making under uncertainty. European Journal of Operational Research 264 (1), 257–269. https://doi.org/10.1016/j.ejor.2017.06.036.
Baumann, C., White, S., 2010. Enhanced dialogue in transport policy making: enabling change towards sustainability through deliberative public engagement. World Conference of Transport Research, Lisboa 2010, 1–22.
Bellamy, R., Chilvers, J., Vaughan, N.E., 2014. Deliberative mapping of options for tackling climate change: citizens and specialists 'open up' appraisal of geoengineering. Public Underst. Sci. 25 (3), 269–286. https://doi.org/10.1177/0963662514548628.
Berechman, J., 2018. The Infrastructure we Ride on Decision Making in Transportation Investment (Vol 53). Palgrave Macmillan, Cham. https://doi.org/https://doi-org.tudelft.idm.oclc.org/10.1007/978-3-319-74606-7.
Beukers, E., 2015. Shaking up the cost benefit analysis process: Issues and directions for improvement when assessing integrated spatial transport plans through a cost benefit analysis. PhD thesis.
Beukers, E., Bertolini, L., te Brömmelstroet, M., 2015. An assessment of interventions for improving communication and trust in cost benefit analysis processes. Impact Assessment and Project Appraisal 33 (1), 28–42. https://doi.org/10.1080/14615517.2014.941142.
Bills, T.S., Walker, J.L., 2017. Looking beyond the mean for equity analysis: examining distributional impacts of transportation improvements. Transport Policy 54 (December 2016), 61–69. https://doi.org/https://doi.org/10.1016/j.tranpol.2016.08.003.
Bueno, P.C., Vassallo, J.M., Cheung, K., 2015. Sustainability assessment of transport infrastructure projects: A review of existing tools and methods. Transport Reviews 35 (5), 622–649.
Cass, N., 2006. Participatory-deliberative engagement : a literature review. Renew. Energy, 1–49 (August).

Chilvers, J., 2008. Deliberating competence theoretical and practitioner participatory appraisal practice, Science, Technology and Human Values, advance online publication.
Clark, J., Burgess, J., Harrison, C.M., 2000. I struggled with this money business: Respondents perspectives on contingent valuation. Ecological Economics 33, 45–62.
Czajkowski, M., Hanley, N., LaRiviere, J., 2015. The effects of experience on preferences: Theory and empirics for environmental public goods. American Journal of Agricultural Economics 97 (1), 333–351.
De Waal, F.B.M., 2006. Primates and philosophers. Princeton University Press, New Jersey.
De Waal, F.B.M., 2008. Putting the altruism back into altruism: The evolution of empathy. The Annual Review of Psychology 59, 279–300.
De Bruijn, H., Veeneman, W., 2009. Decision-making for light rail. Transportation Research Part A: Policy and Practice 43 (4), 349–359.
De Hartog, J., Boogaard, H., Nijland, H., Hoek, G., 2010. Do the health benefits of cycling outweigh the risks? Environmental Health Perspectives 118 (8), 1109–1116.
Dean, M., Hickman, R., Chen, C.L., 2019. Testing the application of participatory MCA: the case of the south Fylde line. Transport Policy 73, 62–70. https://doi.org/10.1016/j.tranpol.2018.10.007.
Dekker T, Koster PR, Mouter N. 2019. The economics of participatory value evaluation. SSRN Electronic Journal [Internet]. Available from: https://doi.org/10.2139/ssrn.3323645.
Dietz, T., Stern, P.C., Dan, A., 2009. How deliberation affects stated willingness to pay for mitigation of carbon dioxide emissions: An experiment. Land Economics 85 (2), 329–347.
Esteves, A.M., Franks, D., Vanclay, F., 2012. Social impact assessment: the state of the art. Impact Assessment and Project Appraisal 30 (1), 34–42. https://doi.org/10.1080/14615517.2012.660356.
Ferreira, A., Beukers, E., Te Brömmelstroet, M., 2012. Accessibility is gold, mobility is not: a proposal for the improvement of Dutch transport-related cost-benefit analysis. Environment and Planning B: Planning and Design 39 (4), 683–697. https://doi.org/10.1068/b38073.
Fishkin, J.S., Mansbridge, J., 2017. Introduction. Daedalus 146 (3), 6–13. https://doi.org/10.1162/DAED_x_00442.
Frame, B., O'Connor, M., 2011. In: Integrating valuation and deliberation: The purposes of sustainability assessment. Environmental Science and Policy (Vol. 14). Elsevier Ltd, pp. 1–10. https://doi.org/10.1016/j.envsci.2010.10.009.
Geurs, K., Van Wee, B., 2011. Discussing equity and social exclusion in accessibility evaluations. European Journal of Transport and Infrastructure Research 11 (11), 350–367.
Geurs, K.T., Boon, W., Van Wee, B., 2009. Social impacts of transport: literature review and the state of the practice of transport appraisal in the Netherlands and the United Kingdom. Transport Reviews 29 (1), 69–90. https://doi.org/10.1080/01441640802130490.
Hajer, M.A., Pelzer, P., 2018. 2050—An energetic Odyssey: Understanding techniques of futuring in the transition towards renewable energy. Energy Research & Social Science 44, 222–231.
Handy, S., 2008. Regional transportation planning in the US: an examination of changes in technical aspects of the planning process in response to changing goals. Transport Policy 15 (2), 113–126. https://doi.org/10.1016/j.tranpol.2007.10.006.
Harsanyi, J.C., 1975. Can the maximin principle serve as a basis of morality? A critique of John Rawls' theory. Am. Polit. Sci. Rev. 69 (02), 594–606.
Heinen, E., Panter, J., Mackett, R., Ogilvie, D., 2015. Changes in mode of travel to work: A natural experimental study of new transport infrastructure. International Journal of Behavioral Nutrition and Physical Activity 12, p. 81.

Hickman, R., Dean, M., 2018. Incomplete cost–incomplete benefit analysis in transport appraisal. Transport Reviews 38 (6), 689–709. https://doi.org/10.1080/01441647.2017.1407377.

Hicks, J., 1939. The foundations of welfare economics. Economic Journal 49 (196), 696–712.

Hüging, H., Glensor, K., Lah, O., 2014. Need for a holistic assessment of urban mobility measures - review of existing methods and Design of a Simplified Approach. Transportation Research Procedia 4, 3–13. https://doi.org/10.1016/j.trpro.2014.11.001.

Jara-Díaz, S.R, 2007. Transport economic theory. Elsevier Science, Amsterdam.

Jones, P., Lucas, K., 2012. The social consequences of transport decision-making: clarifying concepts, synthesising knowledge and assessing implications. Journal of Transport Geography 21, 4–16. https://doi.org/10.1016/j.jtrangeo.2012.01.012.

Kaldor, N., 1939. Welfare propositions of economics and interpersonal comparisons of utility. Economic Journal 49 (195), 549–552.

Kates, R.W., Clark, W.C., Corell, R., Hall, J.M., Jaeger, C.C., Lowe, I., others, 2001. Sustainability science. Science 292 (5517), 641–642.

Kelemen, E., Saarikoski, H., 2015. Method factsheet deliberative valuation. pp. 4–7.

Kenter, J. O. (2014). Deliberative and non-monetary valuation: A review of methods. Laurence Mee Centre for People and the Sea, (October), 1–43. https://doi.org/10.13140/RG.2.1.1430.7606.

Kenter, J.O., O'Brien, L., Hockley, N., Ravenscroft, N., Fazey, I., Irvine, K.N., Williams, S., 2015. What are shared and social values of ecosystems? Ecol. Econ. 111, 86–99. https://doi.org/10.1016/J.ECOLECON.2015.01.006.

Kenter, J.O., Bryce, R., Christie, M., Cooper, N., Hockley, N., Irvine, K.N., et al., 2016. Shared values and deliberative valuation: Future directions. Ecosystem Services 21, 358–371.

Khreis, H., Warsow, K.M., Verlinghieri, E., Guzman, A., Pellecuer, L., Ferreira, A., Nieuwenhuijsen, M., 2016. The health impacts of traffic-related exposures in urban areas: understanding real effects, underlying driving forces and co-producing future directions. J. Transp. Health 3 (3), 249–267. https://doi.org/10.1016/j.jth.2016.07.002.

Klasen, S., 2008. The efficiency of equity. Review of Political Economy 20 (2), 257–274. https://doi.org/10.1080/09538250701819719.

Koopmans, C.C., Mouter, N., 2020. In: Mouter, N. (Ed.), Standard Appraisal Methods. Advances in Transport Policy and Planning (Vol. 6). Elsevier, Amsterdam.

Kügemann, M., Polatidis, H., 2019. Multi-criteria decision analysis of road transportation fuels and vehicles: a systematic review and classification of the literature. Energies 13 (1). https://doi.org/10.3390/en13010157.

Lindenau, M., Böhler-Baedeker, S., 2014. Citizen and stakeholder involvement: a precondition for sustainable urban mobility. Transportation Research Procedia 4, 347–360. https://doi.org/10.1016/J.TRPRO.2014.11.026.

Lucas, K., Jones, P., 2012. Social impacts and equity issues in transport: an introduction. Journal of Transport Geography 21, 1–3. https://doi.org/10.1016/j.jtrangeo.2012.01.032.

Lusk, J.L., Norwood, F.B., 2011. Animal welfare economics. Applied Economic Perspectives and Policy 33 (4), 463–483.

Macharis, C., Bernardini, A., 2015. Reviewing the use of multi-criteria decision analysis for the evaluation of transport projects: time for a multi-actor approach. Transport Policy 37, 177–186. https://doi.org/10.1016/J.TRANPOL.2014.11.002.

Mackie, P., Worsley, T., Eliasson, J., 2014. Transport appraisal revisited. Research in Transportation Economics 47, 3–18.

Manaugh, K., Badami, M., El-Geneidy, A., 2015. Integrating social equity into urban transportation planning: A critical evaluation of equity objectives and measures in transportation plans in North America. Transport Policy (37), 167–176.

Mardani, A., Zavadskas, E.K., Khalifah, Z., Jusoh, A., Nor, K.M.D., 2016. Multiple criteria decision-making techniques in transportation systems: a systematic review of the state of the art literature. Transport 31 (3), 359–385. https://doi.org/10.3846/16484142.2015.1121517.

Miccoli, S., Finucci, F., Murro, R., 2014. A monetary measure of inclusive goods: the concept of deliberative appraisal in the context of urban agriculture. Sustainability (Switzerland) 6 (12), 9007–9026. https://doi.org/10.3390/su6129007.

Millennium Ecosystem Assestment, 2005. Ecosystems and human well-being. Ecosystems 5. https://doi.org/https://doi.org/10.1196/annals.1439.003.

Mottee, L.K., Howitt, R., 2018. Follow-up and social impact assessment (SIA) in urban transport-infrastructure projects: insights from the Parramatta rail link. Australian Planner 55 (1), 46–56. https://doi.org/10.1080/07293682.2018.1506496.

Mottee, L.K., Arts, J., Vanclay, F., Howitt, R., Miller, F., 2020. Limitations of technical approaches to transport planning practice in two cases: social issues as a critical component of urban projects. Plan. Theory Pract. 21 (1), 39–57. https://doi.org/10.1080/14649357.2019.1696980.

Mouter, N., 2017. Attitudes of dutch politicians towards cost-benefit analysis. Transport Policy 54, 1–10.

Mouter, N. (Ed.), 2021a. New Methods, Reflections and Application Domains in Transport Appraisal. Elsevier. Retrieved from https://www.sciencedirect.com/bookseries/advances-in-transport-policy-and-planning/vol/7/suppl/C.

Mouter, N. (Ed.), 2021b. Standard Transport Appraisal Methods. Elsevier. Retrieved from https://www.sciencedirect.com/bookseries/advances-in-transport-policy-and-planning/vol/6/suppl/C.

Mouter, N., 2021c. Willingness to allocate public budget and Participatory Value Evaluation. Chapter 4. In: New methods, reflections and application domains in transport appraisal. Series: Advances in Transport Policy and Planning (Vol. 7). Elsevier, Amsterdam.

Mouter, N., Chorus, C.G., 2016. Value of time: A citizen perspective. Transportation Research Part A 91, 317–329.

Mouter, N., Annema, J.A., Van Wee, B., 2013. Attitudes towards the role of cost-benefit analysis in the decision-making process for spatial-infrastructure projects: A dutch case study. Transportation Research Part A 58, 1–18.

Mouter, N., Annema, J.A., Van Wee, B., 2015. Managing the insolvable limitations of cost-benefit analysis: Results of an interview based study. Transportation 42 (2), 277–302.

Mouter, N., van Cranenburgh, S., van Wee, G.P., 2017. Do individuals have different preferences as consumer and citizen? The trade-off between travel time and safety. Transportation Research Part A 106, 333–349.

Mouter, N., van Cranenburgh, S., van Wee, G.P., 2018. The consumer-citizen duality: Ten reasons why citizens prefer safety and drivers desire speed. Accident Analysis & Prevention 121, 53–63.

Mouter, N., Ojeda Cabral, M., Dekker, T., van Cranenburgh, S., 2019. The value of travel time, noise pollution, recreation and biodiversity: A social choice valuation perspective. Research in Transportation Economics 76.

Mouter, N., Koster, P.R., Dekker, T., 2021. Contrasting the recommendations of participatory value evaluation and cost-benefit analysis in the context of urban mobility investments. Transportation Research Part A: Policy and Practice 144, 54–73.

Murray, L., 2011. Deliberative research for deliberative policy making: Creating and recreating evidence in transport policy. Social Policy and Society 10 (4), 459–470. https://doi.org/10.1017/S1474746411000212.

Nahmias-Biran, B.H., Martens, K., Shiftan, Y., 2017. Integrating equity in transportation project assessment: a philosophical exploration and its practical implications. Transport Reviews 37 (2), 192–210. https://doi.org/10.1080/01441647.2017.1276604.

Næss, P., 2006. Cost-benefit analyses of transportation investments. Journal of Critical Realism 5 (1), 32–60. https://doi.org/10.1558/jocr.v5i1.32.

Ness, B., Urbel-Piirsalu, E., Anderberg, S., Olsson, L., 2007. Categorising tools for sustainability assessment. Ecol. Econ. 60 (3), 498–508. https://doi.org/10.1016/j.ecolecon.2006.07.023.

Nicolaisen, M.S., Olesen, M., Olesen, K., 2017. Vision vs. Evaluation - Case studies of light rail planning in Denmark. European Journal of Spatial Development 65.

Nyerges, T., Aguirre, R.W., 2011. Public participation in analytic-deliberative decision making: Evaluating a large-group online field experiment. Annals of the Association of American Geographers. 101 (3), 561–586. https://doi.org/10.1080/00045608.2011.563669. Routledge.

Pereira, R.H.M., Schwanen, T., Banister, D., 2017. Distributive justice and equity in transportation. Transport Reviews 37 (2), 170–191. https://doi.org/10.1080/01441647.2016.1257660.

Persky, J., 2001. Retrospectives: Cost-benefit analysis and the classical creed. Journal of Economic Perspectives 15 (4), 199–208.

Quigley, R., Thornley, L., 2011. Literature Review on Community Cohesion and Community Severance: Definitions and Indicators for Transport Planning and Monitoring. Quigley and Watts Ltd, Wellington. (June), 1–52. Retrieved from https://www.nzta.govt.nz/assets/resources/community-cohesion-and-community-severance/docs/community-cohesion-and-community-severance.pdf%0Ahttp://www.nzta.govt.nz/resources/community-cohesion-and-community-severance/docs/community-cohesion-and-community-s.

Raymond, C.M., et al., 2014. In: Comparing instrumental and deliberative paradigms underpinning the assessment of social values for cultural ecosystem services'. Ecological Economics (Vol. 107), Elsevier B.V, pp.145–156. https://doi.org/10.1016/j.ecolecon.2014.07.033.

Raz, J., 1986. The morality of freedom. Clarendon, Oxford, U.K.

Saarikoski, H:, Mustajoki, J., Barton, D.N., Geneletti, D., Langemeyer, J., Gomez-Baggethun, E., Santos, R., 2016. Multi-criteria decision analysis and cost-benefit analysis: comparing alternative frameworks for integrated valuation of ecosystem services. Ecosyst. Serv. 22, 238–249. https://doi.org/10.1016/J.ECOSER.2016.10.014.

Sagaris, L., 2018. Citizen participation for sustainable transport: lessons for change from Santiago and Temuco. Chile. Research in Transportation Economics 69 (April), 402–410. https://doi.org/10.1016/j.retrec.2018.05.001.

Sagoff, M., 1988. The economy of the earth. Cambridge University press, Cambridge.

Schweigert, F.J., 2010. Strengthening citizenship through deliberative polling. J. Community Pract. 18 (1), 19–39. https://doi.org/10.1080/10705421003761223.

Sen, A., 1995. Environmental evaluation and social choice: Contingent valuation and the market analogy. The Japanese Economic Review 46 (1), 23–37.

Seo, K., Golub, A., Kuby, M., 2014. Combined impacts of highways and light rail transit on residential property values: A spatial hedonic price model for Phoenix, Arizona. Journal of Transport Geography 41, 53–62.

Shortall, R., 2020. Deliberative appraisal methods. In: Advances in Transport Policy and Planning (1st ed., Vol. 7). Elsevier Inc. https://doi.org/10.1016/bs.atpp.2020.07.003.

Shortall, R.S., 2021. Deliberative Appraisal Methods. Chapter 3. In: New methods, reflections and application domains in transport appraisal. Series: Advances in Transport Policy and Planning, 7. Elsevier, Amsterdam.

Summers, J.K., Smith, L.M., 2014. The role of social and intergenerational equity in making changes in human well-being sustainable. Ambio 43 (6), 718–728. https://doi.org/10.1007/s13280-013-0483-6.

Sunstein, C.R., 1994. Incommensurability and valuation in law. Michigan Law Review 92, 779.
Szabó, Z., 2011. Reducing protest responses by deliberative monetary valuation: Improving the validity of biodiversity valuation. Ecological Economics 72, 37–44.
Te Brömmelstroet, M., Nikolaeva, A., Glaser, M., Nicolaisen, M.S., Chan, C., 2017. Travelling together alone and alone together: Mobility and potential exposure to diversity. Applied Mobilities 2 (1), 1–15.
TfL, 2014. Silvertown Tunnel: Social Impact Assessment. October, pp. 1–21.
Tresch, R.W., 2014. Public Finance: A Normative Theory, third edition. Elsevier, NY.
Van Wee, B., Börjesson, M., 2015. How to make CBA more suitable for evaluating cycling policies. Transport Policy 44, 117–124.
van Wee, B., 2012. How suitable is CBA for the ex-ante evaluation of transport projects and policies? A discussion from the perspective of ethics. Transport Policy 19 (1), 1–7. https://doi.org/10.1016/J.TRANPOL.2011.07.001.
van Wee, B., Hagenzieker, M., Wijnen, W., 2014. Which indicators to include in the ex ante evaluations of the safety effects of policy options? Gaps in evaluations and a discussion based on an ethical perspective. Transport Policy 31, 19–26. https://doi.org/10.1016/J.TRANPOL.2013.11.002.
Vanclay, F., 2003. International principles for social impact assessment. Impact Assessment and Project Appraisal 21 (1), 5–12. https://doi.org/10.3152/147154603781766491.
Vanclay, F., Esteves, A.M., Group, C. I, Aucamp, I., Services, C, Franks, D.M., 2015. Social Impact Assessment: Guidance for Assessing and Managing the Social Impacts of Projects. International Association for Impact Assessment (April), Acquisition, L., Acquisition, L., Resettlement, I).
Vassallo, J.M., Bueno, P.C., 2021. Chapter two - sustainability assessment of transport policies, plans and projects. In: Mouter, N. (Ed.), New Methods, Reflections and Application Domains in Transport Appraisal (Vol. 7). Academic Press, pp. 9–50. https://doi.org/https://doi.org/https://doi.org/10.1016/bs.atpp.2020.07.006.
Vatn, A., 2009. An institutional analysis of methods for environmental appraisal. Ecological Economics 68 (8), 2207–2215.
Walker, L., Curl, A., 2021. Social and distributional impact assessment in transport policy. International Encyclopedia of Transportation, 361–367.
Ward, E.J., Dimitriou, H.T., Dean, M., 2016. Theory and background of multi-criteria analysis: toward a policy-led approach to mega transport infrastructure project appraisal. Research in Transportation Economics 58, 21–45. https://doi.org/10.1016/j.retrec.2016.08.003.
Wegner, G., Pascual, U., 2011. Cost-benefit analysis in the context of ecosystem services for human well-being: A multidisciplinary critique. In: Global Environmental Change (Vol. 21), Pergamon, pp. 492–504. https://doi.org/10.1016/J.GLOENVCHA.2010.12.008>.
Whitmarsh, L., Haxeltine, A., Wietschel, M., 2007. Sustainable transport visions: expert and non-expert stakeholder perspectives on sustainable transport. In: International Conference on Whole Life Urban Sustainability and Its Assessment.

CHAPTER TEN

Innovative field research methodologies for more inclusive transport planning: Review and prospect

Gina Porter* and Claire Dungey
Durham University, Durham, United Kingdom
*Corresponding author: e-mail address: r.e.porter@durham.ac.uk

Contents

Abstract

This chapter focuses on innovative field research methodologies developed over the last few decades that have the potential to support and promote more inclusive transport planning. The review covers methodologies that have been tried out in the Global North and in the Global South, with specific reference to applications in the context of mobilities/transport research and policy, and considers the potential for future applications with specific reference to the Global South. In the Global South transport planning still typically takes the form of a technocratic exercise conducted by a "tyranny of experts," national and international, whose enthrallment with automobility may severely impede their appreciation of the mobility needs of the public they are appointed to serve (as Klopp and Cavoli, 2018: 105, citing Easterly, 2013, note with reference to African city planning). The everyday experiences, perceptions and needs of the poor, notably slum residents, and of wider vulnerable groups (women, children, older people, the infirm) are often not only marginalized but stigmatized (particularly through association of low income areas with criminality), both by government and private sector

Advances in Transport Policy and Planning, Volume 8
ISSN 2543-0009
https://doi.org/10.1016/bs.atpp.2021.06.006
Copyright © 2021 Elsevier Inc.
All rights reserved.

planning partners. For more socially equitable mobility solutions to be adopted in the cities of the Global South, broader application of field research methodologies that can engage effectively with a wide spectrum of potential transport users (including marginalized groups) is needed. Significant quantities of sound empirical evidence from such research will be required before the majority of policymakers, urban planners and city managers/personnel start to fully engage with the social dimensions of transport planning. Whether the "new normal" following the COVID-19 pandemic will provide the requisite opportunities to build such engagement currently remains uncertain.

Keywords: In-depth interviews, Focus groups, Participatory action research, Peer research, Mobility diaries, Ethics

1. Introduction

The transport, mobility, and accessibility needs and concerns of low-income communities and vulnerable populations (women, children, older people, people with a disability) are still rarely adequately considered when transport plans are prepared, whether they reside in the Global North or South (Gorman et al., 2019; Kett et al., 2020; Porter and Turner, 2019; Porter et al., 2020; Uteng and Turner, 2019). Where travel data are collected, the focus is commonly restricted to commuting patterns but these do not represent the diversity of travel needs faced by these groups. State political interests and associated resource allocations are certainly a major factor in such neglect (Parnell and Pieterse, 2016) but the failure of conventional transport field research methodologies has also played a part. Transport planning practice is still dominated typically by engineers in both Global North and South. In African urban contexts Klopp and Cavoli (2018): 105, citing Easterly (2013) describe how, so often, they are tied up in a planning imaginary that is dominated by a "tyranny of experts" (national and international) and prioritizes the promotion of automobility.

Field research methodologies commonly utilized in transport planning still continue to revolve around large-scale quantitative surveys, with travel pattern surveys typically forming the central focus of investigation (see for instance Fouracre et al., 2006; Richardson et al., 1995), albeit now generally set within a broader transport system inventory and the likely inclusion of some land use and socio-demographic data. Such large-scale surveys of current travel patterns are deficient because they only chart the movements of those who are able to travel—they give no indication of the unmet needs of those unable to travel in the current dispensation, nor of the everyday challenges that transport users (even more advantaged users) may face as they endeavor to reach work/livelihoods, services such as health care and education and other places important to their well-being. Moreover, capture of those personal emotions that can be key to the shaping of transport experiences, decision-making and routines tends to be entirely missing from this type of approach: yet, as Sheller (2007: pp. 176, 179) observes with reference to car use, "the driving body" is "an assemblage of… embodied dispositions and social practices"…"there is a crucial conjunction between motion and emotion, movement and feeling." By contrast, qualitative research methods have significant potential to expose not only the underlying transport-related issues and unmet needs that more vulnerable people may face in their daily lives, but the impacts these may have in terms of emotional well-being and likely life trajectories.

This chapter focuses on a range of qualitative approaches, while recognizing that well-designed mixed methods approaches, where qualitative and quantitative field research activities are carefully combined to complement each other, can contribute to an even richer methodological repertoire with the potential to add even greater strength to investigations. Interestingly, many of the more innovative qualitative field research methodologies discussed in this chapter have their origins in development work conducted in the Global South that takes a participatory approach (Chambers, 1994). Aimed at giving marginalized people a voice, the impetus for this work often came from third sector practitioners whose remit was centered on supporting and engaging with vulnerable populations. Transfer of participatory research approaches to the Global North has often followed at a significantly later date (Korf and Oughton, 2006; see also Schwanen, 2018). It might thus be anticipated that the transport sector in the Global South would be leading the Global North in the adoption of qualitative approaches. However, this has rarely been the case, at least in part because so many Global South current heads of profession were trained c. 25–30 years ago in the Global North and remain firmly entrenched in and committed to the ways of working they learned at that time. Disturbingly, many of the current transport training programs in the Global North that are patronized by students from the Global South maintain a focus largely on quantitative methods and motorized flow.

We start the discussion with a brief introduction to static interviewing methods, notably in-depth one-to-one interviews and focus groups, both of which techniques have been used by social scientists for many decades in qualitative enquiry, including in transport research. We then move to more recently adopted innovative approaches that may offer added potential for transport planning investigations, starting with a review of basic mobile "go along" methods. The earliest versions typically involved pedestrian-focused studies, conducted by researchers on foot. More recently, such work has extended to research conducted by traveling with passengers on motorized vehicles (both on public transport and, to a lesser extent, in private cars). Whatever the transport mode, there is a tendency to draw heavily on the techniques that are commonly termed participant observation (Dewalt and Dewalt, 2002). Although long central to anthropological investigation, participant observation as a technique is still rarely part of the repertoire of transport researchers (though see Jiron et al., 2020 for a recent collaboration between transport studies researchers and anthropologists in Chile).

This is followed by a discussion of techniques which involve the researcher taking a step back from immediate field engagement as data collection moves more directly into the hands of research participants themselves. These methods including participatory photography (where the traveler takes photos of their journeys, then reviews these and associated experiences with the researcher) and broader "co-investigation" approaches where community researchers are trained in research techniques such as in-depth interviewing of their peers and the production of personal mobility diaries in the communities in which they reside. The discussion then moves to Participatory Action Research approaches [PAR] that can involve making specific interventions in the mobility/transport arena and assessing their impact. The penultimate sections of the chapter consider digital approaches to participatory research and how these are expanding in response to the challenges to face-to-face research imposed by COVID-19. In-depth interactions with vulnerable groups, whatever the research mode, almost inevitably raise complex ethical questions—these form the focus of a final section.

2. Stationary researcher-led field studies

Mobile methodologies have gained popularity in recent years (part of the new mobilities paradigm promoted particularly by Sheller and Urry's, 2006 persuasive work) and are discussed in Section 3 of this chapter. However, it is important to also consider what can be gained from traditional stationary *in-depth interviews* with vulnerable individuals, and with other potential stakeholders, if only as a preamble to subsequent mobile investigations (and in combination with the careful observation of context that should be an essential complement to all transport/mobility data collection). Such "sit-down" interviews are often conducted when travelers are waiting at transport hubs, for instance at bus or rail stations; some take place within respondents' homes.

In the in-depth interview we move away from the formal survey questionnaire toward structured and semi-structured interviews in which, typically, the respondent's active participation is elicited as a means to enabling intensive exploration of themes. The semi-structured interview using a checklist often proves particularly valuable as a first stage in understanding unmet mobility needs and mobility constraints because it encourages open conversation and the potential to access issues that the researcher has not anticipated. Following standard interviewing preliminaries (reasons for the interview, consent form with a statement regarding anonymity, an initial collection of relevant basic information about the respondent such as age, gender, occupation etc., agreements regarding the mode of recording the discussion) the researcher typically works with a check-list interview guide of perhaps 10 key questions built around one or two major themes. Often the starting point will be the respondent's current daily travel patterns and practices, key accessibility needs, everyday mobility challenges and unmet needs. The checklist is likely to change over time as new key questions and themes emerge.

To provide a few examples, a mix of in-depth interviews was used in conjunction with edited videotape of five different traffic conditions in one UK street in an early study by Hine (1996) to more fully assess the impact of traffic on pedestrian behavior. In a more specifically political study, Legacy (2016) offers an example of the application of in-depth interviewing, accompanied by social media, commercial media and policy document analysis, in Melbourne, Australia. This was used to chart how campaigners responded to a politicized (automobile focused) urban transport plan, opposing a 6 km inner-city road tunnel plan that was about to be implemented by elected officials without public consultation. Although individual personal narratives may be discounted by policy makers, in research of this kind the compilation of evidence from a diversity of individuals, such that the sum of voices is greater than the individual parts, may be more difficult to ignore.

Other examples demonstrate the potential of static interviewing for exploring people-centered transport issues in low-income country contexts. A number of these are specifically focused on gender issues in transport, a topic which has rarely been central to transport planning activities. An early city study by Seedat et al. (2006) used just a small set of in-depth interviews (with 10 young women students in Johannesburg and 9 in Delhi) to demonstrate, very effectively, the value of such small-scale investigations in highlighting the need for more integrated transport planning and crime prevention and safety interventions. Sadly, such detailed focus on women's walking experiences in urban Africa remains surprisingly rare and the widespread harassment to which Seedat et al. (2006) refer remains a significant factor inhibiting women's mobility in both cities.

There is also remarkably little information regarding women's experiences of working in the transport sector in low income country contexts. Here Naysmith and Rubincam's (2012) semi-structured interviews in South Africa with just (5) female truck drivers (all in person) and (35) road freight employers (some interviewed by phone), show the valuable insights such exploratory work can provide regarding the constraints women face in the sector. In this case the research led to subsequent production of a film and multi-media exhibition. More recently, a mix of informal and semi-structured interviews was utilized in research with drivers, passengers and industry stakeholder interviews (along with GPS and surveys) by Evans et al. (2018) in work to understand the informal motorcycle taxi businesses of Kampala (an issue now of widespread importance to transport planners across much of sub-Saharan Africa).

Semi-structured interviews can also be used to build a more nuanced understanding of travel behavior through mobility biographies. In a development of the standard life history approach, these offer an opportunity to explore, through narrative-interpretative inquiries, how people's everyday mobilities may change over the life-course. Plyushteva and Schwanen (2018) demonstrate the value of this approach through in-depth studies with women who are long-term residents in Manila and London. Travel behavior is thus examined with specific reference to the relational settings and associated negotiations in which journeys emerge and to other factors of contextual change, facilitating conditions, intrinsic motivations, and the interactions between structural factors and human agency (see also Uteng and Turner, 2019). Taking a slightly different approach Vecchio (2020) uses 20 semi-structured interviews built round three themes (subjects; valued activities; mobility practice) to build micro-stories of people's mobile lives in peripheral settlements of Bogota. He suggests these stories, which emphasize the interdependencies of mobility with others (principally family members), can provide a potential first input for the design of urban mobility policy in the neighborhoods where they were collected. Through such an approach small-scale mobility intervention experiments might be introduced, for instance, thus helping overcome the "difficulty of representing marginal areas of a city and the structural limitations of tools such as Origin-Destination surveys" (which pick up basic trips by individuals but will not identify the challenges, tactics and relational networks that may enhance or impede mobility).

Focus groups are commonly used as a complement to in-depth interviewing in the participatory research repertoire. Their hallmark is the explicit use of group interaction to produce data and insights: as such they can offer a valuable complement to participant observation and individual interviews. With vulnerable groups they may also offer the advantage of being less intimidating than a one-to-one meeting with an outsider and perhaps enable participants to feel they can keep more control of proceedings (Langevang, 2007). With around 6–10 participants per group, common practice is to start with a relatively homogeneous group (especially regarding social class, maybe also gender) and pursue a relatively structured discussion with high moderator involvement. Focus groups discussions (FGDs) may suffer some potential disadvantages: as with in-depth individual interviews there is the concern that, given such small numbers, these produce essentially personal narratives that may be discounted by policy makers, especially where FGD participants belong to marginalized groups. Also, participation may be restricted where people defer to authority, especially dominant and controlling FGD members, or in situations where public participation in the local context is weak. Sensitive material is usually better handled in individual interviews.

Eleven two-hour professionally facilitated FGDs were central to Lucas's research in Tshwane Metropolitan Region (Lucas, 2011) aimed at exploring issues of transport and social exclusion. This research, commissioned by the South African Department of Transportation, brought together sets of 8–10 people in a group for 2h. Following a series of prior field visits and conversations with local people, a topic guide was produced for the FGDs. The participants, who were selected to represent a range of different socially disadvantaged groups and settlement types, were asked first to talk about wider concerns about the areas in which they live, and this then led on to talk about physical access to services, their transport problems and how this affected their lives. Lucas' work demonstrates the potential of FGDs in this development context very effectively, but also points to the vital connectivities between transport and other sectors of government that have to be addressed if such research is to achieve the social inclusion to which it aspires: needless to say, this is still very far from its target globally.

Ibeas et al. (2011) suggest a slight variation on the FGD, the Mega Focus Group [MFG], operated along the same lines as a standard focus group but with 40–60 participants. They describe the potential of the MFG as a first stage in promoting citizen involvement in sustainable mobility planning: the MFG is used to garner preliminary opinions of public and private transport that can help determine the feasibility of promoting more sustainable means of transport—public owned bicycles—as an alternative to private cars and standard buses. They apply this approach in Santander, Spain, where it also proved an important tool for the subsequent identification of interest groups for incorporating in smaller standard size focus groups where specific issues related to the adoption of bicycles could be tackled more effectively. The information they obtained encouragingly became incorporated into the mobility plan for the city, involving the management of the public bicycle system, design of a bike lane network and readjusting of some bus line frequencies. This study shows how MFGs offer an opportunity to extend citizen involvement and give a firmer sense of local community insights. Moreover, since it is likely to be harder than with an FGD for the researcher team setting up the meeting to oversee the composition of the group as a whole, this could bring benefits in terms of perceived independence of findings. However, managing large groups for the purposes of ascertaining key community issues can be challenging, and there is still the potential for powerful voices to manipulate outcomes.

Focus groups with a small number of participants can also enable valuable static *participatory mapping exercises*. Although such mapping typically started life as NGO-led rural exercises in the Global South, it also has relevance in urban contexts globally, for instance helping with preliminary identification of parts of the neighborhood with difficult surfaces for people using wheelchairs to negotiate, locations that women find particularly hazardous to travel through at certain times of day or night, or road crossing points where children fear traffic dangers en route to school. Group work during the mapping process encourages discussion and debate which, if observed and noted by the researcher[s], can add valuable additional information beyond the map produced. Stewart (2017) shows how a combination of focus groups and recent developments in accessibility modeling are opening new possibilities to improve participation of local communities in accessibility-based transport planning through digital interactive tools and collaborative scenario building (Pereira et al., 2018).

3. Mobile "go along" methods with direct researcher participation

Mobile studies, in which the researcher accompanies or follows the respondent can be traced back to the mid-20th century (notably work in US urban planning by Lynch, 1960). They have gained popularity in recent years, promoted by Sheller and Urry's (2006) mobilities work and the impetus that the "mobilities turn" has given to new thinking in transport studies (Porter et al., 2017: 41). Watts and Urry, 2008, p. 867 describe these approaches under the broad heading "mobile ethnography," since they involve "travelling with people and things, participating in their continual shift through time, place and relations with others." Mobile studies are often focused beyond transport per se, for instance around understanding family environments (Walker et al., 2014), physical or mental health (Carpiano, 2009; Copelton, 2010; Doughty, 2013), the significance of place and power (Palmgren, 2018 on walks in shopping malls) or for broad city planning and urban renewal projects (Kowalewski and Barlomiejski, 2020). Participant observation tends to be even more key to these mobile interviews than it is in in-depth interviewing and focus group discussions—the researcher's noting of their own sights, sounds and feelings can contribute vital contextual understanding.

Walking interviews: In inter-disciplinary mobility-focused studies conducted with children in Ghana, Malawi and South Africa (Porter et al., 2010a,b, 2017) the research emphasis was on exploring the transport and mobility issues that the children faced in their rural and peri-urban communities, but also aimed to understand the wider context in which young people's mobile lives played out and the interrelationships between movement on the journey and the moorings from which that movement was undertaken (Cresswell, 2010). The approach is described as mobile ethnography since it combined interview with some of the contextual insights of traditional ethnographic method, examining participants' interpretations of their context while experiencing those contexts personally (Porter et al., 2010a,b, Porter et al., 2017:41–46; see also Carpiano, 2009). Walks conducted with children traveling home from school—sometimes 5 km distant—in the study sites in all three countries (where the teams had worked since 2006) demonstrated the important benefits of the walking interview for understanding young people's lives and the diversity of mobility constraints they face (such as exhaustion following pedestrian load-carrying of heavy produce for family members before the walk to school, or fear of graveyards and the supernatural, robbery and rape).

Despite the evidently unequal power relationship of adult researchers, the researchers in this study found they could more easily build rapport with the child respondents [aged c. 9–18 years] than had been possible in static contexts. Shy children did not need to make eye contact as they walked side-by-side with the academic research team, while silences were natural when traveling across uneven ground (giving time for considered reflections or responses to our questions). Moving from recording of observations associated with walking exercises to planning decisions on the ground (whether in transport or wider settlement/area planning) is not straightforward, but getting a local councilor along to participate in one of these walking groups in Eastern Cape, South Africa, as the children trekked to their homes in a remote village c. 5 km from school—a route incorporating a long, lonely hilltop climb—may have contributed to the subsequent government decisions to build a new road to this settlement, and the siting of a new school in the village itself (Porter et al., 2017).

Walking as a participatory methodology for transport-focused research is particularly apposite when researching the mobility of more vulnerable people since these tend to be among the groups who, of necessity, walk because they cannot afford either personal transport equipment or fares on public transport. Moreover, since walking produces a shared rhythm of movement (Lee and Ingold, 2006) it encourages conversation, companionability and the sharing of understandings. As Ingold and Vergunst (2008), p. 1 observe, "social relations ... are not enacted *in situ* but are paced out along the ground."

Walking as a transport research tool seems to have mostly emerged rather later in urban than in rural contexts. Hodgson's (2012) research in Leeds, UK, with just 29 respondents, which included walking round their neighborhood and emphasized social practices of walking, was important in drawing attention to the clear disjuncture with planners' provision and policy in this context. In this case, policy was found to focus principally on infrastructure design, not the needs of walkers or the interactions between walking and sociality, or women's fear of attack.

Mcfarlane and Silver (2017) use a slight variant of the walking interview, what they term "follow-along participant observation," with six participants from a low-income neighborhood in Kampala to explore constraints on urban life. They spent days with these six participants, as they navigated the city, both observing them from a distance and sometimes making observations from close by. Observations at traffic jams and around route choices, for instance, helped them build insights into the textures of city life. A local photographer provided an accompanying photo-documentary. Combined with interviews, focus groups and workshops, this approach—focused as it is on social infrastructure and its wider connectivities to the city and the state—clearly has the potential to feed into urban and transport planning activities.

Such walking interview methods will not suit everyone, as Castrodale (2018) shows with reference to research with people with a disability in Canadian university locations and Porter et al. (2015) discovered when working with older people on a mobilities study in Tanzania. In Castrodale's study, respondents refer to accessibility concerns including physical barriers like steep steps, but there are also attitudinal barriers around feelings of heightened exposure to surveillance and likely stigmatization. In the Tanzania case, the older people peer researchers said firstly that the prospect of walking would be too daunting physically for their elderly respondents but also made the point that such walks would be difficult for them personally. This made sense in the rural context of farm compounds and unmade roads where the residents they were interviewing lived and also given the age group of both the researchers and respondents concerned. Nonetheless, walking interviews have potential in many situations not only to help address the impact of power imbalances between respondent and researcher and identify key elements necessary for improved pedestrian travel planning, but can also provide a valuable mnemonic device, prompting the respondent with reminders about points and issues that may have been overlooked in a previous static interview.

"*Ride alongs*," that take accompanied travel by researchers or their equipment into the motorized transport arena are less common. While these are rarely conducted formally by transport professionals or drawn on in transport studies, they have the potential to provide significant insights unavailable by other means, because of the in-depth participant observation that tends to be their hallmark. An early example comes from work by Watts and Urry (2008). They conducted what they term a "thin ethnography" of 12 timetabled train and bus journeys in the UK: this included high-speed train lines, rural and urban buses, and express coach services. One of the two traveled on the same timetabled journey five times (either on sequential days or on the same day every week), and made notes, photographs, and short videos over 260 + hours of travel time. By repeating the same journey, they experienced similar concerns to regular commuters on these routes. The timetable remains, they argue, "a crucial actor in the journey (often present to the passenger through WAP (wireless application protocol), wi-fi, text messaging, and other mobile data services, as well as in printouts and paper)" (Watts and Urry, 2008, p. 868). At the same time they note that travel time as a passenger experience extends beyond the clock time of the timetable: "Saving travel time is not necessarily a matter of reducing the minutes between departure and arrival, but can involve attending to how the social and material practices of travel compress passenger travel time." There are resonances here with current debates in the UK around travel time and the planned HS2 train route.

Bissell (2009), principally taking an autoethnographic approach centered on participant observation, but also including interviews with other travelers and photography, draws on his experiences of 116 rail journeys in the UK to point out some of the visual aspects of the journey that are important for transport services planning. This includes factors such as the security associated with being able to see one's luggage and evaluate and avoid what are perceived as potentially unpleasant (e.g., inebriated) or even dangerous fellow passengers. His findings suggest the value of open plan carriages without dividers and seating arrangements, including low backed seats that allow surveillance, rather than walled compartments. More recently, Middleton and Byles (2019) have developed a self-directed video methodology using GoPro cameras and go-alongs in their research with visually impaired young people across London.

In lower-income countries there are even fewer examples of studies focused on transport services taking an ethnographic approach. D'Hondt (2009), through participant observation on c. 500 journeys on minibuses, explores the interactions that occur during drop-offs between minibus operators and the commuter passengers who frequent them on city-wide journeys in Dar es Salaam. Xiao (2018) uses a distinctly auto-ethnographic approach in an equally challenging context: the *danfo* (minibus) system and other transport systems in Lagos. His work shows that the experiential dimension of urban transport merits closer scrutiny. Self-narrative (combined with open-ended interviews with other users, conductors and drivers) can help demonstrate the complexities faced both by passengers and drivers as they navigate urban mobilities that cross the formal and informal sectors in Lagos. His narrative identifies, for instance, some of the major problems that passenger face and the tactics they employ. Even at major bus terminals and stops, they typically wait outside without shelter or amenities (which encourages people who can afford to do so to pay a higher fare to avoid walking or a long wait in bad weather).

In a current research project with young women transport users and transport employees[a] led by the first author, accompanied journeys in Tunis undertaken by a female member of our team with transport workers (mostly with women ticket sellers on the buses), have highlighted the stresses they face in this work. One interview took place with a woman driver in her early 1930s working on the city's light rail metro system as she drove her tram out from the city centre.[b] This brought to the fore a series of security incidents and concerns during the journey, which took the train into one of Tunis's lowest income neighborhoods. It is unlikely that we could have picked up the strength and nuances of her concerns around specific stretches of line and tunnel in a static interview.

Other studies have focused on "go-alongs" in personal vehicles. Research in which a respondent is accompanied in their personal vehicle by the researchers' video and audio recorder allow Harada and Waitt (2013) to better understand transport choices (in the context of climate change) and explore unforeseen aspects of driving in a small Australian city. They use—and specifically compare—mobile methods with conventional semi-structured interviews, emphasizing the value of ride-alongs for understanding the way participants think about their car and pick up emotional registers and bodily reactions.

Once we move to cycles or motorcycles designed for a sole rider, participatory approaches directly engaging the researcher or their recording equipment as passenger/accompanying rider are more challenging and tend to encourage a focus on GPS tracking, sometimes with follow-up stationary interviews (for instance, Pooley, 2013 for cycles in the UK; Evans et al., 2018 for motorcycles in Kampala). GPS mapping has also been central to producing public transport maps in Nairobi, with both policy and planning impact (albeit hard-won). In this case the research took a collaborative mapping approach in which local students traveled matatu routes with GPS-enabled cell phones, supported by (presumably stationary) interviews and focus group discussions with drivers (Klopp and Cavoli, 2018).

[a] see https://transportandyouthemploymentinafrica.com

[b] This was arranged with her employer and including approval of both employer and driver for a video interview during the journey.

4. Co-investigation practices that enable direct participation by research participants

There are many contexts in mobilities research where direct participation by the researcher is constrained and it is necessary to step back from direct field engagement. We have pointed above to some of the practical difficulties of accompanying moving research subjects, but there are often other impediments that work against sound data collection, not least locations where it may be difficult for non-local researchers (even if resident in the same city) to obtain adequate information. This is likely to be particularly the case in very low-income neighborhoods where incomers are viewed with suspicion and field work can possibly expose the researcher to hostility, even violence. Work with vulnerable groups such as children or older people may also be constrained because of perceived power differences and associated suspicions. In these circumstances it can be far more effective to move primary data collection directly into the hands of research participants themselves.

Participatory photography methods such as Photovoice have often been used in vulnerable communities because they can offer such a powerful tool for participants to present their own view of the world. Photovoice is a visual research methodology that provides participants with cameras to help them to document, reflect upon, and communicate issues of concern; it tends to be focused on promoting social change. There are many good examples of participatory photography where study respondents have taken photos at stopping points or during their journeys, then reviewed these and associated context with the researcher to help build a clear picture of their travel and transport experiences. Ward et al. (2015) use this approach to explore the transport experiences of young Maori, Pacific and Asian non-drivers in Auckland, New Zealand, and their ideas for infrastructure improvements. Subsequently Ward et al. (2015) use photovoice to examine the influence of transport on the well-being of (16–18 years) teenagers schooling in another city in New Zealand (Invercargill). Here, given the high cost of licensing and driving a car, most of the students were happy to walk and saw this as contributing to their wellbeing (in some cases despite relatively lengthy treks and common traffic safety concerns). In similar vein, Bowles (2017) teaches women porters in Accra, Ghana, how to take photographs with a 35 mm pre-loaded camera and demonstrates the power of their photo-narratives to throw light on embodied transport practices that are unlikely to be encountered by or considered in conventional transport planning, yet whose work is critical to the movement of goods in the constrained locations where they operate. However, it is important to note potential ethical and safety issues associated with participatory photography, particularly the importance of ensuring participants receive adequate training around potential security issues and the crucial importance of obtaining clear (preferably written) consent before they take photographs of individuals in their community. Taking pictures can be dangerous for the photographer, even for those who are long-term residents in a neighborhood, for instance if illegal activities are being photographed. Issues around photography are further discussed in Section 8.

Peer research: A broader community "co-investigation" approach has been used extensively in a series of African mobility/transport studies with vulnerable groups led by the first author. In this approach, working in collaboration with local universities and local and international NGOs, residents in the study community are trained in research techniques so that they can conduct in-depth interviews with their peers and also produce personal mobility diaries (Porter, 2016); for work with children see (Porter and Abane, 2008; Porter et al., 2010a,b, 2017); with older people see (Porter et al., 2013, 2014, 2015; Mulongo et al., 2019); with young unemployed women see https://transportandyouthemploymentinafrica.com/

In each of the studies listed above, people were recruited from the study community concerned (often via NGOs already working there): 70 young people aged 11–19 years were recruited from sites across Ghana, Malawi and South Africa for the child mobility study; 12 older people from one village in Kibaha district, Tanzania; 18 young unemployed women in an ongoing project in low-income areas of Abuja, Cape Town and Tunis city regions. In each case the peer researchers undertook a quite intensive 1-week training, incorporating desk and field exercises, then worked independently with people of similar age (though not in every case the same gender) in their communities over a period of weeks or months (depending in part on personal interest and other commitments). Support was always at hand (by phone or in person) from project staff and field assistants who had helped with the initial training.

Other recent studies which build on this peer research approach has been developed in a mobilities project in Istanbul led by Nihan Akyelken her work with peer researchers is very effectively demonstrated in a video available at: https://www.youtube.com/watch?v=CoJ_EUgjeQc.

Whatever the precise characteristics of the vulnerable group, careful establishment and agreement of ethical practices at the outset is essential, as is a persistent eye to ensure that such standards are maintained throughout the program of research (Porter, 2016; Porter et al., 2015).

Bringing peer researchers into the policy and practice arena: Work with peer researchers has proved invaluable not only in building understanding of the issues faced by vulnerable groups in sensitive contexts but also then in taking these issues to relevant policymakers and practitioners who may be able to help progress key issues. At the inception of the peer researcher projects led by the first author (described above), establishing a Country Consultative Group (CCG), consisting of c. 20 relevant participants from transport ministries, other relevant ministries (e.g., women and children's affairs, education, health etc.), NGOs and CBOs, transport unions, together with the peer researchers and the academic research team, provides critical infrastructure for ensuring that peer researchers will be able to engage directly with key transport sector organizations (Porter, 2014).

With direct relevant evidence to hand the peer researchers are, in essence, "citizen scientists": they often have the confidence to speak with authority to the CCG about the mobility issues that are faced in their communities. Typically the CCGs meet at intervals of 4–6 months during the research from its inception phase onwards and help to shape the research. This also encourages ownership of the project and its findings. At the final project workshop of the older people research study in Dar es Salaam, for instance, attended by local and national government officials from the health and transport sectors, as well as diverse NGOs, the peer researchers were able to argue their case for stronger government support to older people with remarkable confidence (Porter et al., 2015). Such genuinely participatory processes, which not only provide clear evidence but can also help bring the issues at stake to wider public attention, thus arguably have a substantial role to play in improving social justice in Africa's transport sector.

5. Participatory Action Research involving direct interventions

Participatory Action Research tends to be characterized not only by a focus on working with people (as opposed to on them) but also by associated joint researcher/community intervention experiments. Until recently this approach in which researchers and study community members work together as co-participants has only rarely been adopted in transport studies.

However, it can offer a really valuable route to understanding and resolving the complexities associated with promoting change in the transport sector.

Some years ago the Africa Transport Programme (SSATP, 2005: 153) noted how user participation was "*considered essential to the success of the NMT* [Non-Motorised Transport] *pilot projects*" they ran in Africa. They established user platforms to articulate and prioritize user needs in their projects, and ensure their active involvement in planning interventions etc., despite some resistance from engineering professionals (ibid 153–156). Over ensuing years, however, communities seem to have mostly been relegated once again to the borders of transport planning—whether with reference to walking, cycling, or motorized transport.

An early participatory action research study in Ghana into Intermediate Means of Transport (IMT) provided a clear example of the breadth and depth of learning that intervention studies conducted with communities can offer to the research process (Porter et al., 2012). Failed projects had been numerous in the IMT sector, despite the seeming relevance of IMTs such as hand- and bicycle-carts, in contexts where motorized vehicles were beyond the financial capacity of the majority (especially women). Even so, they continued to be promoted as a low cost, "appropriate" solution by various agencies (Salifu, 1994; Starkey, 2001). Baseline research with communities in five coastal Ghana villages with poor road access was followed by a transport intervention in collaboration with the villagers and Ghana's Ministry of Food and Agriculture. This involved introduction of different kinds of IMT equipment and detailed monitoring of their impacts by resident research assistants in collaboration with the communities over an 18-month period. This proved very effective in improving understanding of patterns of adoption and non-adoption of transport technologies among poor rural women. It revealed, in particular, many important issues around differences between prior stated preferences and actual gendered patterns of adoption and non-adoption in this context which have wider application (Porter et al., 2015).

Another action research study, similarly focused on understanding a transport conundrum—why roads in relatively good condition in rural areas may not be used by minibuses—was undertaken in Malawi (Raballand et al., 2011). In this case a minibus service was subsidized over a 6-month period over a distance of 20 km to serve five villages. The researchers allocated prices for use of the bus randomly, and through this experiment demonstrated that at very low prices, bus usage was high and decreased rapidly with increased prices. However, based on the results of take-up and minibus provider surveys, the experiment showed that, at any price, low (with high usage) or high (with low usage), a bus service provider never breaks even on this road due to the overall low level of passenger resources available to pay fares. This helped explain why walking or cycling is so widespread on most rural roads in Sub-Saharan Africa and demonstrated why motorized services need to be subsidized: without subsidy even a road in good condition is likely to be left without a bus service at an affordable price for local people.

The authors of this chapter are currently engaged in a Participatory Action Research study with unemployed women in low income areas of three cities—Tunis, Abuja and Cape Town. This study (commenced late in 2018 but currently partially stalled by COVID-19), involves a mix of UK and in-country academics working closely with peer researchers (as noted in a previous section—see footnote a for the web reference), their communities, an International NGO, local gender and/or transport-focused NGOs and Country Consultative Groups. Having undertaken in depth baseline field research with peer researchers, we are exploring the potential to improve women's access to safe transport services and improve their employment prospects in the transport sector through piloting and assessing a series of skills-based interventions. One set of interventions will focus on aiding women transport users to access work more easily, another set to improve women's potential to access work in the transport sector, based on our research findings. The design of each pilot is context specific, being shaped both by baseline findings and ongoing work with our Country Consultative Groups.

Attention to the potentialities of PAR now seems to be slowly gathering pace in the transport planning arena, seemingly in part a response to Sheller's (2018) persuasive calls for greater attention to mobility justice. Verlinghieri (2020), for instance, has been working with grassroots movements in two cities (Rio de Janeiro, Brazil and Aquila, Italy) that face significant transport planning challenges. In this case the intervention is focused on promoting more participatory arenas where marginalized groups can have a voice: it emphasizes the mobility crisis as a political crisis. Similarly, Sagaris et al. (2020) take a PAR approach in two Chilean cities, working with advocacy/grassroots neighborhood associations to frame sustainable transport and social justice in policy agendas; their work is built round a series of participatory workshops and surveys. The potential complexities of PAR, evident from both those studies, are further demonstrated in a broader mobility context charting refugee mobility across European borders

(Starodub, 2019). Nonetheless, the power of PAR to understand, engage with and promote positive change toward mobility justice looks set to encourage its wider uptake in the next decade.

6. Digital methodologies

Since the start of the Covid-19 pandemic in late 2019, many research projects have been disrupted, paused, or abandoned following national lockdowns which have restricted options to conduct face-to-face research (Sy et al., 2020). In countries where national lockdowns have been put in place much research has gone entirely online, posing new questions about appropriate field methodologies especially with reference to working with vulnerable groups (Braun et al., 2020; König et al., 2020).

Some online tools for collecting data such as surveys or social media scraping and computer assisted content analysis had been utilized for many years prior to the pandemic (Fielding et al., 2008). Within the field of transport planning, digital methodologies had been used as a way of exploring users' perceptions of accessible and safe road systems (Griffin and Jiao, 2019). Crowdsourcing, for instance, is an online tool that takes a bottom-up approach whereby users can voice their opinions about suitable or safe transport routes. However, as Griffin and Jiao (2019) suggest, participatory spatial technologies need to include the engagement process, and not just focus on the technology itself. They thus refer to a PPGRS (a public geography information system) or "wikimap" that allows people to click on a location on a computer-based map to inform transport planners about the routes they prefer and the problems they identify. This can include difficult routes for walking and cycling. The app prompts the user to rate a ride as positive or negative, calculates the overall rating of all routes, and records the total amount of users on each roadway.

Using smartphones as a tool for generating findings can, in some instances, promote the inclusion of lower income groups, particularly if they are more likely to participate in online forums than in-person meetings. In the TRIPS project (Transport Innovation for vulnerable-to-exclusion people needs satisfaction), conducted in seven European pilot cities in 2020, transport users with access needs came together with transport organizations, technology and system integration experts to work on inclusive mobility solutions (König et al., 2020). The project is framed as a "co-design for all" methodology that involves users in the decision making—for instance, by forming working groups, implementing social media analysis, and conducting qualitative interviews. However, in this case, the researchers note that the Covid-19 pandemic has necessitated a shift to using entirely online methodologies. Instead of interviewing respondents face-to-face or observing users taking public transport, the team have shifted their focus to studying social media content regarding users' mobility issues and conducting an online questionnaire. The team have analyzed social media content regarding accessibility needs before, during and after traveling on public transport (such as by bus, metro, ridesharing or bike-sharing). Social media platforms were also scanned using search terms such as "mobility-impaired," "'disabled", "visually impaired" or "taxi," "metro" or "subway." Qualitative interviews were conducted via phone or video regarding choice behavior, barriers, and participation in transport design.

Anik et al. (2020), using a slightly different approach, explore how young people can become more involved in transport planning in Dhaka, Bangladesh. Their research considers the premise that young people may be reluctant to express themselves in focus groups but be more comfortable participating in social media forums to voice their opinions on a topic. Study participants used Facebook to express their views regarding transportation. A tool to analyze user's inputs was used (Sociograph) and follow up focus group interviews were conducted with non-group members regarding the social media content (Anik et al., 2020). The extracted text from social media platforms as well as the focus group data were compiled separately and analyzed through text mining (word cloud construction and topic modeling). Afterwards an online survey was conducted asking participants to prioritize the preference and perception of various characteristics (Analytic Hierarchy Process) which was followed up with a similar survey with transport professionals (Anik et al., 2020).

A wider view of digital technology in transport planning takes us to the concept of the "smart city" that has developed over the last two decades. This generally incorporates civic engagement via technology, and is often driven by "big data." However, the concept tends to be largely driven by Global North perceptions of the technologically advanced city as the most "desirable." Large amounts of data are collected through ICT technologies and then analyzed by machine learning for better efficiency (Lee et al., 2020). Ethical concerns have been raised about the methods utilized, for instance in terms of privacy and internet security (Bunders and Varro, 2019). Moreover, the poor may risk being marginalized, especially when segments of the population cannot afford to buy smart technologies (Lee et al., 2020). Careful attention to questions around who has access to the data, who is included in the data collection and whose interests are served is crucial. Although some initiatives have focused on "smart cities for the poor," these projects often have a short-term funding period and users may lose interest quickly, even when training has been offered in ICT technologies. It has also been taken for granted that everyone had the means to travel to training facilities which is not always the case (Lee et al., 2020). Finally, it must be noted that a return to focusing on numbers per se (the main commuting flows etc.) will further detract from investigations into user experiences and the diversity of their needs.

7. Wider considerations regarding field research in the context of Covid-19

Many researchers are now starting to reflect on how their planned projects are being—or need to be—modified during Covid-19. This unprecedented situation arguably provides a space to consider different methodologies for addressing in/justice in transport and mobilities (Verlinghieri and Schwanen, 2020) but it also raises new challenges. While face-to-face interviews may have been the research method approved by ethics committees, amendments will be required. Recent publications have focused on the risks of over-presenting certain groups who have access to digital technologies such as smartphones as well as the internet. It is also important to consider the digital literacy of research participants, particularly regarding the communication of informed consent. Online consent forms need to be clear, with simple instructions (Sy et al., 2020). If using video platforms, the research participants should have the option of using either audio or video calls.

Whatever the potential mode of contact and engagement, respondents can be reluctant to be interviewed during the pandemic, given potential stresses around issues such as health, food supply and income: for instance, they may have little time for interviews due to the need to constantly search for employment and income. Moreover, respondents may find it difficult to establish new relationships through digital communication as opposed to face-to-face contact (Góralska, 2020). There can also be privacy issues when interviewees face stasis, sitting in a home crowded with relatives and without a space where they can talk privately and without interruptions (Liegghio and Caragata, 2020; Parkes et al., 2020)—though, of course, this point can also apply to face-to-face interviews.

Despite the potential issues noted above, remote methods may be more accessible to those people with physical mobility constraints and may offer more anonymity and privacy, if the online platforms are secure (Sy et al., 2020). One innovative research tool that is gaining prominence during the Covid-19 pandemic is the digital podcast tool. Scholars in Australia, Canada, the US, the UK, India, Iran, Germany, Singapore and New Zealand provided audio recordings of how their cities had been impacted during the pandemic, and these audio files were collected and edited into a podcast. The project involved asking participants what a city sounds like—for instance, the sound of transport and whether the sounds had changed due to lockdown (Rogers et al., 2020).

Mobility diaries can offer another approach to constraints on face-to-face fieldwork during the prevailing pandemic. The solicited diary method (Meth, 2003) which involves asking respondents to write accounts of their daily lives has benefits when direct access to respondents is difficult and topics covered may be sensitive. This method is different from a personal diary given that it is written in response to a request from a researcher and the diarist can select the material to include, albeit with likely specific reference to the commissioning researcher's interests. It contrasts with private diaries that might involve more sensitive material, where ethical questions could arise around researcher use of such data. Respondent diaries can be analyzed thematically by the researcher, notably to pick out prevailing issues in conditions of restricted mobility (Moises, 2020).[c]

In a crowdsourced document developed during the Covid-19 pandemic, Lupton (2020) emphasizes that the diary method can be structured like a questionnaire or semi-structured interview or by asking for free-flowing information. Diaries can both be events-based (e.g., when lockdown occurs) or can be used over months or hours. Diaries can both be photo-based, or a collage, and can be spoken or written. Our own experience of supporting young women in such diary writing in our current study cities (Abuja, Tunis, Cape Town) during Covid-19 suggests that giving feedback during the process, as well as keeping in regular touch with respondents, is vital. With such support and feedback, it is possible to develop insights into the changing mobility needs and patterns of respondents that could have considerable significance for future transport planning.

[c] Hodgson (2012) used mobility interviews in her research with low-income interviewees—these both involved walking with respondents, and a 3-day communication diary that identified their mobility needs.

8. Ethical considerations

This chapter has emphasized the value of participatory research and it is clear that interest in building field investigations with direct citizen participation in living labs is now growing rapidly among urban and transport planners worldwide (Herrmann-Lunecke et al., 2020; Willems et al., 2020; also see, for instance, Mintchev et al., 2019 for Lebanon). While this is a very positive move it also introduces significant hazards, such that some notes of caution are required. As Moose (2003) observes, the dangers of a rhetoric of partnership and rituals of collaboration are substantial. There is no point researchers conducting research with vulnerable groups if the evidence collected is subsequently ignored: it is vital that transport professionals are committed and central to the participatory research process itself (Porter and Turner, 2019).

The approaches we recommend for sound data collection also demand very close attention to appropriate ethical procedures (to protect all participants, including researchers themselves). It is important to ensure that vulnerable groups are brought directly into transport planning as active participants who can speak from their own evidence, but this is by no means always straightforward. Covid-19 lockdowns, in particular, may have a significant negative impact on the participation of peer researchers/policymakers in the review/analysis due to cancellations of meetings and new regulations: some researchers who practice participatory approaches are beginning to wonder whether lock-down may result in lock-out. It is important to consider that both researchers and research participants may be dealing with challenging circumstances in their personal and professional contexts (within and outside the current Covid-19 era). Thus deciding to continue or pause a project may require careful considerations and ethical review (Sy et al., 2020).

Participatory research always needs to be carried out with very careful consideration of the landscapes of power, politics and vested interests in which it is located (Cooke and Kothari, 2001; Mohan and Stokke, 2000; Porter et al., 2015, Porter, 2016). Moreover, the politics of field study arguably increasingly extend beyond individual interactions and local community to national and international levels. In low income country transport contexts, where the playing out of vested interests is often all too apparent, such warnings have particular resonance, especially in the current pandemic. Liegghio and Caragata (2020) consider how they had to shift their methods during the COVID-19 pandemic when conducting research with vulnerable groups in Canada. They reflect on their concern about using video interviews, since this could be interpreted as information extraction without the relational element conveyed in an in-depth face-face interview. Moreover, they write about their concerns to pause research with vulnerable groups versus the need to stop face-to-face interviews due to the virus. While the researchers could afford to suspend knowing about participants' struggles, they concluded that this could come at a huge cost for their target respondents—young people living in low-income housing—and the possibility of policy impact (Liegghio and Caragata, 2020). Their resolution is to use *photovoice* (discussed briefly above; Ward et al., 2015) but the training was adapted during the pandemic. They moved to remote online conference methods, with a follow up discussion on these platforms regarding the photos they had taken. Such methods, in contexts where there is access to social media and a stable internet connection, can help research participants express themselves and build voice during difficult times.

As Tiidenberg (2020) points out, ethical considerations must go beyond tick-boxing (such as only relying on informed consent sheets) to a broader discussion of the implications of research to avoid harm and exploitation. Social media affordances of permanence, searchability, duplicability and scalability can change the meanings of a picture that is shared with a friend into a moral dilemma. Information that is shared on the internet can make a participant especially vulnerable. It is hence important that the participant's personal information is only accessed as authorized by the participant, and that the participant cannot be identified in the research data.

In our current research project with young women transport users and transport employees we asked our peer researchers to write diaries about their experiences during lockdown but also when there were various relaxations of lockdowns. We made it clear from the onset that they should not share photos without consent (e.g., of people breaking lockdown rules) and only travel if they needed to anyway. Diaries can foster anxiety and are potentially dangerous if they contain reference for instance to illegal activities, as Meth (2003) points out with reference to her own work on a gender and violence project in South Africa. In our own work, we soon realized that there was a tendency for people to take videos and pictures on phones and share events on WhatsApp about police brutality that are potentially dangerous for those identifiable—possibly also for the person who took the photos. This was not something that we had anticipated at the outset. The lockdown situation stressed our respondents and they wanted to share what was happening, even though they had been trained on photo consent issues prior to the pandemic. An ongoing ethical review is therefore necessary especially when participants communicate on online platforms or share diaries.

9. Conclusion

In this chapter we have reviewed a diversity of qualitative field methodologies that have been built up—albeit by a minority of transport researchers—over the last two decades or so. Many of the approaches we describe are specifically aimed at addressing the mobility needs of those low-income communities and other vulnerable people—women, children, older people and people with disabilities—who are so often ignored when new transport interventions are planned. We recognize that the application of these qualitative field methods is unlikely to be simple and straightforward or uncontentious, hence the necessary inclusion of a section devoted to associated ethical complexities. Even so, we hope that transport planners whose focus is primarily on quantitative approaches will reflect on the potential of such methods as a complement to their current methodological repertoire and find them worthy of inclusion in their efforts to achieve more satisfactory, socially equitable mobility solutions.

Covid-19 has inevitably impinged on this review of methods. The fact that Covid-19 is not only a health crisis, but also a transport and mobility crisis, became glaringly evident at an early stage in the pandemic. We are now at a moment in time when there is an opportunity to rethink approaches to transport planning and, in particular, to plan more socially equitable mobility solutions based on a broad application of field research methodologies that can engage more effectively—and sensitively—with a wide spectrum of potential transport users. This will require concerted effort by transport practitioners with vision and commitment to social justice. However, it has to be admitted that these are uncertain times: whether the "new normal" following the COVID-19 pandemic will provide the requisite contextual opportunities—not least in the wider political economy—to enable such engagement is depressingly uncertain.

References

Anik, M.A.H., Sadeek, S.N.f., Hossain, M., Kabir, S., 2020. A framework for involving the young generation in transportation planning using social media and crowd sourcing. Transp. Policy 97, 1–18. Available from https://doi.org/10.1016/j.tranpol.2020.06.006.

Bissell, D., 2009. Visualising everyday geographies: practices of vision through travel-time. Trans. Inst. Br. Geogr. 34 (1), 42–60. Available from https://doi.org/10.1111/j.1475-5661.2008.00326.x.

Bowles, L.R., 2017. Doing the snap: storytelling and participatory photography with women porters in Ghana. Vis. Anthropol. Rev. 33 (2), 107–118. Available from https://doi.org/10.1111/var.12129.

Braun, R., Blok, V., Loeber, A., Wunderle, U., 2020. COVID-19 and the onlineification of research: kick-starting a dialogue on responsible online research and innovation (RoRI). J. Resp. Innov. 7 (3), 680–688. Available from https://doi.org/10.1080/23299460.2020.1789387.

Bunders, D.J., Varro, K., 2019. Problematizing data-driven urban practices: insights from five Dutch 'smart cities. Cities 93, 145–152. Available from: https://doi.org/10.1177/0969776419893731.

Carpiano, R.M., 2009. Come take a walk with me: the "Go-Along" interview as a novel method for studying the implications of place for health and well-being. Health Place 15 (1), 263–272. Available from https://doi.org/10.1016/j.healthplace.2008.05.00.

Castrodale, M.A., 2018. Mobilizing dis/ability research: a critical discussion of qualitative go-along interviews in practice. Qual. Inq. 24 (1), 45–55. Available from https://doi.org/10.1177/1077800417727765.

Chambers, R., 1994. The origins and practice of participatory rural appraisal. World Dev. 22 (7), 953–969. Available from https://doi.org/10.1016/0305-750X(94)90141-4.

Cooke, B., Kothari, U., 2001. Participation: The New Tyranny? Zed books, London, New York.

Copelton, D.A., 2010. Output that counts: pedometers, sociability and the contested terrain of older adult fitness walking. Sociol. Health Illn. 32 (2), 304–318. Available from https://doi.org/10.1111/j.1467-9566.2009.01214.x.

Cresswell, T., 2010. Towards a politics of mobility. Environ. Plan. D Soc. Space 28 (1), 17–31. Available from https://doi.org/10.1068/d11407.

Dewalt, K.M., Dewalt, B.R., 2002. Participant Observation: A Guide for Fieldworkers. Altamira Press, Walnut Creek.

D'Hondt, S., 2009. Calling the stops in a Dar-es-Salaam minibus: embodied understandings of place in a drop-off routine. J. Pragmat. 41 (10), 1962–1976. Available from https://doi.org/10.1016/j.pragma.2008.09.020.

Doughty, K., 2013. Walking together: the embodied and mobile production of a therapeutic landscape. Health Place 24, 140–146. Available from https://doi.org/10.1016/j.healthplace.2013.08.009.

Easterly, W., 2013. The Tyranny of Experts: Economists, Dictators, and the Forgotten Rights of the Poor. Perseus Books, New York.

Evans, J., O'Brien, J., Ch Ng, B., 2018. Towards a geography of informal transport: mobility, infrastructure and urban sustainability from the back of a motorbike. Trans. Inst. Br. Geogr. 43 (4), 674–688. Available from https://doi.org/10.1111/tran.12239.

Fielding, N.G., Lee, R.M., Blank, G., 2008. The SAGE Handbook of Online Research Methods. Sage, London, Los Angeles, New Delhi, Singapore, Washington DC, Melbourne.

Fouracre, P., Sohail, M., Cavill, S., 2006. A participatory approach to urban transport planning in developing countries. Transp. Plan. Technol. 29 (4), 313–330. https://doi.org/10.1080/03081060600905665.

Góralska, M., 2020. Anthropology from home: advice on digital ethnography for the pandemic times. Anthropol. Action 27 (1), 46–52. Available form https://doi.org/10.3167/aia.2020.270105.

Gorman, M., Jones, S., Turner, J., 2019. Older people, mobility and transport in low-and middle-income countries: a review of the research. Sustainability 11 (21), 6157. Available from https://doi.org/10.3390/su11216157.

Griffin, G.P., Jiao, J., 2019. The geography and equity of crowdsourced public participation for active transportation planning. Transp. Res. Rec. 2673 (1), 460–468. Available from https://doi.org/10.1177/0361198118823498.

Harada, T., Waitt, G., 2013. Researching transport choices: the possibilities of 'mobile methodologies' to study life-on-the-move. Geogr. Res. 51 (2), 145–152. Available from https://doi.org/10.1111/j.1745-5871.2012.00774.x.

Herrmann-Lunecke, M.G., Mora, R., Sagaris, L., 2020. Persistence of walking in Chile: lessons for urban sustainability. Transp. Rev. 40 (2), 135–159. Available from https://doi.org/10.1080/01441647.2020.1712494.

Hine, J., 1996. Pedestrian travel experiences: assessing the impact of traffic on behaviour and perceptions of safety using an in-depth interview technique. J. Transp. Geogr. 4 (3), 179–199. Available from: https://doi.org/10.1016/0966-6923(96)00003-8.

Hodgson, F., 2012. Everyday connectivity: equity, technologies, competencies and walking. J. Transp. Geogr. 21, 17–23. Available from https://doi.org/10.1016/j.jtrangeo.2011.11.001.

Ibeas, A., Dell'Olio, L., Montequin, R.B., 2011. Citizen involvement in promoting sustainable mobility. J. Transp. Geogr. 19 (4), 475–487. Available from https://doi.org/10.1016/j.jtrangeo.2010.01.005.

Ingold, T., Vergunst, J.L., 2008. Ways of Walking: Ethnography and Practice on Foot. Ashgate Publishing, Ltd., Aldershot, United Kingdom.

Jiron, P., Carrasco, J., Rebolledo, M., 2020. Observing gendered interdependent mobility barriers using an ethnographic and time use approach. Transp. Res. Part A Policy Pract. 140, 204–214. Available from https://doi.org/10.1016/j.tra.2020.08.018.

Kett, M., Cole, E., Turner, J., 2020. Disability, mobility and transport in low-and middle-income countries: a thematic review. Sustainability 12 (2), 1–18. Available from: https://doi.org/10.3390/su12020589.

Klopp, J., Cavoli, C., 2018. The paratransit puzzle. Mapping and master planning for transportation in Maputo and Nairobi. In: Uteng, T., Lucas, K. (Eds.), Urban Mobilities in the Global South. Routledge, New York, pp. 94–110.

König, A., Alchiauskaite, L., Sionen, F., Hatzakis, T., Andersen, K., 2020. Co-production of knowledge for designing inclusive digital mobility solutions—the methodological approach and process of the TRIPS project. In: ICCHPOpen Access Compendium Future Perspectives of AT, eAccessibility and eInclusion, pp. 179–188.

Korf, B., Oughton, E., 2006. Rethinking the European countryside—can we learn from the South? J. Rural Stud. 22 (3), 278–289. Available from https://doi.org/10.1016/j.jrurstud.2005.09.005.

Kowalewski, M., Barlomiejski, R., 2020. Is it research or just walking? Framing walking research methods as "non-scientific". Geoforum 114, 59–65. Available from https://doi.org/10.1016/j.geoforum.2020.06.002.

Langevang, T., 2007. Movements in time and space: using multiple methods in research with young people in Accra, Ghana. Child. Geogr. 5 (3), 267–282. Available from https://doi.org/10.1080/14733280701445853.

Lee, J., Ingold, T., 2006. Fieldwork on foot: perceiving, routing, socializing. In: Collins, P., Coleman, S. (Eds.), Locating the Field. Space, Place and Context in Anthropology. Berg Publishers, pp. 67–86.

Lee, J.Y., Woods, O., Kong, L., 2020. Towards more inclusive smart cities: reconciling the divergent realities of data and discourse at the margins. Geogr. Compass 14 (9), 1–12. e12504. Available from https://doi.org/10.1111/gec3.12504.

Legacy, C., 2016. Transforming transport planning in the postpolitical era. Urban Stud. 53 (14), 3108–3124. Available from https://doi.org/10.1177/0042098015602649.

Liegghio, M., Caragata, L., 2020. COVID-19 and youth living in poverty: the ethical considerations of moving from in-person interviews to a photovoice using remote methods. Affilia 36 (2), 149–155. Available from https://doi.org/10.1177/0886109920939051.

Lucas, K., 2011. Making the connections between transport disadvantage and the social exclusion of low income populations in the Tshwane Region of South Africa. J. Transp. Geogr. 19 (6), 1320–1334. Available from https://doi.org/10.1016/j.jtrangeo.2011.02.007.

Lupton, D., 2020. Doing Fieldwork in a Pandemic. https://nwssdtpacuk.files.wordpress.com/2020/04/doing-fieldwork-in-a-pandemic2-google-docs.pdf. (Accessed 12.10.2020).

Lynch, K., 1960. The Image of the City. MIT Press, Cambridge, London.

Mcfarlane, C., Silver, J., 2017. Navigating the city: dialectics of everyday urbanism. Trans. Inst. Br. Geogr. 42 (3), 458–471. Available from https://doi.org/10.1111/tran.12175.

Meth, P., 2003. Entries and omissions: using solicited diaries in geographical research. Area 35 (2), 195–205. Available from https://doi.org/10.1111/1475-4762.00263.

Middleton, J., Byles, H., 2019. Interdependent temporalities and the everyday mobilities of visually impaired young people. Geoforum 102, 176–183.

Mintchev, N., Baumann, H., Moore, H., Rigon, A., Dabaj, J., 2019. Towards a shared prosperity: co-designing solutions in Lebanon's spaces of displacement. J. Br. Acad. 7 (S2), 109–135. Available from https://doi.org/10.5871/jba/007s2.109.

Mohan, G., Stokke, K., 2000. Participatory development and empowerment: the dangers of localism. Third World Q. 21 (2), 247–268. Available from https://doi.org/10.1080/01436590050004346.

Moises Jr., C., 2020. Online data collection as adaptation in conducting quantitative and qualitative research during the covid-pandemic. Eur. J. Educ. Stud. 7 (11), 78–87. Available from 10.46827/ejes.v7i11.3336.

Moose, D., 2003. The making and marketing of participatory development. In: Giri, A., Van Ufford, R.Q. (Eds.), A Moral Critique of Development: In Search of Global Responsibilities. Routledge, London and New York, pp. 43–75.003.

Mulongo, G., Porter, G., Tewodros, A., 2019. Gendered politics in rural roads: gender mainstreaming in Tanzania's transport sector. Proc. Inst. Civil Eng. Transp. 173 (2), 87–96. Available from https://doi.org/10.1680/jtran.18.00153.

Naysmith, S., Rubincam, C., 2012. Women in the driver's seat: an exploratory study of perceptions and experiences of female truck drivers and their employers in South Africa. J. South. Afr. Stud. 38 (3), 579–599. Available from https://doi.org/10.1080/03057070.2012.708997.

Palmgren, A., 2018. Standing still: walking interviews and poetic spatial inquiry. Area 50 (3), 372–383. Available from https://doi.org/10.1111/area.12410.

Parkes, J., Datzberger, S., Howell, C., Kasidi, J., Kiwanuka, T., Knight, L., Nagawa, R., Naker, D., Devries, K., 2020. Young People, Inequality and Violence during the COVID-19 Lockdown in Uganda. Available from, https://doi.org/10.31235/osf.io/2p6hx.

Parnell, S., Pieterse, E., 2016. Translational global praxis: rethinking methods and modes of African urban research. Int. J. Urban Reg. Res. 40 (1), 236–246. Available from https://onlinelibrary.wiley.com/doi/abs/10.1111/1468-2427.12278.

Pereira, L.M., Hichert, T., Hamann, M., Preiser, R., Biggs, R., 2018. Using futures methods to create transformative spaces: visions of a good Anthropocene in southern Africa. Ecol. Soc. 23 (1), 1–14. https://doi.org/10.5751/ES-09907-230119.

Plyushteva, A., Schwanen, T., 2018. Care-related journeys over the life course: thinking mobility biographies with gender, care and the household. Geoforum 97, 131–141. Available from https://doi.org/10.1016/j.geoforum.2018.10.025.

Pooley, C.G., 2013. Promoting Walking and Cycling. Policy Press.

Porter, G., 2014. Exploring collaborative research methodologies in the pursuit of sustainable futures. In: Sillitoe, P. (Ed.), Sustainable Development: An Appraisal From the Gulf Region. Berghahn, Oxford, pp. 419–435.

Porter, G., 2016. Reflections on co-investigation through peer research with young people and older people in sub-Saharan Africa. Qual. Res. 16 (3), 293–304. Available from https://doi.org/10.1177/1468794115619001.

Porter, G., Abane, A., 2008. Increasing children's participation in transport planning: reflections on methodology in a child-centred research project. Child. Geogr. 6 (2), 151–167. Available from https://doi.org/10.1080/14733280801963086.

Porter, G., Turner, J., 2019. Meeting young people's mobility and transport needs: review and Prospect. Sustainability 11 (22), 6193. Available from https://doi.org/10.3390/su11226193.

Porter, G., Hampshire, K., Abane, A., Munthali, A., Robson, E., Mashiri, M., Maponya, G., 2010a. Where dogs, ghosts and lions roam: learning from mobile ethnographies on the journey from school. Child. Geogr. 8 (2), 91–105. Available from https://doi.org/10.1080/14733281003691343.

Porter, G., Hampshire, K., Abane, A., Munthali, A., Robson, E., Mashiri, M., Tanle, A., 2010b. Youth transport, mobility and security in sub-Saharan Africa: the gendered journey to school. World Transp. Policy Pract. 16 (1), 51–71. Available from 10.35648/20.500.12413/11781/ii227.

Porter, G., Abane, A., Lucas, K., 2020. User Diversity and Mobility Practices in Sub-Saharan African Cities: Understanding the Needs of Vulnerable Populations. Volvo Research and Educational Foundations. http://www.vref.se/download/18.74c15c6d173d8c1d0b2ea183/1607408440344/1-User%20diversity%20and%20mobility%20practices%20in%20Sub-Saharan%20African%20cities%20-2020.pdf.

Porter, G., Blaufuss, K., Owusu Acheampong, F., 2012. Gendered patterns of IMT adoption and use: learning from action research. Res. Transp. Econ. 34, 11–15. Available from https://doi.org/10.1016/j.retrec.2011.12.005.

Porter, G., Tewodros, A., Bifandimu, F., Gorman, M., Heslop, A., Sibale, E., Awadh, A., Kiswaga, L., 2013. Transport and mobility constraints in an aging population: health and livelihood implications in rural Tanzania. J. Transp. Geogr. 30, 161–169. Available from https://doi.org/10.1016/j.jtrangeo.2013.05.001.

Porter, G., Heslop, A., Bifandimu, F., et al., 2014. Exploring intergenerationality and ageing in rural Kibaha Tanzania; methodological innovation through co-investigation with older people. In: Vanderbeck, R., Worth, N. (Eds.), Intergenerational Space. Routledge, London, pp. 259–272.

Porter, G., Tewodros, A., Bifandimu, F., Heslop, A., Gorman, M., 2015. Qualitative methods for investigating transport and mobility issues among commonly socially excluded populations: a case study of co-investigation with older people in rural Tanzania. Transp. Res. Procedia 11, 492–503. Available from https://doi.org/10.1016/j.trpro.2015.12.041.

Porter, G., Hampshire, K., Abane, A., Munthali, A., Robson, E., Mashiri, M., 2017. Young People's Daily Mobilities in Sub-Saharan Africa. Moving Young Lives. Palgrave Macmillan, London.

Raballand, G., Thornton, R., Yang, D., Goldberg, J., Keleher, N., Müller, A., 2011. Are Rural Road Investments Alone Sufficient to Generate Transport Flows? Lessons from a Randomized Experiment in Rural Malawi and Policy Implications. The World Bank.

Richardson, A.J., Ampt, E.S., Meyburg, A.H., 1995. Survey Methods for Transport Planning. Eucalyptus Press, Melbourne.
Rogers, D., Herbert, M., Whitzman, C., Mccann, E., Maginn, P.J., Watts, B., Alam, A., Pill, M., Keil, R., Dreher, T., 2020. The city under COVID-19: podcasting as digital methodology. Tijdschr. Econ. Soc. Geogr. 111 (3), 434–450. Available from https://doi.org/10.1111/tesg.12426.
Sagaris, L., Berrios, E., Tiznado-Aitken, I., 2020. Using PAR to frame sustainable transport and social justice on policy agendas. A pilot experience in two contrasting Chilean cities. J. Transp. Geogr. 83, 102654. Available from https://doi.org/10.1016/j.jtrangeo.2020.102654.
Salifu, M., 1994. The cycle trailer in Ghana: a reasonable but inappropriate technology. Afr. Technol. Forum 7 (3), 37–40. Available from https://doi.org/10.1016/j.trpro.2015.12.041.
Schwanen, T., 2018. Thinking complex interconnections: transition, nexus and Geography. Trans. Inst. Br. Geogr. 43 (2), 262–283. https://doi.org/10.1111/tran.12223.
Seedat, M., Mackenzie, S., Mohan, D., 2006. The phenomenology of being a female pedestrian in an African and an Asian city: a qualitative investigation. Transp. Res. F Traffic Psychol. Behav. 9 (2), 139–153. Available from https://doi.org/10.1016/j.trf.2005.09.005.
Sheller, M., 2007. Bodies, cybercars and the mundane incorporation of automated mobilities. Soc. Cult. Geogr. 8 (2), 175–197. Available from https://doi.org/10.1080/14649360701360063.
Sheller, M., 2018. Mobility Justice. The Politics of Movement in an Age of Extremes. Verso, London.
Sheller, M., Urry, J., 2006. The new mobilities paradigm. Environ. Plan. A. 38, 207–226. Available from https://doi.org/10.1068/a37268.
SSATP (Sub-Saharan Arica Transport Policy Program), 2005. Non-Motorized Transport in African Cities: Lessons From Experience in Kenya and Tanzania. World Bank, Africa Region. SSATP Working Paper no. 80.
Starkey, P., 2001. Promoting the Use of Intermediate Means of Transport-Vehicle Choice, Potential Barriers and Criteria for Success. Rural Travel and Transport Program. SSAT Working Paper No 20.
Starodub, A., 2019. Horizontal participatory action research: refugee solidarity in the border zone. Area 51 (1), 166–173. Available from https://doi.org/10.1111/area.12454.
Stewart, A.F., 2017. Mapping transit accessibility: possibilities for public participation. Transp. Res. Part A Policy Pract. 104, 150–166. Available from https://doi.org/10.1016/j.tra.2017.03.015.
Sy, M., O'Leary, N., Nagraj, S., El-Awaisi, A., O'Carroll, V., Xyrichis, A., 2020. Doing interprofessional research in the COVID-19 era: a discussion paper. J. Interprof. Care 34 (5), 1–7. Available from: https://doi.org/10.1080/13561820.2020.1791808.
Tiidenberg, K., 2020. Research ethics, vulnerability, and trust on the internet. In: Hunsinger, J., Allen, M., Klastrup, L. (Eds.), Second International Handbook of Internet Research. Springer, Dordrecht, pp. 1–12.
Uteng, P.T., Turner, J., 2019. Addressing the linkages between gender and transport in low-and middle-income countries. Sustainability 11 (17), 4555. Available from https://doi.org/10.3390/su11174555.
Vecchio, G., 2020. Microstories of everyday mobilities and opportunities in Bogotá: a tool for bringing capabilities into urban mobility planning. J. Transp. Geogr. 83 (C), 102652. Available from https://doi.org/10.1016/j.jtrangeo.2020.102652.
Verlinghieri, E., 2020. Learning from the grassroots: a resourcefulness-based worldview for transport planning. Transp. Res. Part A Policy Pract. 133, 364–377. Available from https://doi.org/10.1016/j.tra.2019.07.001.

Verlinghieri, E., Schwanen, T., 2020. Transport and mobility justice: evolving discussions. J. Transp. Geogr. 87 (102798), 1–7. Available from https://doi.org/10.1016/j.jtrangeo.2020.102798.

Walker, M., Fredericks, B., Mills, K., Anderson, D., 2014. "Yarning" as a method for community-based health research with indigenous women: the indigenous women's wellness research program. Health Care Women Int. 35 (10), 1216–1226. https://doi.org/10.1080/07399332.2013.815754.

Ward, A.L., Freeman, C., McGee, R., 2015. The influence of transport on well-being among teenagers: a photovoice project in New Zealand. J. Transp. Health 2 (3), 414–422. Available from https://doi.org/10.1016/j.jth.2015.06.004.

Watts, L., Urry, J., 2008. Moving methods, travelling times. Environ. Plan. D Soc. Space 26 (5), 860–874. Available from https://doi.org/10.1068/d6707.

Willems, J.J., Molenveld, A., Voorberg, W., Brinkman, G., 2020. Diverging ambitions and instruments for citizen participation across different stages in green infrastructure projects. Urban Plan. 5 (1), 22–32. Available from https://doi.org/10.17645/up.v5i1.2613.

Xiao, A.H., 2018. 'Oyinbo, Wole!': urban rhythms and mobile encounters in the Lagos transport systems. Urban Forum 30, 133–151. Available from https://doi.orp/10.1007/s12132-018-9345-4.